ARABIAN GULF SECURITY
INTERNAL AND EXTERNAL CHALLENGES

ARABIAN GULF SECURITY
INTERNAL AND EXTERNAL CHALLENGES

THE EMIRATES CENTER FOR STRATEGIC STUDIES AND RESEARCH

THE EMIRATES CENTER FOR STRATEGIC STUDIES AND RESEARCH

The Emirates Center for Strategic Studies and Research (ECSSR) is an independent research institution dedicated to the promotion of professional studies and educational excellence in the UAE, the Gulf and the Arab world. Since its establishment in Abu Dhabi in 1994, the ECSSR has served as a focal point for scholarship on political, economic and social matters. Indeed, the ECSSR is at the forefront of analysis and commentary on Arab affairs.

The Center seeks to provide a forum for the scholarly exchange of ideas by hosting conferences and symposia, organizing workshops, sponsoring a lecture series and publishing original and translated books and research papers. The ECSSR also has an active fellowship and grant program for the writing of scholarly books and for the translation into Arabic of work relevant to the Center's mission. Moreover, the ECSSR has a large library including rare and specialized holdings, and a state-of-the-art technology center, which has developed an award-winning website that is a unique and comprehensive source of information on the Gulf.

Through these and other activities, the ECSSR aspires to engage in mutually beneficial professional endeavors with comparable institutions worldwide, and to contribute to the general educational and academic development of the UAE.

The views expressed in this book do not necessarily reflect those of the ECSSR.

First published in 2008 by
The Emirates Center for Strategic Studies and Research
PO Box 4567, Abu Dhabi, United Arab Emirates

E-mail: pubdis@ecssr.ae
Website: http://www.ecssr.ae

ISBN: 978-9948-00-946-7 hardback edition
ISBN: 978-9948-00-947-4 paperback edition

CONTENTS

DEMOGRAPHIC CHALLENGES FACING THE GULF COUNTRIES

FIGURES AND TABLES

FIGURES

TABLES

ABBREVIATIONS AND ACRONYMS

AA	Anti-Aircraft
AASROC	Asia–Africa Sub-Regional Organizations Cooperation
ACD	Asian Cooperation Dialogue
AEW	airborne early warning
APC	armored personnel carrier
ARF	ASEAN Regional Forum
ASEAN	Association of South-East Asian Nations
AUP	Advanced Unitary Penetrator
AWACS	Airborne Warning and Control System
BAPCO	Bahrain Petroleum Company
BMENA	Broader Middle East and North Africa Initiative
C4I	Command, Control, Communication, Computers and Intelligence
CBR	chemical, biological, radiological
CBRN	chemical, biological, radiological, nuclear
CENTCOM	(US) Central Command
CENTO	Central Treaty Organization
CEP	circular error probable
CSCE	Commission on Security and Cooperation in Europe
CSR	corporate social responsibility
DIFC	Dubai International Financial Center
EFP	explosively formed penetrator
EFTA	European Free Trade Association
ESCWA	Economic and Social Commission for Western Asia
EU-3	France, Germany and Great Britain
FATF	Financial Action Task Force
FDI	foreign direct investment
FMP	foreign military presence
FTA	Free Trade Agreement
GAFTA	Greater Arab Free Trade Area
GATS	General Agreement on Trade in Services
GATT	General Agreement on Tariffs and Trade

[xiii]

GCC	Gulf Cooperation Council
GCI	General Commission for Investment
GDP	Gross Domestic Product
HPM	high-power microwave
ICI	Istanbul Cooperation Initiative
IEA	International Energy Agency
IISS	International Institute for Strategic Studies
ILO	International Labor Organization
IMF	International Monetary Fund
INS	Inertial Navigation System
IPO	Initial Public Offering
IR	International Relations
IRBM	intermediate range ballistic missile
IRGC	Iranian Revolutionary Guards Corps
IS&R	Intelligence, Surveillance and Reconnaissance
ISG	Iraq Study Group
JDAM	Joint Direct Attack Munition
KSA	Kingdom of Saudi Arabia
LNG	liquefied natural gas
LSM	landing ship (medium)
mbpd	million barrels per day
MEI	Middle East Institute
MEI	Middle East Initiative
MFN	Most Favored Nation
MLRS	multiple launch rocket system
MOIS	Ministry of Intelligence and Security
MOP	Massive Ordnance Penetrator
MoU	Memorandum of Understanding
MRBM	medium range ballistic missile
NATO	North Atlantic Treaty Organization
NPT	(Nuclear) Non-Proliferation Treaty
OAFV	officers' armored fighting vehicle
OIC	Organization of the Islamic Conference
OPEC	Organization of the Petroleum Exporting Countries

OSCE	Organization for Security and Cooperation in Europe
PIJ	Palestinian Islamic Jihad
PLO	Palestine Liberation Organization
PRC	People's Republic of China
QFC	Qatar Financial Center
R&D	Research and Development
SAM	surface-to-air missile
SAMA	Saudi Arabian Monetary Agency
SAVAK	National Organization for Intelligence and Security
SCIRI	Supreme Council for the Islamic Revolution in Iraq
SEATO	South-East Asia Treaty Organization
UAV	unmanned aerial vehicle
UN	United Nations
UNCTAD	United Nations Conference on Trade and Development
UNDP	United Nations Development Program
UNSC	United Nations Security Council
USAF	United States Air Force
WMD	weapons of mass destruction
WTO	World Trade Organization
WTTC	World Travel and Tourism Council
WWF	World Fund for Nature

FOREWORD

In recent years the countries of the Arabian Gulf have witnessed increasing levels of insecurity and instability, largely as a result of three issues: the 2003 Iraq War, the Iranian nuclear program and the rise of religious extremism.

These developments have added to other longer-term concerns, such as the ongoing Arab-Israeli conflict and the search for a balance of power in the Gulf. These concerns have long contributed to regional instability and, together with more recent events, have refocused international attention on the Gulf region.

Furthermore, several local and domestic developments which affect the national security of the Gulf Arab states have come to light, including the demographic imbalance in many Gulf countries and increasing anxiety regarding the economic security of the Gulf in view of the rapid development of the region. These issues coincide with the continuing process of integration with the world community through exposure to international markets and the global economy.

The Gulf Arab states are undergoing a phase of transformation. Naturally, such a transformation entails threats to security and stability. To confront these threats, there is a need to establish a security system which will serve to preserve the political stability and socio-economic welfare of these states, balancing military preparedness and "soft power" techniques on the one hand, and local needs and the interests of the international community on the other.

To discuss the internal and external challenges facing the Gulf region, and to launch a dialogue on the need to form a comprehensive security system for the region, the Emirates Center for Strategic Studies and Research (ECSSR) convened its 12th Annual Conference under the title "Arabian Gulf Security: Internal and External Challenges."

This book comprises a valuable collection of the papers presented at the conference. It discusses new security threats to the Gulf region – most importantly in the military sphere – assesses the opportunities and threats relating to the presence of foreign forces in the region, and sheds light on the instability emanating from Iran and Iraq. Internal security problems faced by the Gulf states which have wider, cross-border repercussions are also examined, including terrorism, organized crime, and imbalances in the demographic structure resulting from labor migration.

This volume also discusses the challenges associated with development, international integration and openness to the global economy, and attempts to assess the changes affecting the security of the Gulf and review their universal effects on the future of the region and the world. Furthermore, it endeavors to raise the issue of the establishment of a regional security framework for the Gulf involving countries from outside the region, as well as international organizations.

I hope that the publication of this book will highlight the importance of developing a security formula that is acceptable to all the countries of the region, and shed some light on this vital issue that is so central to the future of the region and the prosperity of its people.

I would like to take this opportunity to thank the authors for their valuable contributions, and express my hope that this volume will be of benefit to both Arab and foreign readers. I would also like to commend the efforts exerted by the team of editors, translators, proof-readers and typists who worked to produce this book in its present form.

Jamal S. Al-Suwaidi, Ph.D
Director General
ECSSR

INTRODUCTION

Towards a Regional Security System in the Gulf

The year 2007 marked a new phase of transformation in the security environment of the Gulf region. The US–British invasion of Iraq, with its uncalculated consequences, has put untold strain on regional stability and undermined the pre-existing security system. As the situation in Iraq has escalated, so has the crisis concerning the Iranian nuclear program. Owing to the lack of any settlement of the conflict between Iran and the international community, the countries of the region are pervaded by fears of US military action against Iran, which could lead to an entirely new war that would have destructive repercussions on the entire region.

Although the concept of a regional security system for the Arabian Gulf has been on the table for a long time, the toppling of the political system in Iraq has created new challenges and unprecedented threats. This has necessitated a review of regional security arrangements among the countries of the region and with the world's major powers.

The dynamics of Gulf security have undergone changes at the international, regional and local levels. At the international level, the American military presence has been reinforced. This has more succinctly defined the GCC's security options: either embrace a unique American hegemony in the region, or involve other international actors that are concerned with the stability and security of the region.

The regional nature of Gulf security has also changed significantly. With the elimination of the 'old' Iraq, which was considered a regional counter-balance to Iran, the fear among the Gulf Arab states of Iranian dominance has increased. Thus, the process of developing regional security has become a source of serious concern to these countries.

The other aspect of Gulf security, which has been destabilized by the changes imposed on Iraq, is the internal security of the Arab Gulf countries. The governments of these countries are wary of the ramifications of democratic transformation in Iraq on their traditional political systems. Furthermore, there are fears concerning the development of a "Shiite Iraq," and a subsequent increase in sectarian warfare between Sunnis and Shiites in Iraq, which may spread to the shores of the Gulf societies themselves.

Undoubtedly, the removal of Iraq from the regional balance of power has titled it in favor of Iran. The Islamic Republic's acquisition of nuclear technology, and especially its ability to enrich uranium, could grant it dominance over the Gulf region. Acquiring military strength and obtaining recognition as a major regional power in the Middle East represent the cornerstone of Iran's goals in the security sphere. However, no country in the region or outside it should foster the illusion that undermining Iranian ambitions, or even changing the political regime in Iran, will solve the security problems of the Gulf.

The Gulf region is subject to three perceptions – and consequently three visions – of Gulf security. Iran believes that the US presence in the region is the greatest cause of instability. It considers Gulf security to be a private affair, and claims that external powers should not interfere in the formulation of Gulf security arrangements. The United States perceives Iran as the greatest danger to Gulf security and rejects Iranian dominance as much as that of any other international power that contests its control of the region. However, while the Arab Gulf states reject the dominance of any regional power (formerly both Iran and Iraq, now only Iran), they favor working out an international formula to maintain Gulf security and stability, i.e. with the contributions of all the concerned international powers.

Doubt and mistrust between the two shores of the Gulf represent a grave problem to both parties—the Iranians and Arabs. Similarly, US–

Iranian animosity impedes the influence of Iran in any future security structure of the Gulf region.

The ideas and policies governing Gulf security go back to the Cold War era and derive their view of security from the concepts of deterrence and balance of power. Yet in any regional security arrangement, security must be based on principles like reassurance and inclusiveness.

Several promising visions of Gulf security have been raised; embodied in concepts such as confidence-building, cooperation and integration. Instead of basing security on Cold War era concepts and policies, regional security arrangements can be worked out on the basis of principles like reassurance and inclusiveness.

This arrangement could be fulfilled by resurrecting the unfinished project devised at the end of the Iran–Iraq war. The final clause of United Nations (UN) Security Council Resolution 598, which put an end to eight years of war, called for a conference comprising Iraq and Iran, their neighboring Gulf countries and the major external powers. However, the conference was never held. This was partly because of Iraq's aggression against Kuwait in 1990 and the consequent regional divisions as well as the fact that the United States has played the role of an "external counterweight" in Gulf security.

A conference of this type could have fulfilled the needs of all the parties concerned with Gulf security by acknowledging universal interests in the Gulf region. The most significant of these interests are the continuous flow of oil from the region to global markets, as well as recognition of the essential role of Iran in Gulf security and meeting the demands of the GCC states that no single power dominates the Gulf region.

Since then, the need to establish a multilateral regional security framework has grown. Many scholars and analysts have promoted the establishment of regional institutions or forums in the style of the Organization for Security and Cooperation in Europe (OSCE) or the regional forum of the Association of South-East Asian Nations (ASEAN).

This does not mean copying other security structures and applying them to the Gulf region. The eight littoral Gulf countries, in addition to international actors concerned with Gulf security and stability, should agree a security framework which fulfills the common interests of all these countries. In fact, establishing such a framework is conducive to balancing US influence in the Gulf region as well as Iranian hegemonic goals.

Observers increasingly feel that the Gulf countries ought to exert more effort to reinforce regional security. Cooperation on the basis of individual cases, whether at the regional level or with the participation of external actors, can reinforce mutual confidence. Naturally, this cooperation is not a substitute for a multilateral regional security system. However, it can be taken as a first step in the quest for a framework of security and stability covering several areas of mutual interest.

For their part, the GCC states must reformulate their approach to security in order to reinforce their abilities to deter interference in their affairs by neighboring or extra-regional powers. Crises and challenges that threaten Gulf security, which is an extension of Arab national security as a whole, should motivate the formation of a unified Gulf strategy that places more emphasis on the role of the GCC states—a role which affects stability throughout the region and fortifies the national security of its countries.

KEYNOTE ADDRESSES

Security Challenges in the Gulf Countries

HH Lt. General Sheikh Saif bin Zayed Al Nahyan

We may take inspiration from my father, the late Sheikh Zayed bin Sultan Al Nahyan – whose name is borne by the hall in which this conference is convened – regarding the lessons and views of Man, his role in this life and his mission on earth as the primary achiever. Man has been blessed by God with capabilities and potentials that have empowered him to be both creative and charitable. These attributes distinguish human beings from other creatures.

I recall the position of Sheikh Zayed during the war in Bosnia and Herzegovina. When his sons in the UAE Armed Forces were sent to oversee peacekeeping and security operations in the Balkans, they were unsure as to which people should be provided with aid. In response, Sheikh Zayed impressed upon the Commander of the UAE force that God had created all humanity and that "we are dedicated to serve all people without distinction with regard to faith or race; people are equal." These humanist principles on which Sheikh Zayed's position was based are the same principles that people must adhere to in dealing with each other in their daily lives.

Just as our Creator has endowed man with benevolent attributes and elements of good, He has also endowed man with malevolent qualities and elements of evil. Some of these malevolent qualities have led to the emergence of the pestilence of terrorism which ravages the world today.

[9]

Both politicians and legal personnel worldwide differ in their definition of terrorism, but it is not a new phenomenon; it is as old as history. The first act of terror was the murder of Abel by his brother Cain. It was a terrifying tragedy which killed one-sixth of the inhabitants of the earth. As in the case of Cain and Abel, ignorance is the most significant cause of modern terrorism—ignorance leads to sin.

"Public order" represents interconnected, complementary aspects of economics, politics, society, culture and security. Undoubtedly, the economic and political factors are both very important. Indeed, the cultural factor is no less important, but the societal factor has the greatest effect because it is the nucleus of the state. Since I am primarily concerned with security matters, however, I would like to talk about this particular aspect of public order—although I do not mean to belittle the importance of the other areas.

The security apparatus shoulders huge challenges and responsibilities, including the task of reorganizing and developing the structure of the apparatus to keep pace with economic, cultural, social and political progress.

The Middle East, and the Arabian Gulf region in particular, has witnessed significant qualitative changes in terms of lifestyle over the last five decades. During the past decade the progress achieved by government institutions and bodies has been consistent and concurrent, occurring at all levels and in all fields—especially at the economic level. However, the security sector has not developed at the same rate. Therefore it is vital that the security services undergo the necessary structural development to reflect the qualitative development achieved by other state entities, both public and private.

One of the challenges facing the security services is the development of strategies, mechanisms and organizational structures. This will result in clarity of vision and methodology on all security, administrative and functional levels, and will produce the desired connectivity between organizational and security units. Such interaction between the different institutions of the security sector at the state level increases the readiness to build effective contacts with counterparts at a global level. This is of growing importance as crime becomes increasingly globalized. Of course, we are all aware that there are several obstacles to improving the mechanisms of security coordination between the different countries of the world. We are still working to remove these obstacles by formulating common strategies and viewpoints.

Yet another security challenge is the rapid evolution of crime both in terms of type, and modes of commission, as criminals benefit from modern technological advances. Hence the security apparatus will have to deal with this development and master these sophisticated technologies in order to fight and preempt crime.

Therefore, I call on officials to accord particular importance to the development of the police and security spheres and adopt new and contemporary concepts in police work by employing advanced techniques and capabilities rather than conventional security and police methods. This will inevitably lead to the development of mechanisms of cooperation that guarantee success in the face of local, regional and international security challenges.

Security in the Gulf Region

HE Abdulrahman Al Attiyah

Our region faces an extremely complex and challenging security situation. The first decade of the 21st century has witnessed unprecedented expansion in the use of force in international relations, especially in the Middle East region, the most recent manifestation of which was the Israeli aggression against Lebanon in July 2006.

Furthermore, the Middle East has witnessed the application of double standards, which, sadly, have been adopted by the United States in particular when handling the affairs of our region. This approach has resulted in a blatant disregard for established principles of international law, and several violations of international resolutions.

Many chronic regional issues have lingered without any solution for several decades. Foremost among these is the Palestinian question, which has become even more severe as a result of Israel's methods of bloody violence, racial segregation, forced displacement, appropriation of property and disregard for international resolutions. This situation has bred frustration and turbulence throughout the entire Middle East region and has endangered the regional security situation by providing radical forces with the opportunity to turn the situation to their advantage.

The security situation in the Gulf region is undoubtedly unique, as is made clear by the following:

- This region is still characterized by an inherent state of imbalance and complex overlaps between regional and international elements. The region has witnessed several devastating regional wars as a result of attempts by various parties to impose regional hegemony. The occupation of Iraq and the dissolution of its army have led to the temporary removal of Iraq from the critical formula of regional equilibrium and the onset of instability that favors certain neighboring countries.

- Our region faces more severe dangers and threats than it did before 2003. This leads us to ask the following question: where is the democratic paradise promised by the United States? US actions have only led to sectarian and racial conflicts that continue to claim hundreds of lives on a daily basis.

- At the heart of the regional security dilemma is the difficulty of achieving an equilibrium of power in the region, based on a framework of regional security that will rebuild confidence among its participants.

- The GCC countries have found that a transitional regional security partnership – established and enhanced by friendships and regional/international security arrangements based on mutual respect and interests – is necessary to handle the imbalance of power in the region and the aspirations of regional and international forces and their conflicting future goals.

- Owing to its economic resources, our region has a strong connection with the stability and prosperity of the world economy. The increasing intensity of international interests in the region has led to the internationalization of the security formula in the region.

- The security dilemma in the Gulf region is further complicated by the fact that the policies of some countries make it difficult for others in the region to formulate worthy alternatives. Iran – and Iraq under Saddam Hussein – opposes the inclination of the GCC states to seek assistance from international powers to balance the region's security equation, arguing that Gulf security affairs should be restricted to the states of the Gulf. We might recall that the GCC countries have been at the forefront of those calling for this, as was mentioned in the statement of their first summit in 1981. However, Iran and Iraq did not propose a viable alternative regional security vision, and their words were contradicted by their actions. The actions of these two countries over the past decades espoused the opposite of what they had called for; this led to complications and to a strengthening of the international component of Gulf security.

To say that relations in the framework of these arrangements are easy and free of sensitivities and pressures would be an overstatement. Each politico-security relationship has a price, and undoubtedly adds political and financial overheads. Conversely, where is the easy, water-tight alternative? Perhaps this conference will assist us in formulating a path to such an alternative.

Following these preliminary remarks, allow me to briefly examine the situations of Iran and Iraq within the regional security sphere. Owing to their strategic location and their demographic, economic and military weight, these two countries have special status with regard to the calculation of the security equation in the Gulf region. They should also be considered as two primary parties in terms of energy security in the region owing to their respective oil production capacities.

On the other hand, as a whole, relations in the region have suffered as a result of acts of instigation and deliberate exaggeration by foreign parties, aimed at igniting dangerous conflicts in the region. In my estimation, the awareness and vigilance of all countries in the region has been heightened to avoid policies that inspire conflict. This awareness will lead to the adoption of formulas for regional cooperation based on authentic commitment to good neighborly relations, parity, and solving contentious issues by peaceful means. This is the only option that will allow us to establish strong pillars of regional security and stability.

Iran is a vital partner in achieving security and stability in the Gulf region on the basis of its geographical proximity to GCC countries. It is difficult for the countries of the region to ignore the obvious geographical strength of Iran, which makes it even more important that a formula for understanding and coexistence between the two sides of the Gulf is reached. These two sides are connected by common geography, religion and heritage, and therefore an inescapable organic, 'geopolitical' relationship.

However, there remains the issue of the three Iranian-occupied UAE islands (Abu Musa and the Greater and Lesser Tunbs). This matter has not been resolved because no progress has been achieved in direct regional and international contacts with Iran to encourage it to contribute to the solution of this issue, thereby reinforcing the security and stability of the region. If progress in settling such longstanding disputes is achieved via peaceful negotiations and referral to the International Court of Justice, it will result in a qualitative transformation of the relations with Iran.

Concerning Iraq, the current critical, ambiguous situation poses several questions regarding the implications of the Iraq issue for the security of the Gulf. One option has been posed by various different circles—namely, finalizing a strategy and schedule for the withdrawal of the occupation forces from Iraq.

It is necessary that all states commit themselves to respecting the unity, sovereignty and independence of Iraq and reject sectarianism and division in the country. There is an urgent need for reconciliation between the different constituents of the Iraqi population, and for amending articles of the constitution in a manner that guarantees equity among Iraqis in terms of their rights and duties, thus forming a national basis upon which security and stability can be built. The most pressing issues are the disarmament and dissolution of militias, the creation of a government that is representative of all Iraqis, and the establishment of citizenship and competence as the basic criteria of appointments instead of sectarian allegiance.

US intimidation has been counter-productive since the failure of the American strategy in Iraq – and in the Middle East in general – which has changed from 'supporting democracy' to 'supporting stability.' That is why a common vision must prevail, built not on exaggerated dangers but on the basis of common understanding between the countries of the region.

We, in the GCC, respect the choices of the Iraqi people concerning their system of governance, and we confirm again that no one has the right to interfere in their internal affairs. When forming the political character of the future state of Iraq, it is important to maintain Arab identity and for government to bolster its commitment to Arabism to prevent the splintering of the state.

No exploration of the different aspects of Gulf security is complete without a brief analysis of the Iranian nuclear crisis. The GCC stance towards this issue is as follows:

- We oppose the introduction of military nuclear programs by any country in the region because this could lead to a new and hazardous arms race.

- It is still possible to form a political solution to the Iranian nuclear crisis. This will require a brave and unorthodox vision, and a rational and realistic look at the different options available.

- In solving this crisis we absolutely reject military confrontation as a solution—with all its negative repercussions and likely consequences.

To achieve regional balance and to guarantee world security and stability, no exceptions can be made regarding countries that seek to possess weapons of mass destruction. You may recall in this respect the sincere call by the leaders of the GCC to make the Middle East region, including the Gulf, an area free of weapons of mass destruction.

Conflicts in the Middle East are not confined to the region, and often develop a universal character which involves states beyond the regional perimeter. Arab countries, collectively or individually, have preferred to

[17]

take a stance of "wait-and-see" when dealing with such conflicts, cautiously observing the course of events and favoring negotiation in their resolution. However, such a stance seems difficult to maintain.

In light of the Middle East's crises, it is difficult to imagine the states of the region being content to rely on an external regional security umbrella that affords no internal protection. These countries must exert serious efforts in solving the problems afflicting the region without leaving such matters to be handled by others.

I pose these remarks and viewpoints at your respected conference in the hope that they motivate thinking and may inspire productive dialogue on formulating a realistic collective vision for the future security of the Gulf countries.

Challenges and Dangers Facing the Gulf Region

HRH Prince Turki Al Faisal bin Abdulaziz Al-Saud

I encountered the subject of this conference on a daily basis when I was the Ambassador of the Custodian of the Two Holy Mosques to the United Kingdom of Great Britain and Northern Ireland and later the United States. What follows is an outline of the ideas and visions that have occurred to me over the last four years, in an attempt to address this difficult issue that is so vital to the people of the Gulf region.

The Gulf Cooperation Council (GCC) is facing a crisis that could adversely affect its stability and endanger its economic, political and social security. This crisis has become so clear that discussions on it have gone far beyond the regional sphere. It has become the subject of numerous writings and analyses seeking to uncover its motives and propose solutions. Some of these writings have been driven by hatred and hostility, aggravating doctrinal and political differences between both sides of the Gulf, i.e., the Sunni Arab countries on one shore and Shiite Iran on the other.

Such writings and analyses by political commentators and experts far removed from the region have projected Iran as a Shiite axis that seeks to spread its influence throughout the region known as the "Fertile Crescent." In effect, this means undermining the centuries-long peaceful co-existence of the different segments of Arab society, with their different doctrines and creeds. According to these analysts, Iran has emerged as a

[19]

dominant force in the region. Such negative analysis has also gained acceptance because of the emergence of nascent forces in the region that have links with Iran, and have defied those who have dared to oppose their orientation. In fact, these forces have resorted to violence to settle scores with their Sunni brothers, by calling them either *Wahhabis* or *Takfiriyyin* (those who accuse others of apostasy) and they have spread misinformation to the effect that Sunni groups either assisted in or ignored persecution against their community during the reign of Saddam Hussein in Iraq. It is only fair to say that Saddam was unbiased in his persecution of all Iraqis, regardless of their origin or faith.

Some elements of the Sunni world have also made loathsome calls to kill and torture those whom they call the "refusers"; meaning the Shi'a. Both parties have clashed in Iraq, which has become a focal point of hatred and abomination. In this context it is necessary to focus on the reality of the Iranian threat, its connection to the events taking place in Iraq and Lebanon, as well as its repercussions on the security and stability of the GCC countries.

We witnessed the meeting between King Abdullah bin Abdulaziz Al Saud, Custodian of the Two Holy Mosques, and President Mahmoud Ahmadinejad, in which they agreed to quench the fire of sectarianism which is blazing in Iraq and Lebanon. To this end, I would rather look on Iran as a neighboring and friendly country, which is tied to us via historic links, economic interests and social similarities. The doctrinal dispute between Iran and the GCC countries must not lead to hostility or hatred; as such disputes are age-old and cannot be settled overnight. Rising above this conflict will require wisdom, recourse to the foundations of the Islamic faith and, above all, tolerance. This must include launching a public awareness campaign to show that coexistence is necessary for providing regional security, and to underscore the futility of resorting to hiding behind doctrinal divisions at a time when people require assimilation and good relations in order to secure the welfare and stability of the peoples of the entire region. Iran and the GCC countries form a brilliant weave comprising Sunnis and Shiites, which can be likened to the most beautiful Zarabi (carpets) produced in Tabriz, Na'in or Shiraz.

We must face the reality that a major element of the doctrinal dispute in the region has become a political issue that could, if neglected, pose a major danger and intensify fear and suspicion on each side. If we were to surrender to such fears and suspicions, neither the Iranian nor the Saudi influence in Iraq, Lebanon or Palestine would be meaningful, especially if each party sought to face and take on the other in these states. There should be cooperation and partnership between neighboring countries, working together in order to fend off the crippling crises the region faces today.

We should tackle this issue in a direct manner by transforming such negative influences into positive investments in Iraq, Lebanon and Palestine, thus reinforcing development in these countries. What is more, this should be achieved via combined efforts. We look forward to a Saudi investment in Mashhad or Shiraz paralleled by an Iranian investment in King Abdullah Economic City or in Jubail, thus breaking down mutual fear and doubt.

All Gulf countries, not only those of the GCC, face innumerable challenges and difficulties that require rational solutions—not the provocation of alleged disputes such as conflict between Sunnis and Shiites in Iraq, or the quest for a "Shiite crescent" here or a "Sunni tide" there. Iran suffers from unemployment, rising economic and social difficulties and a steady growth in population. Such issues exist in the GCC countries as well—albeit on a different scale. Addressing these challenges requires sustained effort and action using our God-given talents and knowledge, as well as cooperation and stability in order to implement development plans.

Those who search for unrealistic, metaphysical solutions derived from historical tradition, such as waiting for a *Mahdi* [equivalent to the second coming of Jesus in the Christian sense] or establishing an "Islamic Emirate," reveal their incapacity to deal with current challenges via human and worldly agencies in accordance with the divine rules set by Allah for populating the earth, which define work, then more work, and still more work, sincerity, diligence and good advice as prerequisites. Success is bestowed by Allah when these rules are followed (say, "Work righteousness; God will see your work, and so will His messenger and the believers").

The aspirations of the peoples of the region, the majority of whom are youths, cannot be met by numbing their spirits and telling them to wait for a "feast from Heaven," or by spreading extremist ideas among them, thereby paralyzing their productive capabilities and creating in them a sense of dependence, fanaticism and conflict.

Therefore, the first challenge facing both sides of the Gulf is the need to take recourse to the book of Allah *Ta'ala* (Most High) and the *Sunna* of the Prophet (peace be upon him), and follow his example by utilizing constructive political thought that relates to earthly matters without being saturated by metaphysical concerns. Thereafter, we should open our doors to cooperation and constructive partnership, as well as economic, social and cultural exchange in order to face real challenges.

The GCC countries seek to bolster the security of all the countries of the region, both spiritually and economically. Therefore, the Kingdom of Saudi Arabia (KSA) and its partners in the GCC have stressed the necessity of finding a fair solution to the Palestinian issue, which remains the combined concern and focus of our nations. There is also the necessity of working towards a Middle East region free of weapons of mass destruction, as well as the reinforcement of the legitimate right of all countries in the region to make use of all types of energy resources, including the peaceful use of nuclear power. The international community must not harbor double standards, and should not deprive us and Iran from gaining access to this form of energy—indeed, the international community condemns us when we try to acquire nuclear knowledge and overlooks the fact that Israel possesses nuclear weapons.

Although my aforementioned statements are full of "wishful thinking," one must acknowledge that the wisdom needed to succeed is indeed present on both sides of the Gulf. I also hope that we are able to solve the issue of our embarrassment to show any desire for material interests. Relations between countries based on material interests are beneficial and positive, and cannot be measured according to comparisons with human affinities between siblings or friends. To illustrate my point of view, I give the example of relations between Saudi Arabia and the Gulf countries—which are excellent brotherly relations. However, Dubai and Bahrain are closer to the Kingdom than the other members of the GCC due to huge Saudi investment and increasing commercial exchange between them and the KSA. In this context, economic integration between the Kingdom and all countries of the Arabian Gulf region sits at the top of Saudi Arabia's development priorities.

Another example of mutual interest lies in Lebanon, prompting the Kingdom to take a keen interest in the Lebanese situation, from the time of its independence to the last clash between the government and the opposition, that has exceeded acceptable limits and pushed the country to the brink of political *Fitna* (sedition), and worse, sectarian sedition. While the main party to the conflict, i.e. Hezbollah, is ideologically and organically linked to Iran, the KSA and all the Gulf countries were, and still are, connected to Lebanon as a whole. Our allies are not only Sunnis because the pre-eminent position that the Kingdom holds in the Islamic world necessitates openness to all Arabs without distinguishing between one sect and another, or even between Muslims and non-Muslims.

In order to avoid competition and discord, the Kingdom deemed it necessary to open a dialogue with Iran, instead of entering into a conflict with it over Lebanon. Any such conflict would have harmed the people of Lebanon, the relationship between the two big neighboring powers on each side of the Arabian Gulf, and relations between Sunnis and Shiites, which are already suffering from preexisting tensions. We have not yet exerted sufficient efforts to mend relations between Sunnis and Shiites in

[23]

a way that characterizes the basic tenets of civilized coexistence within the context of the spirit of tolerance called for by our righteous religion. Even if we fail to mend this relationship, we must try to prevent a war between the followers of both doctrines.

Undoubtedly, any conflict arising between the KSA and Iran in Lebanon would extend beyond Lebanon's borders, and would fuel extremist elements on both sides that rely on sedition and conflict to nurture their twisted rationale—which is incompatible with true Islam. These elements stir up past secessions, create conflicts among people, supplant reconciliation, and revive past differences and divisions. Another role is played by foreign actors, who thrive on our conflicts and hide behind our discord to justify their existence among us. Therefore, we are conferring with all Lebanese parties, giving them advice, listening to their concerns and trying to find common ground, while ensuring that the sovereignty of Lebanon remains intact. Furthermore, we are not advancing our interests at the expense of the interests of the Lebanese people.

One cannot deny the existence of the ongoing Lebanese crisis, but its severity has been reduced somewhat, thanks to Saudi–Iranian contacts. With the cooperation of different Lebanese partners, these contacts have led to the successful avoidance of critical pitfalls, which almost destroyed everything. These efforts are still underway, and we hope that these will be successful very soon.

The principle adopted by the KSA in negotiations is not based on military force or political pressure. It is based on the fact that all people of the region want to live with dignity, security and stability, so that every citizen is able to make a living, has a home to live in with their family, has access to proper education for his or her children and enjoys good health. This is sound logic, and if we agree upon it with other parties, we can solve all our problems. In such an atmosphere, there will be no more disagreement over establishing an international court in the case of the assassination of the late Lebanese Prime Minister Rafik Hariri. If this court were to play its role, it would not be for political reasons but to bolster the security that concerns every citizen in Lebanon. Furthermore, the conflict based on the rights of Shiites in Lebanon is meaningless since it is only evident that they deserve the rights enjoyed by all other members of Lebanese society, in order to participate in the building of Lebanon and benefit from its advantages. They should not be aggressive against others or marginalize partners in any government; sharing in the decision-making but not dictating it.

As for the problem in Iraq, there is a dire need for Gulf/Arab–Iranian cooperation in order to close the rift as quickly as possible without waiting for the settlement of the crisis in Lebanon—even if such a settlement will provide common ground to build on. The situation in Iraq cannot be deferred until the crisis in Lebanon is resolved. Iraq's blood is being shed daily and cooperation is needed to bring its people together.

Sadly, there are political forces in Iraq that have not learned the art of coexistence, power-sharing and bestowing rights to rightful parties. Instead, they attempt to eliminate, exclude and alienate others. These forces need help in taking the first step toward justice, equality and freedom for the members of Iraqi society, and we should not allow them to take advantage of us in order to settle their scores. They should not be allowed to coerce one another and employ extremism and doctrine to camouflage their political ambitions and satisfy their thirst for leadership and authoritarianism. We demand that these forces stop trying to outbid each other on an ethnic or doctrinal basis, and instead develop faithful and honest intentions. We should avoid using them, exploiting their needs and their differences to settle scores with far enemies, and refrain from using these differences as bargaining chips with opportunistic neighbors.

Finally, I would like to warn you about a real danger that continues to bear down on us. This danger will not dissipate unless we take a firm stance against it; a stance that rejects it and does not give it justification or employ it in any form. This is the danger of extremism and religious zealotry— whether this is violent and uses arms, or verbal and uses words and

[25]

manifestos to spread hatred and animosity. We must not permit a situation that allows its proponents, who are under arms, to unleash death and devastation on our societies. Our governments, religious scholars and opinion leaders should take this stance. As Sunnis, we have been burned by the fires of Al-Qaeda and the sedition it has unleashed. The Shiites now are the victims of the acts of a new sect among them called *Jund El Sama* [Soldiers of Heaven], which carries out evil and harmful acts as witnessed from Al-Najaf in Iraq to Zahedan in Iran.

Extremism and excessive acts are lethal, whether they are perpetrated by Sunnis or Shiites, Christians or Jews. When extremists are present among conflicting parties, negotiations cannot succeed, agreements are not respected and confidence cannot be built. Let Iraq be the first platform where we establish a firm position against extremism in all its forms, be it Sunni or Shiite. Such extremism has driven a wedge between Iraqis and propelled them towards a state of polarization, which has resulted in premonitions of ethnic cleansing that could destroy Iraq as a unified homeland and a state of brotherhood which has existed as an Arab-Islamic state for more than 1,400 years—not a mere 100 years, as the West alleges.

I also call for a similar, complementary stance that condemns extremists' use of death – their favorite and most powerful weapon – and stops them from spreading the culture of suicide attacks and public bloodshed committed against those who oppose them. We all disagree with them. We have stopped counting the number of daily victims in Iraq – men, women, the elderly and children – whom they kill without fear of committing the cardinal sin—murder. Left to them, all our countries would become like Iraq. I would like to remind you of the courageous stance taken by the scholars of the Kingdom, a strict stand that condemns all kinds of suicide attacks, be they against Muslims or non-Muslims, a colonialist enemy or a soldier protecting his homeland. Alas, some of our scholars condone such tactics by describing them as 'martyrdom,' but these acts are not without the sin of committing suicide. It is only in our times that suicide attacks are perpetrated, which indicates a historical rejection of them.

No one can dispute the commitment of the scholars of the Kingdom of Saudi Arabia to the *Salafi* methodology in issuing *fatwas* (legal religious edicts). Their *fatwas* should constitute a comprehensive and unified Islamic stance against the culture of death that has deluded many of the *Umma*'s [Islamic nation's] young men and undermined the pure and tolerant spirit of Islam.

Let me say it loud and clear: instead of dreaming of or dreading a "Shiite Crescent," we can work together to build a "Fertile Crescent" that spreads from Iraq to Lebanon, where Syria will have a leading role, Jordan a share and Palestine an important corner; where development, welfare and happiness will prevail and from which all Gulf countries will benefit. Let it be a crescent of agreement, not disagreement.

However, there is a wound between the shores of the Gulf which continues to bleed—that of the Iranian occupation of the three UAE islands (the Tunbs and Abu Musa). How can we agree with Iran in Iraq and Lebanon while it still occupies our land? I hope that Iran faces the fact and admits that such an occupation cannot last, and I ask the people of Iran, its government and its leadership to be fair and unprejudiced towards us. This illustrates how cruel the aggression can be among friends and neighbors!

Arabian Gulf Security:
Internal and External Challenges

HE Terje Rød-Larsen

It must be emphasized at the outset that this presentation is being made in my capacity as President of the International Peace Academy and not on behalf of the United Nations.

This ECSSR Annual Conference focuses on a particularly timely theme. Its relevance is manifested when we consider the regional environment: north, to Iraq; northeast, to Iran; and west, to the Arab-Israeli/Israeli–Palestinian and Lebanese–Syrian arenas. It is evident that the entire Middle East region is in a deepening crisis.

Deepening Crisis: From One Centre of Gravity to Four Epicenters

In a way, it is trivial to say that the Middle East is in crisis, as this region has always had to contend with crises. However, in my view, the Middle East today confronts challenges that have more complex dynamics, and are more extensively disruptive and dangerous than in the past several decades. Multiple issues are a manifestation of the fast-developing and multi-dimensional crisis and fragility that pervades the region:

- The bloody war in Lebanon last summer and its effects on the country's stability.

- The tragic Iraqi imbroglio, with its potentially extensive regional implications.

- The looming crisis over Iran's nuclear program and its impact on a new arms race in the region and beyond, including the possible collapse of the Non-Proliferation Treaty (NPT).
- The still unresolved Israeli–Palestinian conflict.

It is unnecessary to point out that these predicaments hold significance for not only the inhabitants of this region but also those beyond it. Instability and conflict in the Middle East inherently have global repercussions because this region is more important, both in geo-strategic and geo-economic terms, than any other in the world.

The Middle East is also a region in which local, regional and global dimensions are intertwined like no other: everything that concerns one society in the region affects all others. Middle Eastern crises are immediately exported into every capital throughout the Muslim world. They also touch hearts and minds in every capital in the Western world. Regional conflicts are of a global scale, but not *between* societies, civilizations, or sectarian groupings. Instead, the dividing lines are *within* societies, within cultures, even within communities, be they ethnic or sectarian.

Middle Eastern predicaments are also often international crises, either in a latent or manifest sense. In the old days, many of the crises in the region were directly and inextricably linked with the Cold War at the global level. And even though the Cold War is over and superpower rivalry is no more, the world's sole superpower is deeply involved in the region. Some would argue that it has indeed become a regional power: it is no longer an outside actor just *sometimes* involved in the region. The argument would run that the United States is now so deeply engaged here that it cannot possibly isolate itself, or be ignored by any party in the region. The intimately interwoven crises of the Middle East profoundly shape the nature of world politics and the course of international relations. The converse is also equally true; world politics forcefully shape the nature of political developments in the region.

Allow me to focus, however, more specifically on what I think is a more central and distinct new element in the dynamics of crisis and fragility in the Middle East. For decades, the *key issue* dominating and shaping this region was the Arab–Israeli conflict. This conflict constituted one centre of gravity, around which the region revolved. It shaped and overshadowed everything; it fundamentally impacted Arab domestic politics, and intra-Arab as well as intra-regional relations. It defined the overall politics and international ties and linkages of the region.

My thesis is that this situation has changed paradigmatically over the course of the last four or five years. The Arab–Israeli conflict is no longer the sole defining crisis in the region. Of course, it remains essential, and needs to be resolved desperately because it continues to be a fundamental prerequisite for changing political and diplomatic dynamics. Such a change must be based on the Arab Initiative, relevant Security Council resolutions, and the Road Map.

However, instead of one center of gravity, there are now four epicenters of crisis, conflict and instability in the Middle East. These differ in their origins and patterns of confrontation but at the same time are deeply interrelated. The four epicenters are Iraq, Lebanon and Syria, Iran and the Israeli–Palestinian arena. With the emergence of these epicenters over the last few years, the geopolitical map of the Middle East has changed fundamentally.

Consequently, there is a fundamental need to alter both the analyses and the recipes for crisis management and conflict resolution in the region. I believe that such a change has already begun, especially here in the Gulf. Two new political configurations have recently taken shape: first, the informal mechanism of the Arab Quartet, of which the United Arab Emirates is a member alongside Saudi Arabia, Egypt and Jordan; second, the meetings of the six GCC states along with Egypt and Jordan— the so-called "Six-plus-Two" group. This reveals that many in the region perceive a heightened need not only for discussion but also for unity in the Arab world. Such unity is seen as a precondition for addressing the

[31]

manifold new challenges confronting the Arabian Gulf and the Levant. The nature and central issues posed by the four epicenters, as I perceive them, are briefly outlined below.

Iraq: A Challenge to Wider Regional Stability

There is no doubt that both for the states of the Arabian Gulf and other actors in the region and beyond, Iraq is the key crisis in the Middle East today. Needless to say, the Iraqi arena is not directly linked with the Arab–Israeli conflict.

Initially, there were many discussions over the legitimacy and international legality of the war in Iraq. I believe this discussion is now outdated and no longer has practical relevance. The instability in Iraq has increasingly become a problem that affects everyone. The current instability threatens to spread through the entire region surrounding the country. It is therefore not just a problem that the United States confronts but one that affects everyone.

The Iraqi problem will ultimately have to be addressed at two mutually reinforcing levels. The first is at the domestic level. Ways have to be found to bring the different Iraqi communities together. They must be helped and persuaded to thrash out their differences. They should be allowed to re-build a common destiny.

The second level at which the Iraqi problem will have to be addressed, is the regional level. This regional process will have to accompany, underpin and reinforce any such domestic process. Iraq's neighbors will have to play a constructive role. That will be a difficult feat to achieve as the ability of some to hinder progress has already been seen. Many already fear the consequences if the efforts to stabilize Iraq fail. Regional instability might spread and affect everyone. The regional conference initiated by the Iraqi government is therefore an important venture, and a promising one. However, it must also be accompanied by similar efforts at the domestic level.

Lebanon: Microcosm for Regional Struggles

Iraq today brings to mind Lebanon—another country that once was and has again become an arena in which outside players stage their confrontations, indirectly and through proxies. After the civil war, Lebanon remained an incomplete project of state-consolidation. With the withdrawal of Israeli troops in May 2000, new momentum was created. This led to Security Council resolution 1559 and eventually to Syria's military withdrawal in March/April 2005.

I had the privilege to serve as the Special Envoy of the United Nations Secretary-General and act, on his behalf, as the negotiator on both the Israeli and the Syrian withdrawals. We also assisted the Lebanese in organizing the first free and fair elections in Lebanon.

However, a contest remains over who has what influence and what role in Lebanon—reflecting a fundamental struggle over the nature and extent of Lebanon's sovereignty and independence. This struggle is inherently a regional struggle. It involves and affects, for instance, Syrian and Iranian interests, which in turn makes it relevant for the national security interests of Egypt, Jordan and the GCC countries, besides others in the region. Lebanon's direct relevance to security in the Arabian Gulf may be best illustrated by the efforts of Saudi Arabia and Iran to broker a compromise between the two main camps in Lebanon. These efforts reflect and appear to indicate public recognition for a growing Iranian role in the region. The renewed importance accorded to the Sunni and Shi'a identities may be observed throughout the region, revealing the emergence of a new fault-line in the Middle East.

Iran: A New Center of Gravity

Indeed, it seems that one of the key changes over the last few years is not only a fundamental reordering of the balance of power in the Middle East, but also a seismic shift in regional geopolitics. This shift will have far-reaching implications as Iran has now emerged as a major player in the region.

[33]

Last summer, when I accompanied Kofi Annan, then UN Secretary-General, on his travels to this region amid the crisis over the war between Israel and Hezbollah, it was repeatedly impressed on us how the eyes in the region were fixed not only on Tel Aviv, but were also equally trained on Tehran.

Thus, in my analysis, Iran represents the fourth epicenter of crisis. The Iranian nuclear program and ambitions have raised many questions, both in the wider international community and in this region. Fears and doubts have been voiced, rightly or wrongly, over whether the world is witnessing a revival of age-old Persian nationalist ambitions.

Let me state clearly that, just like any other state signatory to the non-proliferation treaty, the Islamic Republic has the indisputable right to develop nuclear energy for civilian purposes. Yet, it must do so within the confines of the nuclear non-proliferation regime. Iran needs to answer the questions that have remained unaddressed so far.

If these questions are not addressed, the implications will be very significant and deeply worrying. First, the already weak global non-proliferation regime will erode further and is likely to collapse. Second, an arms race may ensue, perhaps beginning in the region but certainly not confined to it for long.

Sometimes, perceptions are much more important than realities, because it is the former that drive actions. This is one such instance. The main issue is not necessarily about what is really happening in Iran's nuclear facilities. If the raised questions remain unanswered, then many of the regional political actors may conclude that the real issue at stake is one of Iran's hegemonic, emerging ambitions. In the region, a new fault-line is appearing between aspirations of Arab unity, stability and peaceful regional and international cooperation versus the widely perceived aspirations of aggressive expansionism and hopes of regional dominance and hegemony. If these trends are allowed to deepen, they will expose and widen rifts across the region.

Inter-Linkages between the Epicenters

Thus far, reference has been made to three of the four epicenters of crisis and instability in the Middle East in relative isolation. However, it is hardly necessary to emphasize how these epicenters have grown and become increasingly interlinked.

Examples illustrating the linkages between these arenas abound. Reference has been made to Saudi and Iranian mediation efforts in Lebanon. There has also been a brief mention of the Arab Quartet and the Six-plus-Two mechanism, which groups together the GCC with Egypt and Jordan. Both these vehicles are significant manifestations of a growing recognition of shared concerns and interests among these actors. However, it is perhaps equally significant to note who does not form part of these mechanisms.

There is one further example of how the arenas and conflicts in the Middle East, although separate in their roots, have become intertwined. This interlinking is demonstrated in the fourth epicenter of crisis and instability in the Middle East—the Israeli–Palestinian arena.

The Israeli–Palestinian Arena: Ripe for a Revived Peace Process

The issues in this arena remain essentially the same as they have been for a long time, and yet have become much more complicated in recent years. With the election of Hamas to the Palestinian Authority, questions have emerged not only regarding the recognition of Israel but also the commitment to previously signed agreements and the renunciation of violence. These are, of course, the three conditions that the Middle East Quartet stipulated in January 2006.

However, this question also has much to do with broader regional dynamics. Many Palestinian decisions are no longer made in Ramallah or Gaza but in Damascus, where Khaled Meshaal, the head of the Hamas politburo resides. Moreover, there has been increasing contact between Hamas and Iran. For the Israelis, and some states in the international community, this has raised questions about the feasibility of efforts to revive the Israeli–Palestinian peace process.

These questions are important and valid. And yet, it seems, precisely because of the new wider regional dynamics, there is a genuine momentum now to re-start the Israeli–Palestinian peace process.

I will not name here a senior Arab official who told me some time last year that in the light of the questions raised by developments in Iran, the Israeli–Palestinian conflict had basically turned into a real estate conflict— one that really could and needed to be settled immediately, once and for all, based on broadly accepted blueprints, such as the Arab Initiative. My friend added that this would in turn bring justice and improved living conditions to the suffering Palestinian people. It would bring security and an end to the bereavement suffered by Israelis through the establishment of the State of Palestine alongside Israel. This move should be paired with universal recognition of both. According to my friend, this would mean that policymakers in the Arab world could focus on issues that are really of more immediate and tangible concern.

There can be no question that all arenas of crisis in the Middle East need to be addressed in parallel. Only a holistic, comprehensive approach can ultimately stabilize the region. In the long run, I believe, this will mean the establishment of a regional security architecture that integrates all and affords space to everyone. In the short run, however, comprehensive solutions are very difficult to realize. The Lebanon war last summer and the prolonged political crisis in the country may come to be seen as precursors of future developments. Unfortunately, things may get much worse before they get better.

Therefore, I believe significant progress can be made to begin stabilizing the region in one particular arena: the Israeli–Palestinian one. This may be an arena which in many ways is far removed from the Arabian Gulf, the key concern of this conference. However, due to its symbolic significance, its emotive appeal, and its signaling effects, progress in the Israeli–Palestinian arena will powerfully and positively affect the other conflicts. This theatre of confrontation may not only indicate the easiest way forward, but also become the most important dynamo for further stabilization efforts.

I believe that the way forward is a package of two concurrent steps. Many do not remember that it is actually the PLO, according to all signed agreements, not the Palestinian Authority, which retains foreign policy functions on behalf of the Palestinian people. This is an important part of the Oslo Accords. As a result, I don't think there can or should be much discussion about it: PLO Chairman Mahmoud Abbas and the Government of Israel should engage in negotiations. In this context, I think it is significant that the Palestinian Authority Prime Minister, Ismail Haniya, has stated repeatedly that he does not object to any such talks.

Negotiations should focus on immediate action but also open up discussion and seek possible agreement on the principles of a final status arrangement. As outlined in the Road Map, the immediate action should be Israeli territorial concessions in the West Bank and the establishment of a Palestinian state. This state would then have the same international status as Israel.

In order to make such a process work, any agreement reached in negotiations would be put to a referendum among the Palestinian people before implementation. Once supported at the popular level, both states should be recognized by all other states. This should also lead to immediate state-to-state negotiations on settling all remaining issues. Elections to the new and permanent Palestinian state institutions would take place in parallel.

Wider Regional Significance of a Revived Israeli–Palestinian Process

The process leading to the establishment of the State of Palestine should by guided by the Arab Peace Initiative and its realization. This initiative, adopted unanimously by the Arab League at its March 2002 summit in Beirut, has not received Israeli endorsement. However, it does remain a key pillar of any forward move. As you may recall, the Quartet's Road Map explicitly addresses and builds on the Arab Peace Initiative. I believe and know for a fact that many in Israel now see the benefits and advantages of this initiative.

Consequently, progress in the Israeli–Palestinian arena is not only directly relevant to Gulf security, but for the Arabian Gulf states. These states can play a very significant role in achieving such progress, with a beneficial impact on their security concerns and needs. With the recent efforts of the Arab Quartet, which includes the United Arab Emirates and the work of the Six-plus-Two group, the Gulf states have done a lot of important groundwork. The fact that the UAE is now recognized as a leading diplomatic actor in the region is a testimony to these important achievements—and certainly, this recognition will only grow further.

To conclude, I would quote the late Founding Father of the United Arab Emirates, Sheikh Zayed bin Sultan Al Nahyan. Ten years ago, while opening a conference here in Abu Dhabi, Sheikh Zayed referred to the need for Arab unity: "It is time," he said, "to mend fences, forgive each other, and leave the door open for all Arabs to return to the Arab ranks."

Sheikh Zayed went on to say that the Arabs would settle their dispute with Israel once the legitimate rights of the Palestinian people were addressed, saying in that instance, "the Arabs would cooperate with [Israel], because they have no greed for the rights of others."

Sheikh Zayed's wisdom still looms large and should guide us all.

An Overall Perspective of Gulf Security

*HE Staff Lt. General Fahad Ahmad Al-Amir**

The fact that this Conference examines urgent security issues in the Arabian Gulf, and brings together various elites to put forward their views and perceptions of those issues within a sober and result-oriented dialogue, indicates a great sense of responsibility towards the region's future security, stability and the interests of its people.

It is no secret that the Arab Gulf countries are extremely important. In addition to their significant strategic location, they own nearly two-thirds of the world reserves of oil and gas which are sources of energy, drivers of economies and transportation, and basic military requisites in times of both peace and war. They are also important players in terms of the security and stability of the world economy, which explains the intense competition between various influential powers to control them. Furthermore, they play a significant role in the dynamics of the region's economies themselves.

We view security from an overall perspective since there is a close relationship between security and stability on the one hand, and modernization and development on the other. In order to address security challenges, particularly those of an internal nature, development

---

* Staff Lt. General Fahad Ahmad Al-Amir designated Staff Brigadier General Ahmad Mahmoud Al-Rahmani, Director of Joint Military Operations at the Kuwait Armed Forces, to deliver his address at the Conference on his behalf.

requirements must be met, and local imbalances and shortcomings in various fields – political, economic, social, etc. – must be addressed. We believe that developing a regional security environment is important if we are to be adequately prepared to respond to external challenges and threats.

As for internal challenges, we believe that the imbalance in the population composition constitutes a basic problem in the Arab Gulf states. These countries have opened their doors to an expatriate labor force which today accounts for a majority of the active labor force in the Gulf states. This has been accompanied by a lack of interest on the part of nationals in technical and vocational education. As a result, these states are unable to rely on their nationals to implement development plans.

Overdependence on the expatriate workforce has long-term cultural, political, economic, social and security-related implications. The processes of naturalization for immigrants and nationalization of the workforce constitute fundamental challenges to the GCC countries, especially because such processes relate to other important issues such as education and training.

Education presents the Gulf states with a chronic dilemma. Generally speaking, the education sector in these states continues to grow quantitatively rather than qualitatively and in many respects does not meet contemporary requirements. Furthermore, there is a wide gap between educational output and development need, and the lack of a strategic vision for the development of the education sector has led to a reduction in both the level and quality of output. In this respect, the importance of harmony with the requirements of globalization and the necessity of giving more attention to modern technological and technical sciences become apparent.

Development is a continuous process in which inputs and outputs interact through various courses of production. Productive sectors in the Arab Gulf states have grown remarkably over the last few years. This requires that the inputs of the development process be modernized on a regular basis. Labor force is doubtless the most important of these inputs. Therefore, training and human capacity-building should be considered among the priorities at this stage. A direct link should also be established between training goals and development targets. This requires a re-assessment and organization of training fields with a view to acquiring the knowledge, expertise and skills needed by national cadres to access the labor market.

Notwithstanding the achievements and gains of the training sector in the Gulf states, there still exist some failures that limit its efficiency and effectiveness, including the lack – thus far – of a comprehensive training plan that encompasses all types and levels of training and seeks to strike the desired balance in developing and qualifying the national labor force.

Among the negative symptoms which characterize the national labor force in our countries are: the high levels of unemployment; the prevalence of an attitude of dependency; a change in attitude towards work from productivity and a search for value in the effort spent, to a mere job to be done; the reluctance of the young to take on manual work; and the spread of abominable practices such as the tendency towards extravagance in consumption.

Furthermore, the Gulf states' tendency to guarantee the provision of employment services under the umbrella of wealth distribution has enormously harmed the work ethic of citizens and led to laziness and a lack of innovation, modernization and motivation in many sectors. It has also led to disguised unemployment and an unproductive workforce which in turn has encouraged many private employers to resort to foreign workers in order to safeguard production. Although this phenomenon is on the decrease, sluggishness in addressing its causes will lead to long-term social imbalances and negative security impacts.

Another challenge is posed by the phenomenon of extremism that plagues the world at large – and this region in particular – and which stems from a culture of single-mindedness and exclusion. There is an urgent need to diagnose the reasons behind this phenomenon, its motives and the means with which to combat it, especially in view of its security-related and potential social effects including: the partitioning of society, severing the

[41]

links that secure its unity and harmony; an absence of law and discipline; a lack of freedom of opinion and expression; the domination of intransigence and isolation; and a departure from sound doctrines and human values.

Governments and civil society institutions must unify their efforts to combat this phenomenon. Such efforts must focus on: revising prevailing negative cultures; modernizing education systems; disseminating tolerant values; encouraging liberties; consolidating democracy and human rights; and reinforcing the foundations of law and order.

As for terrorism, which is born of extremism, it is growing at an alarming rate and constitutes a challenge that cannot be underestimated. Terrorism drains a great deal of resources and effort that could be invested in development. The Gulf region has been greatly affected by the repercussions and impacts of terrorism. This necessitates compliance with strategies which aim to combat this phenomenon, address its causes, investigate its motives, and enhance regional cooperation with a view to creating a more secure and stable world.

The GCC states have adopted a number of resolutions and initiatives in this respect, including: the security strategy of the GCC states for combating extremism and terrorism at the 22nd Summit of the GCC Supreme Council, held in the Sultanate of Oman in 2001; the endorsement of the GCC Anti-Terrorism Pact at the 24th Summit of the GCC Supreme Council, held in the State of Kuwait in 2003; and the agreement by the 90th GCC Ministerial Council, held in Saudi Arabia in 2004, to support a number of steps and mechanisms to combat terrorism. Yet we are still in need of more comprehensive cooperation and a wider coordination of efforts to root out terrorism, establish the principles of moderation and adopt a common strategy for Gulf national security to stand up to terrorism and other threats.

As for external challenges, we believe that the long-lasting instability in the region poses the greatest danger of all. The successive wars which the region has experienced have undoubtedly contributed to the loss of numerous opportunities for construction and development, established a culture of violence and led to regional division. The implications and effects of those wars are still present, foremost of which is the inability of the region's states to re-build confidence among themselves.

Although the toppling of the former Iraqi regime has removed a major threat to the GCC countries, the situation in Iraq heralds sectarian and ethnic dangers that continue to attract regional and international security interventions, amounting to a continuation of the state of instability in the region.

The EU–GCC security partnership is a reflection of the European interest in the security of the Arabian Gulf region, from the participation of European states in the 1991 war to liberate Kuwait and the signing of bilateral security agreements with the GCC states to secure European participation in Gulf security, to the holding of a NATO-initiated strategic dialogue with the six GCC states within the framework of the Istanbul Cooperation Initiative (ICI), launched during the Organization's summit in Istanbul in 2004. The aim of this was to enhance regional security and stability through the establishment of a foundation for a new partnership with the Organization.

Openness to Europe, and to NATO in particular, represents a qualitative change that should be viewed separately to the region's individual armed disputes. Focus should instead be put on peaceful and developmental cooperation to qualify the Gulf armed forces to play roles which guarantee a more efficient and cooperative environment and establish security and stability in accordance with international concepts and standards.

The concept of the Greater Middle East has recently been put forward. We believe that the vision promoted under this concept entails many challenges and risks for the Arab Gulf states. This concept is undoubtedly not without basis. That is why there is a need to be ready to interact with its political, economic, social and even geographic implications and effects.

The Iranian nuclear issue has introduced yet another state of controversy, tension and crisis to the area, the impacts of which will affect the states of the region as a whole and negatively influence their development. If we truly believe in the right of nations to acquire nuclear technology in all its forms in accordance with international rules and standards, this case represents a serious challenge to the Gulf region. We hope that efforts will continue to further harmonize the viewpoints of the relevant parties and that a solution will be reached via peaceful means that will spare the region further distress and provide its peoples with more opportunities for development and prosperity.

Concerning the security situation in Iraq, factors such as sectarian conflict, growing violence, incompatible interests and tendencies, increasing acts of terrorism, political instability and influence exercised by external powers all entail great dangers that will not be confined to within Iraq's borders but will affect the entire region and hinder Iraq's integration into the regional environment. The undertaking by the region's states of more effective roles to maintain Iraq's unity and stability is necessary to meet serious challenges and to avoid the implications and negative effects of the situation in Iraq.

With regard to the above issues, the following points should be taken into account:

- Considering the importance of Gulf oil and the smooth flow from its sources to the world, we believe that the Gulf states should firstly take all necessary measures to build confidence among themselves and then agree on a protocol to secure maritime and trade traffic through the Strait of Hormuz, putting forward solutions to cases where navigation through the strait becomes dangerous or problematic.

- GCC states should adopt practical development strategies that respond to current socio-economic challenges, pay particular attention to synergy in formulating development plans and programs, complete all economic integration projects among them and attempt to remove obstacles to the establishment of the GCC common market and monetary union.

- Efforts should continue towards: developing education systems that will facilitate the overall development targets of GCC states; linking education with practical needs for certain professions and jobs in Gulf societies; adopting ambitious technical and vocational education plans that will secure the gradual substitution of national labor force for expatriate labor force; developing awareness, encouraging production and confronting negative consumption patterns; and advancing political, economic and administrative reform in the GCC states.

- It is necessary to complete the ongoing military capacity-building in the GCC states through: developing joint military capabilities and realizing the Peninsula Shield Force, with the latter possibly forming the nucleus of a joint Gulf army; adopting a joint Gulf military strategy to deter all potential external threats; intensifying cooperation between the GCC and friendly states in rooting out terrorism; and reaching an appropriate formula for security arrangements in the Gulf region.

- With regard to the Iranian nuclear program, we believe it is necessary to continue with political/diplomatic efforts to harmonize the viewpoints on both sides of the Gulf and between the Islamic Republic of Iran and the international community to protect the Gulf region from undesirable conflicts.

- Concerning the situation in Iraq, we believe it is necessary to work on settling all differences that led to the present situation in Iraq through enhancing dialogue between the constituents of Iraqi society, revising the political process, dissolving militias, supporting Iraqi government efforts to combat terrorism, enhancing the security and military capabilities of Iraq, and upholding communication with neighboring states in pursuit of those objectives.

Ultimately, we strongly believe in the importance of dialogue, joint action and continuous engagement – be it between the GCC states themselves or with Iraq, the Islamic Republic of Iran or other international parties – in reaching a common understanding on the region's major issues and that confidence-building measures will help to spare the region from more wars and calamities in the future.

[45]

IRAN, IRAQ AND GULF SECURITY

1

Iran: Weakling or Hegemon?

Anthony H. Cordesman

There is ongoing debate among national security experts as to whether and to what extent a country should be judged by its intentions or its capabilities. Both intentions and capabilities are always uncertain, even in the short term, and become progressively more uncertain with the passage of time. Domestic politics change perceptions and strategy, reality intervenes and alters plans, and external factors reshape both intentions and capabilities over time. States may or may not act as they claim or plan to, nor even behave as rational actors. In practice, crises sometimes lead to radical changes in intentions that can escalate or mutate as a given crisis develops.

In this respect, Iran is no different to any other state. It is, however, politically more volatile than many of its neighbors, and more driven by ideology and religion. The tension between President Mahmoud Ahmadinejad and Supreme Leader Ali Khamenei is only one example of how difficult it is to be sure of Iran's current intentions, much less its future ones. Its security structure is still divided between its regular forces, the Iranian Revolutionary Guard Corps (IRGC), and its intelligence services. Its economy is weak and chronically mismanaged, and population pressure continues to pose a problem despite a diminished birth rate.

It is unclear just how divided the various factions in its national security community really are. There are some claims that the Iranian National Security Council, or some structure within the Iranian government, exercises relatively tight control over Iran's strategy, plans and actions. At the same time, others claim that Iran now has an adventurist President and a more cautious Supreme Leader; that the Revolutionary Guards sometimes act on their own; and that groups like the Al Quds force take covert action or use proxies without full consultation or agreement within the central government. There are indicators to support all of these positions but no concrete evidence to confirm any of them.

Iran's intentions are further complicated by its dependence on imports for advanced high-technology weapons; its uncertain ability to fund major arms purchases; its difficulties in obtaining parts and upgrades for its existing systems; and its uncertain ability to execute plans to develop its own military industrial base. Iran often drafts ambitious plans and goals. Its ability to execute them, however, has proven consistently limited and many of its claims regarding weapons purchases, development and production are dubious. Moreover, the claimed size and nature of its military exercises and other military activities are often more matters of propaganda than a measure of either its intentions or capabilities.

As for the uncertainties caused by Iran's domestic politics, calling any state a "semi-pluralistic, semi-populist, oligarchic theocracy" should be enough to explain both today's internal divisions and the future uncertainties surrounding Iran's regime and intentions. Iran will probably never again change its leadership as a result of external efforts at regime change, but its political structure is simply too contradictory, divided and inherently unstable for some form of internal regime change not to be inevitable. That change may well be evolutionary rather than radical, but it will occur.

Neither Weakling nor Hegemon

Many aspects of Iran's current and future capabilities, however, are as uncertain as its current and future intentions. On the one hand, Iran is surrounded by strong external powers, many of whose intentions are equally unpredictable. These include a strong US military presence in the

Gulf; Pakistan with its nuclear arms; Turkey with some of the most capable military forces in the region, an Iraq in the middle of a civil war, southern Gulf states that are individually weak but could become collectively strong, Russia, unstable central Asian powers, peripheral Sunni powers like Egypt, Jordan and Syria; and peripheral threats like Israel.

Seen from this perspective, Iran has at least as much reason to think defensively as it does offensively. It may have offensive opportunities for regional political reasons and choose to exploit them if they occur. At the same time, it is weak as an offensive military power compared to most of its neighbors and any combination of the United States and the Southern Gulf states. Iran certainly has the strength to play a spoiler role, but very limited capacity to finish any major offensive conflict that it starts on favorable terms.

As for becoming a regional hegemon, this can only happen if Iraq's neighbors so weaken themselves as to create a virtual power vacuum. Iraq is the only state that currently has such potential weakness and it is unclear that Iran could dominate even a Shi'ite-controlled Iraq. Being Arab may well be more important than being Shi'ite. More importantly, few elites share power gracefully or for long.

It seems useful in this context to point out the real definition of a "hegemon." "Hegemon" is the Greek word for "leader," and the dictionary definition of hegemony is the ability to exert, "preponderant influence or authority over others." Iran may sometimes be able to do this, but only if another nation chooses to allow it, finds this to be to its advantage or is temporarily too weak or too badly led to resist. It lacks the current force to do more and can only shift the balance in its favor if other states fail to react.

Using the other party for self-advantage and competing to see who can do the best job of using who is not "hegemony"—it is "opportunism," and the difference between offensive and defensive opportunism is as unreal as the difference between offensive and defensive bullets. While no one can predict Iran's intentions, it is probably as pointless to demonize it as to sanctify it. Iran does what it must, when it must, and seeks to get away with what it can, when it can. Iran's leaders may be an awkward cross between the characters in a play by Samuel Beckett and one by Luigi Pirandello, but they all probably broadly understand the limits of Iran's position in spite of their theocratic character, as do most or all of Iran's neighbors. If there are gaps in this aspect of regional *realpolitik*, they probably occur only in Israel and the United States.

At the same time, Iran's limited offensive capabilities do not make it a military weakling. Saddam Hussein's horrible miscalculations about Iran's weakness and internal divisions at the start of the Iran–Iraq War should be a warning of what can happen if Iran is invaded or forced into anything approaching total war. Its strengths in overt conflict are more defensive than offensive, but Iran has already shown it has great capability to resist outside pressure or any form of invasion and has done so under far more adverse and divisive conditions than exist in the country today.

Moreover, the US-led invasion of Iraq is a warning that even when outside efforts to depose a regime are successful, they can trigger forces that become virtually uncontrollable unless an immediate successor regime can command both popular support and the ability to govern. In practice, the law of unintended consequences should be as much a deterrent as Iran's military strength.

Axis of Evil versus Opportunities for Opportunism
Accordingly, when it comes to analyzing Iranian capabilities, it seems most functional to focus on Iran's current and future opportunities for opportunism, and not whether Iran is part of an "axis of evil" or simply acting in its own defense. Here too, however, there is a need for caution and perspective. Israeli and US commentary and some Arab rhetoric have often exaggerated such capabilities as much as it has highlighted Iran's hostile intentions and ambitions. At the same time, some of Iran's defenders have described the nation as a benign multicultural martyr to external misunderstanding in ways that border on the absurd.

Seen from this perspective, Iran could present five major kinds of current and potential threats:

- *As a conventional military power:* Iran has limited capabilities today but could become a much more threatening power if it modernized key elements of its forces and its neighbors did not react.

- *As an asymmetric threat that can seek to intimidate or attack using unconventional force:* Iran has established a large mix of unconventional forces that can challenge its neighbors in a wide variety of asymmetric wars, including a low-level war of attrition.

- *Iran's asymmetric and unconventional capabilities allow it to use proxies and partners in the form of both state and non-state actors:* Iran's support of Shi'ite militias in Iraq, ties to elements in the Iraqi government, partnership with Syria, and links with Hezbollah in Lebanon are all practical examples of such activities.

- *As a potential nuclear power armed with long-range missiles:* Iran is a declared chemical weapons power. Its biological weapons efforts are unknown but it seems unlikely that it remained passive in reaction to Iraq's efforts. It has openly made the acquisition of long-range missiles a major objective, and its nuclear research and production programs are almost certainly intended to produce nuclear weapons.

- *Iran presents a potential religious and ideological regional threat in an Islamic world polarized along sectarian lines.* Despite all the talk about a clash between civilizations, the potential clash within Islam seems far more dangerous. The risk that Sunni and Shi'ite extremists can provoke a broader split between sects and nations could push Iran into a more aggressive religious and ideological struggle.

Iran as a Conventional Military Power

Iran has limited capabilities today but could become a much more threatening power if it modernized key elements of its forces and its neighbors failed to react. Iranian training and doctrine has slowly improved over time, although Iran has little practical experience with advanced command and control, targeting, Intelligence, Surveillance and Reconnaissance (IS&R), and electronic warfare capabilities; and its efforts to improve its capability in joint operations and sustainability have had only limited success.

Iran does have a large, if divided force structure. It currently has some 545,000 active and 350,000 army reserves, not counting the Basij militia. Its army has an active strength of around 350,000 men, although 220,000 are low-grade conscripts and its corps of technicians and non-commissioned officers is poorly trained and given limited initiative.

Iran's Conventional Land Forces

The Iranian army has four corps, with the equivalent of 12 divisions, four of which are armored. It has one Special Forces brigade, two brigade-sized commando "divisions," and a small airborne brigade. Its equipment includes some 1,600–1,750 main battle tanks, some 720 other armored fighting vehicles, 650 armored personnel carriers, over 300 self-propelled artillery weapons, over 2,000 major towed artillery weapons, and roughly 900 multiple rocket launchers. It has large numbers of mortars and anti-tank guided weapons—many of which are highly effective systems. The bulk of the army's equipment, however, is still worn, obsolescent to obsolete, and difficult to sustain in maneuver and combat.

The Iranian army has considerable mass and ability to operate in relatively static defensive roles. It is not, however, a modern maneuver force by any means. Only a third of its main battle tanks are modern enough to have moderate capability and most of its other tanks, officers' armored fighting vehicles (OAFVs), and armored personnel carriers (APCs) are worn and obsolete. It is reliant on towed artillery forces with weak to poor targeting and fire control, and its 50-odd remaining attack helicopters are worn and have limited operational capability. Its short-range air defenses are ineffective against modern attack aircraft with long-range targeting and precision fire capability. Most of its conventionally armed multiple launch rocket systems (MLRSs) and surface-to-surface weapons seem to have cluster warheads, but are too inaccurate and lacking in lethality to use against anything other than static forces and area targets and are therefore more likely to produce harassment effects than kills.

There are an additional 100,000 men in the land/air branch of the IRGC but this too is a largely conscripted force organized into many small formations with grandiose unit designations like "division." It has some armor and artillery, but is largely an infantry force. Only selected elements trained in missions such as operating Iran's longer-range surface-to-surface missiles, operating as advisors and embedded forces in other armies or militias, special missions and unconventional warfare have moderate to high capability. However, the IRGC can potentially draw upon hundreds of thousands of young men in the Basij militia for local defense missions.

Iran's Conventional Air Forces
The 35,000 man-plus Iranian air force has shown considerable skill in keeping its outdated fleet of aircraft operating, modernizing some sub-systems and avionics, and adapting new weapons to aging platforms. Its core electronic warfare, IS&R, and Command Control, Communication, Computers and Intelligence (C_4I)/battle management systems, however, have low to moderate capability and are severely limited by the age and inherent limitations of the avionics on its aircraft.

It has over 260 combat aircraft, but operational availability is about 50–60 percent for US supplied types, all of which are now three decades old or older and none of which have had access to generations of US upgrades. Operational readiness for its Russian and PRC-supplied aircraft may be 75–80 percent, but only some 10–12 Su-25K, 18–23 MiG-29A, and 20–25 Su-24MK aircraft represent anything approaching modern aircraft, and all are export versions of Russian fighters with limited avionics. Even with the addition of some 18–22 operational F-14s and 30–50 operational F-4Es, this is a limited force of less than 100 combat aircraft with moderate modern war fighting capability, and it would have severe problems generating and sustaining high numbers of sorties.

The Iranian air force does have some modern air-to-air and air-to-ground missiles, although much of its inventory is aging severely and has limited capability. It still operates 5 P-3MP Orions with airborne warning, air control, maritime patrol, and remote anti-ship missile targeting capability, but their operational status is unclear and their electronic warfare capabilities are limited. Overall reconnaissance, electronic warfare, battle management and targeting capabilities are poor to moderate. The Iranian air force remains severely limited in terms of equipment.

There are some 15,000 men assigned to land-based air defense forces. Iran's main surface-to-air missile defenses include roughly 150 IHawk surface-to-air missile launchers, 45 SA-2 and additional PRC-clone launchers, and 10 obsolescent long-range SA-5 launchers. It has some operational FM-80 Crotale, 20–30 Rapier, and 3–15 Tigercat shorter-range systems. It also has large numbers of man-portable surface-to-air missiles (some modern) and Anti-Aircraft (AA) guns.

Iran has found some ingenious ways to modernize the sensors, battle management and electronic warfare systems supporting this force, and to improvise a crude form of netting to integrate some fire units. The new TOR-M1 surface-to-air missiles it is importing from Russia reportedly have been delivered and test-fired. However, these are the first truly modern systems it has received since the fall of the Shah and they are best suited for short-to-medium range point defense. Barring massive deliveries of Russian S-300 or S-400 surface-to-air missiles, sensors and battle management systems, the Iranian system is vulnerable and largely obsolete.

Iran's Conventional Naval Forces

The 16,000–20,000 strong Iranian navy suffers from many limitations. It has learned how to keep its three Kilo-class submarines operational, but its larger surface ships (three aging missile frigates and two aging gun corvettes) are obsolete and it has limited amphibious capability for anything other than raids or Special Forces missions against exposed targets in the Gulf, and its amphibious exercises are largely set piece shams. (It has three landing ships [medium] LSMs with a total lift capacity of around 300–350 troops and 30 major armored weapons.)

The navy does have significant numbers of mine vessels, smaller patrol ships (some armed with anti-ship missiles), and maritime patrol aircraft and mine-laying helicopters. In overall terms, however, it is now far less capable of fighting a conventional battle at sea than it was when it was decisively defeated by the US Navy in the "tanker war" of 1987–1988.

Iran's Conventional Weaknesses and Strengths

This force mix scarcely makes Iran any kind of regional military "hegemon," and the region would have years of warning before Iranian forces could acquire and absorb considerable numbers of new weapons. It can certainly improve its defensive capabilities and the attrition it can impose on an attacker, but it would require the United States to virtually abandon the Gulf for Iran to be able to win a regional arms race that would give it the air and naval capabilities to gain serious offensive capabilities in conventional war, and even then, a cohesive response by the GCC would seriously challenge any capability that Iran could develop.

Geography is also a critical factor. Iran would virtually have to be invited in to cross the Gulf with significant forces. It has little or no foreseeable incentive to strike at most of its other neighbors, and many border areas in which it might advance present other geographic problems apart from offering little or no strategic advantage. Iran certainly has the ability to wage war, but it does not have the capability to win most wars in ways that give it any advantage.

The two exceptions that must be kept clearly in mind are Iraq and the defense of its own territory. Iran is a highly populated country of over 65 million people with centrally located cities, and its forces are strong enough to make it anything but a defensive "weakling." As the Iran–Iraq War and Gulf Wars show, much depends on popular support, but any invasion of Iran that produced a strong nationalist response, rather than a broad-based uprising against the regime, would almost certainly turn into a bloody and pointless war of attrition.

This would be the kind of war where even major tactical victories against Iran would not offer lasting strategic advantage and would tie the attacker down in exposed positions. As will be discussed shortly, the defeat or large-scale destruction of Iran's conventional forces would not deprive it of the ability to retaliate using unconventional forces, proxies, or partners. It also might drive Iran to respond over time with far greater efforts to acquire nuclear weapons.

Iran and Iraq

It is also important to point out that Iran does have the ability to rapidly deploy a large mix of conventional and unconventional forces into Iraq. Iraq's current military forces are divided and extremely weak and Shi'ite and Kurdish dominated. If Iran was invited in following a US and British withdrawal by a Shi'ite dominated government, and had popular support from most of Iraq's Shi'ite Arabs, it could quickly dominate most areas with a Shi'ite majority, defeat insurgent or Sunni resistance in most areas outside Anbar and Mosul, and defeat Kurdish forces in any clash over Kirkuk.

Iraq is largely a power vacuum. If Iran and Iraq cooperated to secure a Shi'ite dominated "federation," Iran could play a major offensive role with only limited warning and preparation. However, much would depend on Iraqi government and Iraq Arab Shi'ite support in such a scenario and on the willingness of the United States to permit the movement of Iranian conventional forces.

It should also be noted that no Sunni Arab state is currently organized to project large ground force contingents into most of the populated areas of Iraq, although Jordan and Syria could project significant ground forces into the West. Turkey could project a corps-sized force into Northern Iraq (and did so at the time of Saddam Hussein), but its fear of the Kurds is unlikely to make it intervene on the part of the Arabs even if invited.

Iran as an Asymmetric Threat

Even nations as powerful as the United States have learned to their cost that the conventional balance is only one balance in modern warfare. Iran has responded to its conventional weaknesses by seeking three different forms of asymmetric capabilities that it could try to use either to intimidate or attack:

- The use of its own regular and IRGC forces for unconventional warfare.

- The development of long-range strike systems and weapons of mass destruction.

- The creation of ties to proxies and partners that it can join or use in asymmetric conflicts.

The Threat in the Arabian Gulf

Iran has built up a large mix of unconventional forces in the Gulf that can challenge its neighbors in a wide range of asymmetric wars, including low-level wars of attrition. These include a wide range of elements in the regular forces and IRGC as well as some elements in the Ministry of Intelligence and Security (MOIS), or Vezarat-e Ettela' at va Aminat-e Keshvar (VEVAK), which was installed following the Islamic Revolution to replace the now-disbanded National Organization for Intelligence and Security (SAVAK). In 2006, the MOIS employed about 15,000 civilian staff. Its major tasks included intelligence collection and operations in the Middle East and Central Asia, domestic intelligence and monitoring of clerical and government officials as well as the prevention of conspiracies against the Islamic Republic.

Its air forces remain vulnerable in any form of mission, but are less vulnerable near Iranian bases, sensor coverage and surface-to-air missile (SAM) coverage. Its naval forces include its three Kilo-class submarines, which can harass or seek to interdict ships moving in and out of the Gulf, a wide range of mines and vessels that can be used as mine layers or to release free floating mines. They also include roughly 140 light patrol and coastal combatants, including 11 French-designed Kaman-class missile patrol boats with 2 to 4 CSS-N-4/YJ-1 "Sardine" anti-ship missiles each. These are sea skimming, solid fueled missiles with a 42–50 kilometer range, 165 kilogram warheads, Inertial Navigations Systems (INS) and active radar similar to the Exocet, and can be used to harass civil shipping and tankers, and offshore facilities, as well as attack naval vessels. Iran may well have far more advanced Russian and Chinese-supplied missiles and claims to be developing advanced anti-ship and anti-fixed target missiles of its own.

Iran made claims in the spring of 2006 that it was testing more advanced weapons for such forces. These included a sonar-evading anti-ship missile that can be fired from submarines as well as surface combatants that IRGC Rear Admiral Ali Fadavi claimed no enemy warship could detect, and "no warship could escape because of its high velocity." Iran also claimed to be testing a new missile called the Kowsar with a very large warhead and extremely high speed to attack "big ships and submarines" that it claimed could evade radar and antimissile missiles. While such tests may have been real, Iran has made so many grossly exaggerated claims about its weapons developments in the past, that it seems they were designed more to deter US military action and/or reassure the Iranian public rather than for their actual capabilities. It followed up these actions in the late summer of 2006 by testing new submarine launched anti-ship missiles.

It has a 20,000 man naval branch in the IRGC that includes some 5,000 marines. This branch of the IRGC has 10 Houdong missile patrol boasts with CSS-N-8/C-802/YJ-2 missiles with 165-kilogram warheads, active and inertial guidance, and a maximum range of 120 kilometers. It operates mobile land-based CSS-C-3/HY-2/Sea Eagle/Seersucker anti-ship missiles that can be rapidly emplaced on the Iranian coast or islands in the Gulf shipping channel. These systems have ranges of 95–100 kilometers, very large warheads, and autocontrol and radar homing guidance. They can be targeted by a remote air link, and the exact level of upgrading of these missiles since their initial delivery during the Iran–Iraq War is unknown.

The IRGC has large numbers of Boghammar and other patrol boats with recoilless rifles, rocket launchers, man-portable surface-to-air missiles, and anti-armor guided weapons. The IRGC routinely uses small civilian ships and vessels in unconventional operations in various exercises, including mine-laying and raids on offshore facilities. This force has facilities at Bandar-e-Abbas, Khorramshar and on the islands of Larak, Abu Musa, Al Farsiyah, Sirri and the Halul oil platform. It can make use of additional facilities at Iran's main naval bases at Bander e-Abbas, Bushehr, Kharg Island, Bandar e-Anzelli, Bandar e-Khomeini, Bandar e-Mahshahr and Chah Bahar. These forces can rapidly disperse and shelter in caves and hardened sites. Small ships can be very hard to detect with most radars even in a normal sea state, and civilian ships can easily change flags and meld in with commercial traffic.

Closing the Gulf?

These light naval forces have special importance because of their potential ability to threaten oil and shipping traffic in the Arabian Gulf and the Gulf of Oman, raid key offshore facilities, and conduct raids on targets on the Gulf coast. Many Gulf energy facilities are extremely vulnerable, and the GCC states are exposed to any form of attack on their desalination and coastal power facilities, and precision strikes on critical high-capacity, long-lead time replacement items in energy facilities and power grids. This vulnerability might also allow Iran to carry out very successful air attacks in a surprise raid with precision weapons, using IRGC "suicide" aircraft, and future unmanned aerial vehicles (UAVs) and precision cruise missiles. It is also possible that Iran could conduct coastal raids with IRGC and/or Special Forces that go deeper into Southern Gulf territory.

Iran could not "close the Gulf" for more than a few days to two weeks even if it was willing to sacrifice all of these assets, suffer massive retaliation and potentially lose many of its own oil facilities and export revenues. Its chronic economic mismanagement has made it extremely dependent on a few refineries, product imports and food imports. It would almost certainly lose far more than it gained from such a "war," but nations often fail to act as rational bargainers in a crisis, particularly if attacked or if their regimes are threatened.

However, even sporadic, low-level attacks on Gulf shipping and facilities, could allow Iran to wage a war of intimidation in an effort to pressure its neighbors. As a recent International Energy Agency (IEA) study shows, the current and future volume of oil export traffic would make any threat that sharply raised oil prices, deterred smooth tanker flows, and otherwise interfered with energy exports of great importance, particularly in a world where every developed economy is critically dependent on global trade and the continuing flow of Asian heavy manufactures that are steadily more dependent on Gulf oil.

Table 1.1

The Importance of Gulf Oil Exports

Area of Export Flow	Current Flow (mbpd)	Share of World Oil Demand in (Percent)		
		2004	2030 (Reference)	2030 (Lower Demand)
Strait of Hormuz	17.4	21.2	28.1	19.4
Straits of Malacca/Far East	13.0	15.8	23.7	23.3
Bab el-Mandab	3.5	4.3	4.5	4.9
Suez	3.9	4.7	4.8	5.3

Source: Adapted by Anthony H. Cordesman from material provided by Ambassador William C. Ramsay, Deputy Executive Director, International Energy Agency, February 6, 2007.

Other Contingencies

At the same time, as previously discussed, Iran could use its entire mix of forces in conducting unconventional and asymmetric defenses of its own territory, and in conducting deep penetration and border raids and attacks on its neighbors. Iran's material and resource limits may affect its major weapons systems and military sophistication and modernization. Its internal division may delay or limit some aspects of its military coordination and effectiveness, as does its dependence on conscripts. It is clear from Iran's military literature, however, that it keenly studies both asymmetric warfare techniques and asymmetric vulnerabilities and opportunities, and while its exercises are of patchy quality, some elements of the Iranian forces are highly effective in testing asymmetric methods of operation.

Iran's Use of State and Non-state Actors as Proxies and Partners

Iran can also make use of both state and non-state actors. Iran's support of Shi'ite militias in Iraq, ties to elements in the Iraqi government, partnership with Syria, ties to the Hezbollah in Lebanon, support of Shi'ite Afghan elements, and arms supply and training of elements of Hamas and the Palestinian Islamic Jihad (PIJ) are all practical examples of such activities. So are past efforts to destabilize the Hajj, and support Shi'ite unrest in Bahrain and Saudi Arabia.

Proxies and Partners

These can be both foreign forces directly under Iranian control (proxies) and forces that cooperate with Iran to their own or a common advantage (partners). The issue of who is using whom is largely moot if all the actors involved are both willing to cooperate and feel they benefit from such cooperation.

A special element of the IRGC called the Al Quds force is often associated with Iranian efforts to arm, train and advice foreign states and non-state actors. In practice, however, Iranian intelligence is often involved or such efforts are operated under diplomatic cover, with the involvement of commercial entities and dummy corporations and even elements of Iran's regular forces. This is scarcely a unique mix of operations, and one adopted by many other countries. Deniability – plausible or implausible – is the major reason for both the complexity of such efforts and attempts at concealment.

[63]

The Strengths and Weaknesses of Such Operations

Like direct forms of asymmetric operations, the use of foreign actors can be both defensive and offensive. It can also serve ideological and religious causes. It is also extremely difficult to establish motive and the scale of such efforts under many conditions, particularly since they can be conducted without attribution to Iranian government support (false flags) or under conditions where the Iranian government can claim any documented incident was a rogue operation it did not authorize.

The problem that Iran faces in most such operations is that they can harass, but not achieve decisive strategic results. The end result is a "spoiler" operation that may damage an opponent, or cause local or regional instability, but does not really benefit Iran. Iranian influence does not give Iran control. The Hezbollah operation against Israel, and Israel's destruction of most medium and long-range rocket forces that Iran and Syria had laboriously built up, is a case in point. Supporting anti-US elements in Iraq does not necessarily benefit Iran in the long run. Implausible deniability provokes direct or indirect hostile responses, and Iran can find itself dragged into a far more serious conflict or crisis than it intends through the acts of its "partner."

Much depends on the specific case and the skill with which Iran acts. Sheer distance and the tactical buffer caused by the need to bypass or overfly Arab states, gives Iran some freedom of action in supporting Hezbollah, Hamas and the PIJ. This also allows Iran to build up its capabilities and influence by appearing to take the Arab side—although not if its efforts in nations like Lebanon provoke Arab states to see such actions as threatening their security or provokes Israel to the point where its tenuous restraint turns into hostile action.

The Iraq Option

Low-level operations that intimidate a Gulf state or other neighbor without making it react in hostile ways can also succeed, although they involve careful balance and judgment. Simply building up military and security relations can provide both a defensive option and a potential threat to other powers without being a direct provocation.

If there are strategic options where such methods could play a direct role, they seem to lie in three areas, two of which are marginal. Iran could seek to attack the United States or any other power by using non-state actors, particularly if they seemed at least partially hostile to Iran. Iran may have supported Al Qa'ida in Iraq for precisely this reason. Supporting Shi'ite elements in Afghanistan would be another way of securing its interests against any resurgence of the Taliban and Iran could do so without having to confront the United States or NATO.

The most serious opportunity is Iraq, for all the reasons touched upon earlier. It is also one of the only two serious opportunities that Iran has to move from a largely defensive power to one that has significantly expanded its power and influence. The other is the effort to acquire long-range missiles and nuclear weapons discussed in the following section.

Like all of Iraq's neighbors, Iran has an incentive to avoid direct major military intervention that might well provoke a broad regional conflict, which could trigger large-scale US intervention, and which ultimately might alienate the Iraqi Arabs that Iran came to aid. It does, however, have every incentive to see Iraq come under the effective control of a strong Arab Shi'ite government that would be a reliable partner and at least partially dependent on Iran.

Iran has had strong ties to the Supreme Council for the Islamic Revolution in Iraq (SCIRI) and Al Dawa since these exile movements started fighting during the Iran–Iraq War, and trained and equipped their forces from the early 1980s to 2004. It has built up some ties to the Sadr's Mahdi militia, despite political and religious differences. It actively supports some elements of the Shi'ite leaders in the Iraqi government, and can increasingly play on both the sectarian civil conflict in Iraq and Iraqi fears that the United States may withdraw.

There have also been British and American charges that Iran has supported both Shi'ite and Sunni elements hostile to British and US forces, and armed them with shaped charge bombs, advanced triggering devices, night sights, and other weapons whose transfer had been traced to the Mandali and Mehran border crossings to the northeast and southeast of Baghdad. They have also charged that Iran had regularly provided money to Shi'ite extremist groups and military training, and that this was done by the Al Quds force in the Revolutionary Guards, which reported to Iran's Supreme Leader.

For example, on February 11, 2007, US experts gave a background briefing in Baghdad in which they said that Iran had armed Shi'ite militants in Iraq with sophisticated armor-piercing roadside bombs that had killed more than 170 American troops. These weapons included simple systems like mortars, but also included more sophisticated weapons known as "explosively formed penetrators" or EFPs, where the "machining process" used in the construction was said to have been traced to Iran. The experts said that the supply trail began with the Al Quds force, which had armed Hezbollah, and which had begun to use EFP weapons against Israel in the 1990s.

The briefing also included a PowerPoint slide program and sample mortar shells and rocket-propelled grenades that the military officials said were made in Iran after the fall of Saddam Hussein. The EFPs, as well as Iranian-made mortar shells and rocket-propelled grenades, were said to have been supplied to what US experts described as "rogue elements" of the Mahdi Army militia of anti-American Shi'ite cleric Muqtada al-Sadr, a key backer of Shi'ite Prime Minister Nouri al-Maliki. They did not fully respond to questions as to whether similar weapons had been provided to the Badr Brigade, the military wing of the SCIRI, but it seemed clear that this was an issue.

A US intelligence analyst stated that Iran was working through "multiple surrogates" – mainly in the Mahdi Army – to smuggle the EFPs into Iraq. He said most of the components were entering the country at crossing points near Amarah, the Iranian border city of Mehran and the Basra area of southern Iraq. The previous week, the United States had announced that a Shi'ite lawmaker, Jamal Jaafar Mohammed, was a key actor in the main conduit for Iranian weapons entering the country.

US officials did say that said there was no evidence of Iranian-made EFPs having fallen into the hands of Sunni insurgents who operate mainly in the Anbar province in the west of Iraq, Baghdad and regions surrounding the capital. They also said that there was no clear evidence that Iran was the source of the SA-7, SA-14 and SA-16 shoulder-fired anti-aircraft missiles in Iraqi insurgent and militia forces, although they provided evidence that Iranian-made Misagh-1 man-portable missiles had been used by insurgents in Baghdad in November and December of 2006.

The United States has seized members of the Al Quds force operating in Iraq. For example, one of the six Iranians detained in Irbil in January 2007, Mohsin Chizari, was the operational commander of the Al Quds force there. Iranian advisors have been found in areas like the Ministry of the Interior, and many of the senior officials in the Iraqi government are former exiles who lived in Iran at some point. All of these events could lead to a major expansion of Iranian influence, particularly if a US withdrawal creates a power vacuum in Iraq or the current low-level sectarian and ethnic civil war makes Iraqi Shi'ites dependent on Iran.

Iran as a Nuclear Power armed with Long-Range Missiles

Iran's second possible option for achieving a major increase in its regional influence and power is to acquire weapons of mass destruction. Iran is a declared chemical weapons power. Its biological weapons efforts are unknown but it seems unlikely that it remained passive in reaction to Iraq's efforts. It has openly made the acquisition of long-range missiles a major objective, and its nuclear research and production programs almost certainly are intended to produce nuclear weapons.

Iran's major long-range missile development program is the Shahab series, which now seems to include both solid and liquid fueled intermediate range ballistic missiles (IRBMs) and medium range ballistic missiles (MRBMs). While Iran claims some of these systems are deployed, it continues to test new variants with ranges of 2,500–3,000 kilometers and improved warhead designs and accuracy. Iran has also obtained long-range Soviet bloc cruise missiles such as the KH-55 Granit or Kent. This system has a range of 2,500–3,000 kilometers. It has a theoretical circular error probable (CEP) of about 150 meters and a speed of Mach 0.48–0.77, and while Iran may have bought some 12 systems for reverse engineering purposes, it is possible that they could be carried and fired by its Su-24s.

Its progress in actually producing usable nuclear weapons and warheads for such systems is uncertain, but US intelligence experts estimate that it is unlikely that Iran will have any form of nuclear device before 2010. Given the accuracy of its longer-range missile systems, it would virtually have to arm them with a nuclear weapon for them to be more than terror weapons, although advanced chemical and biological cluster munitions could be an option.

US Preventive and Preemptive Strike Options

The very fact that Iran has embarked on such efforts has led to serious discussions of Israeli and US preventive or preemptive options, although senior US officials and officers have repeatedly said that their country is currently committed to supporting European and UN diplomatic options, and sees no urgent need for action.

Such operations would be difficult for Israel and challenging for the United States. Iran would find it difficult to defend against US forces using cruise missiles, stealth aircraft, stand-off precision weapons and equipped with a mix of vastly superior air combat assets and the IS&R assets necessary to strike and re-strike Iranian targets in near real time. For example, each US B-2A Spirit stealth bomber could carry eight 4,500-pound enhanced BLU-28 satellite-guided bunker-busting bombs— potentially enough to take out one hardened Iranian site per sortie. Such bombers could operate flying from Diego Garcia in the Indian Ocean, the RAF Fairford base in Gloucestershire, United Kingdom, and Whiteman US Air Force (USAF) Base in Missouri.

The United States also has various other hard target killers, many of which are still under development or classified. Systems known to be deployed include the BLU-109 Have Void "bunker busters,"—a "dumb bomb" with a maximum penetration capability of four to six feet of reinforced concrete. An aircraft must overfly the target and launch the weapon with great precision to achieve serious penetration capability. It can be fitted with precision guidance and converted to a guided glide bomb. The Joint Direct Attack Munition (JDAM) GBU-31 version has a nominal range of 15 kilometers with a CEP of 13 meters in the GPS-aided Inertial Navigation System (INS) modes of operation and 30 meters in the INS-only modes of operation.

More advanced systems include the BLU-116 Advanced Unitary Penetrator (AUP), the GBU-24 C/B (USAF), or the GBU-24 D/B (US Navy), which has about three times the penetration capability of the BLU-109. It is not clear whether the United States has deployed the AGM-130C with an advanced earth penetrating/hard target kill system. The AGM-130 Surface Attack Guided Munition was developed to be integrated into the F-15E, so it could carry two such missiles, one on each inboard store station. It is a retargetable, precision-guided standoff weapon using inertial navigation aided by GPS satellites and has a 15–40-NM range.

The United States does, however, have a number of other new systems that are known to be in the developmental stage and can probably deploy systems capable of roughly twice the depth of penetration with twice the effectiveness of the systems known from its attacks on Iraq in 1991. The newest development in the BLU-series is the 5,000 pound BLU-122, supposed to have been operational in 2007. Furthermore, there is the Massive Ordnance Penetrator (MOP), weighing almost 30,000 pounds and able to carry 5,300 pounds of explosives. According to some estimates, the optimum penetrating distance for the MOP is up to 200 feet. A possible alternative to these weapons are directed-energy and high-power microwave (HPM) weapons, none of which are currently beyond testing phase.

It is not clear whether such weapons could destroy all of Iran's most hardened underground sites, although it seems likely that the BLU-28 could do serious damage at a minimum. Much depends on the accuracy of reports that Iran has undertaken a massive tunneling project with some 10,000 square meters of underground halls and tunnels branching off for hundreds of meters from each hall. Iran is reported to be drawing on North Korean expertise and to have created a separate corporation (Shahid Rajaei Company) for such tunneling and hardening efforts under the IRGC, with extensive activity already under way in Natanz and Isfahan. The facilities are said to make extensive use of blast-proof doors, divider walls, hardened ceilings, 20-centimeter-thick concrete walls, and double concrete ceilings with earth filled between layers to defeat earth penetrates. Such passive defenses could have a major impact, but reports of such activity are often premature, exaggerated, or report far higher construction standards than are actually executed.

At the same time, the B-2A could be used to deliver large numbers of precision-guided 500-pound bombs against dispersed surface targets or a mix of light and heavy precision-guided weapons. Submarines and surface ships could deliver cruise missiles for such strikes, and conventional strike aircraft and bombers could deliver standoff weapons against most suspect Iranian facilities without suffering a high risk of serious attrition. The challenge would be to properly determine what targets and aim points were actually valuable.

As discussed earlier, Iran's air defenses have quantity, but little quality. This would enable US or Israeli attacks, but this situation could change over the next few years. Iran purchased 20 Russian 9K331 Tor-M-1 (SA-15 Gauntlet) self-propelled surface-to-air missiles in December 2005, which were reportedly delivered and test-fired by the IRGC in January 2007. Some reports also indicate that Iran is seeking to use more modern Soviet SA-300 missiles and Russian systems to modernize its entire air defense system. If Iran could acquire, deploy and bring such systems to a high degree of readiness, they would substantially improve Iranian capabilities.

Iran's air forces are only marginally better able to survive in air-to-air combat than Iraq's forces were before 2003. Iran's command and control system has serious limitations in terms of secure communications, vulnerability to advanced electronic warfare, netting, and digital data transfer. According to the International Institute for Strategic Studies (IISS), Iran does still have five operational P-3MP Orions and may have made its captured Iraqi IL-76 Candid airborne early warning (AEW) aircraft operational. These assets would give it airborne warning and command and control capability, but these are obsolescent to obsolete systems and are likely to be highly vulnerable to electronic warfare and countermeasures, and long-range attack, even with Iranian modifications and updates. There are some reports that Iran may be seeking to make a version of the Russian AN-140 AEW aircraft, but these could not be deployed much before 2015.

Iran's air defense aircraft consist of a maximum operational strength of two squadrons of 25 export versions of the MiG-29A and two squadrons of 25–30 F-14As. The export version of the MiG-29A has significant avionics limitations and vulnerability to countermeasures, and it is not clear whether Iran has any operational Phoenix air-to-air missiles for its F-14As or has successfully modified its IHawk missiles for air-to-air combat. The AWG-9 radar on the F-14 has significant long-distance sensor capability in a permissive environment, but is a US–made system in a nearly 30-year-old configuration that is now vulnerable to countermeasures.

Iran might risk using its fighters and AEW aircraft against an Israeli strike. It seems doubtful that Israel could support a long-range attack unit with the air defense and electronic assets necessary to provide anything like the air defense and air defense suppression assets that would support a US strike. A US strike could almost certainly destroy any Iranian effort to use fighters, however, and destroy enough Iranian surface-to-air missile defenses to create a secure corridor for penetrating into Iran and against key Iranian installations. The United States could then maintain such a corridor indefinitely with the help of restrikes.

Iranian Options for Retaliation

This does not mean it would be easy or desirable for the United States to exercise its military options. US forces are preoccupied in Iraq, and the lack of security in Iraq makes a full military attack against Iran all too unlikely. US military options are not risk-free, and the consequences of US strikes are enormous. Meanwhile, Tehran has several retaliatory options:

- Retaliate against US forces in Iraq and Afghanistan overtly using Shahab-3 missiles armed with chemical, biological, radiological (CBR) warheads.

- Use proxy groups, including those of Abu Musab al-Zarqawi and Muqtada Al-Sadr in Iraq to intensify the insurgency and escalate the attacks against US forces and Iraqi security forces.

- Turn the Shi'ite majority in Iraq against the US presence and demand that US forces leave the country.

- Attack the US homeland with suicide bombs by proxy groups or deliver CBR weapons to Al Qa'ida to use against the United States.

- Use its asymmetric capabilities to attack US interests in the region, including soft targets such as embassies, commercial centers and American citizens.

- Attack US naval forces stationed in the Gulf with antiship missiles, asymmetric warfare and mines.

- Attack Israel with missiles possibly armed with CBR warheads.

- Retaliate against energy targets in the Gulf and temporarily shut off the flow of oil from the Strait of Hormuz.

- Stop all of its oil and gas shipments to increase the price of oil and inflict damage on the global and US economies.

Many observers argue that a military strike against Iran could add to the chaos in Iraq and may further complicate the US position in Iraq. While the consequences of US military attacks against Iran remain unclear, the Shi'ite majority in Iraq can choose any or all of the following options:

- Ask the United States to leave Iraq.
- Influence Shi'ite militia groups to directly attack US forces.
- Turn the new Iraqi security and military forces against US forces in Iraq.

If Iran becomes a Serious Nuclear Power

The situation will also change dramatically if Iran goes from developing nuclear weapons and long-range missiles to deploying an effective nuclear strike capability. At this point in time, there is no way to be certain what such a force would look like or how capable it would be, but certainly the political–psychological impacts would be enormous. There are many different ways in which Iran can proliferate and deploy nuclear-armed or other chemical, biological, radiological or nuclear (CBRN) weapons, and use them to deter, intimidate and strike other nations. All have only one thing in common: they are all provocative and dangerous to any nation that Iran may choose to try to intimidate and target, *and* they are all provocative and dangerous to Iran.

Even Iranian ambiguity will probably lead Israel and the United States – and possibly India, Pakistan and Russia – to develop nuclear options to deter or retaliate against Iran. Israeli and/or US restraint in striking Iran does not have to stop at the first convincing Iranian threat to use nuclear or highly lethal biological weapons, but it could do so.

As for regional options, Iranian nuclear ambiguity might be enough to trigger Saudi, Egyptian and Turkish efforts to become nuclear powers, and some form of Israeli sea basing to enhance the survivability of its nuclear forces while increasing range and/or yield to strike Iran. Saudi Arabia has already said that it has examined nuclear options and rejected them, but this is no certainty and inevitably depends on Iranian action. The successful deployment of a highly capable Iranian force and Israel's existential vulnerability, would almost certainly lead Israel to develop a retaliatory capability to destroy Iran's cities and kill most of its population.

[73]

Regional powers might show restraint if the United States could provide convincing ballistic and cruise missile defenses and the same form of extended deterrence it once provided Germany with during the Cold War. But these options are speculative and do not yet exist. Successfully deploying a nuclear warhead is one achievement; second-strike capability is another that must be considered by Iranian decision-makers. It borders certainty that Iran's reaching a second-strike nuclear capability will take at least a decade, indeed, if it is ever achieved.

Any form of major nuclear confrontation could be a nightmare for all concerned. Iran's effort to limit or control the game will probably end at the first ground zero. Any actual Iranian use of such weapons is likely to provoke a nuclear response and may well provoke one that is targeted at Iranian cities and its population. Moreover, while Israel may technically be a more vulnerable "one bomb" country, it is highly questionable whether any form of Persian state could emerge from nuclear strikes on Iran's 5–10 largest cities.

The end result is the prospect of a far more threatening mix of CBRN capabilities in the Gulf region—the area that most models project as the main source of continued world oil and gas exports beyond 2015. It includes the near certainty of an Israeli–Iranian nuclear arms race that cuts across Arab territory, US nuclear targeting of Iran in some form of extended deterrence, and the threat of greater polarization between Sunnis and Shi'ites and broader regional tensions and actions that spill over from the confrontation over Iran's nuclear activities. None of these are pleasant prospects.

Iran as a Religious and Ideological Threat in a Polarized Islamic World

For all the talk of a clash between civilizations, the potential clash within Islam seems far more dangerous. The risk that Sunni and Shi'ite extremists can provoke a broader split between sects and nations could push Iran into a more aggressive religious and ideological struggle. One of the unfortunate consequences of 9/11 is that Arab and Islamic states have tended to deal with movements like Al Qa'ida as internal security threats, and avoid the broader issue of ensuring that Islamist extremism does not polarize and divide Islam and the Middle East region. In dealing with the West, many Arab, Iranian and non-Arab Muslim intellectual and religious leaders have also done more to defend their own cultures and Islam than to show they will deal directly with the threat that such extremism can present.

Afghanistan, Algeria, Bahrain, Iraq, Lebanon and Saudi Arabia however, are just some of the warnings of what happens when Islamist extremists threaten to take power, Sunni and Shi'ite Islamists turn upon each other, and other sectarian tensions and discrimination are not firmly dealt with and defused. It is also worth noting that much of the vaunted religious tolerance within Western culture was forced upon that largely Christian culture by some of the bloodiest wars in its history during the reformation and counter-reformation, and just how consistently horrifying the results of anti-Semitism were during the long centuries before it reached its apogee in the Holocaust.

Iran is scarcely free of its own form of Shi'ite extremism, but has also scarcely been dominated by them. As was the case in Bosnia and Kosovo, the collapse of the existing power structure in Iraq without any stable replacement has been the source of open religious warfare and this has been driven largely by Sunni, not Shi'ite extremism. At the same time, Iran has been opportunistic in dealing with events in Iraq, in exploiting its ties to Syria's Alawite regime, and in dealing with the Shi'ite Hezbollah in Lebanon. Iran has supported Shi'ite separatists in Bahrain and Shi'ite unrest in Saudi Arabia's Eastern Province in the past.

The idea of a "Shi'ite crescent" may be more of an unfounded fear than a clear possibility. However, growing divisions that divide Sunni, Shi'ite and the other sects of Islam in ways where Iran is virtually forced to play an opportunistic role are all too credible. The potential cost is also indicated by the fact that while more than 85 percent of the world's Muslims are Sunni, Shi'ites are the majority of the population in

Azerbaijan, Bahrain, Iran, and Iraq. They constitute about 30 percent in Kuwait, about 15 to 20 percent in Pakistan and about 25 percent in Yemen.

The problem could go beyond differences between Sunnis and Shi'ite "twelvers." Some other sects of Islam, like the Ibadis, differ from Sunnis but differ significantly from Shi'ites as well. Some modern Alawites identify themselves as close to the Shi'ite "twelvers," but differ sharply in the details of their beliefs in regard to the status of Ali, and in many other Gnostic and syncretistic beliefs, particularly a belief in metempsychosis. Ahmadi Muslims depart strikingly from other Muslims in their belief in Mirza Ghulam Ahmad as the Mujaddid (Renewer) of Islam. Ismailism presents other problems in establishing Islamic identity because of the diversity of interpretations.

Even without a major Sunni–Shi'ite clash, Islamic extremism could lead to a wide range of asymmetric struggles, and partner and proxy conflicts. If there is one area where dialogue, negotiation and common efforts to promote tolerance and common understanding are truly critical, it lies in doing everything possible to prevent this possibility from becoming real.

Limiting Iran's Current and Future Chances for Opportunism

All of the threats that Iran poses can be contained with the right choice of policies and military actions. Barring major shifts in its regime, Iran is not only capable of being deterred, but is a nation that will probably respond to the proper security incentives over time. The real question may well be whether Iran's neighbors and the United States provide the right mix of deterrence and incentives, and not Iran's current and potential capabilities.

It is not possible in this chapter to discuss all the problems involved in Iran's relations with its neighbors, or to indulge in the region's obsession with using history to produce self-inflicted wounds. There little space to discuss the mistakes on the part of the United States and Israel in demonizing what are often real problems in Iran's behavior. The same is true of the tendency of other nations and private organizations and individuals, to confuse mere dialogue with actual negotiation.

Given the recent history of Iran and the region, however, there are several necessary steps that Iran's Arab neighbors must take to structure the best mix of deterrence and incentives for Iran, and to do so in the context of a broader effort to bring regional security:

- *Rely on actions not words*: If the Arab world has not yet succeeded despite exhaustive talking, it is not for want of trying. Iran's rhetoric, however, has been far more extreme and much less productive, and the same has often been true of the United States. Presidential and Congressional rhetorical excess and empty gestures have provoked Iran without changing its ways and have caused self-inflicted wounds. Israel has done almost as good a job in provoking Iran while exaggerating its importance. Demonstrating a serious mix of deterrent capabilities, tied to a clear pattern of actions that do not threaten Iran or its regime if it is not aggressively opportunistic, is far better than provocative rhetoric or empty promises on any side.

- *Abandon efforts at active Iranian regime change without abandoning efforts to influence evolutionary change*: The Gulf and Islamic world do not need another example of the dangers of attempting regime change from the outside, and empowering incapable exile groups. Iran's political and economic structures badly need modernization, liberalization and reform for the good of the Iranian people, but this should be encouraged peacefully and by quietly supporting internal Iranian reformers.

- *Create truly effective deterrent forces with a strong and unified local component*: It may well be a decade or more before the Gulf Cooperation Council (GCC) can provide a strong mix of regional security and deterrent capabilities on its own. There is, however, a serious danger in simply continuing separate Gulf national efforts, many of which have limited real-world mission capability and deterrent value. There is no reason for the GCC states not to rely on

[77]

the United States but the more they do for themselves, the less direct and provocative that reliance will be.

- *Resolve strategically unimportant disputes and seek clearly defined mutual agreements*: Many of the current tensions between Iran and its neighbors are over border, riverine, island and dividing line issues that either have no strategic importance or where both sides would benefit from arbitration, mediation or turning the issue over to the World Court. As Bahrain and Qatar have shown, persistent efforts to resolve issues on this basis may take years to initiate and complete but can ultimately be successful.

- *Support negotiating efforts to have Iraq comply with the IAEA and UN. However, make it unambiguously clear to Iran that seeking nuclear armed missile forces will trigger a major defensive reaction and the risk of retaliation and/or preemption far more dangerous than the exercise is worth*: It may be years before Iran can develop a serious nuclear threat to its neighbors or one that could trigger a regional conflict, but it should be made clear to Iran now that the most dangerous military action it can take will steadily endanger its security, if not its very existence.

- *Understand that the failure to deal with regional disputes and equity for Shi'ites empowers Iran*: Iran is only strong in its ability to manipulate most state and non-state actors as its partners and proxies when the Arab world is weak or indifferent in resolving its own internal disputes. One key to success is a collective effort to aid Bahrain's "post-oil" economy and its Shi'ites, another is social and economic equity for Saudi Arabia's Shi'ites and broad-based aid for the development of Lebanon.

- *Do not give up on Iraq*: The most important single key to offering Iran security and limiting its opportunism will be to create a stable, independent Iraq. It is doubtful whether outside powers can produce Iraqi consensus but they may well be able to offer aid and incentives that will limit forced migration, help bridge ethnic and sectarian differences and keep a Shi'ite dominated Iraq from tilting towards Iran. There will be a competition for influence and if Arab Sunni states take the side of the Iraqi Sunnis, they will play into Iranian hands.

- *Persist in the Arab League effort to reach a full Arab–Israeli peace and promote King Abdullah's peace plan*: The Israeli-Palestinian conflict and Israeli-Lebanese/Syrian conflicts are additional keys to Iran's ability to create regional problems. This is only one reason to persist in current Arab peace efforts despite the frustrations in dealing with Israel, the United States and the Palestinians. The cause is simply too important to abandon.

- *Talk to Turkey, Syria and Pakistan as well as seeking influence in Afghanistan and Turkmenistan*: Do not ignore Russia. This is a regional game in terms of influence, not a Gulf game. It needs to be played as such.

- *Redefine GCC relations with the United States to create a true partnership*: The United States needs to pay far more attention to its regional friends and allies in shaping its polices towards Iran and its overall security posture in the Gulf, particularly in light of the uncertainties surrounding Iraq and the need for consensus in dealing with Iran. Gulf states, however, need to take more responsibility and stop acting in a fragmented and sometimes divisive way. Iran is only one of the catalysts that should make the United States and GCC states seriously think about the need to develop a coordinated approach to Gulf security, and one based on pragmatism and military realities.

- *Accept the seriousness of the danger posed by both Shi'ite and Sunni religious extremists*: The moderate Arab states, and religious and intellectual leaders of the Arab world, need to work together to meet the challenge posed by extremists in both sects. A clash between civilizations has always been more of a myth than a reality, but allowing Islam to become the scene of a steadily accelerating struggle

[79]

between Sunnis and Shi'ites, dragging in both state and non-state actors, poses a threat that goes far beyond Iran, the Gulf and the risk of any "Shi'ite crescent."

One thing is clear: any effective action to deal with Iran's capabilities and possible future intentions has to be complex, nuanced and sustained. It cannot be accomplished either by threats or by calls for dialogue and grand bargains. It must be done in the context of finding broader solutions to regional security issues and in the context of military realities rather than hopes and good intentions.

Perceptions of Power and Multiplicity of Interests: Iran's Regional Security Policy

Mahmood Sariolghalam

This chapter focuses on two variables to explain Iran's policy toward its southern and western Arab neighbors: how Iranian perceptions of power influence its foreign and security policy and how multiple interests at the national and regional levels confront Iran with a number of policy paradoxes. The discussion also highlights the links between Iran's sophisticated domestic structure and its foreign policy behavior, particularly towards the regional Arab states.

Perceptions of Power

In his classic work *Perception and Misperception in International Politics*, Robert Jervis points out how the perceptions of decision makers influence policy and behavior:

> [I]t is often impossible to explain crucial decisions and policies without reference to the decision-makers' beliefs about the world and their images of others. That is to say, these cognitions are part of the proximate cause of the relevant behavior and other levels of analysis cannot immediately tell us what they will be.[1]

Like most revolutionary states, Iranian foreign policy is predominantly shaped and conducted by the composition of its domestic politics. Internal politics in Iran is characterized by a historically based distrust of foreign governments. It is no accident that the collective term often referred to in official Iranian statements and public pronouncements is not the governments of the region, but rather, the "people." Here, the word "people" is understood as a homogenous entity not differentiated by nuances and layers. The reference to "people" reflects a revolutionary belief system solidly based on populism and is an indication of disillusionment with governments. In other words, ultimate power lies in the mobilization of the masses through general and abstract ideas. It is a common practice for all revolutionary states to speak in universal and highly abstract terms. The Soviet Union and the People's Republic of China under Chairman Mao dealt with the world in a similar vein.[2]

While "third worldism" evaporated in the late 1960s when globalization processes began their sharp upward trend, the concept returned to Middle East politics with the advent of the Iranian Revolution. For historical reasons, the Islamic Republic of Iran has acted in a distrustful and resentful manner towards great powers and avoided dealing with them unless it was essential for procuring crucial materials or for achieving political balance. Therefore, Iran's present behavior cannot be sketched without reconstructing its past. The internal inference processes are thus critical to understanding the continuance of distrustful behavior. Jervis further asserts, "The pressures to apply the lessons from one salient situation to others that resemble it are so powerful that even those who are aware of the pitfalls of this practice may succumb."[3] Jervis then goes on to conclude that events lead to lessons and in turn shape future behavior.[4]

In other words, Iran has kept its revolutionary order intact. Its complex domestic structures are often inadequately understood by analysts and states. Iran's post-revolutionary experience is no different from other revolutionary states. And like that of other revolutionary states, the leadership tends to be preoccupied by the ideas and fixations of their underlying ideological outlook.

At the state and governmental levels, the revolutionary atmosphere has been rigorously upheld and retained its relevancy. Nonetheless, over time and more visibly since the early 1990s, Iran has learned to accommodate the contradictions of its external environment with its belief structures but has never fully allowed its institutions to build cumulative and predictable relations, particularly with other governments. In this connection, Robert Jervis observes:

> Other beliefs are highly resistant to particular categories of discrepant information, often those that are most readily available. Frequently those attacking a position produce information they consider crucial only to be told by the defenders that the information is irrelevant because, as anyone who understood their view would see, it does not bear on the claims they are actually making.[5]

Iran's apparent change in behavior has occurred not because of internal debates or shifts in belief but rather due to economic and security exigencies. In fact, the belief structure in Iran has remained stable and untouched by colossal events such as the demise of the Soviet Union, September 11 and the fall of Saddam Hussein. The forces of indigenization have proved far more pressing than global developments. Because Iran's political system is not linked to global production, technological and marketing systems, there are no compelling reasons for structural accommodation to suit the global system. Huge oil revenues have provided unprecedented financial stability and also added to the irrelevance of the external milieu. In the meantime, containment and appeasement provide the diplomatic mechanisms for dealing with external threats and ensuring political sustainability at home.[6]

The Iranian post-revolutionary polity has also been powerful enough to uphold its revolutionary institutions and ideological atmosphere. Understandably, relations with liberation movements and selected Islamists have endured and have withstood the oscillations of both Iranian and international politics. As with all revolutions, it is uncommon to witness revisions, re-evaluations and flexibility. Occasionally, flexible approaches may be practiced as long as the revolutionary inertia is preserved. In short, in Iran's foreign policy, power is understood as the mobilization of people and support for liberation movements—a vivid departure from the Westphalian system of nation states.

Since the end of the Safavid period (1501–1722), Iran's foreign policy approach and national security doctrine were founded upon its international alliances.[7] Iran's geopolitical salience and its proximity to Russia and the Soviet Union made it a significant player in Middle Eastern–Western relations. However, in the post-revolutionary period the basis of Iran's internal political structure set the approach, tone and priorities of its foreign policy. The country's bitter experience with great powers and the high degree of their infiltration into domestic politics led to politics of distance and isolation.

It may be argued that since 1979 not only have domestic politics shaped Iran's foreign policy behavior but also overshadowed its content and direction. One interesting offshoot of almost all revolutionary states is that they develop sharp divisions over foreign policy approaches to the point where one approach forcefully wins over all the others, thus eliminating competing groups and coalitions. A number of ideological and conceptual standoffs can be delineated in post-revolutionary Iran: liberal versus revolutionary (1979–1981), globalizing versus revolutionary (1989–1997), civil society versus revolutionary (1997–2005) and liberal versus revolutionary (from 2005 onwards). These dichotomies have produced social conflicts which have occasionally become violent and led to a form of organized politics that is preoccupied with elimination rather than accommodation. Whenever ideology replaces national interest, philosophical discourses will dominate policy debates, which in turn become divisive.

The reality is that in contemporary Iran only a revolutionary order can maintain stability and defend the status quo. Iran's regional approach does not constitute an offensive doctrine. Rather, it is based on self defense and a comprehensive deterrence strategy. The Iranian constitution was also constructed to serve revolutionary idealism. However, in Iran today, the vocabulary of leaders remains revolutionary while politics is tailored towards maintaining a status quo and meeting rising popular expectations under difficult regional and international conditions. This trend applies also to China, the Soviet Union, Cuba and Algeria. Unlike the Soviet Union, Iran does not have a monolithic system. Despite limitations, organized groups compete to make an impact. Iranians use vague language to make their points in a country where ambiguity is a virtue and subtlety a social industry. Rhetoric is not just part of Iranian politics but an ingrained part of its culture. Perhaps no other nation has such robust oratorical talent as Iran. However, rhetoric and posturing should not be mistaken for policy.

After almost three decades, the ideas that shaped the Iranian Revolution of 1979 are still alive and afloat. As is the tradition with all revolutions, any deviation from the original path threatens the very raison d'etre of a consolidated revolutionary order. The course of a revolutionary polity is commonly identified with how its individual leaders perceive their own society and the world at large. Nonetheless, this is the first time in centuries that Iranian leaders are in a position to determine their course in foreign policy. For too long and under deteriorating conditions, Iran's foreign priorities were determined by foreign powers. This explains why the most powerful idea that shaped the Iranian Revolution was "an end to foreign intervention." That idea still prevails and Iranian leaders consistently express their distrust of foreigners, especially Westerners. Resentful references to Iran's past experience with the West dominate every politician's speech. The "foreign intervention" complex among the elites and certain segments of society leads one to believe that this perception is not just analytical but rather an embedded feature of Iranian political consciousness.

Attempts to deviate from this historical obsession by turning inward and focusing on institution-building at home have not been very successful. With good intentions and a cosmopolitan direction, former president Akbar Hashemi Rafsanjani sought to focus on economic reconstruction in his two consecutive presidential terms from 1989 to 1997. His deviation seemed logical enough after a long and devastating war with Iraq. His successor, Mohammad Khatami, undertook an even more ambitious project—the launching of civil society and democracy in Iran. His deviation too resonated with the post-Soviet fashion to pursue democratization. Ultimately, neither president succeeded. They both discounted the underlying axiom that the principles of the Iranian constitution and its supporting institutions are designed solely to hinder "foreign influence and intervention" in the country. Not only did the endeavors of the two former presidents reflect a departure from the fixations of a revolutionary order but more conclusively, Iranian society proved to be too divided to shoulder these national drives. Iran's presidential election of June 2005, however, brought the derailed revolutionary order back to its original track. Though some may analyze Iranian politics in terms of groups struggling for power, fundamental differences in interpretations over ideology and Islam cannot be discounted in this process.

The usual dictum is that revolutions resist reform and are not flexible enough to make transitions. The Chinese Revolution clearly stands out, thanks to a leadership that was inspired more by Chinese nationalism than Marxist dogmatism. There is a striking correlation between the Iranian and the Chinese revolutions: both countries were humiliated in the 19th and the 20th centuries, both experienced revolutions, and these led to endogenous political power and stressed political sovereignty. The Chinese, however, quickly realized that economic wealth is the bedrock of any power and to accumulate it, countries had to be connected to the core Western world. A more critical Chinese realization was the ground rule that the more a country is structurally linked to the US economy, the more it will enjoy prospects for prosperity. In only 18 years, Chinese exports increased from a meager $20 billion in 1987 to $851 billion in 2005. From 1998 through 2005, some $350 billion of foreign investment was attracted by China. The economy of China today is one third that of Japan and one seventh that of the United States. One cultural hallmark has been decisive in this economic success. There is a sustained national consensus between the state and society in China that the future of the country depends on its integration with globalization processes. Moreover, the Chinese were confident enough to resist structural political and cultural change in the face of intense involvement in the global economy.[8] However, in Iran, there is a lack of consensus over its economic direction and engagement with the international community.

In contrast, the root perception on power as reflected in Iran's foreign policy is self-sufficiency and indigenousness. These concepts constitute the political legacy of the revolution. Revolutionaries of all types are usually so convinced of their cause and way of thinking that they barely allow room for diversity of thought. Revolutionaries are not conceptually trained to question their assumptions. For them, there is only one solution for every problem and one answer for every question. For more than a quarter of a century, Iran's political structures and its overall national direction have remained solidly revolutionary. Both the revolutionary legacy and its current rigidity emphasize a strategic distance from the great powers – especially the United States – in order to ensure absolute sovereignty. Russia, China and the European Union are viewed as less threatening and useful for tactical relationships. Iranian policy makers' dramatic lessons from the country's relations with big powers before the revolution overshadow contemporary thinking and policy approaches. Fears of agenda setting by foreigners reinforce the policy of strategic distance. Therefore, Iran is interested in expanding its power domain as long as it does not have to share it with great powers.

Turning to the second variable, Iran cannot remain endogenous by the nature of its geo-politics, geo-economics and cultural spread. Economic extroversion and security introversion in policymaking produce a paradox. Iran's economy is overwhelmingly dependent on oil revenues and therefore the country is forced to engage the global oil industry. Yet, Tehran's foreign policy stresses ideological issues rather than the cooperation necessary for economic growth. The result is a combination of paradoxes and contradictions in Iranian behavior. It appears that these two premises underline Iran's approach towards its southern and western Arab neighbors. On the one hand, Iran wishes to cooperate and expand its interconnectedness in cultural and economic domains with Arab countries. On the other hand, however, Tehran is engaged in a cold war with the United States—a country that enjoys strategic relations with Iran's Arab and non-Arab neighbors. The outcome is a separation of its security policies from its economic and political cooperation in the Arab-Iranian matrix that at times turns into hostility and diminishes the prospects for even normal relations. In the Arab domain, the economic and the security policies are interlinked and encourage global engagement. In the Iranian domain, however, the two realms originate from two highly polarized frames of reference.

At the conceptual level, the polarity and divergence between Iran's security and economic policies stem from an identity crisis, which has repercussions in other layers of Iranian society. The identity crisis is a problem prevailing in almost all Muslim societies. It is being positively addressed in Turkey and Malaysia where there is a consensus, both on the street and in the corridors of power, to join the processes of economic and political globalization and allow individuals who wish to practice Islamic rituals the liberty to do so. As Fareed Zakaria contends, liberalism is a prerequisite to democracy and even private economic pursuits.[9] The Muslim world is no exception. Freedom of association and organization will empower societies against strong states because the organization of citizens is the key to change. Long-term stability in Iran will be the result of a conceptual dialogue and a political settlement between the Islamists and the liberals. As mentioned before, with regard to Beijing's success, the foundation for such a settlement is nationalism, which should be learned from the Chinese communists and applied in the Iranian case. This is why the concept of "regime change" in US political circles as a policy prescription towards Iran is a superficial and short-term approach to a complex problem. In the end, Iranians themselves need to rise above ideological quarrels and focus on what is useful for their country's advancement. Iran is an ancient country and is a slow moving giant in the process of ordering its internal divisions. If economic progress is any guiding principle for political settlements and cultural change, other Muslim countries like Malaysia or neighboring Turkey can certainly serve as examples.

The Multiplicity of Interests

Adding complexity to the picture is the impact of the Iranian economy on its politics. As a *rentier* state where the government does not need the support of its citizens to justify policies, state–society relations in Iran under any ruling group will necessarily be a one-way street. Today, just like almost all OPEC countries, some 85 percent of the economic activity in Iran is conducted by the state. The command of the government over national resources and petroleum income leaves insufficient room for private economic activity. Under such a political economy model, with or without the Islamic Republic, the pursuit of economic growth in Iran is an illusory project. No matter which group or movement rules Iran, the issue of economic distribution is the most salient political challenge. The pursuit of development and national economic interests require an active and empowered private sector. As Milton Friedman points out in his classic *Capitalism and Freedom*:

> ... if economic power is joined to political power, concentration seems inevitable. On the other hand, if economic power is kept in separate hands from political power, it can serve as a check and a counter to political power.[10]

The political future of Iran lies in how its economy evolves, to what degree citizens become less dependent on state employment and what would expedite the rise of a vibrant and organized private economic sector. Otherwise, no state with independent revenues would be compelled to delegate authority and feel obliged to hold itself accountable for its foreign policy decisions.

Iranian society, however, has undergone dramatic changes even while the state has maintained revolutionary stability and consistency. It is essential to go beyond the clerics to fathom Iranian society. The machinery of the Iranian government is not run by the clerics. Furthermore, Iran's diplomatic corps and the majority of the parliament members are not clerics. Western media and analysts tend to concentrate on the Iranian clerics as the most relevant analytical unit to understand Iranian politics. However, the political influence of officials with engineering and medical degrees in post-revolutionary Iran should not be underestimated.

[89]

There is a sizable group of professionals, many Western-educated and mostly engineers, who believe that liberal economic growth and openness in societies are "alien concepts and a conspiracy to regain control of Iran." Their religious orthodoxy is much deeper than the clerics and is barely questioned or challenged even during their life span. Their conceptual poverty in social, economic and political issues has partly caused Iranian politics to experience endless processes of trial and error. As engineers working in the diplomatic service, cultural institutions, national television and the economic ministries read the latest translated books in the social sciences and engage in self-teaching, the country undergoes another wave of short term self-doubt and a new phase of theoretical self-examination. Engineers and physicians generally do not recognize diversity of views, nuances and varied diagnoses and applaud the simplification of complex issues. For them, there is only one answer to every question and one solution to every problem. Engineers artificially feel confident to decide and set criteria for political correctness. Physicians too, enjoy the media spotlight while they explain the roots of the Arab–Israeli conflict and many other intricate global issues without having read an original book about the subject or having been trained to distinguish between data presentation and data analysis. Ironically, all recognized fundamentalists throughout the Muslim world are either engineers or physicians. There is not a single notable fundamentalist who has been trained in economics, sociology or political science.

Iranian radicalism can be traced more to the practices of the Iranian Tudeh (Communist) Party than the Islamists. In the Shah's prisons, members of the Tudeh Party and other communist groups were able to indoctrinate their Islamist inmates with radical ideas and methodology. In the social sphere of Iranian society, the clerics are the only organized group with a strong sense of camaraderie, grassroots support and national reach. Various intellectual groups are more or less dispersed, urban-based and confined to making deductive ivory tower analyses.

In Iranian politics, there are elections almost every year. People are trained in illiberal democracy. Even better, there is rotation of power. As many as 6,000 officials are rotated following a presidential election. There are also policy debates and both moderate and radical views are represented in domestic and foreign policy discussions. However, all this activity takes place in a predominantly singular school of thought. What impedes all these trends from becoming cumulative is the reality that Iranian conduct is not linear but rather sinuous.

Nonetheless, politically, the collaboration of the clerics with engineers and physicians produces more reliable levels of stability and conformity. However, both in the reformist and the conservative camps, the binary logic of engineering has reinforced the ideological proclivities of the leaders. The project-based rationale of engineering in Iranian domestic politics as well as foreign policy has generated a mechanical approach and a short-term perspective on complex human processes. It is no surprise that even the reformists under former president Mohammad Khatami, dubbed their mission a "project for democracy," as though it were another dam or highway construction project. After more than half a century of democratic practice, the Japanese still believe their democracy is an unfinished process that has yet to reach European levels. An engineering mindset leaves little space for nuance, subtlety, sophistication, gray area options in problem solving or a long-term definition of life. In addition to this, there is an ingrained subconscious tendency towards procrastination, sensation and tempestuousness in Middle Eastern political life. Therefore, the role of the non-clerics and the influence of typical political culture need to be recognized in the analytical matrix of understanding Iranian politics.

Yet, it is pertinent to point out that Iran is not exactly another Soviet style state. Over the last two decades, some urban sectors of Iranian society have changed for the better. Despite the fact that the society is highly stratified, levels of tolerance among citizens have expanded. There is far more diversity in Iranian society than in any other country in its neighborhood. Members of the Iranian Parliament engage in lively and unhindered debate over economic issues. Such levels of liberty cannot easily be witnessed in other developing countries. The movie industry raises salient social and cultural issues in amorphous and subtle Iranian ways—a rare practice in the Middle East. The spectrum of newspapers in the country portrays how divergent worldviews are.

In Tehran, one can identify startling cultural variations, from Islamic orthodoxy to Beverly Hills-style lifestyles. There is no consistent and universal imposition of state prerogatives over the society. Nonetheless, there is a minority segment in Iranian society that has distanced itself from the state and lives a luxurious life. The *nouveau riche* rarely watch Iranian television and usually spend their vacations abroad. They interact with Iranian visitors from Los Angeles and Bethesda in cozy north Tehran cafés, discussing the latest concerts in Dubai and the fashion shows in Milan. Still, the economic umbilical cord keeps a majority of them dependent on the state. Yet another segment of the public religiously and enthusiastically supports the ideological order. The paradox is that all these variations are concurrent. This rainbow portrait of society gives Iran an exotic aura. Many of the aforementioned features are not institutionalized and many trends are transitory. Nonetheless, there are two lasting institutions: love of material life and a passion for proximity to power—idiosyncrasies that may be prevalent throughout the whole Middle Eastern region.

Contrary to conventional wisdom, Iranian clerics are open to discussion, diverse views and conceptual challenges in their seminary settings. If the traditions of Shi'ite clerics are examined from a historical perspective, radicalism either as a way of thinking or as a political method are deemed as irrational exuberance. Ayatollah Sistani, an Iranian-born Iraqi cleric and his Iranian mentor, Ayatollah Khoi, stand out as vivid examples. In his book entitled *The Shi'a Revival*, Vali Nasr asserts that these two Grand Ayatollahs kept their loyalty to the principled conservatism of the traditional position by maintaining a distance from day-to-day politics and focusing on preaching. This is the position that the Shi'ite *Ulema* had embraced since the Safavid dynasty—what Nasr characterizes as the 'old school.' Furthermore, Nasr contends that Ayatollah Sistani views Shi'ite clerics as teachers and defenders of the faith—roles that are filled not only by having an Islamic government but by protecting and promoting Shi'ite piety under whatever government Shi'ites may happen to have.[11] Therefore, the idea of the *Shi'ite Crescent* sweeping through the Middle East is unsubstantiated. True, Shi'ites everywhere in the Muslim world are being empowered. However, this movement is more a reflection of globalization, urbanization and citizens' increased levels of expectations rather than a grand regional political movement.

From the beginning, the religious dimensions of the Iranian Revolution were not accepted by the Sunni world. The goal of the Islamic Republic to align itself with the "Muslim world" quickly turned out to be an illusion. Iranian post-revolutionary political tendencies did not necessarily coincide with those of the Sunni world. For the most part, Sunnis kept close to the West and were willing to learn from their experiences in the processes of modernization and to contribute to those processes in a global context. The dictum of the Iranian Revolution was to keep a strategic distance from the West and rely on self-sufficiency. The politics of the Iranian Revolution were closer to leftists and anti-imperialists—ironically, more anti-imperialist than the leftists and more anti-Israeli than the Arabs. The Shi'ite–Sunni divide is not a new phenomenon but there is more global awareness of it because the US entanglement in Iraq has imparted greater salience to these divisions. For many Arab countries, the Shi'ite issue is essentially an internal security matter but beyond that, it is a concern over Iran's ideological and revolutionary influence. Iran's generosity towards the Shi'ites, however, does not necessarily translate into Tehran's unquestioned and unconstrained influence. Understandably, provincialism in diplomacy has inhibited Iran from reaping the benefits of its extensive involvement with Shi'ite communities. Hezbollah may represent an exception, but Iraqi and other Shi'ites in the Arab world view Iran as a source of political and logistical opportunity rather than an inspiration or authority on matters of religion or identity.[12]

Moreover, the Iranian Revolution was more about anti-despotism, ousting the Shah's regime and spreading an anti-American and anti-Israeli sentiment rather than projecting a Shi'ite worldview. Iranian leaders did understand the impediments to their religious reach. Relations with Pakistan, Egypt, Saudi Arabia and other Arab states all indicate that politics mattered far more to Tehran than religious tendencies. Relations with Egypt were discontinued not because of its Sunni majority but because the Camp David Accords were signed by Anwar Sadat. To the Iranian revolutionary leadership, Wahhabism in Saudi Arabia mattered less. The Wahhabi–Shi'ite standoff could never be resolved anyway. It was the American domination of Saudi Arabia that caused oscillation in the relationship. Iran's alliance with Syria had more to do with the anti-Israeli stance of Damascus and its anti-Israeli policies than the Alawi religious orientation of the ruling Syrian elites. Even among the Shi'ite enclaves where Iran's influence did prevail, anti-Americanism was a far stronger force than Shi'ite religious practices. Iran's religious reach is of course salient, but to achieve great power status, Iran needs to concentrate on its economy, distance itself from exclusive military power and begin to enrich its soft power. More importantly, if Iran does not accommodate the West, it cannot hope to accomplish great power status in its proximity. Perhaps with the sole exception of Turkey, Iran has experienced turbulent relations with all of its Muslim neighbors. Only Armenia, a Christian state, stands out as a friendly neighbor. Iran's popularity with the Arab masses is a reflection of its anti-American and anti-Israeli policies and not its system of government.

Foreign Policy Labyrinth

The legal framework and revolutionary atmosphere in Iran have led to a number of paradoxes in Iranian foreign policy behavior. Article 153 of the Constitution specifies that "it is forbidden for any hegemonic power to dominate Iran's natural resources, economy, army and other pillars of the state." In the age of globalization, this idea of withstanding foreign influence causes critical impediments to cooperation. In Iranian global conduct, three intertwined paradoxes are obvious:

- Iran desires to be a normal state carrying out its ordinary functions at the international level while simultaneously striving to be a revolutionary state with a defiant rhetoric.

- Iran questions the unjust nature of the international system as administered by major industrial countries while seeking to influence that very system.

- Iran attempts to develop its economy while failing to accept the role of the multinational corporations or Western governments in facilitating its entry into the international technology, capital and commodity markets. Moreover, Iran wishes to maintain its rhetorical foreign policy while it reaches out for economic cooperation.

In a simple dichotomy, Iran alternates between revolutionary idealism and political realism. These oscillations breed discontinuity, increase vulnerability and limit diplomacy to tactical interactions. An underlying dilemma is whether revolutionary institutions can project realism and adopt a long-term definition of statecraft. For other countries, the duality of state institutions in Iran raises uncertainties and ambiguities in pursuing common objectives.

A central threat perception among the Iranian elite shapes Tehran's security doctrine—US opposition to the Islamic Republic of Iran. Three aspects of Iranian policies have received consistent global attention: Iran's support for militant Palestinian groups, opposition to Arab–Israeli peace negotiations and Tehran's nuclear program. All these policies stem from a revolutionary legacy. However, the offensive posturing of the 1980s has given way to a defensive one in the 1990s and beyond. In fact, Iran today is a status quo power. Linkages in Iraq, Afghanistan, Lebanon and elsewhere are components of an Iranian containment policy pursued by the United States.

A notion now doing the rounds in the United States is regime change in Iran. Perhaps with the exception of a brief period during the second Clinton Presidency, US policy towards Islamic Iran has never delinked the settlement of the nuclear problem from pursuit of regime change. However, in case of regime change, the question that arises is: what will replace the current polity in Iran? The roots of the Islamic Republic of Iran can be traced to a long history of struggle to acquire political sovereignty. Iranians living in the country prefer gradual reforms. US intervention in Iran will certainly be rejected by Iranians from all walks of political life. The last time the United States intervened in Iran in 1953, Prime Minister Mohammad Mossadegh was overthrown and Islamic fundamentalism as a political practice was born. Therefore, the concept of regime change by the United States towards Iran is neither theoretically sound nor politically possible. Security issues are at the core of the US–Iran nuclear confrontation. The United States cannot hope to dissuade Tehran from crossing the nuclear threshold while continuing to promote its regime change theory, however implicit and rhetorical. Likewise, for the purpose of easing security tensions, Iran cannot expect to hold a respectful dialogue with the United States without altering its attitude towards the Palestinian conflict. A change in Iran's approach towards this issue is pivotal in any potential understanding and rapprochement between Tehran and Washington. No US administration can reconsider its Iran policy without Tehran's willingness to gradually alter its rhetoric.

The Nuclear Stand-Off

Why does the Iranian government insist on independent and domestic uranium enrichment? Iranians feel they deserve to be recognized as a regional power in the Middle East. Power and recognition is the cornerstone of Tehran's security behavior. Nuclear capability is believed to provide Iran with security guarantees and scientific superiority in a troubled and unstable neighborhood. Iranians also raise economic justification for their nuclear program. By 2018, estimates indicate that Iran will have a population of over a 100 million. Almost two thirds of that population will be below the age of 30. The economy will then require diversification of national energy resources to maintain expanding growth rates and surging domestic energy needs. But this is not the whole picture. Iran feels insecure, surrounded by either US troops in Iraq and Afghanistan or by the US military presence in the region. Security paranoia in Tehran leads to a confrontational policy towards the United States. There is actually a precedent for an American approach based on dealing with Iranian policies rather than its polity. In the Shanghai Communiqué of February 28, 1972, former US President Richard Nixon and Chinese Premier Zhou Enlai concluded as follows:

> There are essential differences between China and the United States in their social systems and foreign policies. However, the two sides agreed that countries, regardless of their social systems, should conduct their relations on the principles of respect for the sovereignty and territorial integrity of all states, non-aggression against other states, non-interference in the internal affairs of other states, equality and mutual benefit, and peaceful coexistence.

Nuclear negotiations with Iran cannot be dissociated from security talks. Although Tehran must overcome many technical hurdles prior to mastering uranium enrichment its scientists appear confident enough to rely on promising indigenous know-how. Any military solution to Iran's nuclear program will be registered in the Iranian psyche as Phase II of the 1953 US intervention in Iran. Such an approach will help intensify the "sovereignty sensitivity" of all Iranians, will reactivate political radicalism in the region and postpone Iran's national economic development. Hopefully, in both Tehran and Washington, realism will outpace ideology.

Iran's Regional Arab Policy

The foregoing analysis indicates that Iran's regional policy towards both the Arab and non-Arab worlds stems from the country's perceptions of its

[97]

security, the Western world and domestic tendencies. In other words, a macro level analysis of Iran's global perceptions is reflected in its regional approach. Iran no longer views the nature of Arab regimes as a significant factor in formulating its bilateral and multilateral relations with them. Since the Rafsanjani presidency, Iran has established a policy of expanding cordial relations with Arab governments. Yet, lingering differences over the Palestinian issue, Hezbollah in Lebanon, Iraq and the US military presence in the Middle East have produced divergences between Iran and the Arab consensus. As long as the Islamic Republic considers the United States an opponent and friction between them continues to overshadow regional politics, no long standing, strategic and unhindered Iran–Arab relations can be foreseen. Distrust and perceptions of unreliability are serious problems on both sides. Iran's domestic and foreign policy structures are both founded on promoting indigenousness and maintaining a strategic distance from great powers while a majority of Arab governments are strategically linked to such global powers. Therefore, there are incontrovertible asymmetries hindering integration processes between the two sides. Nonetheless, Iran does have a genuine national security interest in having a stable Iraq on its border. Iranian and Saudi initiatives have eased the tensions in Lebanon between the government and Hezbollah. With active Saudi diplomacy emerging, King Abdullah also possesses the clout to bring Iran on board the Palestinian consensus-building process.

Iran today has the second largest Jewish community in the Middle East after Israel. The difference between Iran and much of the Middle East is that there are no anti-Jewish social structures in Iran. Iranian Muslims have lived alongside Christians and Jews for centuries. For an average Iranian, whatever his religion, the major issues, which are shared by those in other developing states, are job security, employment, education, national pride and international prestige. However, Iran's anti-Israeli policy is not just based on its national interests. Anti-Israeli sentiment is a passion, which can be raised to a dramatic level in Iranian politics. Realism is no guide in shaping Iran's stance towards the Palestinian–Israeli conflict.

Notwithstanding the harsh rhetoric on both sides, Iran and the United States do share a wide range of interests. Two of Iran's staunch enemies – the Taliban and Saddam – were toppled by the United States. Tehran and Washington share a common interest in promoting an integrated Iraq with a 'one man, one vote' political system. The unhindered flow of oil is a strategic objective of both countries. Confrontation with Iran is thus unnecessary and a military strike will reset the politics of the country on a military course. In his book entitled *Does America Need a Foreign Policy?* Henry Kissinger forcefully argues, "There are few nations in the world with which the United States has less reason to quarrel or more compatible interests than Iran."[13] Stated differently, words do not matter while interests are lasting. What is said behind the podium is far less relevant. It is the geopolitics and geo-economics of states that persuasively set direction and define horizons.

From the standpoint of the world community, it is too damaging for Iran and the United States to communicate through rhetoric and flamboyant statements. Under current strained conditions, Washington must exercise more responsibility because it has more power. However, as a global actor, the United States generally fails to fathom the domestic politics of other countries before mapping out its strategy. The American mind subconsciously presumes that because the country is so powerful others must adhere to its agenda. However, Iran is a unique case, and with its sophisticated political system and its rainbow-hued and multilayered political life, it should not be understood in terms of typical Middle East politics.[14]

The current Iranian elites, both clerics and non-clerics, had one fundamental objective when they were in their 20s and 30s—ensuring Iran's independence and national sovereignty. That objective has been achieved. However, the current issue is how political sovereignty can be turned into meaningful interaction with the rest of the world. More than 50 percent of wealth in Malaysia is owned by non-Malaysians. Interdependence, outsourcing and regional integration are the current trends. The critical question is: how can a revolutionary mindset move beyond its circuit? With the exception of China, history provides no assurances. From a linear and historical perspective, Iran is on the right path. Iranians are rummaging through fiction and non-fiction to explore new strengths and appetites. The Iranian Revolution served as an upheaval to mull over, re-evaluate and reinvent the truth. It goes against reason to hinder the evolutionary path of a talented nation.

Iran's development is a work in progress. Regrettably, however, its economic development is overshadowed by its overwhelming security concerns. Iranian leaders have little choice but to pay adequate attention to the country's wealth creation and technological growth and in this sense, initiate a new national security orientation. Iran's emerging elites in the next decade will have to focus particularly on wealth accumulation given the fact that the country will possess a population possibly exceeding 100 million by 2018. Although Iranians take their own decisions, making the political process almost purely endogenous, it is clear that the forces of globalization will influence the national agenda for good governance. Progress, not only in Iran but throughout the entire Middle East, will depend on the extent to which states are politically prepared to grant more individual space and unleash economic activity. The political consequences of such a move would be colossal for the whole region. Ultimately, structural improvement in Tehran's relations with the Arab world will hinge on Iran's improved image at the global level. Iran has the great potential for semi-industrialization, having both natural and human resources at its disposal. However, both its economic development and normal relations with neighbors are linked to a change in the definition of its national security doctrine.

3

The Security Situation in Iraq and its Repercussions in the Gulf Region

Abdullah Al-Shaiji

For decades, Iraq had been a threat to the Arab Gulf states, especially the state of Kuwait. Even before its invasion of Kuwait in 1990, Iraq had constituted a security concern to these countries due to its considerable military advantage. Indeed, it can be said that the regime of Saddam Hussein formed the biggest threat to the security, stability and prosperity of the entire Gulf region. Today, Iraq is still a source of instability and a threat to regional security, although in a different way to the menace posed by Saddam Hussein's regime.

Iraq currently constitutes a new type of threat to the GCC countries, and this threat comes from two sources. First, Iraq has become a failed state. Second, Iraq could become an inspiration and incubator for terrorist and extremist elements such as Al-Qaeda and other organizations influenced by Al-Qaeda's beliefs and ideas. These organizations could pose a threat to the GCC states and their interests since they have allied themselves with the West, and in particular the United States.

What happens in Iraq is of great significance to the whole region. Within this context, one can understand the warning that US President George W. Bush reiterated when he disclosed his new strategy in Iraq at the beginning of 2007. He warned the Arab states of the Gulf, Egypt and Jordan that the United States' defeat in Iraq would help create a safe haven for terrorism and would represent a strategic threat to the survival of these countries. The US Vice President, Dick Cheney, also highlighted the implications of Washington's failure in Iraq and said that such implications would not be restricted to Iraq. The United States and moderate governments throughout the Middle East would also suffer.

The Situation in Iraq and the US Strategy

With the ongoing war in Iraq entering its fifth year, the Arabian Gulf is on the brink of a frightening abyss. Furthermore, in view of Iran's refusal to stop enriching uranium, the possibility of a confrontation between Iran and the international community is looming on the horizon. The United Nations Security Council has unanimously passed two resolutions to impose international sanctions on Iran, and a third resolution is being prepared. There are fears that the United States will launch some form of military action against Iran, which is reflected in the sharp escalation of tension between the two sides, the increase in the US military build-up in the Arabian Gulf and elsewhere in the region, and the precautionary and emergency measures taken by some countries, such as the State of Kuwait and the Kingdom of Bahrain, to deal with the repercussions of a potential military confrontation.

Thus, the Gulf region is becoming "an inflammable powder keg," – as described by the Saudi Monarch, King Abdullah Bin Abdulaziz Al Saud, during his inaugural address at the opening of the GCC Supreme Council Summit in Riyadh in December 2006 – and crises are recurrent in this most important region of the world.

Statements made by US military commanders sum up the tragic situation in Iraq, which is witnessing sectarian fighting and a dreadful security deterioration. Despite numerous security plans, the country is heading for chaos and disintegration. In February 2007, the US Defense Secretary, Robert Gates, admitted that four ferocious wars were raging in Iraq simultaneously; a Shi'ite–Shi'ite war for the control of Basra and the southern parts of Iraq to gain control over oil resources; a Sunni–Shi'ite war, an insurgency war led by Sunni and anti-American elements, and finally the war waged by Al-Qaeda. The latter has two goals: to support and help the Sunni insurgency and to escalate and exacerbate Sunni–Shi'ite violence. In a hearing at the end of February 2007, Michael McConnell, Director of the US National Intelligence Service, told the US Senate that developments in Iraq were heading in the wrong direction, and that the term "civil war" would best describe the main elements of conflict in Iraq, including the deteriorating sectarian division, forceful displacement of population and patterns of violence.

A security experts group, known as the Baghdad Brain Trust, concluded in March 2007 that the United States has six months to win the war in Iraq—or face a Vietnam-style collapse in political and public support that could force military strategists into a hasty retreat as a result. In addition to previous evaluations, there are other disturbing statements, such as the one from General John Abizaid, the former commander of the United States Central Command (USCENTCOM) in November 2006, warning against the possibility of a third world war if Islamic extremism was not stopped. He made a comparison between Al-Qaeda today and European fascism and Nazism in the 1920s and 1930s, which sparked off World War II.

British researcher Gareth Stansfield, in a study published by Chatham House in London on May 17, 2007 entitled "Accepting Realities in Iraq," draws a bleak picture of the situation in Iraq and of the consequences of US security prescriptions. The Bush surge strategy and the implementation of the Baghdad security plan are the latest of such prescriptions. The study stresses that Iraq is witnessing not one civil war, but several civil wars, and that Iraq is becoming a battlefield for proxy wars. The country faces the possibility of political, economic and social fragmentation along sectarian, tribal and ethnic divides. The Iraqi government is only one among many "state-like" actors. What exacerbates the situation in Iraq is that it is being transformed into a stage for settling accounts between international and regional powers. This further contributes to the destabilization not only of Iraq's security, but also the security of the Gulf region as a whole.

Within the same context come the recommendations of the Iraq Study Group (ISG), known as the Baker–Hamilton Commission, which were published in December 2006. These recommendations stressed the need for a change in US strategy in Iraq and recommended the withdrawal of the majority of US forces by the beginning of 2008. In April 2007, the US Congress passed a bill linking funding of the wars in Iraq and Afghanistan to a timetable for the withdrawal of US forces from Iraq. The bill stipulates that the pullout should begin in early October 2007 and should be completed by the end of March 2008. President Bush vetoed the bill. He also threatened that he would veto any similar bill that the Democrat-controlled Congress might pass and refused to set artificial deadlines that would "help enemy fighters achieve victory," as he put it. This opened a political confrontation between the Bush administration and Congress over the war in Iraq.

The Baker–Hamilton Commission also recommended that an international conference on Iraq should be convened. This conference was held in Sharm el-Sheikh in May 2007 and more than 60 states, international and regional organizations participated in the conference, including the United States, major Security Council members, major industrialized nations, Iraq's neighboring countries, and representatives from the Arab League, the United Nations and the European Union. The closing statement recommended that help should be provided for Iraq and that its security, stability, unity and integrity should be maintained.

It seems now that the Bush administration has reviewed its position, and has decided to respond to the stance of the Democrats who control Congress and the demands of realistic Republicans such as Henry Kissinger, John Scowcroft and James Baker, who demand that the United States should start a dialogue with Iran and Syria. The United States and Iran participated in the Sharm el-Sheikh conference in May 2007 and later the two countries held talks at ambassador level in Baghdad to discuss the situation in Iraq.

The real problem with the US strategy in Iraq is that it does not make a link between enforcing security via security plans, such as the recent

Baghdad security plan, and activating the political path. The main challenge is the ability of Prime Minister Nouri Al-Maliki's government to start national reconciliation and to amend the constitution in a way that provides reassurances for different groups on complicated issues, such as federalism, dismantling armed militias and solving the problem of Kirkuk. These are the demands of the international community and the countries that attended the international pledging conference for Iraq.

As Iraq's neighbors, the GCC states have adopted a clear position toward the crisis in Iraq. The closing statement of the GCC summit held in Riyadh in December 2006, expressed support for Iraq's integrity, sovereignty, independence and identity, and rejected claims of fragmentation and disintegration. The statement stressed the principle of non-interference in Iraq's internal affairs by any party attempting to influence its internal affairs in order to achieve certain goals—such attempts would not help Iraq's national unity. The statement also rejected any attempt by any party to extend its political and cultural influence inside Iraq in a manner that would strengthen division and sectarianism and would threaten the region's stability.

The summit also demanded the immediate dissolution of armed militias in Iraq and an end to outlawed armed operations, which would contribute to increasing tension in Iraq. The summit's closing statement also reiterated the belief that national reconciliation between various components of the Iraqi people is a fundamental prerequisite for the realization of stability in Iraq.

The Situation in Iraq and the Security of the Gulf Region

The Middle East is littered with crises on various fronts. Iraq is being fragmented and is heading toward civil war with destructive implications and repercussions for the region. Lebanon is divided and there are no prospects for a peaceful settlement in Palestine. Through its bullish policies, Iran wants to see US forces leave the region so that it can become the predominant power that sets the agenda of the region and controls its security. This is against a background of growing feeling that the US administration has become increasingly impotent in the last two years of George W. Bush's term. Furthermore, with their eyes on the White House in the 2008 elections, the Democrats are tightening the noose around President Bush.

According to the "neocons," Iraq was supposed to become the example and the model through which the whole region would be transformed in a way that serves US interests. They believed that the Middle East would be turned into an obedient region in which terrorism would be defeated, democracy would prevail and renegade states would be alienated. This would be the beginning of a period of unchallenged US domination for generations to come. Developments in Iraq have proved that this kind of theoretical analysis was shallow, superficial and idealistic, and the painful reality in Iraq refutes such a theory. Today, Iraq has become a mix of three elements: failed state, part civil war, and part regional war.

The security situation in Iraq has deteriorated greatly in 2006 and the country is heading for disaster. More than one hundred attacks and operations are carried out daily; on average, 3,000 Iraqis are killed every month; and about 40 Iraqis are abducted every day and their bodies discovered dumped on roadsides. The number of prisoners has risen to more than 30,000 in addition to a surge in sectarian and factional killing, and forced displacement inside and outside the country. The UN agencies describe this as the biggest forced displacement since the Palestine tragedy.

Concerned that the repercussions of the Iraqi dilemma would reach the region's countries through the export of terrorism, displaced people and fugitives, the Kingdom of Saudi Arabia has launched a project to build a multi-level security wall equipped with hi-tech equipment along its border with Iraq. The wall will be more than 814 kilometers long. Also, the State of Kuwait has announced that it will build a security wall along its border with Iraq, which stretches 217 kilometers.

The important question is: what is the future of any relationship between the GCC states and Iraq, which seems to be heading for division along sectarian, factional and ethnic lines? More than four years have passed since the beginning of the war on Iraq. Still, the prospects for Iraq's disintegration and its repercussions are the main source of concern for all countries in the region; from Kuwait in the north to Oman in the south.

The GCC states are in a state of "uncertainty." First, they do not approve of the US presence in Iraq. In his address to the Arab summit, which was held in Riyadh in March 2007, King Abdullah Bin Abdulaziz Al Saud described this presence as an "illegitimate occupation." Second, these states do not support an immediate US military withdrawal from Iraq because this would lead to further fragmentation and would threaten the region's security and stability. Third, they do not want to see Washington opening up to Iran because that would mean more US concessions to Tehran at the expense of the region's states and would give Tehran greater freedom to maneuver. The embargo that is imposed on Iran would be lifted and consequently Tehran would become bolder and more confident to interfere in the affairs of the GCC countries. This would have a negative effect on the stability of these states, especially in view of the sectarian realignment in Iraq and suspicions about Iran's role in extending Shi'ite influence in the region.

In Paris in November 2006, the Emir of Kuwait, HH Sheikh Sabah Al-Ahmad Al-Jaber Al-Sabah, warned that a US withdrawal from Iraq would lead to a civil war. He said that the impact of such a war would reach Kuwait, and the whole world would pay the price. Such warnings reflect the fears of the GCC countries in this respect. Added to this is the strong message that the Saudi security advisor, Nawaf Obaid, voiced in his article in *The Washington Post* on November 29, 2006. In that article he said that the Kingdom of Saudi Arabia would not stand by while massacres are committed against the Sunnis in Iraq. Abdul Aziz Al-Hakim, head of the biggest Shi'ite group in Iraq, warned that the Sunnis would be the biggest losers if a civil war erupted in Iraq. The article also pointed out that the Saudis would intervene even if this led to a war in the region, since taking no action would have more dire consequences with regard to Iranian hegemony.

Although the Kingdom of Saudi Arabia stressed that the article did not reflect the official Saudi position, and although Obaid was removed from his post, this position reflects the concerns of the Sunni majority in the Arab and Islamic world toward what Iraq might face in the future. This is also confirmed in the Chatham House study mentioned earlier, which points out that the Kingdom of Saudi Arabia and the Gulf states are concerned about Iranian hegemony in Iraq and that "Saudi Arabia might not stand by if the United States now withdrew from Iraq, principally because such an action would herald the commencement of a full-scale Sunni–Shi'a civil war in Iraq, with the possibility of Iran and Saudi Arabia fighting each other through proxies in Iraq."

The main criticism of the GCC countries in general is that they are in a state of collective resignation and are incapable of submitting an initiative to actively influence developments in Iraq. This has prevented them from playing a significant and strategic part that is compatible with their economic and financial weight, especially since they are most affected by what is happening in Iraq.

Apparently, the GCC countries do not have many choices. They also lack the capability to deal with the Iraqi crisis. This has left the arena open to Iran to play an effective role in the course and conclusions of events. Iran is using Iraq as a bargaining chip to strengthen its position with regard to other issues, especially its nuclear program, and in its efforts to dominate the region. There are fears that a "grand deal" might be struck between Washington and Tehran, where it is feared that such a deal would see Washington reluctantly acknowledge Tehran's role in the region in a way that would satisfy its ambitions for control and hegemony. The United States could make such concessions because it needs help to extricate itself from Iraq.

The Unexpected Consequences of America's War against Iraq and the Fall of the US Plan in the Region

The repercussions of the Iraq war, described as "unintended consequences," have caused great damage to the US plan for the "Greater Middle East" that expands from Morocco in the west to Pakistan in the east. As has been proved, President George W. Bush was under the misguided illusion espoused by the Neocons. They persuaded him that a swift victory in Iraq would serve as a basis for US hegemony in the region, guarantee control over its oil, protect Israel, and frighten hostile regimes such as Iran and Syria and organizations labeled as terrorist, such as Hamas, Islamic Jihad, and the Lebanese Hezbollah. As for allied and moderate regimes such as Egypt, Jordan and the Arab states of the Gulf, they would be forced to transform democratically and to implement political reforms, with Iraq setting an example to follow and a model for the entire region. As Paul Wolfowitz, the former US Deputy Secretary of Defense put it, democracy would spread, emanating from Iraq and would cover the whole region reaching Iran and Syria.

However, four years have passed since the fall of Baghdad and President Bush has declared "mission accomplished" and announced the end of military operations in Iraq. Indeed, the situation in Iraq has changed. The US project has failed and with it has fallen the United States' prestige and its capability to influence the course of events in the Middle East. One of the most striking features of this failure is that the United States has agreed to hold direct talks with Iran to find a way out of the crisis in Iraq. In the past, it repeatedly announced publicly its refusal to conduct such talks.

The Iraq war has inflicted huge damage on the United States. Washington has lost its image as the most important power capable of dealing with the issues of the region and imposing a solution in the Middle East. Its main concern now is to find a way out of Iraq, especially after those countries participating in the "alliance," such as Britain, have announced that they intend to withdraw their forces from Iraq gradually. Other countries such as Italy, Romania and Denmark have already withdrawn their troops.

[109]

What follows are the most significant "unintended consequences" of the US war against Iraq:

- The United States has lost the capability to influence developments in the Middle East and Washington's enemies in the region feel that it is incapable of settling crises. Although they admit that Washington is still strong and influential, they believe it is no longer the strongest and the most influential force in the region. In other words, the United States is a "dominant" but not the "predominant" force. US strategists such as Zbigniew Brzezinski and Richard Haass have also highlighted the retreat of the US role.

- Instead of focusing on the principles of "change and imposition of democracy and reform," US policy has shifted to a more realistic approach and shows a return to the old bases and fundamentals of the US strategy in the region. This policy is based on the exchange of freedoms for stability, a return to the status quo, and the giving up of ideas and demands for reform. Two years ago, President Bush and Secretary of State Condoleezza Rice were criticizing this same position whenever they spoke about the mistakes of US policy in the region. This old policy has been realized and is an admission that the ambitious US project has failed.

- A real clash has emerged between the two ideological trends in the US administration. The neocons have lost their momentum after the resignation of the former US Secretary of Defense Donald Rumsfeld. Moreover, the Democrats have forced the US ambassador to the UN, John Bolton, to resign from his post. Rumsfeld's Under Secretary of Defense for Policy, Douglas Feith, was also forced to resign. All of them played major roles in engineering and pressing for the war on Iraq.

- The Iranian plan in the Middle East is taking precedence over the US project and Iran is benefiting from setbacks that the United States has suffered in Iraq. It has forced the United States to sit down and discuss the situation in Iraq, which can be seen as a victory for Iran and shows that Iran's attempts in Iraq have borne fruit.

- There are genuine fears of a confrontation between the international community and Iran over Iran's nuclear program and the policy of brinksmanship it is following, reflected by an escalation in the language of confrontation and challenge. The Security Council has unanimously passed two resolutions to impose economic sanctions on Iran and to punish those involved in the running of its nuclear and ballistic missiles programs. The United States has created new regional circumstances by eliminating Iran's two regional rivals—the Taliban regime in Afghanistan to the east in 2001, and Saddam Hussein's regime to the west in 2003. This has created a strategic void and put an end to the balance of power in the region, which is a crucial element of its stability. Iran has benefited from this situation and has filled this void strategically, politically, and in terms of security. Iran is becoming increasingly emboldened in pursuing its bid to realize its agenda and its ambitious project to become the predominant power in the region.

- In confronting the axis of hardliners in the region led by Tehran and supported by Syria, an axis of moderate states has been created through what Condoleezza Rice described as laboring for a new Middle East. Her announcement came during the Israeli war on Lebanon in 2006. This has created a gap between the moderate regimes that allied themselves with Washington and the West, and their peoples who view these regimes as subservient to the West. The so-called hardliners are winning the battle for the hearts and minds of the populations in moderate Arab countries.

- The trend to liken the Iraq war to Vietnam, with all its bitter memories, suffering, incompetence and defeat, is gaining momentum. Even some politicians and military commanders are reiterating this view and US public opinion is convinced now that the war in Iraq is moving in the wrong direction. This is a clear condemnation of the course of the war and its consequences.

- In-fighting inside the US political system between the Republican administration and the Democrats is intensifying. The Democrats owe their victory in the US congressional elections in November 2006 to American military setbacks in Iraq. They also have their eyes on the White House in the 2008 presidential election. Therefore, they are clearly and understandably trying to press for binding legislation that links the funding of the war in Iraq to timetabling a military withdrawal to be completed in the summer of 2008. The Democrats backed away from their initial demands to link funding to scheduled military withdrawal by the end of May 2007. However, this does not mean a final victory for the US administration, but more of a temporary retreat for the Democrats, who will come back stronger and more determined to face President Bush. The number of Republicans who are concerned about their political future and their chances in the 2008 elections is increasing and are expected to abandon President Bush and his sinking ship in Iraq. No doubt the repercussions of the crisis in Iraq will cast a shadow on the results of the upcoming US elections.

- After rejecting the recommendations of the Baker–Hamilton committee regarding opening up to Iran and Syria, the US administration reversed its position and sat with representatives of these two countries in the conference of Iraq's neighboring countries in Baghdad in March 2007, and the conference on Iraq in Sharm el-Sheikh in May 2007. Within the same context came the significant meeting between the US and Iranian ambassadors in Baghdad to discuss the situation in Iraq on May 28, 2007.

- Talk about plans for a gradual withdrawal or redeployment is increasing. As the White House spokesman Tony Snow commented, ideas are being considered that invoke the case of South Korea as a model for the US military presence in Iraq for decades to come.

Conclusion

Under the shadow of a continuous and bloody war in Iraq and the looming prospect of a new war against Iran, the atmosphere of two wars in the Gulf region can only generate more fear and concern. Indeed, the Kuwaiti parliament held a session to discuss the country's preparations to face the dangers of a new war in the region over Iran's nuclear program. There are genuine concerns that the Gulf region will become an arena for, and a victim of US wars and Iranian revenge.

Recent statements by Gulf officials highlight the dangers of a US–Iranian confrontation for the region as a whole. For example, the Kuwaiti Prime Minister, Sheikh Nasir Al-Mohammad Al-Ahmed Al-Sabah, said in an interview with the Egyptian *Al-Musawwar* weekly in early March 2007 that "any military action against Iran would have dire consequences for the region's security, economy and environment. In a way, it would further exacerbate regional and world tensions." On the fringe of the World Economic Forum, held in Amman in May 2007, Sheikh Nasir reiterated Kuwait's position in rejecting a military solution because "a military solution would bring destruction for the region and for the whole world."

The GCC states are seriously concerned as they see threats of war are escalating against a backdrop of political and military mobilization against Iran. Although these states will pay the price for any new confrontation in the region, they feel helpless to influence or change events in a way that would realize stability in the region in general and would reinforce their national security.

The crises and challenges that face the Gulf region's security should prompt the people concerned to join ranks and to develop a unified Gulf policy and strategy. This should produce a role for GCC states, not to affect the course of events in the Gulf region only, but also to contribute to finding a common ground and appropriate atmosphere to reach a just, final and comprehensive settlement for the Palestinian cause, which is the main source of all problems in the Middle East.

[113]

4

Gulf Security Following
the Invasion of Iraq

Gareth Stansfield

Much has been written about the changing dynamics of Gulf security
since 2003. With the removal of the Ba'ath regime from power in
Iraq, the Gulf states were faced with an unpalatable problem that had
remained largely hidden during the previous three decades of US
involvement in the security of their region. For the United States, from the
1970s through to the 1990s, Gulf security had been viewed through realist
lenses, focusing on securing oil, maintaining security and ensuring that no
other power could encroach on the region. An understanding of the
political, economic and social dynamics within Gulf states was almost
totally absent from the US view of security, yet it was these concerns that
largely dominated the threat perceptions of the Gulf states themselves.
The elevation of these concerns to the forefront of the discourse on Gulf
security was one of the main regional impacts brought about by the
invasion of Iraq, thus opening the door to changes in the way in which
their security could be managed and understood at a variety of levels.

At the international level, the already significant US military presence
in the region was strengthened. However, this was a double-edged sword;
while a US presence could temper any conventional threat posed to the
region by Iran – including any territorial designs on Arab Gulf states'
possessions that Tehran may have been harboring – an overwhelming US
presence in the Gulf could easily be met with antipathy by Gulf

populations and, politically and economically, inhibit the options available to Gulf Arab leaders for engaging with members of the wider international community who had clear interests in developing links with their oil-rich states. In essence, Gulf leaders would now have to choose between embracing US hegemony in the Gulf and seeking security by engaging a range of actors from the wider international community.

Regional Gulf security was also profoundly altered by regime change in Iraq. Certainly since 1980, if not earlier, the Gulf security architecture had been largely built upon the presence of two principal political and military forces (Iran and Iraq), the existence of Saudi Arabia as a key component of the global economic system and the presence of other Gulf states as important oil exporters with long-standing links to Western powers—namely the United Kingdom but also, increasingly, the United States. With the effective removal of Iraq as a state capable of projecting its military, political and economic power in the Gulf, the natural regional counterbalance to possible Iranian hegemony had been removed. How the regional Gulf security architecture would then be constructed was a source of concern for Arab states in particular.

The final, and I would argue most important, aspect of security that was destabilized by the changes imposed on Iraq was the domestic realm in Gulf states. While regional capitals maintained their concerns over the presence of US forces and the aspirations of Tehran, it was arguably internal considerations that motivated governments to a greater degree. Two inter-related issues stood out as being of particular concern. The first was how to plan for US success—if and when US plans to democratize Iraq were realized. What would a US-designed democratic system in the Gulf mean for the rest of the region? Would the remaining states be coerced by the international community or pressured by their populations to follow suit and similarly democratize according to the much vaunted 'democratic domino' theory forwarded by US neo-conservatives before the invasion of Iraq? If so, what would this mean for the traditional political order that characterized the Gulf states? The second part of this puzzle was even more worrying as it was tied intrinsically to regional security concerns. With the removal of the Ba'ath regime, the Shi'as of Iraq were well placed to take advantage of their numerical predominance there, whether through force or via the ballot box, and to turn what had been a bastion of Arab nationalism with a Sunni hue into something altogether more Shi'a in its outlook, stoking fears that such a stance would invariably see the influence of Iran increase. How the rise of a 'Shi'a Iraq' would impact upon Shi'a populations in the Gulf region – especially in Bahrain and Saudi Arabia – was an issue that began to be discussed with increasing regularity in the days preceding March 2003.[1]

Inter-linked Levels of Security

These three levels of security form the framework by which Gulf security following the invasion of Iraq will be analyzed and assessed in the remainder of this chapter. It is now no longer the case – indeed, if it ever were – that different 'levels' of security (i.e. domestic, regional and global) can be considered as discrete categories of analysis. This is especially true when the focus is the Gulf region. The interconnectivity of non-state characteristics weakens the viability of analytical approaches that rely heavily on realist International Relations (IR) frameworks, with "some of the most pressing threats to the state [deriving] from domestic politics, which, in turn, implicate the possibility of regional stability."[2]

The post-2003 situation in the Gulf and the ensuing traumas of international politics have also exposed a struggle within the discipline of IR, and particularly with reference to how states interact, and how 'security regions,' 'security communities,' or 'zones of peace' are formed.[3] The debate in many ways is not new, and has at its core the issue of whether a focus upon structure, or upon more normative 'identity' factors has more analytical worth. In some ways, a focus upon the Gulf region is useful for investigating this debate. It can be argued that an approach which focuses upon inter-state relations is useful, but now insufficient, for building an understanding of post-2003 Gulf regional security; yet realist theories of

IR remain distinctly appropriate when considering the higher-level actions of the superpower, or 'great powers.' The balance between the sub-state, trans-national elements of Gulf societies and the influence of 'systemic' elements of the international system determine the political direction of the region. Untangling the relationships between the two, and how the inherent tension between them is managed, provides a more nuanced understanding of the security development of the Gulf. There is, I venture, no other comparable region to the Gulf since 2003 that manages to combine the distinctive regional color of an idiosyncratic region with the very real pressures exerted by the superpower and great powers.

Perhaps the most comprehensive theory unifying both realist and constructivist approaches is the Regional Security Complex Theory of Barry Buzan and Ole Wæver. In brief, they outline four levels of analysis that must be addressed when considering security in regions.[4] These levels are:

- *Domestic considerations*: these include questions over whether the state is 'strong' or 'weak' due to stability of the domestic order and the correspondence between state and nation. Specific vulnerabilities sometimes make other states a threat even if they have no hostile intentions. This is obviously an important level to focus upon and drives much of the security concerns of Gulf capitals themselves. How nations are constructed, how nation and state-building projects are progressing, and the effect of changes in the power-structures of other regional states – most notably Iraq – could impact upon the domestic stability of Gulf states are all crucial in this regard.

- *State-to-state relations*: in terms of the Gulf, such relations are complex and inter-related. Ties of ethnicity (such as 'Arab' or 'Persian') interact with confessional status (and particularly the increasingly important notions of sectarianism in Islam) and pre-state regional identities that continue to survive (most notably, a *Khaleeji* [Gulf] identity common to the region, whatever shoreline one resides upon).

- *Interaction with neighboring regions*: this is discussed by Buzan and Wæver as being of relatively limited importance due to the nature of security being driven by *internal* regional considerations. However, an argument could be made that the Gulf region's interaction with its neighbors should be considered of increased importance owing to its central position in the 'Islamic region,' and the acts of states not geographically located in the Gulf region which impact upon the security of Gulf member states (and particularly with reference to Turkey and Syria on Iraq, and Pakistan and Afghanistan on Iran).

- Finally, and of crucial importance in assessing Gulf security, is the role of global powers in the region, and how the global and regional security structures interplay.

When questions pertaining to Gulf security are raised, the inter-relationship that exists between different levels of analysis is clear, and suggests that considering security in the Gulf *as a region* may indeed be the most appropriate way of proceeding. It is quite impossible, for example, to discuss the impact of post-2003 events in Iraq without referring to the concerns of the international community, the regional imbalances imposed by Iraq's effective removal as a meaningful state actor in the region, or why political elites in Gulf states view with trepidation the rise of a Shi'a-dominated state in Iraq. It is only by viewing them as interconnected rather than discrete problems that a more complete understanding of the 'regional security complex' can be generated. Indeed, it is these interconnections that form the regional security complex itself. How events and dynamics that occur at the spatial level of the region, or in the individual countries therein, and then feed into situations that exist at a wider spatial level – and perhaps in a 'systemic' sense where realist theories of IR are particularly enlightening – is a dynamic that is important to consider.

There is also a distinct temporal element to note when addressing the changing nature of Gulf security. In effect, the focus upon the 'domestic,' perhaps 'non-state' elements of security only really gained prominence following the upheavals caused by regime change in Iraq and the unleashing of different catalysts of change.

In the pre-2003 security architecture of the Gulf region, three inter-related issues tended to structure discussions about Gulf states' security:

1. the containment of the Ba'ath regime in Iraq by UN-imposed sanctions;
2. the controlling of Iranian aspirations and the managing of Iranian influence by the United States and Arab Gulf states respectively; and
3. ensuring the continued and uninterrupted supply of oil to world markets.

While commonly referred to in academic literature on the subject, these elements of the security architecture did not indicate how security was being perceived by the states of the region. If such concerns were added, it would entail significant additions to the list, including:

1. issues focusing on the investment of Iran in the economies of Arab Gulf states—in effect, the political economy of Iranian–Arab Gulf relations;
2. the transformation of the internal governing structures of states, with particular attention paid to the democratization/liberalization pressures applied by Western countries;
3. dealing with the imbalances caused by large numbers of remittance workers; and
4. for some states, considering how changes brought by democratization and changes in domestic political economy may change the Sunni/Shi'a balance in the state itself.

To understand this change in 'security outlook,' it is first necessary to discuss briefly how the pre-2003 security architecture developed and assess the 'determinants' upon which Gulf states viewed their security and those dynamics which threatened their continued stability. The changes that engulfed Iraq following the removal of the Ba'ath regime will then be reviewed, with particular reference to those issues that posed potential threats to Gulf states—Iraq as a 'catalyst' of regional violence; the disintegration of Iraq; and the emergence of a Shi'a-dominated government. This study concludes with an assessment of these potential threats 2007, and how wider Gulf security was being considered during and in the immediate aftermath of the initial US–Iran stand-off over Tehran's nuclear program.

Pre-2003 Gulf Security Architecture

Following the British withdrawal from 'east of Suez' in 1967, Gulf security dynamics can be grouped into three distinct periods. The first of these was up to 1979, and was characterized by US support for Iran and Saudi Arabia. The second period commenced with the Iranian Revolution in 1979 and ran until 1988, and was characterized by US support for Iraq in its war with Iran. The final period began with Iraq's invasion of Kuwait and culminated with the invasion of Iraq by US-led forces in 2003, and is characterized by the policy of the 'dual containment' of both Iraq and Iran.

From 1969, Gulf security was structured around the 'twin pillars' of Pahlavi Iran and Saudi Arabia. Rather than maintain a heavy presence in the region, the US instead supported key allies, namely Saudi Arabia and Iran, to be powers capable of dominating the regional security environments, as US surrogates, and thereby ensure the free flow of oil from the Gulf. With the changing currents of the Cold War, Iraq would also be brought into the fold of US-supported countries (albeit in a less obvious fashion), while the Islamic Revolution of Iran in 1979 effectively severed the Iranian-US relationship, but still saw Tehran maintain its position as a regional power.

The subsequent decade saw the US strategy of building 'pillars' in the 1970s become refocused on balancing the threat posed by Iran to the interests of the United States and her Arab allies.[5] The principal tool by which this threat would be balanced was the provision of financial support and intelligence to Saddam's Iraq in its conflict with revolutionary Iran. With the two most militarily powerful states in the region focusing their efforts on each other, the security of the rest of the Gulf was maintained—however, it was a security system built upon pitting two powerful countries against each other, and would again need to be reformulated when the Iran–Iraq War came to an end in 1988.[6]

The war between Iran and Iraq had the end result of leaving neither side defeated, and neither side victorious. For the Gulf states, this was an outcome that had both positive and negative aspects. On the one hand, with neither side winning, there remained no undisputed regional hegemon. On the other, a 'draw' meant that two very large military establishments remained in place, with each regime claiming victory and with each considering how to best pursue its national interests. The problems imposed on Iraq by this non-victory were particularly acute. With some 100,000 dead, a badly damaged infrastructure and an oversized military draining the depleted treasury, the survivability of the Ba'ath regime was highly questionable.[7] Compounding these internal social and economic problems was the fact that Iraq had run up debts to foreign states, at least to the value of US$80 billion, but perhaps to the level of $100 billion, with half of this being owed to Saudi Arabia and Kuwait.

The threat posed by Ba'athist Iraq to Gulf security crystallized in 1990. Following the end of the Iran–Iraq War, Saddam Hussein desperately needed to ensure that his swollen military forces were kept occupied (as returning, defeated forces can quickly turn their attention to those who sent them to war in the first place), and to find a new source of revenue to support the devastated Iraqi economy. This source and focus of military adventure would be Kuwait, which Iraq invaded on August 2, 1990.[8] However, Iraq's attempt to incorporate Kuwait as its nineteenth governorate failed. International condemnation of Iraq's invasion was followed by the assembly of a 'coalition of the willing' to defend Gulf states under the codename Desert Shield. Desert Storm – a military operation to remove Iraqi forces from Kuwait – quickly followed.

The routing of Iraqi forces from Kuwait in 1991 was the beginning of a tortuous decade-long period for the people of Iraq which saw the most comprehensive sanctions regime in history imposed by the United Nations. Coalition aircraft patrolled its skies in the south and in the north, and Iraq's ability to interact in any way with its neighbors was massively weakened.[9] However, the Iraqi state still existed and, as such, provided some 'balance' to Gulf security if only by perpetuating the status quo as dictated by the state structure of the region. Particularly with reference to Iran, the continued existence of the Iraqi state under the leadership of Saddam Hussein served as a counter – albeit a grossly weakened one – to any possibility of the spread of Iranian influence in Iraq and, by extension, the wider Gulf region. Perversely, the presence of Saddam's regime also maintained the status quo in a different way – by ensuring that the United States sustained a significant military posture in the Gulf, with bases in Oman, the UAE, Qatar, Saudi Arabia and Kuwait. While ostensibly looking toward containing the Ba'athist regime in Iraq, the presence of US military forces also served to counter any possible security threat toward the Gulf states emanating from Tehran.

More through luck than design, a reasonably stable security arrangement could be seen to exist in the Gulf in the last decade of the twentieth century, but it was one that had profoundly weak foundations in so far as it relied upon the exertions of a singular superpower (acting, understandably so, in its own self-interests), seeking to 'contain' two states that would, in normal circumstances, be critical components of a regional security system. Into this mix was added the presence of the world's largest hydrocarbon reserves in Saudi Arabia, and the existence of other Arab Gulf states – each with their own significant resources and connections to the international community, and with their own aspirations, fears, and agendas.

These foundations were undermined by the US-led invasion of Iraq in 2003, and were demolished in the subsequent years following the deconstruction of the Iraqi state, the failed rebuilding of the state, and the outbreak of several civil wars. Now, Iraq was no longer able to act as a benign keystone keeping the regional security system intact. Rather, it became a vortex of change, drawing in the involvement of outside powers keen to promote their own national interests. Most importantly in this regard is the rise of political Shi'ism in Iraq. From being a bastion of Arab nationalism with a particularly Sunni hue, Iraq's political identity changed overnight and the state became dominated by Shi'as, with their Kurdish allies in support. The reaction from the Sunnis saw an active and dangerous insurgency (or resistance, depending on your point of view) emerge which inflicted heavy casualties on coalition forces. It is useful at this point to go into a little more detail about the situation inside Iraq, before considering how events there were viewed from the safety of the Gulf.

Iraqi Realities

From the second half of 2006 onwards, observers, senior military figures in the coalition, and politicians, began to make increasingly bleak pronouncements about the situation in Iraq.[10] They had very good reason to be worried. Far from Iraq returning to some semblance of normality three years after the removal of Saddam from power, it had in fact degenerated into a series of brutal [un]civil conflicts, with Iraq's warring factions seemingly further apart than ever, and with the involvement of regional powers (namely Iran, but also Saudi Arabia, Turkey and Syria) all seeking to involve themselves in Iraq's affairs for reasons pertaining to their own national security. In short, Iraq was in a state of civil war, and war by proxy.

The Plurality of Conflicts in Iraq

From the summer of 2006 through to the end of the year, violence in Iraq reached appallingly high levels. However, this time the United States was not primarily to blame. Rather, the nature of violence in Iraq had changed from being 'externalized' against the forces of the occupation, to 'internalized' and between Iraqis themselves. This meant that violence in Iraq had become localized in its nature, but no less vicious because of it. While listing the 'theaters' tends to suggest a degree of order where perhaps little existed, the following breakdown covers most of the conflict situations that had emerged by the summer of 2006:

- A struggle over the control of the state between Shi'as and Sunnis. This manifested itself as a bloody civil war in Baghdad and its environs, and permeated the institutions of the state.

- Conflict over whether Iraq would be unitary (as the Sunnis and Sadrists demanded) or federal (as the Kurds and the Supreme Council demanded).
- Territorial conflict in Kirkuk between Kurds and non-Kurds.
- Continued US–Sunni conflict.
- Continued Shi'a (Sadrist)–US/UK conflict.
- Sunni tribal vs. Sunni Al-Qaeda conflict in Anbar, Nineva and Diyala.
- A Shi'a–Shi'a conflict in Najaf and Basra mainly between Sadrists and Badr forces.
- Rampant criminality across the entire country.

The result of these conflicts was manifold and devastating. To live a normal life proved impossible in Iraq outside the Kurdistan Region—the impact of which was to further feed the forces of polarization that had already largely segregated Iraq's communities into distinct Sunni and Shi'a zones, and consolidated the existence of the now largely autonomous Kurdistan Region in the north.

Gulf Security after 2003

From the perspective of the Gulf states, the invasion of Iraq by US-led forces in 2003 presented a difficult choice—whether to support the removal of a regime that had long posed a threat to them by a US-led coalition, or denounce any such attempt to remove the dictatorship of Saddam Hussein, thus satisfying the demands of their own peoples. Informing the thinking of the Gulf states was a deep-seated fear that any change in the status quo of Iraq may well have a deeply destabilizing effect upon their own security. These concerns were multi-dimensional: the Gulf states feared the effects of failure – if the US decided to withdraw, perhaps due to a vigorous defense by Iraqi forces – and the reinvigoration of a Ba'athist regime which, by its victory, would be firmly entrenched in Iraq and able to rebuild its influence in the region; they also feared Saddam's defeat and how their role in assisting the United States would be received by Arab public opinion. US success would also bring with it a change in the governing structure of Iraq and an alteration in the balance of power between groups there. Concern was particularly focused upon the interaction of tribes and, more importantly, the threat posed to Iraq's dominant Sunni heritage from a politicized and majoritarian-minded Shi'a leadership.

With the benefit of hindsight, were the Gulf states right to harbor such concerns? In what ways is the post-2003 Gulf security environment different to that of 2002 or earlier? In some ways the difference is stark, since the Iraq that was, arguably, is no more. From being a significant actor in the region capable of influencing events to a considerable degree, it is now questionable whether the Iraqi state itself exists as a meaningful actor even inside Iraq's boundaries. Far from being the sole arbiter of coercive power, the Iraqi state is now one of only several such powers that exist within the country.

While this is the case, the threat posed by Iraq to Gulf security pre-2003 has to be qualitatively different to the threats that have emanated from it since the invasion. 2003 is an appropriate watershed on which to base this distinction. It is certainly possible to argue that Iraq, far from being a source of regional instability in the 1990s, was effectively removed by the imposition of the US policy of 'dual containment' and the UN-imposed sanctions regime of the 1990s. However, the crucial point to make is that even with the most draconian sanctions regime ever designed being imposed upon Iraq, 'the state' and the regime survived and still had the capacity to manage internal forces and remain capable of denying neighboring powers influence in its domestic political realm—a situation quite different to that of post-2003. As is now well known, Iraq only became a safe-haven for Al-Qaeda-associated groups after 2003. It is highly questionable whether it was such before then.

With the elections of January 2006, Iraq became a 'Shi'a state' – i.e. a state in which the narrative was now one directed by the new 'dominant nationhood' of the Shi'a. It was, in many ways, a watershed moment for

Iraq and the wider region. With these elections, Iraq made its first tentative steps toward embracing a post-Ba'athist future, but they were steps that were in a profoundly different direction to those taken in the past. It was in these elections that it became clear that Iraq's future would now be one in which the Shi'a community would enjoy an unprecedented level of involvement—with the state itself increasingly seen as the preserve of the Shi'a religious establishment and their Kurdish allies. How this change will affect the Gulf remains a cause of serious concern in Arab Gulf capitals, particularly with reference to both the spread and enhancement of Iran's influence in Iraq, and the invigoration of Shi'a communities in Arab Gulf states.

This latter issue is of particular importance. Previously, from the viewpoint of US policy-makers, Gulf security concerns were considered in terms of inter-state relations. However, with the changes apparent in Iraq, Gulf security should now be viewed at a more fundamental level. Rather than focusing on the international relations of the region, security is increasingly involving the preservation of the domestic political status quo and is now measured in terms of threats to Gulf governments. Whether from Shi'ism, US-defined democratization, Al-Qaeda, or the fluctuations in the global economy, the sterile dimensions of international affairs have been polluted by the domestic concerns of the governments in power. A second focus considers how the US presence in the Gulf region has been forced to adopt a new posture toward Iran due to the failure of 'regime change' in Iraq and the occupation of that country. From the perspective of the Gulf states, Iraq's instability will have potentially dangerous ramifications for regional security. If the United States succeeds in stabilizing Iraq, will it then be used as base from which to influence the affairs of Iran and Syria—possibilities which will have a harmful impact upon the stability of Gulf states? Or will a stable Iraq by definition be a Shi'a-dominated one, with equally worrying ramifications for Gulf states? If the United States fails, how will this affect its struggle with Iran? If Iraq fragments into different independent states, what would be the impact of this on the security of Gulf countries?

Shi'a Concerns in the Gulf

Fear over how issues relating to Shi'ism may destabilize the Gulf can largely be reduced to two principle categories. The first is what many analysts describe as the "rise of the Shi'a crescent," with Shi'a communities in Arab Gulf states all viewing the rise of their co-religionists in Iraq as models to emulate in their homelands. Such actions can of course be influenced by Iran to a considerable degree, and it is this Damoclesian threat hanging over at least three Gulf states that raises the question of the intentions of Tehran.

The threat is arguably very real. The switching of Iraq from being a state firmly identified as being ruled by a Sunni Arab core, to one in which the Shi'a religious establishment with its opaque links with Tehran now operates the levers of power, followed by the deterioration of security in Iraq and the polarization of communal identities to the point where it is now theoretically correct to talk of 'civil war' in Iraq, has led many observers to speculate about the beginnings of a wider civil war in the Middle East that sees Shi'a 'challenges for power' not only in Iraq, but in the Gulf and Lebanon.

It is presumably these types of anxieties that have led several Arab Gulf states to involve themselves more fully in the political process in Baghdad. Indeed, Saudi Arabia remains so concerned about possible scenarios that could come to pass if and when US forces leave Iraq that it has publicly declared that it would have no choice but to support the Sunni community there in any power-struggle that would develop between them and the Shi'as. The Saudi motivation is clear—any change in the balance of political power in Iraq may have an effect upon the stability of the ruling regimes of the Gulf. Therefore, a Sunni–Shi'a dispute in Iraq has a very real and potentially transformative affect upon the other states of the Gulf.

The second category revolves around fears of a proxy war against the United States being fought in Iraq that could spill over into a wider confrontation between the United States and Iran in the Gulf. Quite simply, Tehran has no chance whatsoever of being able to defeat the might of the US military in anything remotely resembling a conventional-style conflict. If the United States chose to attack Iran – presumably in a manner more reminiscent of the bombing-lead attacks that were inflicted on Iraq in 1991 and on Serbia in 1999 rather than the 'overwhelming force' attack that saw the ground invasion of Iraq occurring concomitantly with the air assault in 2003 – Iran would be lucky to inflict any casualties on its opponent.

Yet, Iran has managed to successfully 'fight' the United States inside Iraq, through supporting Shi'a proxies in particular, in a manner that undoubtedly influences US decisions as to whether it could attack Iran more openly over the stand-off that emerged in mid-2007 over Tehran's WMD program. Any planning of an attack against Iran taking place in the Pentagon had to factor into the military equation the certainty that Iran can exact a terrible revenge upon the US presence in Iraq. It can also further destabilize Lebanon, heighten the already serious problems faced by NATO in Afghanistan, and even influence events in Palestine if it so wished. Conflict with the United States by proxy in the Middle East is something that Iran can undertake, and perhaps even win.

The 'Shi'a-ization' of the Iraqi State

The demise of the Ba'ath regime in Iraq not only removed from the political map of the region the dictatorship of Saddam Hussein, it also fundamentally altered the character of political power in the state. With a near-century long history of Sunni Arab domination of state institutions, the overthrow of Saddam effectively and swiftly brought a new 'dominant nationhood' into power in Iraq. The Shi'a, for most of Iraq's history as a state and for the preceding period of Ottoman rule, had been largely excluded from holding meaningful positions of influence in the state. Similarly, the Kurds had also been excluded from participation at the highest levels of government.

Writing in 2007, it is clear that the situation in Iraq has changed. While Iraq is still in a state of turmoil (irrespective of 'the surge' embarked upon by the US and Iraqi military), it is clear that the Shi'a, as a political constituency, will remain a – if not *the* – pre-eminent group in the state. For some analysts, this fact is indicative of a new era emerging in

Middle Eastern and Islamic world politics – an era in which the Shi'a will become a more prominent and vocal force in the affairs of Arab states, thereby fundamentally altering the complexion of political life in the region, and especially in the Gulf.

Operating across the 'regional' and 'domestic' areas of the theoretical framework, and perhaps in the space between them, is the role of Shi'ism in regional politics. Considerable attention has been devoted to what some analysts have described as the Shi'a "reaching for power,"[11] or the emergence of a 'Shi'a crescent' starting in Iran and ending in Lebanon. For these observers, the terrible events in Iraq cannot be considered in isolation to the rest of the region, as merely the localized happenings of a country subjected to years of dictatorship, sanctions and now occupation. Rather, events in Iraq are intrinsically tied to wider regional networks. Vali Nasr noted with some prescience in 2004 that "Iraq's sectarian pains are all the more complex because reverberations of Shi'a empowerment will inevitably extend beyond Iraq's borders, involving the broader region from Lebanon to Pakistan."[12] Indeed, according to this logic, instead of Iraq being the first 'democratic domino' in the Middle East, it now has the potential to be a 'Shi'a domino.'

Unwittingly, perhaps, regime change in Iraq may therefore result not only in the rebalancing of power between the Shi'a and Sunnis there, but also impact upon the balance of power between Shi'a and Sunnis across the region. From the US perspective, this fact – of their being a threat to the balance of power between Sunnis and Shi'as – is a problem for several reasons. First, a change in the balance of power suits Iran far more than it suits any other regional player, and this is, in the current circumstances, an anathema to the interests of Washington. Second, and perhaps more importantly, the United States has, along with virtually all other powers with interests in the Middle East, consistently ignored the salience of Sunni–Shi'a power struggles which, as Nasr again notes, "is neither a new development nor one limited to Iraq. In fact, it has shaped alliances and determined how various actors have defined and pursued their interests in the region for the past three decades."[13]

The ramifications of this struggle for the Gulf region could be profound. While the division on the map seems clear enough, with Shi'a Iran being on the eastern side of the Arabian Gulf, and the Sunni Gulf states being on the western side, the reality is more complex. Arab Gulf states, and most notably Kuwait, Saudi Arabia and Bahrain, have sizeable Shi'a populations – in the case of Bahrain a distinct majority – which are characterized as comprising a 'Shi'a arc' stretching from Lebanon to Pakistan. However, it is in the Gulf where they clearly predominate.

The thinking behind such scenarios is straightforward and highly persuasive, particularly when presented to Western audiences that view the structure of political life in the Middle East through prisms of sectarianism and ethnicity, oppression and resurgence, and an expectation that some form of singular identity overwhelms any possibility of multiple identities alone capable of generating bridges between societal cleavages. The scenarios invariably start with the consolidation of a 'Shi'a' regime in Baghdad, which then acts as a catalyst for other Arab Shi'a communities— namely those in Bahrain and Saudi Arabia in the Gulf, and also in Lebanon and the wider region. What is missing in these scenarios, however (beyond references to most Shi'as in the Gulf emulating Grand Ayatollah Sistani of Najaf, or having some hazy tribal links to southern Iraq, or, indeed, being influenced by Iranian revolutionary groups), is the *process* by which such links evolve and how politicized Shi'ism first becomes manifest in the states of the Gulf and then evolves into a position where challenges can be made against the *status quo*. Quite simply, these scenarios have failed to take into account the possible *responses* of the incumbent Gulf regimes, which will probably be taken in order to preserve themselves and adapt to the new environment in which they exist.

There are clearly elements of the 'Shi'a crescent' scenario which are attractive—indeed, few ideas are received quite so energetically as ones which attempt to re-parcel out the territories of the Middle East region in some form of century-late revision of the post-First World War settlement. Yet, is it really possible that there will be, if not a redrawing of the map then a redrawing of the regional system in such a way that sees the rise of a Shi'a Arabian Republic, or a 'Republic of Kurdistan,' or the emergence of some wider 'Sunnistan' that could challenge the power of the already extant states of the Gulf?

I would like to proffer here that such scenarios are enticing, but probably somewhat misleading as they are built upon two largely questionable assumptions. The first is that there exists some collective will on behalf of Shi'as or Kurds in Iraq to destroy the state in which they reside. I would argue strongly that this is simply not the case. Rather, the political leaderships of these groups seem to be committed – certainly for their own self-interests – to promoting Iraq's survival, albeit in a manner that affords them control of the state. The second is that there seems to be little evidence that a meaningful challenge has emerged in any Gulf state from Shi'as toward the governments of the countries in which they live. One would have expected that, nearly five years after Saddam's removal from power, at least some murmurings would have emerged that would suggest a threat to the governments of the Gulf. There has, on the whole, been very little movement indeed.

Why should this be the case? Why haven't the Arab Shi'as of al-Hasa province in Saudi Arabia viewed with admiration and pride the actions of their co-religionists to the north and sought to take matters into their own hands? Admittedly, one of the most important reasons is that the Saudi state has the means to manage such tendencies, either through coercion or patronage. However, evidence from Iraq itself illustrates clearly that there is a lack of political unity among the Shi'as. Indeed, the tenets of Shi'ism do not ease the facilitation of a singular homogeneous social or even cultural movement, let alone a political decision-making structure capable of bringing together peoples across the boundaries that divide states. The ramifications of this fact can be seen on the streets of Baghdad, and particularly in Basra, where different groupings loyal to a range of leaders are engaged in a highly destructive conflict to secure control of Iraq's urban centers and the surrounding hinterland (especially when these areas

[132]

contain oil infrastructure). Basra itself is now heavily divided, with the Supreme Council for the Islamic Revolution in Iraq (SCIRI) dominating the political life of the city, but with the *Fadilah* Party maintaining its control over the official offices of the governorate, and with forces loyal to Muqtada al-Sadr (or at least acting nominally in his name) in areas removed from Basra such as Amara and Kut.

These divisions have a further, ethnic, aspect to them. Far from being unified Shi'as seeking to exert their control over the destiny of the Iraqi state, there is a serious set of conflicts emerging over: (i) resources and economic advancement; and (ii) ethnicity—particularly the difference between those considering themselves 'true' Iraqis, and therefore Arabs, and those considered by them to be 'Persians.' The range of Messianic groups now operating in the south of Iraq, including the Sadr movement and its splinters, are largely mobilized around an Arab nationalist platform and target, in particular, the SCIRI and the British military presence.

The fracturing of Iraq and the existence of a range of actors capable of challenging the state's authority raises what many in the Gulf consider the key cause for future concern. In terms of influencing Iraq's political direction, neither the Iraqi state nor the United States can claim the accolade of being the most important actor; the momentum of the insurgency and the speed with which society is polarizing in Iraq removes any possibility that the United States can act in anything other than a reactive fashion, making it patently unable to then implement any preconceived plans (if there are any) aimed at effecting change in Iraq. Furthermore, the inherent weakness of the fractured state combined with the fact that political power in Iraq has chaotically devolved to those best placed to project their power over specific localities means that a whole range of locally powerful and influential actors are seeking the patronage of a powerful sponsor. For Shi'a parties, this sponsor has to be Iran. For this reason, and because of the long history of social, cultural, religious and economic interaction between Iraq and Iran, it is now not incorrect to describe Iran as being the most influential power in Iraq.

Iran is powerful because it has the means to influence events in Iraq through a wide range of proxies (including the Badr Corps and other Shi'a militias); Iraq's leading politicians from the Shi'a and Kurdish communities are largely beholden to Iran, owing to their years of fighting Saddam's regime with the support of Tehran; and, perhaps most importantly, the inter-linkages that exist between Iran and Iraq at the societal level that are strong and extensive, and cover more than simply the bonds of religious affiliation (which, at times, have actually proved to be quite divisive). They include social, cultural, economic, political and now paramilitary ties that allow Iran to manipulate the political landscape of Iraq in a manner that suits any faction seeking to exert its influence in Tehran. It is these factors that have led the United States to view Iran not only as a threat to regional stability, but as a threat to US plans in Iraq itself. For these two reasons, the animosity between Iran and the United States has continued to grow throughout 2006 and 2007. For the security of the Gulf region, nothing could have been more destabilizing.

Iran and the Gulf

The changing nature of security in the Gulf has therefore brought with it a whole new range of issues relating to the rise of the Shi'as in Iraq, the influence Tehran enjoys among the prominent parties that comprise the new Iraqi government, and the example Iraq now represents to Shi'a communities in the Gulf. However, in keeping with the theory of interconnectedness that permeates Buzan and Wæver's regional security complexes, it is not possible to disaggregate affairs and events in Iraq, and how such events may impact upon the (in)stability of Gulf states, without moving into a wider spatial environment and considering the regional dimensions surrounding Iran.

It is not necessary in this chapter to explore the on-going dispute between the United States and Iran, since it is investigated in more detail elsewhere. Suffice to say that any conflict between the two will have a fundamentally destabilizing effect on the security of the Gulf region, again, in two major ways. The first of these has already been mentioned when considering the politics of Iraq, and this is the conducting of a war by proxy by both Iran and United States in Iraq, and also across the wider Middle East region. It is a battle that could see the United States embroiled in situations as damaging as those we witness regularly in Baghdad, only in places ranging from Lebanon through to Afghanistan. For the Gulf, this obviously has immediate implications owing to the fact that southern Iraq will be a focal point of any such proxy action. Yet, there are also other concerns that Gulf states must factor into their security relations. These include the fact that Iran invests a formidable amount of capital in the Gulf states, and particularly in the UAE. Iran is also a major economic partner for Gulf states, and a very sizeable market. Furthermore, Iranian 'goodwill' will be vital to any 'security community' that may emerge in the near future, especially as Iraq is now no longer capable of challenging the region-wide influence of Iran, and is, perhaps, subject to decisions made in Tehran.

Conclusion

The changes imposed on Iraq represent a watershed in the history of Gulf security. One of the three most important states (Iran, Iraq and Saudi Arabia) that influenced superpower involvement in the region was effectively removed. However, has it been removed fully, or has it merely been transformed? Arguably, Iraq, and events there, still have a profound influence on the nature of Gulf security (and the actions and policies of regional states, great powers and the superpower) but have now entered the security equation at the regional level. At the core of this balance is the condition of the relationship between Sunnism and Shi'ism, and how

[135]

this religious schism is superimposed on to, and empowered by, the regional competition between Iran, other Gulf countries and the United States. Fears of the rise of a Shi'a crescent seem, at present, to have been at least either premature or inaccurate. Indeed, I would suggest the latter. However, it is undoubtedly the case that Sunni–Shi'a differences are permeating the political discourse of the Islamic world in a way not previously seen. As such, it should be expected that Gulf states will continue to remain wary of any possible Iranian influence in their territory.

THE INTERNATIONAL DIMENSION
OF GULF SECURITY

5

From the Cold War to the War on Terror: A US Perspective on Arabian Gulf Security

David Mack

Apart from brief trips to the region, I was quite new to the Gulf when I arrived in Abu Dhabi in 1986 as the US Ambassador to the United Arab Emirates. Of course, I had the benefit of attending the round of briefings routinely given to new ambassadors, including one on Gulf security from General George Crist, Commander-in-Chief of the US Central Command.

General Crist was a warrior-scholar who worked hard to integrate area knowledge with military strategy. However, without meaning to slight the general, I would describe his briefing as being founded on a false premise. It was a threat-generated briefing, and the threat identified in this case pertained to Soviet designs on Iran and the Gulf. In fact, General Crist began the briefing with an area map showing the Soviet Union in red. This was followed by a picture of Peter the Great, the seventeenth and eighteenth-century Russian ruler who greatly expanded the Russian Empire. Under his Russian and Soviet successors, the Muslim lands of Central Asia and the Caucasus were absorbed into the Empire. This historical background gave depth to the false premise that the United States was facing a familiar Cold War scenario of a Moscow government harboring designs for southward expansion through Iran into what strategists referred to as the "warm waters of the Gulf." General Crist's next slide went a step further and illustrated the probable invasion routes of Soviet armies through Iran to the Gulf.

One should bear in mind that this briefing took place in the summer of 1986. Whether or not Soviet expansion into the Gulf region was ever a realistic threat, world events had already altered the underlying realities shaping Gulf security issues. However, governments typically prepare 'to fight the last war' or tend to devise strategies based on previous conflicts.

It soon became evident to me that a far more relevant image for the aforementioned briefing would have been that of the late Ayatollah Khomeini; if Crist's successor, General Norman Schwarzkopf, were conducting the briefing in 1990, the dominant image would have been that of Saddam Hussein; and if General Tommy Franks were giving the briefing in 2001, the image would be that of Osama bin Laden. In 2002 and 2003, Franks would probably have a new picture at his briefings—that of Saddam Hussein once again. Today, I imagine that Admiral William Fallon at US Central Command is likely to be using a picture of Iranian President Mahmoud Ahmadinejad. This is what we might call the 'threat of the month approach' to Gulf security. It raises the risk that the United States is talking about the last threat instead of focusing on the next one. It can create the even greater danger that in US policy, the means tend to swallow up the ends, as the United States forgets the vital interests that lend importance to the area, and ignores likely natural allies.

Many of you will be urged by your governments to think strategically about Gulf security. Today, I will discuss one possible strategy for the United States and for its 'longstanding friends' of the Arabian Peninsula to defend their shared interests. I will not be presenting a US government perspective or even the perspective of the Middle East Institute, which by its charter does not take institutional positions. However, I will explain my personal view, based on experience both in and out of government in relation to this problem. I will also describe how the US government appears to perceive those interests, bearing in mind that there is much churning within policy circles in Washington. Other conference participants will describe how Arab governments in the region view those interests. In my view, the most promising areas are those where these

[140]

perspectives converge or overlap. It is also important to be conscious of areas where the security perspectives of the United States and its friends in the region diverge and try to learn appropriate lessons from these divergences.

As General Crist's briefing showed, it is necessary to recognize that the US government and most US strategic thinkers approach these issues from a global perspective. This is not surprising for a government with global interests and responsibilities. From such a starting point, a US strategist normally seeks to understand how forces and developments in the Middle East affect the global economy and the global balance of power. By contrast, countries in the region are more likely to focus on the regional balance of power and how global factors and external forces might upset that balance. Conversely and more positively, the Gulf Cooperation Council (GCC) states might enlist the governments and private sectors of countries outside the region to help redress a regional imbalance.

An example of Washington's global Cold War thinking was President Ronald Reagan's decision in 1987 to offer US Navy protection to Kuwaiti oil tankers as a deterrent to Iranian activities in the so-called "tanker war." This period was characterized by Iran's attempts to put an end to GCC support for the Iraqi war effort. All US ambassadors in the region, myself included, argued that the United States should respond in a forthcoming manner to the Kuwaiti request for such protection. Our view was based on the US national interest in maintaining a longstanding economic and strategic partnership with the GCC states. President Reagan hesitated and agreed to proceed only after he learned that Kuwait had made a similar request for protection to the Soviet Union. As I might have understood from General Crist's briefing, the United States would go to great lengths to prevent any competition from the Soviet fleet in the Gulf. In the end, the United States did the right thing, but for what I thought to be the wrong reason. The result was *Operation Earnest Will* involving military and political cooperation that established a precedent and provided practical experience for more far-reaching cooperation during the security crisis of 1990–91.

The security cooperation which characterized the administration of President George Bush reached impressive levels. Personal relationships, both at the political level and at the level of top military commanders, also became positive during the great military build-ups for *Operation Desert Shield* and *Operation Desert Storm*. Moreover, President Bush decided to lend his prestige and exert full efforts to secure a lasting peace between Israel and its Arab neighbors, which led to the Madrid Conference and subsequent developments. This apparently indicated Washington's recognition that it could not deal with Gulf security effectively if it did not also seek a lasting resolution of the Palestinian issue and other Arab–Israeli disputes.

During the Clinton presidency, enhanced security cooperation continued but without an equivalent advance in political consensus between Washington and the Gulf states. President Clinton's world view, which emphasized globalization, made sense for the United States. However, this approach met with initial resistance in traditional societies, which feared that the effects of globalization would threaten both their economic independence and their cultural distinctiveness. Clinton's National Security Council Advisor, Martin Indyk, also made the error of characterizing his support for Gulf security as 'dual containment.' The fact that Indyk made this public statement before an American-Jewish audience and without adequate private consultations with friendly Arab governments set off alarm bells across the length and breadth of the Arabian Peninsula. As a result, 'dual containment' soon became little more than a glib slogan that masked disagreements and lack of mutual political consensus. This was ironic since President Clinton's actual policies toward both Iraq and Iran tended to be continuations of those followed by his predecessor. Just as was true during the Cold War, the governments of the GCC countries saw the fate of US–GCC relations as being dependent on the vagaries of US global objectives that they could only envisage.

It is impossible to understand the strategic approach of President George W. Bush without taking into account the tragic events of September 11, 2001. However, even in the preceding months, there were indications that the new US administration was going to adopt policies unilaterally, expecting other friendly governments to fall into line or to be sidelined or even penalized. Some theorists of the new strategic environment at the end of the Cold War took the view that the United States had an obligation to itself and to others to play the kind of role that the Roman and British empires had at their high points. In US domestic politics, great deference was paid to the President and his senior advisors in the aftermath of these alarming terrorist attacks in the US homeland. Americans demanded a decisive response to the 9/11 aggression.

Internationally, the initial response was also positive, as many other governments welcomed strong US leadership. The United Nations and several of its member states cooperated with forceful US measures to deal with the Al-Qaeda elements which had found a safe haven in Afghanistan and were operating elsewhere around the globe. Unfortunately, the Bush Administration missed an opportunity to develop lasting multilateral institutions and a truly collaborative approach to common problems.

The GCC governments provided wide-ranging support in response to the US need for rapid deployment of military and other assets against Al-Qaeda and the Taliban regime in Afghanistan. In addition to the use of facilities, intelligence gathering and exchange was also enhanced. Recognizing that individual citizens and residents in their countries were providing financial and other kinds of support to Al-Qaeda, the GCC governments also undertook a tightening of financial controls and increased domestic monitoring to unprecedented levels. In some cases, the governments moved too slowly, not always recognizing that the Al-Qaeda threat against them and against progressive reforms in their countries was an existential one. In some cases, it was too easy to believe that opponents of the regime who were prepared to resort to violence could be appeased by allowing them to focus on their adversaries in the West. Unfortunately,

[143]

a US media establishment predisposed to judging Arabs and Muslims harshly often failed to reflect the more positive information emanating from knowledgeable US government officials, including statements made in Congressional testimony. Some media outlets, both in the United States and in the Arab world exaggerated signs of a "clash of civilizations" and downplayed evidence of cooperation.

In addition to unilateral decision making, the Bush administration also flirted with ideas of 'regional transformation,' beginning with Iraq and possibly extending to other adversaries, but also including friendly states that had autocratic or traditional political and social systems. President Bush seemed to believe that the long-term security of the United States depended on Middle East governments becoming both democratic and socially progressive. Considered as a very long-term proposition, he may well be right, but in any meaningful timeframe it is clear that both the ideological justification for Washington's policy of regime change in Iraq and its severely flawed implementation have reduced US credibility as an agent of benign change to a historically low level. This policy has also raised critical questions about the reliability of Washington as a strategic partner for those very governments whose support is imperative if Washington is to achieve its short- and medium-term goals in the region.

The reality is that the traditional and unelected GCC leaders responded well in most cases to international policy requirements. With the passage of time, practical cooperation has increased but the lingering legacy is a mutual lack of trust. Therefore, the durability of strategic coordination between the United States and the GCC is still uncertain.

The reality of trans-national terrorist threats to US national security in late 2001 could not be denied. There was also a plausible case to be made regarding the danger of the proliferation of weapons of mass destruction. However, the Bush administration missed an historic opportunity to build a joint strategy based on alliances. Once again, the United States was adopting a threat-based strategy focused on its adversaries rather than its friends.

The foregoing discussion has provided abundant examples of how not to develop a sustainable US Gulf strategy. Now let us consider a different approach.

Thinking about Gulf Security

What is the right way to think of Gulf security? In my view, the starting point is to identify shared interests. This approach does not deny the reality that sometimes the United States and the GCC states either do not share the same interests, or at least do not share them to the same degree. It is necessary to be candid about such differences. However, undue focus on differences of opinion does not provide fertile ground for practical cooperation. Obvious interests between the United States and the GCC states include the following:

Orderly production and flow of oil and gas: The steady flow of oil and gas from the Gulf producers to consumers at market prices is a matter of mutual concern. There is nothing wrong with this emphasis. It has not been a choice dictated by either Washington or by capitals in the region. Rather, it is a reality based on geology and a global economy for which oil and gas from the Gulf are essential. The industrial markets for the bulk of these energy resources are distant, and no single nation can provide adequate security for the production and transportation of the oil and gas of the Gulf and Arabian Peninsula regions.

US–Gulf commercial activity: Another mutual interest lies in the trade and commerce between US companies and their Gulf business partners, both in the government and private sector. This commercial activity is profitable for US firms, and it transfers necessary technology and managerial expertise to the Gulf.

There are also less obvious interests, but ones that a strategist must bear in mind. These include the following:

Educational exchange: Interaction in the field of education is another matter of mutual concern, especially the issue of Gulf students pursuing higher education in the United States. Historically, this student exchange, along with business, has formed the bedrock of US relations with the region. Today, educational exchange has become constrained because of conflicts stemming from political disagreements and US visa restrictions.

Economic and political reforms in the region: Some may question whether the issue of internal reforms in the Gulf countries is an appropriate matter for US government concern, but the Bush administration has chosen to make it a high-profile issue.

Another interest that seems obvious to me but does not always top the agenda for other US strategists is regional stability. What this implies is that change should come in an orderly and gradual manner. Some critics in both the United States and in the Middle East charge that successive US administrations, under the leadership of presidents from both the Republican and Democratic parties, have been too willing to cooperate with entrenched autocratic governments. Critics from both the left and the right of the US political spectrum have suggested that there is a virtue to 'constructive destabilization' of the traditional political and social order in the countries of the Arabian Peninsula. Without denying the desirability of political and social change, I would question whether this is a 'shared interest' in an operational sense. Moreover, I am skeptical about the policy enunciated by President George W. Bush in his second inaugural address of January 2005 that US relations with countries around the world should be based on the extent of their democracy.

Seeking an International Democratic Utopia

It is useful to reflect on the strategic role of the current US government efforts to export its particular notions of political freedom. President George W. Bush has stated that human freedom and the spread of democracy will advance US interests and protect the American people against terrorist threats. In the very long run, he may be right. Yet, it would be unwise to ignore the lessons of history under the influence of the euphoric slogan 'Freedom is on the march.'

For many in both the United States and the Middle East, the words of the President's January 2005 inaugural address were inspiring:

> ... it is the policy of the United States to seek and support the growth of democratic movements and institutions in every nation and culture, with the ultimate goal of ending tyranny in our world.

Human freedom, like economic development or education is desirable on its own merits. We should not, however, oversell the benefits of rapid political change, either for the United States or for the advancement of human rights in a particular country. This would repeat in a more benign way but on a wider scale the mistake Washington made in overselling the war to topple the Iraqi regime of Saddam Hussein. Democracy that is 'Made in America' will not be the answer to complex situations in each country that need to be addressed with sensitivity to the local political and economic landscape. Neither is it desirable to have political change necessarily associated with the high-profile US formula of multiparty elections and popular sovereignty through the ballot box. Desirable goals are more likely to be rule of law, government accountability and transparency of government decision-making. This leaves open the process for reaching those goals.

In some of the most conservative Arab countries – the oil and gas producing and politically traditional states of the Arabian Peninsula – the preferred route may be through cautious top down progress toward constitutional monarchies. Several hereditary rulers in the region have been moving ahead at a pace that may seem slow to many in the West, but worries progressive elements within these countries. The progressives fear that too abrupt a transition to elected parliaments will lead to legislative bodies that are dominated by adherents of political Islam, who will oppose economic and social reforms. It is significant that even in a country such as the United Arab Emirates, whose citizens enjoy virtually no political

[147]

rights in the American sense, people cherish their high degree of personal freedom, family privacy, economic opportunity, private property rights, legal protection from government abuse, access to free media and excellent public services, such as education and health care. Not surprisingly, in such countries, the degree of upward pressure for democracy is minimal.

Moreover, there is a profound cultural disconnect between US and Arab attitudes based on differences of public psychology. As a people, Americans are endowed with energy, impatience and the basic confidence that all problems can be solved. Based on their past history, the Arabs are endowed with reflection, caution and fear of chaos. While Americans perceive reform and democracy as critical requirements for attacking radicalism and terrorism, US friends in the region see undue haste as a prescription for instability and the rise of radicalism. How can we be so certain that the toppling of autocratic regimes in Muslim countries will lead to a better outcome than when the Shah of Iran was overthrown in the Islamic Revolution of 1979? In the long term, that historic change may ultimately benefit both the Iranian people and the United States, but if that is so, it is proving to be a very long term indeed.

Americans should set their sights beyond their past tolerance for autocratic governments that serve US interests temporarily, but they should also be realistic in how they define the process of democratization. The key building blocks for democracy are basic security, rule of law and institutions of civil society. The United States can and should urge governments to move toward goals of greater inclusiveness in the political process, more transparent governance and better access by the citizenry to their governing institutions. It would be wise to show a clear example in our own society of the desirable direction of change. US diplomacy should discreetly encourage progress in similar directions but not presume to tell other countries how to calibrate the pace and tactics of political reform. The United States should also be modest in recognizing the limits of both its leverage and credibility as the agent of change in Muslim countries. It should be acknowledged that durable political change in a given country is unlikely unless such reforms have an organic relationship with its historical experience and respect the traditional culture of the population at large.

Mutual Interests as a More Reliable Strategic Guide

If my suggested starting point of mutual interests is accepted, it should be an overriding US objective to prevent hegemony over the Arabian Peninsula and the Gulf by any power with the capability, and perhaps the motive, to disrupt those interests. This would include the capability to disrupt the production and transport of oil and gas from this region to foreign markets, to interfere with the commercial activity that is gradually integrating the economies of the region into the global trading and investment system, to interrupt the exchange of peoples for mutually beneficial education and to obstruct the orderly process of political and economic reform.

This kind of strategy based on interests would not be aimed at any one threat. Rather it should strengthen the ability of the GCC states to deter interference in their affairs by any larger neighbor or state external to the region that might be potentially more powerful based on its population and military establishment. I leave it to your imagination, but I would suggest that multiple threats are possible even though no particular threat is so imminent that it should dominate long-range strategic thinking.

Viewed from a worst-case scenario, many states and non-state movements might be seen as posing some kind of potential threat based on their considerable actual or potential power, and in some cases on a plausible motive: relative poverty and the need for revenues or resources available to the GCC states, which are relatively better off but comparatively weak in military terms.

Let me give an example. Professor Richard Bulliet of Columbia University, a prominent American scholar of the Middle East, has written several novels in his spare time. One of them, published in 1984, is entitled *The Gulf Scenario*. The story concerns a US consulting firm which had very profitable contracts from the US Department of Defense over the years producing war games for US military and political strategists. The firm had conducted war games for a Soviet invasion of Iran, Iranian attacks across the Gulf and an Iraqi invasion of Kuwait and Saudi Arabia. Looking around for a new source of profit, the firm worked on a war game concerning a Pakistani government plot to take over the United Arab Emirates by subversion. The plot is motivated by the UAE's wealth in stark contrast to Pakistan's poverty. Using the large community of Pakistani emigrant workers, the Government of Pakistan eventually sends in its armed forces to protect Pakistani citizens. The novel moved to an exciting climax when Pakistani intelligence discovered that the proposed war game might upset its actual plans for such an operation. As US Ambassador, I loaned the book to a senior UAE official, who after reading it acknowledged that he found it all too plausible. Strategists have to consider combinations of motive and capability and plan accordingly. States that might be viewed as potential hegemons – and I understand that some might include the United States in this category – need to pursue policies designed to alleviate those concerns.

Moreover, in some cases there is a history of past threats, subversion, intimidation or even actual aggression, as in the case of Egypt in the nineteenth century and Iraq in 1990. Certainly until the destruction of Iraqi military power and the overthrow of the Saddam Hussein regime in 2003, there was a plausible, if debatable, threat from an Iraqi state presumed to harbor plans for revenge and capable of reconstituting weapons of mass destruction. Similarly, there is a history of Iranian subversion, intimidation and territorial claims. Some might argue that Tehran has demonstrated better behavior in recent years. Others will find Iranian actions in Iraq as well as its plans to improve missile capability and obtain a nuclear potential to be very troubling. I admit that I am deeply skeptical about Iranian objectives, but there will be other speakers at this conference who can analyze that in detail. Current behavior in

Baghdad or Tehran has to be considered, but also the potential for a shift to something worse—if internal struggles bring a more hostile regime to power or if anarchy creates safe havens for terrorist activity in the region. Everybody hopes for stable, popular governments committed to peaceful relations with their neighbors, but such optimism is rarely a good basis for strategic planning.

In recent years, strategists have realized that they need to consider the threat of hostile non-state actors as well as governments. Such groups are nihilistic, violence prone, destabilizing and hard to deter. They represent a new element that was not envisaged very clearly by strategists in past decades. However, it is not a new problem. For historical parallels, strategists could consider the assassin movement in the medieval Islamic world or piracy on the high seas in the eighteenth and early nineteenth centuries. At the current time, I would suggest that a strategy for Gulf security be robust and flexible enough to deal not only with Al-Qaeda but also with something non-existent now but possible in an uncertain future, such as a Baluchistan independence movement with the power to block the Strait of Hormuz and seek political concessions from both the oil-producing states and the oil-consuming states in the industrialized world. I am intentionally exaggerating here in order to dramatize the need for an interest-based and highly flexible strategy that would serve the long-term needs of both the United States and the Arab Gulf states.

In too many past cases, Washington has relied excessively on the role of military power. Strategies that neglect other security tools often lead to unintended consequences and miscalculations. It is an error to exaggerate the utility of force while neglecting elements of soft power—diplomacy, educational exchange, economic leverage and inducements to potential adversaries for good behavior as well as disincentives for bad conduct. Since the end of the Cold War, the world has witnessed a surge in US relative dominance in terms of conventional military power. By contrast, the attraction of US values has suffered owing to the neglect of instruments of soft power.

Earlier in this chapter I posited that the United States and the Arab Gulf states share strategic interests. That does not mean that those interests are identical. The United States is a global power and has interests involving Korea, for example, which are not high on the agenda of the Gulf states, although it could be argued that the government in Pyongyang threatens to destabilize the industrial economies of East Asia and thereby imperil the prosperity of the Gulf energy producers. As a former US diplomat I can remember trying to engage the support of counterparts in the Gulf states to check the danger of weapons proliferation by North Korea. Most of our strategic dialogue, however, will involve issues within the Middle East and South Asia regions. There are various tools for promoting these shared interests, which include the following:

- frequent political and strategic dialogue between the United States and regional governments;

- joint security training and military equipment transfers of various kinds; and

- bilateral military cooperation agreed upon by both parties.

Strategic dialogue is in my view the most important tool. It is also the one most often neglected by the United States and desired by the states of the region. Bilateral military cooperation gets much attention but ought to take place in a broader strategic framework than sometimes occurs.

The United States needs the help of its friends in the Arab world. Washington has often sought and usually received concrete military and economic cooperation from governments that have recognized a common security interest. However, very seldom does Washington enter into a meaningful security dialogue in which it listens to the views of its partners. Rather than wait for Washington to launch a new initiative, the GCC states should take measures to assert their own view of what a sound security strategy requires.

Just as we Americans sometimes try to engage the attention of our Arabian Gulf interlocutors on issues such as Iran, they keep reminding us that their own strategic concerns are equally or more likely to be dominated by an issue we would often prefer to ignore, forget or defer—the Arab–Israeli peace process. Unfortunately, we are not always listening.

The Middle East is the homeland from which my own cultural heritage, or what we inadequately call Western civilization, originates. Whether we speak of agriculture, writing systems and algebra or we consider Judaism, Christianity and Islam, the major religions of the children of Abraham—the Middle East is where it all began. There is no higher moral imperative for US policy than to work for peace in this region, particularly between Israel and its Arab neighbors, and most urgently between Israel and the Palestinian people. Various US leaders have neglected this challenge, to the detriment of US policy throughout the region. It is vital that the United States makes an energetic and persistent effort to end the suffering of the Palestinians and provide them with a state that is viable in every sense, including its territorial unity and sovereignty on nearly all of that part of Palestine that was under Arab control on June 4, 1967. We ignore the importance of resolving this issue at our own peril. Without a viable Palestinian state and an end to suffering, peace among the Palestinian factions is highly unlikely. Without that internal harmony, Israel will not have a peace partner nor be able to enjoy the security that it deserves.

It is also true that Washington's neglect of the peace process, or its undue bias toward Israel, undermines US relationships with other states in the region that are necessary for the country to achieve its strategic objectives in the war on terrorism, as well as in ensuring the security of the Arabian Peninsula and Gulf regions. The effort to separate these issues has failed time and time again, and the notion that a military victory over the Iraqi regime of Saddam Hussein would pave the way for peace between Israel and its neighbors was fallacious. I hardly need to comment on the equally bizarre notion that the peace process could remain on the back burner while the United States mobilizes a coalition of Arab states and Israel to confront Iran.

[153]

The Paradox of Iran

In dealing with Iran, the United States should consult more fully with potential partners in the region about what is at stake for them. I welcome the greater diplomatic interaction that seems to have taken place between the United States and Arab governments during the past six months. However, it is worrisome that US public statements have focused so heavily on the issue of Iran's nuclear weapons ambitions and its political structure. Some of us who are old enough will remember a time when Iran ruled by an ambitious Shah, who was then allied with the United States, was asserting hegemonic objectives in the Gulf and was being encouraged by Washington to develop a peaceful nuclear program. It is common knowledge that Iran can employ many means other than nuclear weapons to press its ambitions for regional influence, and some of these are just as unacceptable as nuclear intimidation. Washington should not imagine that a change in either the Iranian regime or its nuclear ambitions would solve the problems of Gulf security. Eventually, Iran's legitimate security interests must be satisfied in a manner that excludes Iranian behavior aimed at dominating its neighbors.

One approach towards integrating Iran into a future Gulf security structure may require resuming the unfinished business at the end of the Iraq–Iran War. The final paragraph of UN Security Council Resolution 598, ending the eight-year war, also called for an international conference of Iraq, Iran, their Gulf neighbors and key outside powers. This conference never took place, partly because of Iraqi aggression against Kuwait in 1990 and the subsequent deepening of regional divisions. Such a conference would possibly lead to the recognition by all concerned of the global importance of the Gulf and the role that its shared resources can play in area-wide economic development. Iran needs to know that it is recognized as having a critical role in Gulf security and encouraged to find a community of interests that is not based on assumed hegemony.

There is some positive change coming out of Washington. In November 2006, we had the first public indication that the Bush administration was reviewing ideas for the security architecture of the Gulf region. John Hillen, at the time Assistant Secretary of State for Political–Military Affairs, addressed the annual conference of the Middle East Institute (MEI). His remarks, available on the MEI website, discuss the thinking of the administration based on consultations over the past year with governments in this region. It was a detailed presentation of a strategy based on enduring US interests and the interests of our partners, bilateral capacity building in various military areas and a call for multilateral consultations and cooperation. In January 2007, Secretary of State Rice joined in a remarkable public statement in Kuwait by the foreign ministers of the GCC, Egypt and Jordan. One sentence registered very strongly with me as being both quite obvious to observers in this region and almost always ignored in Washington. As quoted by a published US State Department document of January 16, 2007, it reads:

> The participants agreed that the Palestinian-Israeli conflict remains a
> central and core problem and that without resolving this conflict the region
> will not enjoy sustained peace and stability.

I would like to quote another public statement which I hope indicates that Gulf leaders are not shy about making their views known to US diplomats and that the latter are listening to their Gulf counterparts. On January 23, 2007, Under Secretary of State for Political Affairs, Nicholas Burns, addressed an audience assembled by the Gulf Research Center in Dubai. The text of his remarks was finally released by the State Department on January 30 and I was pleased to see that it represented a far more nuanced discussion of Gulf security issues than we generally hear in Washington. Among other things, Burns quoted approvingly the wise counsel of the former President of the UAE, H.H. Sheikh Zayed bin Sultan Al Nahyan:

> Our security policy … is based on the necessity for cooperation by the
> countries of the region themselves to resist any danger that threatens our
> security.

This advice is refreshingly different from the overly unilateral approach that tends to focus on a single threat to the exclusion of others, and which too often has characterized US strategic thinking.

The Dilemma of Iraq

This chapter would not be complete without examining the potential of Iraq as a threat to Gulf security. In the near term, at least, the threat no longer stems from potential aggression. Instead, it is the destabilizing potential of an Iraq imploding through sectarian strife, feuding partisan militias and national disintegration. A sound US strategy needs to be based on the harsh realities of Iraq rather than the ideological illusions of some US strategists who imagined that they could somehow turn Iraq into the Norway of the Middle East. Today, instead of building utopian sand castles, the United States must focus on damage control. Indeed, the congressionally mandated Iraq Study Group (ISG) achieved a bipartisan consensus in its December 2006 report that the objectives in Iraq had to be more realistic.

Most people understand that the intoxicating visions of regional transformation and other planned goals for the US adventure in Iraq are unattainable. However, despite the claims of President George W. Bush to the contrary, there is a substitute for victory. It is noteworthy that the administration has already been using more realistic and less messianic criteria for success. This 'mission crawl back' has been driven by facts on the ground, but it has not been articulated by the Bush administration in a consistent and convincing way.

This was part of what the Iraq Study Group (ISG) tried to do, and the ISG recommendations are reflected in much of the current Congressional debate. Changing the nature of the US military presence and reducing its size by gradually disengaging from combat operations against Iraqis, is one part. Unlike some Democratic Party proposals in Congress, the ISG foresaw a further need for a residual US military presence engaged in training, support for Iraqi forces and fighting foreign *jihadis* who remain in Iraq. A second part would be maintaining a robust political and economic engagement in partnership with the international community. International measures would give priority to stability, rather than democracy, and they would focus on containing both the level and the spread of the violence while dealing with the human tragedies and economic burdens of refugee flows both within Iraq and across its borders. The decision by the United States to join with and support the existing Contact Group on Iraq and its neighbors was a positive step.

It was not, however, an answer to the most difficult strategic dilemmas in Iraq. The US National Intelligence Estimate of January 2007 stated that outside actors are not likely to be a major driver of either violence or the prospects for stability because of the self-sustaining character of Iraq's internal sectarian dynamics. There should be no illusions. The governments in Tehran and Damascus do not have clean hands with regard to the violence. However, at the end of the day, neither Iran nor Syria wants to have a failed state or outlaw region on their borders, providing a safe haven for terrorists and setting off a new tidal wave of refugees. Both governments seek indications that the United States has priorities other than regime change in mind for them. For Syria, in particular, an implosion in Iraq would be an existential threat. As for the other neighbors, they need the assurance they will not be abandoned to deal alone with the consequences of an Iraqi implosion, a new Muslim civil war and increasing Iranian power.

Regional cooperation does not offer an easy answer but the lack of an international diplomatic framework to stabilize Iraq, coupled with continuing US threats of regime change in Tehran and Damascus, have ensured that both Iran and Syria see little reason to cooperate. Even though both governments have soiled hands, what was puzzling was the absence of US backing for a multilateral effort to engage them on issues like border control. The bipartisan Iraq Study Group rejected tying the International Support Group to unrelated issues like nuclear development or Lebanon. However, such a multilateral context would require the

United States to downplay its own messianic goals of victory for democracy in Iraq and regional transformation. Instead, it should embrace the goal of stabilizing Iraq in a multilateral context, emphasizing diplomacy rather than military force.

Such measures cannot be taken unilaterally or with only our closest friends. If we have any chance of minimizing the spillover of conflict, it must be in a genuine multilateral context open to all of Iraq's neighbors, along with major states and international organizations. In the context of 21st-century Washington, what was novel about the Iraq Study Group's proposed International Support Group for Iraq is that it would require an unaccustomed degree of modesty for the United States. The time when the United States might have led such an effort has long passed. Here lies the paradox. Few nations will participate in such efforts if the United States is in full control and sets the agenda. However, no international efforts can succeed without strong US backing.

Diplomatic dialogue is not a seal of approval for current or past policies. Rather, it is a tool for engaging both friends and adversaries in finding areas where interests overlap. Beyond damage control and containment, a positive evolution of the situation in Iraq would require mutually reinforcing actions by its neighbors and other states in support of decisions that hopefully will be taken by the sovereign government of Iraq.

The United States should also reposition itself on other Iraq issues where its long-term agenda is suspect and works against its effective leadership of other nations regarding Iraq. The United States should clearly announce that it does not seek permanent bases. The temporary facilities it needs are intended for force protection, not for the purpose of projecting force outside of Iraq. Washington also needs to clarify that controlling Iraqi oil is not a US objective, although it wants equal treatment for US oil companies.

Indeed, the end game that Americans must learn to tolerate will not leave the United States as the dominant foreign presence in Iraq. This will disappoint proponents of a 21st-century US version of the Roman Empire. However, it could be much worse. The United States must try to avoid a scenario whereby implosion in Iraq sets off a regional power struggle in which the dominant victor is a hostile Iran and the losers become dependent US clients. If the United States continues striving for regional *primacy*, it may forfeit the chance for *equal* treatment and future respect.

For the near term, the United States can deploy great *military* power in Iraq and elsewhere in the region. However, never has it been more evident that military power alone, unsupported by a strong diplomatic context, is wholly inadequate. Moreover, the war in Iraq has been unpopular both at home and abroad. As a result of this war, coupled with the neglect of the Arab–Israeli peace process, US soft power is much less than it was in 2003. As US military and economic inputs start to decline, the country needs to compensate for the slack with subtle, daring and effective diplomacy throughout the region. Modesty will have great merit during the coming phase, which will be focused on efforts to stabilize Iraq and halt the spread of violence and suffering. The United States must be present at the creation of this new international framework to lend it credibility, but it would be better if the stage is shared with others.

Force and Diplomacy, a False Dichotomy

In my diplomatic career, I have experienced situations where US foreign policy was overly dominated by use of military measures without the guidance of an adequate diplomatic framework. You might call this 'witless use of force.' At other times, I was in the position of trying to use diplomacy with an adversary who saw that it was not backed up by the potential use of force. You might call that 'toothless diplomacy.' As a State Department official dealing with Iraqi diplomats in the summer of 1990, I would have liked to have had a carrier battle group in the Gulf to participate in the joint air exercise to which a farsighted Sheikh Zayed agreed in July 1990. Two carrier battle groups, along with all the other military assets of the United States and its GCC allies, may be more than adequate. However, it should be remembered that such great military power will only be effective in the context of diplomacy that is both robust and flexible.

At the present juncture, I am glad that the United States has military forces available in the region. I do wish they had not been squandered in Iraq, when they were deployed without adequate planning and consultation with strategic partners regarding non-military factors so critical to the outcome. There is no contradiction between the use of diplomacy and military force. In fact, the two work best in tandem.

A final word of advice is that it is necessary to lay down red lines for the behavior of a potential adversary, and also to consider overlapping interests. Strategists, including military strategists, need to give an appropriate role to diplomacy and economic relations. The military tool is often the least effective and almost always the most risky. To quote the ancient Chinese strategist Sun Tsu, "Military force is most impressive when you do not have to use it." Even in wartime, it should be recalled that there are overlapping interests between enemies, such as preventing the use of poison gas or avoiding mutual destruction. During the decades-long Cold War between the West and the Communist Bloc, Washington and Moscow found grounds for cooperation and even held summit meetings. History records that on more than one occasion, both sides avoided the worst outcome by not resorting to war.

6

A European Perspective on Gulf Security

Johannes Reissner

European interest in the Gulf region will remain at a high level. For years to come, the European continent's dependency on the region's energy resources will be sustained and may even increase. At the same time, there are heightened concerns about the security of the Gulf region and these regional risks are increasingly being perceived as potential risks for European security as well. Yet, regardless of the ways in which Europe and the Gulf are drawing closer, the abilities of the European Union and its member states to improve the Gulf security situation seem to be diminishing.

The question of regional security has gained new dimensions since the events of 9/11, the fall of Saddam Hussein's regime in 2003 and the subsequent security deterioration in Iraq. Accordingly, Gulf security can no longer be conceived at the restricted level of state-to-state relations.

After the fall of the Ba'athist regime in Iraq, the existing indigenous regional balance of power between Iraq and Iran was destroyed. Since the early 1990s, the United States has evolved as the most important "external balancer," a new role that is strongly contested by Iraqi resistance groups and by the Iranian authorities. The Iranian nuclear program is regarded by the West as the most important security threat, not only for the region but also beyond. At the same time, Iran perceives the US presence as the main cause for regional instability. In short, the US–Iranian antagonism has introduced a strong Cold War element into the region, with all its ramifications. Of these, US efforts to build an alliance with the so called moderate Arab states against Iran are only one aspect, which became most evident in November 2007 at the Near-East Conference in Annapolis.

It is obvious that the GCC countries will not abandon the US security shield for some time to come. However, this has no popular support and is counterproductive with regard to the security dimension of society–state relations. Of course, the US presence is only one of the factors disturbing conventional state–society relations. Another contributing factor lies in the fundamental changes stemming from demography, migration, the growing role of ethnic and religious minorities and the quest for political participation. These changes, exacerbated by the Sunni–Shia divide, can foster extremist tendencies and are therefore at the forefront of security concerns.

The impact of globalization constitutes the third factor that needs to be considered in any formulation of Gulf security. This impact, in its economic and communication dimensions, is interlinked with security problems at the state-to-state level and within the society–state dimension. Globalization may elude clear cut definitions even more than the manifold security problems within society–state relations, but it has gained unprecedented importance. Globalization not only provides new opportunities and widens lifestyle horizons, but also opens up new avenues of self-understanding. Peoples of the region can see themselves as part of the global society, and that has an important impact on the politico-cultural relations between Islam and the West.

This chapter explores these three interlinked security dimensions for the Gulf region and analyzes their implications for European efforts to play a constructive role in enhancing security.

Security at the State-to-State Level and the American–Iranian Antagonism

Despite the growing awareness of the risks of asymmetric warfare and the society–state security dimension, the state remains the most relevant actor and the centerpiece of all Gulf security concepts. A great many ideas have been put forward in terms of confidence building, cooperation and integration. However, these ideas are state-centered, and the security concept at work remains predominantly based on notions of balance of power and deterrence. Heading the list of security concerns is the fear of a US military strike against Iran with incalculable consequences and the more diffuse, but nevertheless intense, fear of Iranian hegemony, expressed by the Arab littoral states.

Since the fall of the Ba'athist regime in Baghdad in 2003, which for a long time was considered the regional power balancer against Iran, there is no room for any kind of regional power balance. As Michael Kraig has rightly observed, the regional power balance had already been destroyed by the Iraq–Iran War from 1980–88 "through the exhaustion and hollowing out of the region's two largest states."[1] Since then, the region's security fell more and more into the hands of the United States. With the First Gulf War to liberate Kuwait in 1991, the role of the United States had finally changed from a power beyond the horizon to a power within the region. However, that did not mean the establishment of a *Pax Americana*, but rather the establishment of a US military presence directed against Iraq and Iran.

The strategy developed by the Bush administration since the terrorist attacks on the World Trade Center and the Pentagon on September 11, 2001, has been described as follows:

> a military-based counterproliferation approach based upon a flexible mix of deterrence, coercive diplomacy, global military superiority, and the preventive or pre-emptive use of military force, alongside the spread of US-defined democratic and free-market values.[2]

The lesson learned from Iraq's deteriorating security after the fall of Saddam Hussein is that US military power can sweep regimes away, but does not have the constructive power to generate processes of political and social transformation, which were the proclaimed goals in that case. The pompously announced but short-lived Broader Middle East Initiative only revealed "the folly of trying to create Middle East peace through the "transformation" of an entire region's culture, economics and politics toward US and Western ideals."[3]

There is some inherent logic that, after Iraq, Iran should become the main target for President Bush's strategy of "peace through US global hegemony."[4] Iran had already been marked as "rogue state," "greatest state-sponsor of terrorism" and as part of the "axis of evil." The question of whether this strategy has its roots in dreams of a "new world order," as expressed by Bush Senior after the liberation of Kuwait in 1991, may be left for historical discussion. Nevertheless, it is definitely an outcome of the post-Cold War situation. Today, Iran as a "rogue state" (in Washington's eyes) along with the global threats of terrorism and proliferation, has not gained the strength of the former USSR, but is viewed in a similar role as a "realm of evil."

The premises and ideological assumptions of the US administration's strategy of "peace through global US military superiority" blew the chill winds of a Cold War into the region. Furthermore, "the orientation of US regional diplomacy towards balancing Iran, towards containing and rolling back Iranian influence with all means 'short of war'"[5] created a political situation in which no concept of a security scheme including *all* states of the region has a chance of further development. It reinforces "the traditional notions of *realpolitik*," which "continue to inform the dominant thinking and practice among Gulf states."[6] For the time being, the American–Iranian antagonism and the ways in which it is handled on both sides impedes any efforts to overcome these Cold War notions of *realpolitik* with respect to Gulf security.

The point here is not to blame either Iran or the US presence in the region as the main cause for regional insecurity and instability—that is being done by others on both sides time and again. Instead, it needs to be understood that the US–Iran antagonism as such is the main hindrance to giving effect to the principles of "non-exclusion"[7] and "reassurance."

Both are prerequisites for any kind of regional security arrangement which will be dealt with later. "Reassurance," in opposition to deterrence, can be considered as a concomitant principle to non-exclusion, insofar as deterrence only will make everybody concerned feel excluded. Security must be considered by all parties as a collective good.

The principle of "non-exclusion" as a minimum requirement does not necessarily mean that Israel has to be included in efforts to enhance Gulf security. Nor does it mean that Iran has to be included in finding a solution to the Arab–Israeli conflict. Of course, the conflict over Palestine has its repercussions on Gulf security, and because Jerusalem holds a religious significance for Muslims. However, Israeli pretensions regarding having a say in Gulf security should be rejected in the same manner as Iran's claims of being considered as the spokesperson for Muslims.

For the concept of security it is very important that principles of non-exclusion and reassurance do not rule out measures to ensure deterrence and balance of power in particular cases. It would be foolhardy to overlook the fact that Iran is currently considered a threat to regional stability not only by the United States but by the Arab Gulf states as well. However, there is a difference between a policy of deterrence and the seminal antagonism between the United States and Iran.

For the time being, this antagonism is one of the most obvious impediments to a collective security arrangement between the states in the region. Security based on non-exclusion and reassurance is in some ways more demanding than deterrence.

> The key to reassurance is a reliable normative and institutional structure...It requires an ability to initiate and maintain cooperation among sovereign states on matters that have been traditionally conceived of as the heart of sovereignty: decisions about what is needed to maintain and preserve national security.[8]

From this perspective, security concepts based on reassurance touch upon the dimension of state–society relations.

The State–Society Dimension of Security: Minorities and the Sunni–Shia Divide

As indicated earlier, the relationship between state and society has in many ways emerged as a highly important security dimension for all the Gulf countries. The causes and forms of security-relevant tensions and problems between societies, or sections of societies, and their states are manifold. Undoubtedly external players do play an important role in causing changes in state–society relations and even in undermining the legitimacy of states. The US military presence in the region is a case in point, but certainly not the only one. However, despite the role of external players in stirring up conflicts between societies and states, as outsiders they have only very limited capabilities to contribute in any meaningful way to the resolution of such conflicts. Unsettled and conflicting state–society relations not only constitute a security issue but also impede the development of security strategies between states based on the principles of non-exclusion and reassurance.

A new kind of bourgeoisie has developed in all Gulf countries.[9] Their calls for participation in public life in general and for political participation in particular are getting stronger. Women want to play a more self-determined role in their societies, and the young generation has become more demanding. In addition, religious and ethnic minorities have begun to play a more assertive role within their societies and vis-à-vis the states. It is not appropriate at this point to give a description of the multifaceted claims of different constituencies in the diverse countries of the region. However these claims, deliberately or not, at least potentially undermine conventional understandings of sovereignty and legitimacy.

For a long time, the main reaction to this kind of threat was to brush away claims and demands from the various groups of society as being inspired by outside forces. This kind of reaction is still practiced and there continues to be ample inducement for playing the blame game and making others responsible for unstable society–state relations. However, such reactions are losing their persuasiveness and can be upheld only by force.

[166]

If any general observation can be made about the transformation processes in all the Gulf countries, it is that a shift in the state–society relationship is underway, from a relationship between rulers and ruled to a relationship between states and citizen.

This transformation process may be just in its beginnings. Certainly, it is a troublesome one and more difficulties are to be expected. The future of the process is by no means clear. However, it is an irreversible process, which has developed its own dynamics. Whether it will lead to stable participatory and democratic institutions for the whole region remains to be seen. However, these institutions, whether seen as being in its infancy or more developed, are already having an impact on state–society relations and should not be underestimated.

Growing self-awareness on the part of the region's population can become detrimental for security if it leads to disloyalty towards the state and the country. In particular, that might be the case where ethnic or religious minorities with trans-national affiliations are concerned. They may even put the existing territorial integrity of states under question. Whether this is done intentionally by a particular minority or not, it suffices that governments feel that way, for then, even the simplest concept of cooperative security will have no chance to succeed.

Since December 2004, when Jordan's King Abdullah spoke of the "Shi'ite Crescent", the Sunni–Shia divide has increasingly gained the status of a wall, developing a fault line of its own. However, although this divide is old and contains several deep-rooted animosities, it only forms the background to the conflict but should not be regarded as its catalyst. In this connection, the title of Vali Nasr's nonetheless valuable book *The Shia Revival* is somewhat misleading.[10] A "Shia revival" can hardly be observed, for example, in the Republic of Azerbaijan, where 60 to 70 percent of the people belong to the Shia sect. The self-assertiveness of the Shia and the emergence of the present Sunni–Shia conflicts as an important regional political factor originated in the freeing of the Shia in Iraq from Saddam Hussein's yoke, and in the fact that the Arab states failed to fully integrate their Shia minorities into the nation state.[11] Most particularly, the Sunni–Shia divide constitutes a complex and additional overlay to the Arab–Iranian divide, combined with conflicting political attitudes towards the West, in particular the United States.[12] Israelis, for obvious reasons, tend to construct the Sunni–Shia divide in terms of a "moderate" Arab "axis" against a "radical" Iranian–Shia "axis."[13]

There is no doubt that, given the deep-rooted animosities and prejudices on both sides, the Sunni–Shia divide can be and is easily manipulated for mobilization purposes in troubled times. However, there must be a careful examination of the extent to which the Sunni–Shia divide will shape regional political developments. The difference between the regional and the local should not be overlooked. Fantasies that paint Iran as the mastermind of Shia movements do not reflect reality. Since the much heralded "export of the revolution" during the 1980s, Iranians have learnt that religious affinities do not necessarily transform into a political following. Shia adherents in Iraq as well as in other Arab countries of the Gulf have shown that their aspirations and policies are shaped by local concerns and interests. There is no doubt that certain groups and factions in Iran would like to consider themselves as the "big brother" of the Shia community and that efforts are being exerted to politically influence Shia adherents outside Iran. However, these factions and efforts are matched, at least to a certain degree, by Iran's anti-American and anti-Israel stance, which regards the much discussed Sunni–Shia divide as just another evil machination of the imperialist powers.

It may be argued whether, at least at the level of state-to-state relations, the Sunni–Shia conflict has currently reached its climax or not. After the strong statement of King Abdullah of Saudi Arabia in January 2007 against Iranian attempts to spread Shia Islam in the majority-Sunni Middle East, the King met Iran's President Ahmadinejad in Riyadh on March 3, 2007. Reportedly, the two heads of state most involved in the Shia–Sunni dispute discussed the matter frankly.[14] Only days later, at the 12th ECSSR Annual Conference in Abu Dhabi, HRH Prince Turki Al-

Faisal bin Abulaziz Al Saud clearly denounced the stirring up of sectarian conflict and violence.[15] An additional impetus was given through the international Baghdad Security Conference held on March 10, 2007. It may have encouraged the visit of Iraqi Prime Minister Nuri Al Maliki to Ramadi, a stronghold of the Sunni insurgency, shortly afterward.

With respect to the Sunni–Shia divide, the scope for external actors to do something constructive is minimal. On the contrary, they can play a very harmful role. They can excite and reinforce confessional cleavages or the separatist tendencies of minorities. For this reason, great responsibility is called for, both in public policy and in the media. Politicians, journalists as well as "experts" should be aware of how damaging their grand designs and big words about regional, confessional, ethnic or other fault lines and conflict potentials can be.

Effects of Globalization

To describe and analyze all the various globalization factors that have a direct or indirect effect on Gulf security would need a special volume. However, two aspects must be mentioned and discussed briefly:

- Diversification of economic relations and the emergence of new external actors who will play a growing role in Gulf security

- Impact of global communication on self-perception and the consequent change in attitudes towards development and the West.

Diversification and New Players

In the field of economics the most evident sign of globalization is that the Gulf region has currently many more partners beyond the realm of Western countries than ever before. This casts doubt over the supposedly "Western Orientation" of the Gulf region. It can no longer be taken for granted that the regions of the world seeking to join the global economy will turn automatically to the West.[16] The trade balance of the Middle

Eastern countries has clearly shifted to the industrialized or industrializing countries of Asia. By the year 2000 the United States and Europe had already lost the dominant position they had held since 1980, when their share in exports and imports had reached more than 50 percent. Moreover, this position has declined even further from 2000 to 2005,[17] notwithstanding the remarkable increase of EU and US trade with the GCC countries during the same years.[18] For them, Asia has also gained unprecedented importance.

Despite this development the Asian countries have not yet evolved into direct partners in Gulf security matters. However, their concerns about the stability of the region, which constitutes their energy lifeline, are becoming more and more obvious, and they have begun to play at least an indirect role in its security environment. The focus of their interest is not in particular countries, but in the resources of the region and its stability as a whole. Hence they tend to exert some pressure to focus on regional stability rather than follow particular interests.

China, for example, with its huge need for energy from the Gulf region already functions as a kind of balancer. Saudi Arabia is in a better position than Iran to help China to expand its strategic reserves to the equivalent of three months of net oil imports by 2015. Apart from currently supplying 17 percent of China's total oil imports and making multi-billion dollar investments in its petrochemical sector, Saudi Arabia, as a "swing producer," has the unique capacity to produce oil significantly above its OPEC quota. Experts estimate that if, for the next three year period, Saudi Arabia chose to produce an extra half a million barrels per day of oil for Beijing, that alone would raise China's strategic oil reserve to three months of supply. That explains why China has offered Saudi Arabia extraordinary privileges in its collaboration over the establishment of the strategic oil reserve. Thus, from Beijing's perspective, despite Iran's importance in its energy security and significant bilateral trade ties, it is not the most important country in the region. Translated into the geopolitical plane, the simple truth is that China has to be sensitive about the Saudi stance towards Iran.[19]

The balancing effects of the energy-hungry Asian countries become most obvious in their behavior towards the controversy over Iran's nuclear program. China's careful position in the UN Security Council (UNSC) regarding sanctions on Iran and Japan's reduced investment in Iran because of the UNSC sanctions resolution are cases in point. Balanced relations with all of the Gulf countries may foster the insight that security is a common good. For the Gulf countries, the emerging role of the external players from Asia is also attractive for the following reason: Despite talk about a "multi-polar order," the Asian countries have not combined their economic interests with the concept of a specific "order" and are not inclined to influence the political and social systems of the Gulf countries. The "order" they seek is stability for the sake of energy security and trade benefits.

In this context, India and Russia must at least be mentioned. India might be described as a regional power just over the sea. It considers the Strait of Hormuz and the Gulf as the westernmost frontier of its strategic environment and has developed a strategic relationship with Iran.[20] This relationship is not restricted to interests in Iranian oil and gas. The development of the North–South Corridor from Russia via Iran to India is an important component of this relationship which most probably includes defense and intelligence ties as well.[21] In India's relations with the GCC states, trade and investment will definitely play a growing role, but so will the significant number of Indian expatriates working there (Indians currently number over 30 percent of the population of the UAE). India's overall Gulf strategy can be characterized as maintaining a careful balance between the often conflicting interests of all the regional states.[22]

Russia has recovered from the demise of the Soviet Union and is also interested in playing a role in the region beyond Iran. This interest was amply exemplified by President Putin's visit to Saudi Arabia and Qatar in mid-February 2007. In Riyadh, Putin reached, for the first time, a "verbal understanding" to sell weapons to Saudi Arabia, offered to help the GCC to develop their own civilian nuclear power plant and tried to win Saudi Arabia and Qatar as partners for a Russian-led "gas cartel."[23] What the outcome of this visit will be remains to be seen, but in any case it underscores Saudi Arabia's interest in diversifying its strategic relations.

Impact of Global Communication

Global communication not only affects state–society relations, gives rise to public demands vis-à-vis the state, and thus influences the domestic security environment in the way indicated above. It opens up horizons for conceiving new lifestyles. Deep-rooted living traditions come under question, while the broader understanding of religion and daily religious practices undergo change.[24] Moreover, global communication implies far reaching changes in world views, particularly with regard to notions of development. Just as own traditions are questioned, so also are Western paradigms of development. Concomitant with the splitting of the world into two rival political and ideological blocs after World War II, the idea that Islam constitutes a "system" of its own, which is superior to the systems of capitalism and communism, was formulated. Its less political expression was the idea of an "Islamic way of life." After the demise of the Soviet Union, formulating Islam as a system seemed less compelling. Instead, globalization increasingly worked to its advantage. Muslims and Muslim societies no longer needed to imitate the West in order to feel "modern." Modernity, whether in terms of goods or concepts, became accessible from all parts of the globe. The West was no longer considered as *the* model for development. Although it may still offer certain things, what is drawn from it is decided by the countries and societies themselves. The "Western orientation" of the countries in the region as a natural offspring of globalization is a supposition that cannot be taken for granted either with regard to economic markets, or the ideas market.

Globalization has made it evident that Muslim societies cannot be understood primarily by contrasting them to Western societies. To evaluate or even to judge Muslim societies by mere comparison with the West will only foster confrontational approaches based on essentialist theories of a "clash of civilizations." Both Muslim societies as well as Western societies constitute parts of the global society. The fact that globalization originated in the West has become irrelevant in the present scenario. Western as well as Muslim societies are now facing challenges in dealing with the consequences of globalization. Of course, differences between Western and Muslim societies with respect to their point of departure in the encounter with globalization do play a role. However, just because globalization was initiated in the West does not necessarily mean that Western societies are more apt to cope with globalization.

The security implications of this changed positioning of both societies within the global society cannot be detailed here. Nevertheless, efforts to formulate security should bear this changed scenario in mind. In the age of globalization, to feel at home and secure with one's own world view and way of life has assumed more importance than ever before. The dialectical relationship between the regional (or the local) and the global, makes top down (i.e. from the West downward to the region) concepts of security counterproductive.

For European (and other external players) trying to play a constructive role in Gulf security, the new scenario of positioning Muslim as well as Western societies vis-à-vis global society demands more awareness of regional and local dynamics, and a more modest and sober approach as to what the Europeans might be able to do. Approaches and how they are communicated have become part of the security equation.

What Role for Europe?

With respect to politics and the stability of the Gulf region, Europe finds itself in a somewhat contradictory situation. On the one hand, its dependency on energy from the region will grow.[25] However, as the trade shift from the region to Asia indicates, Europe faces more competition than ever before, and not only in trade. Its impact on the region is also diminishing. Despite the historical involvement of individual European countries in the Gulf, and despite Europe's growing interest in Gulf stability, the European Union does not have a coherent concept for Gulf security and is unlikely to develop one for quite some time. European involvement in Gulf security has been primarily bilateral between EU member states and particular Gulf countries. Interest in Gulf security was mainly trade-driven rather than politically motivated. For Germany, in particular, it is no exaggeration to say that there had been no Middle East policy at all going beyond the Arab–Israeli conflict on the one hand and Germany's relations to Iran on the other.[26]

In the case of Iran, however, European policy was not and is not driven just by trade interests. This assumption was harbored by the United States and Israel, and also large segments of the European public since the launch of the EU's "critical dialogue" with Iran in 1992.[27] This dialogue, along with the "constructive dialogue" from 1998 onwards, are expressions of the European approach, which was diametrically opposed to the containment policy and to the use of force as the only means to counter military threats. From the 1990s onwards until today, European policy towards Iran was caught between the US–Iran antagonism, which the Europeans find unacceptable. From the European perspective, Gulf policy as well as Near East policy has to reflect transatlantic policy at the same time. The efforts of the EU–3 (France, Germany and Great Britain) from October 2003 onwards to find a diplomatic solution for Iran's nuclear dossier had not achieved the envisaged results, and in December 2006, the dossier was transferred to the UN Security Council.

After passing two UN Security Council resolutions (1737 of December 2006 and 1747 of March 2007) the year 2007 saw much saber-rattling not only from the United States but also from France, after the election of President Sarkozy. Despite this, Washington seems to be still committed to a diplomatic solution to the issue of Iran's nuclear program. However, US efforts to build an alliance with the so called moderate Arab states against Iran and to coax Syria out of the Iranian orbit became most evident at the Near East conference in Annapolis on November 28. For the time being, it seems that the Arab states harbor a more prudent attitude towards such an alignment than the Europeans. To implant Cold War sentiments into the region will neither lead to a solution of Iran's nuclear program nor enhance overall Gulf security.

A European Strategy for Gulf Security?

European engagement in Gulf security took an important step forward with the EU decision for an EU Strategic Partnership with the Mediterranean and the Middle East (referred to as the EU Strategic Partnership) of June 23, 2004.[28] Its impact in public was overshadowed by the US Middle East Initiative (MEI) and the Broader Middle East and North Africa Initiative (BMENA), which was endorsed at the G-8 summit in Sea Island, Georgia, also in June 2004. For a moment, there was a "cacophony of competing and contrasting initiatives" which was "bound to generate confusion and stimulate opportunistic behavior on the part of individual governments in search of petty immediate benefits."[29]

Whether the EU Strategic Partnership will have to be viewed as just another benevolent Western initiative remains to be judged by history. Nevertheless, it should be recognized that for the first time all EU member states showed their commitment "to advance its partnership with the countries of the Gulf," including the GCC countries, Yemen, Iraq and Iran (also termed as "east of Jordan"). The EU Strategic Partnership is the outcome of a historical process in which the important steps included the EU–GCC Cooperation Agreement signed in 1989, the Barcelona Process for EU–Mediterranean Partnership launched in 1995 and the European Security Strategy published in December 2003.[30]

The document on the EU Strategic Partnership does not spell out concrete goals, but names certain principles, and indicates political fields of action. By doing so it gives a fair picture not only of basic European approaches to regional development and security but also of how the Europeans assess their possible role in doing something useful about shared concerns.

[175]

By addressing all of the riparian states of the Gulf, the EU Strategic Partnership has bound itself to the above mentioned principle of non-exclusion and aims at "inclusiveness," considered as one of the basic principles for any future Gulf security system.[31] The principle of reassurance found no particular expression. However, "partnership and dialogue" are stressed as the "cornerstones of the strategy," and the whole document breathes the spirit of understanding security as a common good, which is obtainable only by mutual reassurance. The Strategic Partnership focuses on "shared security concerns" and follows a "broad concept of security."

Pragmatism marks the basic approach of the proposed Strategic Partnership. For its successful implementation "a long term and coherent engagement with a pragmatic approach" is required. The "need for differentiation" is emphasized, and it is clearly stated that there is "no basis for a one-size-fits-all approach."

The Strategic Partnership embraces the principle of separation, which is to be seen as an additional expression of pragmatism, and spells out a warning against linking regional conflicts. The resolution of the Arab–Israeli conflict is considered as having a "core strategic priority." However, it is not seen as a precondition for solving other problems, and "progress on the resolution of the Arab–Israeli conflict cannot be a precondition for confronting the urgent reform challenges facing our partners, nor vice versa."

The various fields of the proposed policy agenda for the Strategic Partnership are:

- The Middle East Peace Process
- Political Dialogue–Human Rights and the Rule of Law
- Non-Proliferation, Security Dialogue and Counter-Terrorism
- Migration
- Economic Reforms
- Social Development (education and the role of women)
- Cultural Dialogue.

The above list suggests that the Strategic Partnership aims to be comprehensive, even if environmental security, which plays an enormous role for all riparian states of the Gulf, is not expressly mentioned. However, one may assume that this aspect is included in the term "broad concept of security." It indicates awareness of the importance of so-called soft security, whether humanitarian or environmental.

In clause 11 the document emphasizes "synergy with other initiatives" and declares that "the EU will seek maximum coherence with the United States, United Nations and other external actors in pursuit of the goals of the Partnership." Whatever this will mean in concrete terms, it clearly indicates the European Union's awareness of the transatlantic dimension with regard to everything it does or plans to do in the Gulf region.

With respect to the crucial question of the implementation of the Strategic Partnership, "continuing consultation and review" are proposed. The European Union is well aware that "no single framework exists for partnership," and this reflects the "complexity and diversity of our partners and their situations." It should be added that this also reflects the "complexity and diversity" of the European Union itself—an institution with many member states having their own interests and bilateral relations vis-à-vis the Gulf region. Therefore, the importance of the Strategic Partnership as a first step towards a coherent EU policy approach towards the region should not be underestimated. Its strength lies in the mix of its principles and comprehensiveness on the one hand and its openness with respect to eventual actors on the other. In short, an assessment of Europe's role in the region cannot be deduced from the Strategic Partnership alone. Such an endeavor should examine carefully all the various activities of the EU member states and their bilateral relations with the Gulf countries.

Undoubtedly, the existing framework and instruments for the implementation of the Strategic Partnership are insufficient. Despite many contacts, no institutional framework exists yet for relations with Iraq. The "constructive dialogue" with Iran and the negotiations for an EU–Iran Trade and Cooperation Agreement, which started in 2002 together with a "human rights dialogue," are pending because of the controversy about Iran's nuclear program. The GCC countries and the EU continue to hold their annual Joint Council Ministerial Meetings according to the Cooperation Agreement and conduct some political dialogue.

There is an obvious need to create more and especially more diversified forums for a consistent dialogue at the state level as well as the societal level. Any effort to enhance security is dependent on communication. Being informed about the specific security concerns and threat perceptions of each side is the first step towards confidence building. Differences of opinion can be overcome only if they are spelt out. The EU is ready and eager to develop an instrument of dialogue with the GCC countries in order to fathom ways in which it can be useful.

"Partnership" should be understood as an indication that the ultimate determination to improve security has to come from within the region.[32] In this respect, the conference of Iraq's neighbors, the United States and the United Nations held on March 10, 2007, as well as similar conferences held earlier should be seen, beyond their specific political aims, as useful instruments to foster the idea of security as a common good. In addition, the growing interest of external players from Asia in Gulf security may also play a role in consolidating this principle. However, given the asymmetrical power scenario in the region and the prevailing mistrust between Arabs and Iranians, which is exacerbated by the US–Iran divide and the Sunni–Shia rift, there is a strongly felt need for a multilateral forum or a political platform that can foster diplomacy beyond the level of state visits. The importance of such state visits particularly at the present juncture, is not to be denied. However, they can also become a source of mistrust. Therefore, an institutionalized multilateral forum could provide more transparency.

Is a Multilateral Security Architecture in the Gulf Possible?

As one scholar rightly observes, the promotion of CSCE-like processes or even OSCE-like institutions for the whole of the Middle East became a "benign academic tradition."[33] That does not mean that any concept of

Gulf security in terms of security systems or at least, institutionalized arrangements can be discarded from the outset. Arrangements and institutions can play an important role in enhancing the stability of expectations. However, security discourses that take existing systems as models often tend to forget the underlying basic principles and get lost in a plethora of technical terms. This can have the counterproductive effect that the countries concerned do not feel "on board," and that the security schemes developed by external players do not truly serve their interests.

In the discussion on Gulf security, when CSCE-like processes or OSCE-like institutions are put forward, two basic facts are generally overlooked. The first is that regional security challenges cannot be constructed in terms of antagonistic political and ideological blocs, and the second is that the strategic conversion between Europe and the United States of the Cold War era does not exist any longer. It cannot be denied that the inclination to (re-)construct existing lines of conflict into clear cut dichotomic arrangements still plays an important role, particularly with respect to the Middle East. It is still a widely used practice to play out "moderate" against "radical" Arabs/Islamists. However, to make this kind of thinking the basis for any kind of security concept worth its name, would not only be nonsense, but also dangerous. In addition, the success of the CSCE process still connotes the final break-up of the political and social system of the former Eastern Bloc. With such a paradigm in mind, any effort to create a security system for the Gulf region or the Middle East is bound to fail from the inception.

The US–European strategic convergence which existed during the Cold War and which worked as functional precondition for the OSCE process is much weaker. As Roberto Aliboni points out, it eroded particularly with the rise of Islamism. However, there is still some kind of convergence:

> ...a convergence on the significance of a set of strategic trends and challenges, such as weapons of mass destruction (WMD) proliferation, terrorism and failed states, much less so, however, on their nature (whether they are risks or threats), their reach and significance, their inter-linkage and respective priority and, of course, on how to deal with them.[34]

[179]

Keeping in mind these caveats against imposing models of security structure on the Gulf region, the question that remains is: Would it be useful to envisage a multilateral security forum based on the already mentioned principles of non-exclusion and reassurance? The EU has experience in setting up such sub-regional structures and could be a credible initiator of such a forum. The time and circumstances may be ripe for such an effort. All the Gulf states see an urgent need to reduce the US military presence, albeit for different reasons. Efforts aimed at creating a regional structure are to be understood as complementing the GCC states' bilateral agreements with the United States and the Istanbul Cooperation Initiative (ICI) agreed by NATO in June 2004, which raises vague prospects of security cooperation.[35] Whereas the US military presence in the region is a recognized fact, the issue remains whether the Istanbul Cooperation Initiative is in accordance with the principle of non-exclusion. At least for the time being, there will be no opportunity to have Iran on board.

The ASEAN Regional Forum (ARF) has been simultaneously suggested from different sides as a more suitable model for a multilateral security forum for the Gulf than the OSCE or a CSCE-like process.[36] The advantages of the ARF can be enumerated as follows:

- The ARF encompasses states embroiled in prolonged asymmetrical conflicts, unlike the CSCE process, which was negotiated between entrenched blocs
- The forum includes states with fundamentally different political systems
- The ARF allows different groupings of states to work on different issues
- Work within the forum is based on consensus, begins with issues that promise mutual benefits, and its members do not relinquish sovereign rights
- A major advantage of the ARF model lies in the capacity to integrate external actors having prominent interests in the region either as members or mediators.

Involving extra-regional parties with a stake in Gulf security and stability in a Gulf Regional Security Forum as suggested by Kraig[37] similar to the ARF model does not mean the creation of a new kind of "consortium" of "security guarantors" for Gulf security. For domestic political and military reasons, the European Union, China, Japan and India cannot in the near future play a role similar to, or even try to replace the US Central Command, the US Fifth Fleet, and other US military services in the region.[38] However, their role could and should be to balance US hegemony as well as encourage security cooperation within the region itself.

Sentiment has grown among observers that more efforts by the Gulf countries themselves are needed to enhance the regional security situation. Case-by-case cooperation, whether on a purely regional level or including external players, can help a great deal in enhancing mutual trust in general.[39] Such cooperation of course, is no substitute for multilateral regional security architecture nor does it make the role of external powers dispensable. However, it should be borne in mind that case-to-case co-operation and regional bilateral and multilateral agreements can function as first steps towards building a framework for security and stability in many areas of mutual concern.

7

Foreign Military Presence and its Role in Reinforcing Regional Security: A Double-Edged Sword

J.E. Peterson

In the past two decades, the Gulf has been inundated by foreign military presence (FMP) to a degree never before seen in modern times. Of twenty-one countries in and around the Gulf, only three are without any overt FMP. The United States has a FMP in thirteen of these countries, the UK is in nine, and other external powers have a FMP in nine as well (see Table 7.1). In terms of the number of countries as well as the scope and degree of activities, the FMP is largely, although not exclusively, the domain of the United States. The United States is no longer simply a great power with interests in the Gulf but it has become a Gulf power itself. The FMP of Britain, the last great power to dominate the Gulf, was far less ambitious, far less variegated, and seemingly, far less necessary. Looking farther back in time, the regional footprint of each of the other European powers present in the region between the 16th and 20th centuries was even less. Thus, for obvious reasons, this exposition necessarily focuses mostly on the United States' role in the Arabian Gulf. Moreover, my remarks are mainly directed at the eight littoral countries of the Arabian Gulf.

Why is the Gulf so central to US security policy and FMP? The obvious answer is the concentration of three-quarters of the world's oil reserves in the region. However, geo-strategic calculations play a significant role as well. For 500 years, the great powers of each epoch have vied for power and bases, aiming for the control of the Heartland or

Rimland.[1] In many ways, this imperative has never died and has even survived the Cold War. In the post-Soviet and post-9/11 eras, for example, the United States has expanded its basing in Central Asia and added Eastern European facilities.[2]

Table 7.1

Foreign Military Presence in the Greater Gulf Region

Local Country	United States	United Kingdom	Other
Afghanistan	yes	yes	38 other countries represented in ISAF
Bahrain	yes	yes	–
Cyprus	–	yes	6 other countries + Turkey
Diego Garcia	yes	yes	–
Djibouti	yes	–	France and Germany
Iran	–	–	–
Iraq	yes	yes	30 other countries represented in the multi-national force (MNF) Operation Iraqi Freedom
Israel	–	–	Canada
Jordan	–	–	–
Kuwait	yes	yes	–
Kyrgyzstan	yes	–	Denmark, Russia
Oman	yes	yes	–
Pakistan	yes	yes	–
Qatar	yes	yes	–
Saudi Arabia	yes	–	–
Tajikistan	–	–	France, India, Russia
Turkey	yes	–	Israel
Turkmenistan	–	–	–
UAE	Yes	–	–
Uzbekistan	–	–	Germany
Yemen	–	–	–

Source: *The Military Balance 2007* (London: International Institute for Strategic Studies, 2007) and other sources.

The United States is the predominant source of FMP in the Gulf but it is not the only one. Three tiers of powers exercising FMP can be distinguished. Prior to 1989, the principal players were the two superpowers. Now of course there is only the United States. This creates a new dynamic in that there are no Cold War excuses for establishing and maintaining a FMP in the region. NATO and Western European allies, especially the United Kingdom, form a second tier with ties and access based in part on the legacy of European colonialism. Within the Arabian Gulf region, a third tier of extra-Gulf regional powers have had a presence. Pakistan allegedly stationed troops in Saudi Arabia in the past, has provided seconded personnel to a number of Gulf states and possesses what some have termed the "Islamic bomb." Following the Gulf War of 1990–91, Egypt and Syria briefly enjoyed favor under the "GCC plus two" concept. Although it has no access to the Gulf itself and stations no personnel on its perimeter, Israel in some ways should be considered a Gulf FMP because of its concern, political rivalries, and projection capability. A small degree of FMP exists among the regional states as well. For example, the forces making up the Peninsula Shield force, the Saudi presence in southern Bahrain, and even Iranian interests and activities in Iraq.

It will be obvious that the role and conceptualization of US security policy is central to any discussion of FMP in the Gulf. The genesis of a US global security system lay in the aftermath of World War II, specifically with the decline of Britain as the guarantor of a compatible security system and the emergence of the Soviet Union, and later China, as perceived threats to the Western concept of the world order. Up to that point, however, the United States had few overseas possessions. Since the extent of these possessions increased only marginally (for example, some strategically important Pacific islands and "neo-colonial" outposts in the Philippines, Panama and Guantanamo), the United States was forced to rely on basing rights in the territories of allies and current and/or former colonial possessions, or to lease the use of facilities from host nations. Thus, one author calls the result a "leasehold empire."[3] But in the 1980s the system was regarded by many as overstretched in the same way that previous empires had been: by enormous economic costs and political opposition abroad and at home. The end of the Cold War promised to relieve the pressure on US imperial necessities, but the following years produced more requirements for the projection of US forces overseas

(Saddam's invasion of Kuwait, anarchy in the Balkans, the US-led invasions of Afghanistan and Iraq), even as the nature of those requirements were changing.

The argument for a FMP on the part of a foreign power depends, of course, on its perceptions of security threats in its sphere of influence and the perceived degree of intensity or likelihood of those threats. In addition, a practical consideration must always concern the trade-off between security requirements and political liabilities. For this reason, this paper has been subtitled "a double-edged sword" in recognition that while FMP may bring benefits for either the foreign power or local state or both, it also threatens to create liabilities as well. A discussion of the matrix of benefits and liabilities for both the foreign power and host nations follows an examination of typologies of FMP.

Typologies of Foreign Military Presence

"Foreign military presence" can be extremely difficult to define authoritatively. It is possible to elucidate a great variety – and degrees – of FMP in the Gulf. In fact, this paper suggests that there are at least four classifications or typologies for defining or categorizing types and degrees of FMP. In applying these typologies to the Gulf, it can be seen that the activities of the primary sources of FMP – the United States, and secondarily the United Kingdom – fall into a multitude of categories, no matter how one measures it.

The first typology is concerned with levels (or degrees) of FMP (Table 7.2). On a descending scale, these range from full military intervention and occupation to support of some sort for surrogate forces. Most of the 13 categories I have identified are applicable to the Gulf. Intervention and occupation is of course a feature of the US presence in Iraq. It is a legacy from the next category, the presence of an expeditionary force in the region as a function of power projection. Bases and permanent installations are fulsomely scattered around the region, as are non-permanent deployed units. The United States and other external

[186]

actors regularly engage in joint or multilateral exercises with host nations and the former has orchestrated a network of pre-positioning and access agreements. A number of powers maintain an offshore naval presence while a few also maintain an "offshore" ready deployment capability from neighboring countries or regions. Arms and equipment transfers are abundant while considerable use is made of "technical" facilities (particularly for intelligence and communications) and aircraft over-flights. Two levels of FMP that are not present in the Gulf are mutual or multilateral security treaties or agreements (CENTO is irrelevant and NATO operates only outside the Gulf, in Afghanistan) and support for revolutionary or irredentist movements (although a case has been made by the US government for Iranian covert involvement in Iraq).

Table 7.2
Levels of Foreign Military Presence

☑ : present in the Gulf
✗ : not present in the Gulf
? : uncertain if present in the Gulf

1. ☑ intervention and occupation[4]

2. ☑ proximate expeditionary force in region – power projection

3. ☑ bases and other permanent installations (ranging from full bases, with the FMP enjoying internal sovereignty, to small support functions, such as naval replenishment or technical facilities)

4. ☑ non-permanent deployed units

5. ☑ joint or multilateral exercises

6. ☑ pre-positioning and access agreements

7. ☑ offshore naval presence

8. ☑ "offshore" ready deployment capability (e.g. from neighboring countries or regions)

9. ✗ mutual or multilateral security treaties or agreements (CENTO, NATO, SEATO)

10. ☑ arms and equipment transfers

11. ☑ "technical" facilities (intelligence, space, communications)

12. ☑ aircraft over-flights (generally unseen and uncontroversial but reverses on occasion of aircraft trouble or in time of conflict or crisis)

13. ✗ surrogate forces (support for revolutionary or irredentist movements; Cuba in Africa

Another useful typology deals with categories of presence or activities (Table 7.3). In the Gulf, FMP includes airfields, naval facilities, ground forces, communications and control, intelligence and command, and logistics. Absent categories are missile sites, facilities concerning space operations, research and testing, and probably environmental monitoring.

Table 7.3
Categories of Presence

1. ☑ Airfield – or any other site concerned with the operation of aircraft for military purposes; acquired importance only after World War II as the new "coaling stations of contemporary geopolitics."[5]

2. ☑ Naval – port or any other site concerned with the operation of ships for military purposes, such as repair dockyards, mid-ocean mooring buoys.

3. ☑ Ground forces – any site concerned with the conduct of land warfare, such as army bases, exercise areas, fortifications, fixed artillery; in post-colonial era, applies mostly to NATO and Korea for the United States, although colonial powers continue to have shrinking facilities; there are some Third World bases as well.

4. ✗ Missile – sites concerned primarily with the maintenance and launching of missiles, fixed artillery sites, etc.

5. ✗ Space – sites concerned with the operation or monitoring of military satellites other than communications satellites.

6. ☑ Communications and control – sites concerned with military communications or the control of military systems.

7. ☑ Intelligence and command – sites concerned with intelligence gathering by non-satellite means, and sites exercising command over military systems.

8. ? Environmental monitoring – sites carrying out monitoring of environmental factors of military importance, such as military meteorological stations.

9. ✗ Research and testing – sites associated with military research and with developmental testing of military systems.

10. ☑ Logistic – sites not obviously assignable to airfield, naval or ground force, and concerned with production, storage and transport of military materiel, administration of military forces, and the housing, medical treatment, etc., of military personnel.

Source: Robert E. Harkavy, *Bases Abroad: The Global Foreign Military Presence* (Oxford: Oxford University Press, 1989), 17

Another way of looking at FMP is by administrative status (Table 7.4). The categories here run from enclaves in sovereign territories (such as ex-colonies) to host nation sites at which foreign powers are provided access. It should also be noted that basing access has, historically, been acquired in one of three ways:[6]

- by conquest or colonization;
- by providing security or protection for the host via formal alliances or less formal arrangements that still imply protection; or
- by tangible quid pro quo arrangements: security assistance, arms transfers, subsidies, or what amount to "rents."

Table 7.4
Administrative Status

1. ✗ Sites located in colonies, possessions, territories, etc., where the foreign nation has sovereignty.
2. ✗ Sites located in enclaves in which the foreign nation has sovereign rights.
3. ☑ Sites administered by the foreign nation and located within the host nation according to a treaty or similar agreement.
4. ☑ Sites at which the foreign nation has its own facilities within the host nation facilities, and joint foreign/host nation use of host nation facilities.
5. ✗ Sites financed/constructed/operated/used by forces of multilateral alliance.
6. ☑ Sites with facilities operated by the host nation mainly on behalf of the foreign nation, and generally planned/constructed/financed by the foreign nation.
7. ✗ Host nation facilities which contribute significantly to the functioning of a foreign nation military system.
8. ☑ Host nation sites to which the foreign nation has access and of which it makes permanent or repeated use.
9. ☑ Foreign presence at the invitation of, and administered by the host nation, e.g. for the training of host nation forces.

Source: Robert E. Harkavy, *Bases Abroad: The Global Foreign Military Presence* (Oxford: Oxford University Press, 1989), 20–21.

A final typology examines the strategic purpose of the type of FMP (Table 7.5). These range from nuclear deterrence and defense to a scale of conventional conflicts or low-intensity wars to showing the flag and peacekeeping. It should be obvious that requirements for a forward military presence have become increasingly variable or revised. Emphasis is shifting to global threats from WMD (including Third World possession of nuclear weapons), terrorism, hegemonic rivalry with China, and competition over scarce resources (notably oil but also others, such as iron ore and manganese).[7]

Table 7.5
Purposes of Foreign Military Presence

1. Nuclear deterrence and defense.
2. Conventional conflict.[8]

   a) Generic:

   - ☑ Traditional – familiar force-on-force, large-scale engagements, such as the two World Wars, the Korean War, Desert Storm, the Iran–Iraq War, and the 1967 and 1973 Middle Eastern wars.
   - ☑ Irregular – what used to be termed "low-intensity warfare," wherein the dominant frequency of Marxist insurgencies gave way to "Reagan Doctrine" anti-communist insurgencies and then, in the 1990s, to the prevalence of ethnic warfare.
   - ? Catastrophic – large-scale casualties are caused by weapons of mass destruction (WMDs); can involve interstate warfare or terrorism.
   - ? Disruptive – more difficult to categorize than the others; presumably they could include such things as electromagnetic-pulse attacks that disrupt communications or "cyber-warfare," with or without an identifiable perpetrator; they might also involve major political changes in nations via elections or significant shifts in foreign-policy orientation that could heavily impact on US global presence.

   b) Specific:

   - ☑ During the Cold War, US planning based on Central Europe and the Arabian Gulf with expected Soviet involvement in both, with horizontal escalation (one would spread to the other); as well as Korea.
   - ? More recently, disclosure is politically sensitive and higher likelihood of unforeseen conflict both in terms of type and location.

   c) ☑ Problems of arms re-supply during conflict – shifting permissions according to conflict.

   d) ☑ Coercive diplomacy, air-based intelligence – sometimes still "gunboats" but also forward movement of AWACS, firing of Tomahawk missiles (Sudan and Afghanistan), flying intelligence aircraft off hostile coasts (China), U-2 over-flights.

   e) ☑ Showing the flag.

   f) ✗ Peacekeeping – "A more recent phenomenon is the use of foreign facilities in order to conduct peacekeeping or interposition operations nearby. Here one might cite US access to facilities in Egypt to support peacekeeping in the Sinai, and in Hungary and Albania for operations in Bosnia and Kosovo, respectively. West African ports like Dakar, Senegal have been used to support peacekeeping operations in nearby states, such as Liberia."[9]

Much has been made of the promise of the current "revolution in military affairs" to reduce the need for an overseas presence, but proponents ignore such still-pertinent factors as continuing requirements for maintaining air superiority, for ground troops to seize and hold territory, and for safe ports to unload sea-lifted equipment.[10]

Of course, the four typologies outlined above are not mutually exclusive. More accurately, they are complementary. A particular aspect or type of FMP may be located in all four typologies. FMP also exhibits a considerable degree of fluidity. At a more fundamental level, the last several decades have seen changing requirements for FMP, involving a decreasing need for some categories but an increased requirement for others. These fluctuations have been inspired by a number of factors. Perhaps the foremost revolves around changes in the political/security situation. On a global level, the US requirement for many permanent operating bases was obviated by the end of the Cold War. On the other hand, accelerating regional requirements have escalated the US naval presence from a small "show the flag" presence in the Gulf to a key naval headquarters.

Changes in alliances may either remove the need for access or provide new opportunities to create access. Another key factor is technological advances. For example, naval fuel requirements over the past century have moved from a dependence on coaling stations to oil bunkers and finally nuclear-powered vessels. In the air, aircraft have acquired progressively longer ranges, missiles have superseded strategic bombing, and satellites have added an entirely new dimension.[11] Furthermore, superiority in science, engineering, and information technology has spurred US dominance on the conventional battlefield—never more evident than in the 2003 attack on Iraq.[12] In addition, the United States enjoys "command of the commons"—primarily consisting of space and the sea that belongs to no country and provides access to much of the globe.[13] There is more movement towards basing on US or US-controlled territory (using bomber aircraft based in the United States and Diego Garcia) and sea basing (use of seaborne platforms for operations ashore, akin to assaults conducted on Japanese-held Pacific islands during World War II).

The pertinence to the Gulf of the purposes and activities outlined earlier in the typologies have changed over the years. The Gulf was important for World War II staging, particularly in the "Persian Corridor" to the Soviet Union. Some airfields formerly held importance for staging and communications: the emergence of the Cold War saw the establishment of facilities such as the Dhahran air base that were later deemed unnecessary. Staging was also regarded as important for local or regional conflict, such as Britain's marshaling of its forces to protect Kuwait in 1961. Another key concern was – and seems to remain – the use of regional facilities to facilitate regional interdiction, with Iraq being the best example. In keeping with changing requirements – including both military and political factors – the US Department of Defense has shifted its emphasis to devising a spectrum of basing access.[14] In broad form, this spectrum consists of main operating bases, forward operating sites and cooperative security locations.

> Obviously, the main thrust here is in the direction of a very limited number of main operating bases, so as to lessen the US overseas footprint, and an increase in forward operating sites and cooperative security locations to accommodate lighter and more mobile forces for a variety of contingencies.[15]

Balancing the Positives and Negatives in FMP

The typologies discussed earlier represent the end-result of the process or strategy. Just as important, or even more so, is the decision-making process that defines the strategy regarding FMP on the part of both the foreign power and the local state. On both the strategic and the practical side, FMP involves a process of determining a proper balance between the advantages and disadvantages, benefits and liabilities. This calculation holds true for the host nations as much as it does for the foreign powers.

Separating rational security policy-making from the political and other aspects is not an easy task. Security policy-making in developed countries is often skewed by domestic political concerns and overarching ideological perspectives. Elite perspectives and assumptions shape the domestic decision-making context, particularly with regard to foreign military intervention.[16] Just as in developing countries, action may be taken on the basis of the reputation and intrinsic interests of decision-makers as much as on a rational and objective calculation of national interests. Security policy-making in developing countries is similarly characterized by a complex mix of contributing factors. These include elite assumptions about the international system and the definition or perception of threats to the regime and/or the state; the assessment of military capabilities and strategies to counter emerging threats; harnessing human and material resources to respond to security imperatives while addressing internal socio-economic demands; and the marshalling of public opinion and political forces to support the regime.[17]

Skewing in developing countries is just as great but perhaps for different reasons. For example, it can easily be seen that security policy-making in Gulf states has little popular input because states are not democracies. The elites consider the security relationship with the United States – and Britain – to have priority over other foreign policy concerns even though perhaps the majority of their populations view the United States with suspicion or hostility for its unquestioning support for Israel, its incursion in Iraq, the conduct of its "war on terror," and broader concerns about its role in the world.

Calculation of the utility of FMP can be analyzed in terms of a matrix involving military/security benefits to either or both the foreign power and the host state, and the liabilities or disadvantages to both parties. Military/security benefits to the foreign military power include the possibility of coercive diplomacy.[18] It may also involve maintenance or extension of colonial or quasi-colonial presence/influence/control. An obvious benefit – and often the primary purpose of the FMP – would be the enhancement of global security and defense. An analogous benefit would be better response to or control of local/regional security problems.

FMP facilitates coordination between foreign forces and local forces. The foreign power may use its presence to incorporate the local state into larger or global security concerns or networks. Equally, a FMP can freeze competitors out of a country or region. In a major assumption of security planners in major powers, the FMP assists in power projection capabilities. Pertinent examples include the use of Saudi facilities in the 2001 war in Afghanistan, as well as the use of Saudi and Kuwaiti facilities during the Iraq sanctions regime. Arms sales frequently play a fundamental role in creating access.

Military/security benefits to the local host, in the first instance, lie in the creation of a security umbrella for the local state. This may be either overt or over-the-horizon. Joint exercises, such as *Bright Star* in the Gulf, provide tangible evidence of the security umbrella, demonstrate the commitment of the foreign power to the local state, and provide additional training and experience for local forces. Such a partnership may assist in regime legitimization and the preservation of the local domestic status quo. On a larger plane, reliance on a common FMP may increase cooperation between regional states. Not least, a FMP may have a stimulant effect on the local economy, including facility rents, employment and offsets.

Counterbalancing the benefits are a multitude of at least potential liabilities or disadvantages. For the foreign power, its presence in the host country may increase the vulnerability of its agents and citizens to civil and violent attacks—and may even provide a "red flag" to the local regime's opposition. Basing agreements with authoritarian regimes may yield short-term benefits but tend to do little for liberalization.[19] Furthermore, basing agreements with such regimes may be volatile and subject to host-nation demands or ousters.[20] Foreign powers may find it difficult to convince erstwhile clients that their security interests are congruent with the foreign power.[21] In the reverse of a point made earlier, access often requires the transfer of arms. This is generally good from the foreign power's economic point of view but may have political costs or disadvantages. In a related consideration, maintaining a large FMP in a multitude of countries may constitute serious financial costs for the foreign power.

Finally, while in a strict military/security calculation FMP may make sense for a foreign power, it may prove to be a liability for other reasons. Overwhelming military might in many spheres does not always translate well to regional conflicts where the adversaries enjoy the advantages of greater willingness to suffer, more young males of fighting age, and deeper knowledge of local terrain, weather, and other factors.[22] The FMP may still have the ability to achieve victory, as the United States did in Iraq in 2003, but the costs of waging war may be unacceptable.

Disadvantages and liabilities are just as great, at least potentially, to the local host. Permitting FMP obviously creates an association with the foreign power's foreign policy, which may create or increase domestic and regional opposition to the local host. Any FMP necessarily involves a loss of sovereignty to at least some degree. It may hamper the formation of or participation in regional cooperation accords, particularly when other local states that are not friendly with the foreign power are involved. The institution of foreign military installations and privileges necessarily involves some degree of surrender of territoriality.

The FMP may constitute a pillar of support for non-democratic regimes against their people, thus reinforcing their resistance to reforms and thereby creating an additional factor in the internal political equation. Reliance on common FMP may strengthen more powerful regional states at the expense of weaker ones. This in turn may lead to foreign-policy initiatives by weaker states aimed at gaining a more significant international profile or enhanced relations with the foreign power at the expense of the stronger state. This has been hypothesized as Qatar's strategy in welcoming the US Central Command to establish itself in its territory. Qatar also provides an example where hosting the FMP may require a government to provide facilities at little or no cost, or to entertain arms and supply purchases to keep the FMP satisfied. This is not a problem for Qatar but poorer states will find it a difficult obstacle. Another domestic impact arises when a FMP aggravates or favors one sector of the population above the others, as can be hypothesized for Iranian involvement in Iraq or the Saudi presence in and influence over Bahrain. Even more dangerously, FMP may lead to a skewed threat perception by the local state because of the foreign power's influence or pressure.

Assessment and Applicability to the Gulf

Any assessment of the impact of FMP on the Gulf must begin with an examination of the changing role of US military strategy, particularly as it relates to the Gulf. Since 2001, US military and security strategy has been geared toward fighting what the government terms the "war on terror." This emphasis has prompted a transformation of US forces to meet a threat far removed from that posed by the Cold War. As the Department of Defense's *Quadrennial Defense Review* in 2006 put it:

> The terrorist attacks on September 11 imposed a powerful sense of urgency to transforming the Department ...We have set about making US forces more agile and more expeditionary. Technological advances, including dramatic improvements in information management and precision weaponry, have allowed our military to generate considerably more combat capability with the same or, in some cases, fewer numbers of weapons platforms and with lower levels of manning. We also have been adjusting the US global military force posture, making long overdue adjustments to US basing by moving away from a static defense in obsolete Cold War garrisons, and placing emphasis on the ability to surge quickly to trouble spots across the globe.[23]

Reflecting the perception of terrorism as a major national security threat, the review envisaged that:

> Long-duration, complex operations involving the US military, other government agencies and international partners will be waged simultaneously in multiple countries around the world, relying on a combination of direct (visible) and indirect (clandestine) approaches.

Operations have been geared to global mobility, rapid strike, sustained unconventional warfare, counter-terrorism and counter-insurgency capabilities. The emphasis on joint mobility capabilities should be underscored. In particular, these were envisaged as expeditionary forces with minimal dependence on host-nation facilities.[24] A shift in emphasis from large Cold War bases in Western Europe, Japan and South Korea to forward operating sites and modest capabilities at host-nation facilities had already been laid out in the 2004 Global Defense Posture Review.[25] Among other things, this stimulated additional US interest in developing facilities and security relationships in various Central Asian nations, with which it had previously had little interaction.[26] Not unexpectedly, it has been noted that many of the new or potential facilities sought by the United States are in oil-producing countries or on oil routes.[27]

This new strategy has been criticized on both political and practical grounds. Changing base structure, it is charged, raises questions about Washington's intentions, reflects a shift in emphasis from maintaining regional security to using forces as an instrument of change, decreases local interests in hosting, requires the renegotiation of complex "status of forces" agreements, and will attenuate US commitments and engagements even though future requirements cannot be known.[28]

These developments have a direct impact on US military planning and presence in the Gulf, which in fact appears to serve as a major focus of overall US planning. The strategy outlined in the *Quadrennial Defense Review* emphasizes a move away from "threat-based planning" to "capabilities-based planning." Given that the Gulf is a principal focus of US security concerns, this undoubtedly means greater emphasis on the US foreign military presence in the Gulf contrary to the review's overall emphasis—albeit in dissimilar forms. While the shift in emphasis from "static defense and garrison forces to mobile, expeditionary operations" intimates less need for bases or other formal "garrison" installations in the Gulf and around the world, "expeditionary operations" will require a continued, if not intensified, network of support facilities in the Gulf, as well as elsewhere, of the kinds outlined in the typology given in Table 7.3.

With this in mind, several distinctions in the formulation and purpose of Gulf military planning have important effects on Gulf host nations, which necessarily must adjust their planning in response. The first of these is distinguishing between the US requirements for FMP in the Gulf as a function of its global security concerns and posture (especially as obtained during the Cold War) and its desire for FMP derived from regional or local reasons.

A second distinction to be considered is that between short-term strategy and long-term outlook. How much of US security policy is partisan (dictated by the Bush administration's personal and ideological views) and how much reflects changes in addressing the *longue durée* (long-term) concerns? How much are the US build-up in the Gulf and its military/security activities there determined by irrefutable national interests and how much is political? How can the motivations between the US presence in Iraq and the saber-rattling vis-à-vis Iran be judged? Is the US experience in Iraq an abnormal blip in the US security posture in the Gulf or is it a template for the future?

Overall and over time, US interest and rationale for FMP in the Gulf have displayed changing motivations.[29] In the past, it was a function of the Cold War and a perceived Soviet threat. At present, it is determined by regional crises—such as threats to regional allies, WMD and terrorism. In the future, it might be determined by the revival of a bipolar rivalry scenario, such as the United States vs. China. It will be obvious that at present, the US perceived need for FMP in the Gulf is high, given the level of conflict and combat-related FMP in Iraq and Afghanistan, along with the concurrent requirement for headquarters, rear bases, supply depots, routes, assistance, over-flight rights, and port calls in the GCC and other regional states. In the future, perhaps 5–10 years from now, there is likely to be a lesser need due to heightened political sensitivities in the region and technological advances that allow greater use of bases in the United States and at sea. Future scenarios are naturally dependent on the level of threat (ranging from irregular to catastrophic) and on the nexus of the threat (Iran, hostile regime change in the Gulf states, China, Russia).

Apart from Iraq, US views of regional actors and the need for a FMP in the region have remained markedly steady over the past several decades. In the run up to the Iraq War, of course, the US government had perceived a strong need for action against Iraq. This gradually came to include a perceived requirement for an expeditionary force to topple Saddam. Following the war, the United States has been preoccupied with a need to combat the "insurgency," broadly defined, and the search for an exit strategy. However, the US presence in Iraq also raises the possibility and desirability of permanent US bases in Iraq. Some have alleged that construction on such bases began shortly after the war ended and much has been made of the fact that the US embassy in Iraq is the largest (and certainly one of the most fortified) embassies in the world.[30]

At the moment, Iraq is at the heart of American FMP in the Gulf. The country can be regarded a principal platform of forward power projection. It can be seen as required for expeditionary forces. In terms of the Department of Defense's three-tiered strategy, as outlined above, Iraq's potential utility is far more than simply hosting main operating bases. However, myriad security and political problems countervail the military advantages stemming from Iraq. A majority of Iraqis oppose a continued US presence in the country, which so far has served as a lightning rod for guerrilla and suicide attacks and has not been able to provide a secure basis for reconstruction of the country. Politically, the present Iraqi government faces the prospect of being perceived as a US puppet regime, while much of the Iraqi public holds the same negative view of US foreign policy as the rest of the region and much of the world.

Iran, on the other hand, is seen as a threat to the United States and the global order for many of the same reasons that Saddam Hussein's regime had been accused of, such as WMD allegations and supporting terrorism. Thus Iran by itself presents a requirement for a continued in-theater US military presence, both for intimidation and for strike capability. US intentions towards Tehran may be summarized in ascending order as: (1) containment; (2) intimidation; (3) one or more calculated strikes; (4) a major attack and (5) intervention leading to occupation.

The GCC states fit snugly into the Pentagon's FMP outlook. They supply essential requirements for forward bases, headquarters and rear facilities, pre-positioning, and transit rights. Their role is as a supporting platform with the FMP consisting of all three Department of Defense (DoD) tiers: main operating bases, forward operating sites, and cooperative security locations.

The specifics of GCC security cooperation with the United States bring up many questions and possibilities. For example, does the negotiated US withdrawal from "bases" in Saudi Arabia represent a model for the future? Or is it simply a one-time solution to a short-term policy difference? In contrast, the American FMP in Qatar has grown as part of a deliberate Qatari policy in recent years to enhance the bilateral relationship. Thus, the Qataris have welcomed the forward headquarters of USCENTCOM, air facilities at Al-'Udayd air base, and increasing use of port facilities. Is the Qatari policy the result of an aggressive strategy for securing a guaranteed security umbrella, a means for expanding Qatari influence within the GCC, a slap at rival Saudi Arabia, part of Qatar's overall "branding" policy, or a combination of all four motives?

Elsewhere in the GCC, Kuwait has provided a varied range of assistance to US forces and permitted extensive use of Kuwaiti territory and facilities. This seems less likely to be a motive for enhancing its "security umbrella" than fear of Iraq, followed by a sense of shared responsibility for rebuilding post-Saddam Iraq. Thus, Kuwait embraces all three tiers. Bahrain, as is well known, serves as the headquarters of the US Navy's Fifth Fleet. Meanwhile, the UAE (which allows port calls and the use of Al-Dhafra air base) and Oman (which permits pre-positioning and use of air bases) prefer to maintain low-profile security cooperation with the United States. The situation in Iraq reinforces the dictum that Gulf security must involve more than just a military dimension. Several calls have been made for a "security architecture" that revolves around a forum for discussion among all eight littoral states.[31]

Above all, beyond the current emphasis on fighting the "war on terror" in its various permutations, which involve Iran, Iraq and Afghanistan, the Gulf's importance to the United States will remain denominated in oil, just as it has been for more than half a century. Since access to Gulf oil continues to be defined as a vital national security concern for the United States, the US capability to project force when necessary to protect that access will be an integral component of US security strategy as long as oil is an essential global commodity.[32]

What are the implications for Iraq and Iran in these circumstances? Are both countries primarily subject in the US perspective to invasion and control? Does this inevitably mean expanding FMP in Iraq and creating permanent bases and presence? Does it mean US supervision of the expansion of Iraqi oil output while simultaneously hampering Iranian output? Regarding implications for the GCC states, the intensification of US FMP in the Gulf has meant corresponding pressures on these states to "cooperate" by offering extended facilities to US military components, access rights, over-flights and naval visits. This situation will not change in the medium- to long-term. It is dictated by the emergent US stance as a "Gulf power," not just a superpower with interests in the Gulf.

It is not only the Gulf states that are affected by US Gulf policy and therefore compelled to deal with the ramifications. There are global reactions to US military policy and implications for the Gulf. There are widespread concerns about what is seen as an aggressive unilateralism engendered by 9/11 and the Bush administration. To those who subscribe to this view, the question arises: how long can the US continue to maintain the superiority that confers unipolar status? It can be argued that such aggressive unilateralism is beginning to impel other major powers to engage in balancing behavior already.[33] It should also be remembered that unipolar does not mean hegemonic.[34] It is often alleged that the United States has relied frequently and overly on a military approach to matters of intervention, consequently experiencing political setbacks and failures which have sometimes required greater military and political intervention

[201]

as a result. Vietnam is a prominent earlier case in which the application of technology and overwhelming military force was seen as the US approach to a regional problem.[35] The 1991 war and especially the 2003 war against Iraq demonstrated that the approach has not changed. It follows that the United States does not have a good track record in this arena despite, or perhaps because of, its military prowess and superiority. This is demonstrated in the Gulf today where the United States has essentially destroyed the existing Iraq in an attempt to recreate a new country in America's image. The 2003 war was an unqualified success but the record since then has been largely a dismal failure.

Global reaction, even among US allies, may take any number of forms. There is considerable suspicion that the US motive in becoming involved in Iraq is centered on achieving greater control of Gulf – and thus global – oil supplies.[36] A possible effect of the reaction to US actions could be the acceptance of euros in payment for oil. This would represent a confluence of European promotion of its currency as a foil to US dominance with a Gulf desire for a more stable currency than the US dollar on which to base its income. Another effect might be more widespread non-cooperation with the United States in the United Nations and the possible drafting of opposing resolutions. Furthermore, the smaller states upon whose cooperation the United States depends for successful execution of power projection may become less reluctant to deny the use of their territory for staging, over-flights and other activities in crisis situations. This not only reduces the power of the United States as a unipolar state, it also raises the costs for military projection.

Before 1971, the Gulf was sometimes referred to as a "British lake." Insofar as that description was accurate, there were marked differences between the nature of British hegemony and that of US hegemony today. Certainly, the international and regional situation has been transformed considerably. Current norms dictate that Britain would not be able to pursue the same political, military and economic policies that it did before 1971. The same norms would seem to indicate that US policy would be similarly constrained. Yet, fundamentally, it is clear that the relationship between external power(s) and local states is, in many ways, as unequal as it was in the past. All the littoral states jealously guard their sovereignty although their ability to determine their own courses of action without outside interference is extremely limited. Militarily, adversarial relationships vis-à-vis the United States have no hope of success, as the two wars against Iraq have demonstrated impressively. Politically, opposing the United States proved suicidal for the Saddam regime and is impossible for Iraq under occupation today. Crossing political swords with the United States is fraught with danger for Iran, and is no longer an option for the GCC states (if it ever was).

The consequence of this gaping inequality is the absence of many constraints on US policy and actions. Is this a healthy state of affairs? On the one hand, the United States can be characterized as a benign power seeking in large part to preserve the status quo in order to defend its own narrowly defined national interests and at the same time to protect and advance its conception (presumably shared by its allies) of a compatible and harmonious global order. On the other hand, the US-led invasion of Iraq seemed to demonstrate the primacy of narrow elite interests in formulating regional policy. Furthermore, the Bush administration's hard-line policy against Iran threatens to embroil the Gulf in yet another war – whether it be a full-scale conventional war, a more restricted conflict that would likely mean assaults on bystander nations and international shipping, or a more cat-and-mouse, covert struggle also with the potential for substantial spillover.[37]

The GCC states stand in the middle of this. The regimes and elites have staked their survival on a partnership with the United States. As small states, this inevitably means bowing to US pressure on security issues and little more than polite dissension on divergent political issues. It can be postulated that the Gulf's status as the world's predominant source of oil produces clout. However, the same situation as in 1973 no longer applies (and it will be noted that the Arab boycott of 1973 did little fundamentally to change US policy with regard to Arab–Israeli matters). As Saudi Arabia has both alluded and openly stated, its own self-interest demands that it seek stability and moderate prices in the international oil market in order to protect both its own economic well-being over the long run and its "special" relationship with the United States and the West in both the short- and long-term.

Both sides face serious questions and considerations about the future of FMP. What is the balance sheet for foreign powers in the Gulf? It should be firmly recognized in Washington that US security policy in the Gulf – and thus its framework for FMP in the region – must be based on more than just narrowly defined security considerations. In the Middle East and the Arab world in particular, it must be recognized that cultural differences and political disagreements will inevitably shape local attitudes to any American FMP, whether mutually beneficial or not. Proponents of US action in Iraq point to the institution of elections and a government formed as a result of those elections as an example of US intervention fostering democratization in a region notoriously resistant to it, but the attempt to introduce a foreign political concept in an alien manner produces echoes of the Weimar Republic as much as post-war Japan and Germany. The establishment of FMP in Gulf states is not simply a bilateral agreement between the foreign power and the host but also embraces the impact on alliances (as in the GCC and intra-GCC relations) and the impact on the host nation by its vulnerability to antagonism by larger regional powers (for instance, Iran). Above all, the relationship between the United States as the far more powerful source of FMP and the Gulf states as weaker hosts must be based on notions of equality and negotiation, rather than intimidation and unilateral decision-making.[38]

For their part, the Gulf states must recognize that their dependence on the United States as a security umbrella and economic partner is only a relatively minor role that they play within larger US global security concerns. To have a FMP in the GCC states is an inescapable reality. The question for the GCC states is whether or not a less direct or smaller American FMP is in their interests. Is there any *quid pro quo* that Gulf states can realistically offer the United States for a less direct FMP throughout the region? At what point – if ever – does a divergence in attitudes between elites and the general citizenry towards FMP and the United States in particular, create a critical division within society?

There are inescapable parallels between the past British experience in the Gulf and the present American one. They should not be overdrawn but they are relevant nevertheless. The British role gradually deepened over time. As John Gallagher and Ronald Robinson, the historians of British imperial history, point out:

> The British began to pursue the establishment of a formal, as opposed to informal, empire because of mounting resistance and opposition in the periphery, not because of a change in the objectives being pursued by the British government. British goals remained the same, but indirect influence was no longer sufficient to attain them.[39]

One wonders whether the US presence in the Gulf is experiencing the same "mission creep."

GULF ECONOMIC SECURITY

8

Risk: Perspectives from the Private Sector

Frederic Sicre

Security is not only a matter of concern to politicians, military personnel and citizens but also has a significant impact on business. In fact, one could say that both worlds are intrinsically linked. As security declines, so does the business environment. Inversely, if an investment environment becomes unfriendly, the greater the chance of social upheaval and instability leading to security challenges. This is why every peace process must have both political and economic support. Politics and economics go hand in hand and business must play its part in creating sustainable and secure economies.

Businessmen tend to view security issues in terms of risks that have to be managed, mitigated or simply avoided. Risk is also a function of time. All those seated in this hall are confident about the present, knowing that for the next 20 minutes, we will be having this discussion together. Can you be as confident about where you will be tonight? Some of you may have made dinner plans, scheduled evening meetings or decided to go to the movies. Can you at this moment be one hundred percent sure that you will be there as scheduled? Of course not, because something urgent might come up, your car may break down or an unexpected traffic jam may prevent you from being on time. There are risks you have to manage and your level of confidence in achieving your evening's objective is not as high as your level of confidence regarding the next thirty minutes.

Business thrives on two opposing forces: on the one hand, security such as clear investment rules, intellectual property rights and independent judicial courts; on the other hand, to thrive and prosper, business also needs a certain degree of risk—the greater the risk, the greater the rewards. This is particularly true of the Middle East. Many executives sitting in New York or Frankfurt may perceive the region to be a volatile sea of hostility and military actions. For those living in the Middle East it is clear that there are many islands of stability where profitable investments can be made and good returns made for shareholders. The private equity industry in general and my firm, Abraaj Capital, in particular have been achieving internal rates of return far above the industry average. In part, this is due to our ability to manage risk in areas where others do not dare to venture. As Winston Churchill said, "An optimist sees an opportunity in every danger, while a pessimist sees a danger in every opportunity." Chinese ideology has another way of regarding risk. A Chinese proverb says: "He who is comfortable should move on." This saying illustrates that if we are fully secure, comfortable and can predict with monotonous precision what will happen, then there is no challenge, no progress, none or very limited growth, and little innovation. Taking calculated risks is the answer to both corporate and personal growth.

The World Economic Forum categorizes risk into five broad areas. In an interconnected world, it is necessary to regard risks in the global agenda before focusing on the GCC.

Economic Risks: The first area of risk for business is in the economic sphere. In this category, global businesses are concerned with issues such as rising fuel costs or the US current account deficit, which totals US$225.6 billion. The United States invests far more than it saves (its current account deficit) and the rest of the world saves far more than it invests (a current account surplus). This is the cause of the imbalance in the global economy. It involves a massive flow of capital to the United States from the rest of the world. The magnitude of this transfer is

[210]

unprecedented in recent history and probably cannot be sustained indefinitely. Therefore, when it ends, it could have a destabilizing effect on the global economy. At that point, the dollar will drop and interest rates will soar, pushing the United States into a recession and wreaking havoc on the global economy. Indeed Deloitte Research has warned of this outcome in past publications. Moreover, there is historical precedent for this scenario. In the late 1970s and again in the late 1980s, a large US current account deficit was ultimately unwound through large dollar depreciations, rising interest rates and recessions. This was followed by financial crises in emerging markets. The pessimists believe that this could happen again, but possibly on a larger scale.

Another risk in the West is the growing fiscal crisis due to demographic shifts and ageing populations. The proportion of people over the age of 60 has been growing at a rate 60 percent faster than that of the world population. In 2005, there were only 9 workers per retiree while in 1950 there were 12 workers per retiree. This is called the dependency ratio and it has been proven that every 1 point increase in this ratio produces a 1.5 percent decrease in GDP over time. This in turn has an impact on pension and healthcare costs which in the United States are growing faster than nominal GDP. Between 1990 and 1997 US GDP growth was just 4.9 percent whereas Medicare growth was 10 percent. Over the last 10 years, GDP growth was 4.5 percent whereas Medicare was 7.4 percent—still showing faster growth rates than the economy can sustain over the long term. The risks associated with this phenomenon could lead to increased social tensions as the older segment of the population finds it difficult to access pharmaceuticals and healthcare systems.

Environmental Risks: The second area of risk defined by the global business community relates to the environment. This has assumed particular importance lately, as the world sees increasing signs that global climate change is not just a theory but a reality. Today, experts no longer speak about climate change but of global climate disruption due to human activity. If average temperatures were to rise by 1.5–2 degrees Celsius, sea levels would rise by 20 feet by 2050, displacing as many as 40 million people in India or 60 million in China. These massive population shifts are not only destructive but would put inconceivable pressure on the infrastructures of urban areas, which would be literally flooded with scores of displaced people seeking economic opportunities and subsistence activities. The increasing numbers of hurricanes and tsunamis testify to the fact that Mother Earth is slowly rebelling, creating security challenges for the future. Specialists concurred that Brazil would never see hurricanes. Yet, in 2004 the country witnessed its first hurricane.

Geopolitical Risks: The third area of risk stems from geopolitical factors. These include terrorism, WMD proliferation, civil wars, organized crime and corruption. These aspects have been addressed by other experts during this conference so I will not repeat what has already been said. However, business must be – and is – concerned with geopolitical risk as these can increase the cost of transactions and hamper economic activity.

Societal Risks: The fourth area is societal risk. Today, there is a clear polarization of ideologies in terms of political systems and beliefs. The Middle East has figured prominently in this debate. Is Western style democracy really the answer for development and progress in the rest of the world? Does one model fit all? There is also polarization in ideologies from a religious standpoint. It is only recently that world attention has focused on the great rift that has been created between Sunnis and Shiites.

Another emerging societal risk and challenge is growing protectionism in the West, largely due to the attractiveness and growth of emerging markets. As more and more multinationals outsource their operations to lower cost environments, developed countries are witnessing jobs being exported elsewhere, resulting in popular resentment, which in turn leads to increased protectionism.

[212]

Another interesting societal risk is the gravitational shift from the corporate boardroom to the consumer. In a more transparent world, with technology increasingly available to all, consumers can access far more information than in the past. Companies that, for example, fail to respect the environment or transgress labor rights become the focal point of consumer discontent. Boardrooms have learned that they cannot ignore their shareholders. They are also learning that consumers can vote with their feet, thereby directly affecting their sales and revenues. The consumer is wielding increasing power as the world progresses, and it is extremely important to recognize this fact—for a business that alienates its consumers will die.

Technological Risks: The fifth area of risk is in the field of technology. One example of the security challenges that we face is the seemingly unstoppable progress of nanotechnology and biotechnology. Imagine that in the future, when a child is born a doctor could rapidly analyze its DNA and predict when that child will die—the date, year, and the cause. Over and above the impact this would have on our emotional lives one can imagine the ramifications for the insurance industry or pharmaceutical companies.

As we have seen briefly, the global arena is changing on a daily and weekly basis and these changes entail varying degrees of danger and risk. In today's world an event happening on the other side of the planet can have global economic repercussions, such as Argentina's debt default of 2002 or the Asian financial crisis of 1997. It is the price of interdependence and reversing this trend is not an option. As such, any region or country needs to understand global risks as they ultimately have an impact locally as well.

Let us now take a closer look at the GCC countries. On the economic front, the pegging of GCC currencies to the US dollar does not allow them to reflect their real values. This is compounded by the current strength of the Euro and the British Pound. In addition, GCC economies have seen

[213]

levels of inflation rise due to the economic boom. The UAE has shown the highest inflationary growth from 1.35 percent in 2000 to 13.5 percent in 2006 followed by Qatar with 1.7 percent in 2000 to 10 percent in 2006. As such, this results in a situation whereby earners of GCC currencies have seen rising costs in their day-to-day lives while their purchasing power drops abroad. Many expatriates maintain residences or holiday homes in France, the United Kingdom or Italy. These will become more expensive, creating an increased financial burden and potentially having a negative impact on GCC consumption. If these trends continue, business may also find it difficult to attract top talent from abroad. Moreover, retaining talent may also become an issue as nobody likes to see their consumption power eroded.

On the environmental front, the risks and opportunities are equally great in the GCC. Public awareness about the environment in this region is dismally low. According to the WWF's *Living Planet Report* the UAE is one of the highest producers of carbon per capita in the world and other Gulf states follow closely.

Certainly, the high pace of development and construction in the region has generated larger quantities of rubble, emissions and industrial activity. The growing demographics of cities have had the same effect. However, desalination plants and electricity generators are also having an impact on the environment. Creating increased awareness in our societies of water wastage and electricity consumption can go a long way to reduce the wastage which occurs both in homes and in corporate headquarters. Rewarding and providing incentives to those companies that follow environmentally sound practices can also increase awareness and reduce the destructive effects that the economic boom is having on the environment. In addition, it makes economic sense, Arabtec Construction LLC, the leading UAE-based construction company has seen its costs reduced in some cases by 50 percent through undertaking environmentally sound decisions. Emphasizing the importance of the recycling industry and developing it across the region is not only an imperative but also a great business opportunity, notably when the GCC is reportedly the largest producer of waste per capita in the world.

On the societal front, the critical risk that stands out pertains to education, which is directly linked to the high levels of unemployment in the region. In the broader Middle East, 100 million jobs must be created by 2020 just to sustain the current levels of unemployment in the wider region which is 15 percent. This represents a 4 percent per annum employment growth rate, which has never been achieved anywhere in the world. This is a massive challenge that requires governments and business to work together closely in terms of increasing investment in education, providing men and women with the same opportunities for a good education and, of course, developing the right curricula needed for the right skills to be produced. As the GCC strives to build a modern infrastructure with stunning architectural forms and to diversify away from oil – its natural resource base – it becomes essential to build up local talent and not depend on foreign skills that may not remain forever in the region. Without building modern education systems and providing an opportunity for either academic or vocational training for all, unemployment will not be reduced, social tensions will rise and businesses will not find the skills and resources to manage growing companies in an increasingly competitive world.

Finally, on the technology front, one challenge that this region faces from a business perspective is the low level of research and development (R&D) taking place. R&D to GDP ratios in the Middle East are among the worst in the world. As diversification efforts move forward, it will be necessary to move up the value chain. This is the issue that Ireland has recently been forced to confront. Ireland built its reputation as a low-cost manufacturing platform for global pharmaceutical and information technology companies. Recently, many of these large investors have come to prefer the cost advantages found in Asia or in Central Europe. As such, Ireland has had to invest massively in its higher education systems to create a vibrant research and development environment. Although these investments do not yield results overnight, current GCC liquidity levels do allow the region to set the foundations for increased R&D. The statistics speak for themselves. In 2006, 173,000 patent filing requests were made to the Patents Bureau in the United States, amounting to 465 patent requests daily. In the GCC, over an eight-year period from 1998–2006, only 298 patent requests were made. Therefore in one day, the US patent bureau received twice as many patent requests than the Gulf states did over an eight-year period.

Having examined some risks figuring on the global and regional agenda, it is possible to review briefly how business perceives the risk map in the GCC. There are basically seven risk areas, some of which have already been mentioned.

1. *Human Capital*: Regional governments are aware of the historical deficit of relevant expertise within the region. Some countries, such as Jordan, have undertaken aggressive educational reform, while others still need to accelerate and invest in their own future in this respect. Governments are opening up the educational field to the private sector, which not only accelerates development, but ensures that the right skills are produced to drive a modern economy forward.

2. *Strained Infrastructure*: In the GCC, the rapid economic growth witnessed over the past five years has pushed existing systems to their limits. GCC governments have announced US$733 billion of infrastructure projects over the next decade to address these deficiencies, yet in the meantime many cities are suffering from heavy traffic congestion and power shortages have already made their mark in some GCC states. In the absence of efficient transport systems and a regular supply of affordable energy to operate, business will seek other destinations.

3. *Need for Growth Capital*: Booming demand and increasing levels of consumption and development are causing many companies to operate at full capacity. With the massive Indian and Pakistani markets nearby it is likely that demand will continue to grow. Medium-sized companies play a

critical role in terms of employment and development and can use the unprecedented growth to expand their operations and turn national Arab companies into regional and eventually international players. Accessing growth capital for these companies is important and this is where not only the banking industry but also private equity can play an important role.

4. *Inflationary Pressures*: The fourth challenge is that of the inflationary pressures already mentioned above.

5. *Ownership Structure*: The fifth challenge relates to the ownership structure in the region. Investment by foreign companies and individuals in companies organized within the GCC states is subject to restrictions. Except in Bahrain, Oman and Saudi Arabia in certain circumstances, foreigners are not permitted to hold more than a 49 percent interest in a local company and then only with respect to certain business activities. Some sectors in all six jurisdictions are restricted to companies that are 100 percent owned by nationals. This structure has forced many foreign companies to refrain from establishing offices in the region and many global banks (that do not have local presence) will charge a premium on their loans to mitigate this perceived risk. Although free zones exist in some of the GCC states, WTO regulations will level the playing field. The risk for local businesses, which have enjoyed some form of protection thus far, is to prepare their companies for an era of increased competition, whereby foreign companies will be allowed to operate freely.

6. *Corporate Governance*: The sixth area of concern in the GCC is corporate governance. The GCC region still suffers from poor corporate governance characterized by a lack of transparency, absence of accurate disclosures, irregularity in public accountability, inferior institutional quality and inefficiency in internal control systems. In the absence of a proper regulatory framework, it becomes more difficult to control accounting manipulation, reduce unethical behavior and prevent fraudulent conduct. According to the Arab competitiveness report, the MENA region ranks lowest in the world for public accountability (-0.78 on a scale from 2 to -2, with 2 being the highest). Local governments have recognized the lack of

corporate governance as a major risk to doing business in the region and have set up world-class institutions such as the Dubai International Financial Center (DIFC) and the Qatar Financial Center (QFC) that are fully transparent with independent regulators. In addition, corporate governance standards are being discussed in several financial circles and among authorities in the region. Good corporate governance lowers the cost of capital and encourages foreign direct investment (FDI). Moving forward with these recent efforts is of paramount importance to build confidence in international circles that business can enjoy a level playing field in the region.

7. *Low Corporate Social Responsibility*: The last area of risk is that of the low levels of corporate social responsibility (CSR) programs. Corporate philanthropy and charitable donations have been taking place but this falls short of really demonstrating commitment to the local communities in which businesses operate. CSR is not just about money. It is about creating sustainable programs for the poor, providing education and relief, donating time and resources to allow local communities to build their own programs, which fit their needs and which they can ultimately manage. CSR is also about labor rights, the environment and the elderly in our communities. Whereas corporate philanthropy in the region was quick to react to certain international disasters, including the 2004 Asian Tsunami relief efforts or the Pakistani earthquake, these one time efforts do not address the longer term objectives of poverty alleviation and social uplift. As vibrant economic growth improves the bottom line of many companies in the region, it is a moral and economic imperative for corporations to develop CSR projects. Not only does this make economic sense but it is a moral obligation to provide those who need hope or assistance with the means to build a future for themselves. It really revolves around the oft-quoted Chinese saying: "Give a man a fish and you feed him for a day. Teach a man to fish and you feed him for a lifetime."

9

Economic Diversity and its Significance in Diversifying Income Sources in the GCC States

Jassem Hussain Ali

The issue of economic diversity enjoys special significance when it comes to Gulf income sources, owing to the oil sector's increasing importance as a major source of treasury revenue for the GCC states, in addition to its significance to their exports. In recent years, the oil sector has played an increasingly important role in the economies of the GCC states. However, fully convinced that there is still no alternative to diversification, the GCC countries have embarked on the implementation of a series of economic reform policies. They are aware that this is the only way to face up to emerging challenges such as population growth and the need to create jobs that are compatible with their citizens' aspirations.

The Significance of the Gulf Oil Sector to the World Economy

The GCC countries as a group have a significant impact on the world economy, since the region is a major source of world energy. In 2005, the Gulf states produced approximately 18.5 million barrels of oil per day (mbpd), accounting for 23 percent of the world's oil production. In addition, 41 percent of proven oil reserves are located in the Gulf states. Moreover, gas production in the GCC region in 2005 represented 8 percent of world production and the Gulf states are expected to play a greater part in the coming years in view of the size of their investments in the natural gas sector. Qatar, for example, is expected to become the biggest exporter of liquefied natural gas (LNG) in the world, replacing Indonesia as the leading exporter. Statistically, the Gulf states control 23 percent of the world's reserves of natural gas (Table 9.1). In short, the world economy needs the Gulf states because they are a vital source of oil and natural gas.

Table 9.1
Various Vital Indicators of GCC Countries (2005)

	Vital Figures	World Percentage (%)
Population	35.9 million	0.5
GDP (in current prices)	US$613 billion	1.5
Oil Production	18.4 million b/day	23
Oil Reserves	487 billion barrels	41
Natural Gas Production	197 billion cubic meters	8.0
Natural Gas Reserves	41,375 billion cubic meters	23

Source: Calyon Corporate and Investment Bank, Research Department.

The Implications of Total Dependency on the Oil Sector

The oil sector (crude oil, natural gas and oil products) plays a pivotal role in the economies of the GCC states. However, some of these countries are more dependent on the oil sector than others. In fact, the oil sector represents the lifeline of the GCC economies at present and there is plenty of evidence that supports this point.

The Budget

On average, oil-based income constitutes about 80 percent of treasury revenues in the GCC countries (Table 9.2). Kuwait comes first on the list of GCC countries dependent on the oil sector, while Qatar is at the bottom. According to 2005 statistics, the oil sector formed 92 percent of Kuwait's treasury revenues, while in Qatar the figure fell to about 64 percent. However, these figures are still relatively high by any standard and put the countries' budgets at the mercy of developments in world markets.

Table 9.2

Oil Sectors' Proportionate Contributions to the GCC Countries' Budgets (%)

GCC States (average)	79
Kuwait	92
Kingdom of Saudi Arabia	81
Sultanate of Oman	78
United Arab Emirates	75
Kingdom of Bahrain	73
Qatar	64

Source: Calyon Corporate and Investment Bank, Research Department.

Exports

The oil sector also plays a major part in the GCC countries' exports. Just like its budget, Kuwait's economy is also the most dependent on the oil sector with regard to its exports, accounting for 95 percent in 2005 (Table 9.3).

Table 9.3

Oil Sectors' Proportionate Contributions to the GCC Countries' Exports (%)

Kuwait	95
Kingdom of Saudi Arabia	87
Qatar	83
Sultanate of Oman	83
United Arab Emirates	80
Kingdom of Bahrain	67

Source: Calyon Corporate and Investment Bank, Research Department.

As for the Kingdom of Bahrain, the oil sector has additional significance. Bahrain imports crude oil from the Kingdom of Saudi Arabia through pipelines dating back to 1945. In addition, the Bahrain Petroleum Company (BAPCO) refines imported crude oil into products such as gas, diesel fuel and aviation fuel. Oil imports constituted 53 percent of the total value of Bahrain's imports in 2005, compared to 43 percent in 2004. However, Bahrain purchases Saudi oil at market prices and this explains the relatively high share of the oil sector in Bahrain's trade balance (Table 9.4).

Table 9.4
The Trade Balance of the Kingdom of Bahrain

	2005 (In million Bahraini dinar)	Percentage (%)	2004 (In million Bahraini dinar)	Percentage (%)
Exports	**3,769.2**		**2,827.0**	
Oil Exports	2,926.6	78	2,087.3	74
Non-Oil Exports	754.1	20	677.2	24
Re-Exports	88.5	2	62.5	2
Imports	**2.987.8**		**2,438.2**	
Oil Imports	1,567.8	53	1,039.7	43
Non-Oil Imports	1,420.0	47	1,398.5	57
Outcome	**781.4**		**388.8**	

Source: Central Informatics Organization, Bahrain.

Gross Domestic Product

The oil sector also plays a significant role in the GDP of the GCC countries, but to a lesser extent compared to exports and imports. According to statistics prepared by the Saudi Arabian Monetary Agency

[222]

(SAMA), the oil sector constituted about 48 percent of Saudi Arabia's GDP in 2005. However, a few points should be clarified, particularly about the way the oil sector's contribution is calculated. According to international standards, refining oil and producing oil products, such as diesel fuel, is considered a transformational industry and not part of the crude oil and gas sector. The method might imply, unrealistically, that the local economy of the country is less dependent on the oil sector.

Similarly, oil-based revenues play a pivotal role in government expenditure, which in turn affects GDP. It is well known that public expenditure influences various economic sectors, such as trade and the construction and hospitality industries. Oil-based revenues (which are used to finance expenditure) underpin the general finances of the GCC countries.

The Decline in the Value of the Dollar

This degree of oil dependency has some negative aspects, such as the pricing of oil in US dollars. It is well known that crude oil and oil products such as diesel fuel, natural gas and its gas-based products are priced in US dollars. What matters here is the decline in the value of the dollar in comparison to other major currencies such as the euro and the Japanese yen. The US dollar has lost significant value in the past few years (between 2002 when dealing in the European currency began and up to the beginning of 2007, the US dollar has lost almost 33 percent of its value against the euro). This helps increase US exports to the euro region and to the other countries whose currencies are not linked to the dollar, such as Japan. Therefore, the decline of the value of the dollar (or the rise in the value of the euro) would serve the US economy by rendering US exports cheaper. In the end, the US economy benefits since this reactivates the economic circle, not to mention creating new jobs. In fact, a large part of the GCC countries' imports come from the EU countries, Japan and other countries whose currencies are not linked to the US dollar. European countries, especially

[223]

those in the euro region, are the major suppliers of all GCC countries, and especially Qatar, as shown in Table 9.5. Imports from the United States only account for 13 percent of the total value of Kuwait's imports—the highest figure among the GCC countries.

In addition to the impact of the value of the US dollar, the issue of importing US interest rates should also be mentioned. As the currencies of the GCC countries are linked to the dollar, the central banks of these countries have no leverage in directly influencing interest rates, because they are forced to import US interest rates. Kuwait is the only GCC member that has adopted a basket of currencies in determining the value of its currency. The basket includes the US dollar in addition to other currencies such as the euro.

Consequently, local economies incur loss in some cases, because interest rates move up and down according to the economic situation in the United States and not in the GCC countries. Following the terrorist attacks in September 2001 interest rates fell dramatically, but they went up in the first half of 2007. This was mainly due to fears that the US economy would suffer from inflation partly as result of a rise in oil prices.

Table 9.5
Sources of GCC Imports (%)

	Europe	Asia (including Japan)	United States	Other Countries
United Arab Emirates	39	39	8	14
Saudi Arabia	35	27	11	27
Qatar	51	23	9	17
Sultanate of Oman	26	28	7	39
Kuwait	37	25	13	25
Kingdom of Bahrain	28	19	10	43

Source: Calyon Corporate and Investment Bank, Research Dept. based on World Bank data.

At the Mercy of World Developments

The relatively high degree of oil dependency among the economies of the GCC countries constitutes an economic challenge, since it places them at the mercy of developments in world markets. Oil is a strategic world commodity, yet the oil sector is not included in trade liberalization debates within the framework of the World Trade Organization (WTO)—the last of such debates took place in Doha. Therefore, no consensus could be reached on factors governing changes in oil prices, as is the case with many other commodities such as coffee and cotton. This issue is of special significance since oil products are vital to society for the provision of energy, transportation, industry, etc.

Oil prices are influenced by a number of political, economic and psychological factors. At this juncture in history, political factors include developments in the Middle East (violence in Iraq and the Iranian nuclear dossier), Latin America (Venezuela's threats to cut off oil supplies to the United States), and instability in Africa (oil pipelines sabotaged and oil plundered in Nigeria). Other factors of equal significance include global climate change. Also, the psychological factor, e.g., speculation and rumor, cannot be disregarded. In other words, the region's countries have no control over the variables that influence oil and gas prices.

A Drop in the Significance of Non-Oil Revenues

The previous paragraphs have shown how significant economic diversification is in the GCC countries in view of the oil sector's domination over specific variables such as the national budget and exports. The whole issue becomes more significant when other variables, such as the removal of certain customs tariffs, are taken into consideration. This is the inevitable outcome of economic integration between the GCC countries—especially the formation of a Customs Union. This requires the unification of foreign trade policies of the GCC member states. There is also the issue of bilateral free trade agreements,

[225]

which involves granting relief from customs duties, and would consequently lead to a decline in the relative significance of customs duties and other treasury revenues. The rise in oil prices and the consequent increase in the oil sector's significance coincided with the implementation of the Gulf Customs Union. This also coincided with the desire on the part of GCC countries to engage in free trade agreements collectively or individually.

The Customs Union and its Effect on Other Revenues

The agreement to establish a Customs Union between the GCC countries came into effect in 2003. The project involves following a unified trade policy with non-member countries with regard to issues such as imposing unified customs tariffs on imports. According to the original plan, the GCC countries were supposed to complete the procedures required for the implementation of the Customs Union by the end of 2005. However, the GCC leaders decided to extend the transitional period up to the end of 2007.

Further delays are not unlikely because the GCC countries are relatively slow in executing vital issues related to the Customs Union in view of the significance of customs duties. In fact, many changes took place after the implementation of the customs union. However, the majority of member states have lost some customs duties following the initiation of the customs union agreement at the beginning of 2003. For example, Bahrain used to levy a customs duty amounting to 20 percent on car imports. This duty had to be lowered to 5 percent after the implementation of the Customs Union, and therefore less revenue would go into the national budget.

The detailed implementation of the customs union's agreement has faced numerous challenges—one of which is to find a solution to the issue of an entry point for goods. There is also the issue of agreeing on mechanisms for joint collection of duties, and the issue of distributing customs revenues among the member states. It is certainly not easy for some countries to waive customs duties in view of their relative significance to treasury revenues.

Free Trade Agreements and Tax Exemption Policy

In addition, there is the issue of free trade agreements, which some GCC members are concluding unilaterally with other countries. The Kingdom of Bahrain and the Sultanate of Oman have each concluded separate agreements with the United States to establish free trade zones. When the US–Bahraini free trade zone agreement came into force at the beginning of August 2006, Bahrain had to exempt 98 percent of US imports from customs duty. This constituted a loss of revenues for the Bahraini treasury since the United States is one of Bahrain's most important trade partners. In fact, excluding the oil sector, the United States is Bahrain's most important trade partner.

It is not difficult to understand why some GCC members conclude free trade agreements with the United States, since such agreements provide these countries with an opportunity to enter the US market with no restrictions. The US market is the largest in the world and the United States is a top importer of commodities and services, which in 2006 reached US$1,855 billion for commodities and US$300 billion for services. The total value of the United States' GDP in 2006 reached US$14,000 billion, twice the size of Japan's economy, which is considered the second largest in the world. These GCC countries concluded bilateral free trade agreements with the United States in order to deal with a number of economic challenges, such as the need to maintain certain jobs, to create new jobs for their citizens and to consolidate their competitive capabilities.

The GCC countries have aimed to set up a collective free trade zone with the EU. Free zone talks between the two parties began in 1988, but no concrete headway has been made because the Europeans have insisted on new conditions including avoiding any damage to the environment as well as adherence to human rights and commitments to political reform. However, since the beginning of 2007 the European stance has undergone a radical transformation after the United States concluded a number of bilateral agreements with certain GCC countries. The EU subsequently expressed its desire to conclude the agreement if the GCC were to settle a number of pending issues, such as removing the local majority rule—i.e. to remove the condition that restricts foreign appropriation to 49 percent.

Such free trade agreements, whether bilateral or collective, require granting exemptions from customs duties. This situation results in reducing such revenues and consolidates the relative significance of oil-based revenues. Therefore, economic diversification becomes strategically significant.

Engaging Oil Surpluses in Economic Diversification

The world's dependency on the region's energy resources could be considered to some extent a negative consequence, since this situation could lead to delays in economic reform and the modernization and development of economies. However, the opposite is taking place. A major goal of the GCC is to increase the pace of economic reform and consequently to diversify income sources, while oil revenues provide a vital cover in case economic reforms are hindered for whatever reason. In other words, funds would be available to overcome unexpected problems.

The oil and gas revenues of the GCC countries have grown significantly as a result of the increase in oil prices in world markets. According to the *McKinsey Quarterly* (January 2007), the aggregate revenues of the GCC rose from US$100 billion in 2002 to US$325 billion by the end of 2006. The British weekly, *The Economist*, in its issue of December 9, 2006, mentioned that the GCC countries enjoy a qualitative surplus in their trade balances and it is expected that the oil-producing countries in the Gulf would realize a surplus amounting to US$280 billion in 2007. Surpluses emanating from the oil sector can be used as a means to create the desired economic diversity and it is reassuring to see that there is a strong tendency among the GCC countries to use oil surpluses to realize certain strategic economic goals.

Reducing Public Debt and Consolidating Reserves

The government of Saudi Arabia implements a strict financial policy that involves employing part of its budget surplus of 2006 to reduce the size of its public debt, which has been reduced to about US$98 billion—28 percent of the value of its 2006 GDP. In 2005, public debt constituted 39 percent of the value of GDP, while in 2003 it amounted to 87 percent of GDP. In addition, the Saudi government has transferred more than US$26 billion from the surplus account to its general reserve—the first time in 20 years that Saudi authorities have supplemented its strategic reserves. Consolidating the general reserve meets some of the requirements of the proposed monetary union between the GCC members in 2010. According to the plan, the GCC members must maintain an amount of reserve equal to the value of their imports for four months. No doubt, the policy of reducing public debt and consolidating reserves will benefit future generations and is a praiseworthy move. It would also give the authorities greater freedom to take economic decisions, especially with regard to liberalizing the economy.

Proceeding with Privatization and Economic Liberalization

Oil surpluses contribute to creating the appropriate financial atmosphere for privatization and economic liberalization and help facilitate open competition between companies without external influence or pressure. Privatization and economic liberalization increase revenues for the national treasury and also improve corporate competence, since private sector institutions are prompted by profitability and this involves providing customers with professional services and value for money.

[229]

The government of the Kingdom of Bahrain, for example, signed a contract in 2006 with a consortium of three foreign companies to operate the al-Had electricity and water plant (first and second phases). The consortium comprises International Power plc from Britain, which owns 40 percent of shares and therefore leads the consortium; the Japanese Sumitumo; and the Belgian Suez-Tractebel—each owning 30 percent of the shares. The government-signed contract is for the purchase of electricity and water equipment for 20 years, according to which the consortium will operate the plant while the public sector will be responsible for distribution. The contract also provides for an additional 60 million gallons of water per day under phase three of the al-Had plant project. The cost of the purchase is US$1.25 billion, out of which US$738 million is for the purchase of the plant's assets. In addition, in 2006 Bahraini authorities signed a contract with Muller (part of the Danish Muller Maersk group) for the operation of Salman port in Manama and Khalifah port in the al-Had area. According to the contract, Muller will have the right to operate the two ports for 25 years and exclusively for 15 years.

The GCC should continue, or rather increase the pace of implementing economic reform programs such as liberalization and privatization. The liberalization policy would provide the governments with an opportunity to collect fees for granting rights—as had happened when the communications sector was liberalized. Privatization programs can also support national budgets through the sale of certain public assets, or transferring the task of operating them to private companies. Privatization also provides an opportunity to improve efficiency and thus lower costs, which would make room for investing funds for other purposes.

Attracting Foreign Investment

Any policy of economic reform and liberalization will attract foreign direct investment (FDI). Such investments serve as a vital indicator of how much trust world institutions have in other countries' trade laws and their prospects. According to the United Nations Conference on Trade and Development (UNCTAD) *World Public Investment Report 2006*, the inflows of foreign direct investment into the GCC countries have jumped significantly—up by 60 percent in 2005 to US$20 billion. This kind of FDI is known as long-term investment (investment in the stock exchange does not fall under this definition, because it is subject to change at any moment).

According to the same report, the United Arab Emirates (UAE) has succeeded in attracting US$12 billion (Table 9.6), which equals an increase of 43 percent. Thus, the UAE's economic policies enjoy a high degree of world appreciation, especially the economic policies of Dubai. In total, some 60 percent of FDI in the GCC countries has gone to the UAE. Second among the GCC countries is the Kingdom of Saudi Arabia, which succeeded in attracting US$4.6 billion of FDI in 2005, compared to less than US$2 billion in 2004. These results have been realized against the backdrop of the Kingdom joining the WTO and conducting the required modification and development of laws and procedures, which in turn has contributed to improving the investment environment for foreign investors.

As for the other member countries, Qatar has succeeded in attracting US$1.5 billion – an increase of 23 percent – and has attracted many companies engaged in the energy sector. The Kingdom of Bahrain comes fourth, attracting more than US$1 billion, and realizing 21 percent growth. This came against a backdrop of implemented economic reforms, involving the transfer of public sector assets to the private sector, including international companies. The Sultanate of Oman has also succeeded in increasing FDI from US$200 million in 2004 to US$750 million in 2006. Finally, the State of Kuwait has managed to increase FDI from just US$24 million in 2004 to US$250 million in the following year as a result of the success of its economic liberalization policy, including in the finance sector.

According to the UNCTAD report, the worldwide flow of FDI reached US$916 billion, recording a 29 percent increase. It attributes this to three factors: economic growth; growth in the world demand for oil; and attempts made by various countries to improve their investment environment through legislative reforms. Moreover, there is increasing global acknowledgement of the benefits of FDI in relation to local economic challenges such as employment, raising wages and enhancing competition.

The FDI share of the Western Asia region, which includes the GCC countries, has reached US$35 billion, recording a rise of 85 percent—the highest among any of the regions analyzed. However, the share itself is considered low as it constitutes less than 4 percent of the total FDI in 2005, yet out of the total amount of FDI that arrived in Western Asia, 34 per cent has gone to the UAE.

It is therefore appropriate to discuss in more detail the issue of attracting FDI to the GCC countries, since such investments are an indicator of the success of their economic liberalization policies.

Attracting Inward FDI to the Gulf Countries

According to the UNCTAD report, the UAE ranked 15th in the world with regard to attracting inward FDI (out of 141 countries covered by the report) in 2005. Thus, the UAE has succeeded in rising 10 positions within one year owing to the progress achieved in economic liberalization. The Kingdom of Bahrain has had similar success and ranked 22nd position. Meanwhile, Qatar ranked 54th, the Sultanate of Oman 91st, the Kingdom of Saudi Arabia 110th, and Kuwait 132nd. Kuwait has lagged behind because of a dispute between the government and parliament over economic reforms, especially with regard to allowing foreign companies to invest in the oil sector. (The Kuwaiti constitution does not allow foreign companies to possess shares in the oil sector.)

According to the FDI Potential and Performance indices outlined in the report (these indices depend on 12 variables with regard to economic policies and situation), the State of Qatar ranked 10th position worldwide (out of 141 countries covered by the report). This positive result reflects worldwide appreciation of the growth potential of the Qatari economy, especially in natural gas, crude oil, industry and services sectors.

The UAE occupies 27th position—a drop of four positions. The Kingdom of Bahrain also dropped one position and is ranked 30th, while the Kingdom of Saudi Arabia dropped four positions to 35th; Kuwait dropped two positions to 42nd; and the Sultanate of Oman dropped three positions to 57th worldwide.

The FDI Potential indicator is more important than the FDI Attraction indicator, because the first refers to the future, whereas the second refers to the past. Various countries in the world are working on improving their investment environment—the majority of GCC states have been relatively late in this respect. Certainly, there is a growing world appreciation of the significance of foreign direct investment and its contribution to tackling local economic challenges, such as job creation.

Table 9.6
Inward FDI in the Arab States of the Gulf (US$ million)

	2005	2001
United Arab Emirates	12,000	1,184
Saudi Arabia	4,628	504
Qatar	1,469	296
Kingdom of Bahrain	1,049	80
Sultanate of Oman	715	5
Kuwait	250	-111

Source: UNCTAD, World Investment Report 2006.

Sales Tax

Is it time to impose value-added tax on commodities in the GCC states? The opinion of this paper is: yes. Today's economic realities mean that decision makers are required to think seriously about imposing this kind of tax, as many other countries in the world do. There are various reasons to move in this direction, including the loss of treasury revenues when GCC states join collective or bilateral agreements requiring the reduction or cancellation of customs tariffs.

The International Monetary Fund (IMF) has suggested that the GCC countries should introduce sales taxes in order to achieve many fiscal goals, such as enhancing the sources of budget incomes. However, it is said that every rule comes with its exceptions. For example, it is not right to impose a sales tax on requirements for children such as formula milk, etc. However, it is possible to implement customs duty on certain luxury items intended for children, such as computer CDs. Countries can also impose an escalating tax on certain goods and commodities with the aim of encouraging a reduction in their consumption, as is the case with tobacco.

Confronting the Demographic Challenge

The rate of population growth in GCC countries is high and is another factor behind the necessity of income source diversification. According to the 2005 census, the population of all GCC countries reached 36 million—representing about 0.5 percent of the total world population (Table 9.1). However, what characterizes the GCC countries is the exceptionally large proportion of youth in the population. GCC citizens below 15 years of age represent about 32 percent of the population on average. Indeed, in the Kingdom of Saudi Arabia, 39 percent of the total population is under 15 years of age (Table 9.7). This demographic fact represents a challenge with regard to planning for education and training, and creating jobs that can keep pace with the growing number of people who will enter the workforce.

Indeed, the population of the GCC countries is growing by 2.5 percent per year on average. However, this rate increases after adding the growth of the expatriate workforce. Such population growth puts pressure on the expenditure trends of the national budget, since more funds are allocated to areas such as education, health services and others.

This demographic challenge might be considered a major reason for economic diversification. As governments' responsibilities to their people grow – reflected in providing job opportunities that comply with citizens' aspirations in terms of salaries and working conditions – so must these governments create new economic arenas.

Table 9.7

Population in the GCC States under 15 years of age (%)

GCC (average)	32
Saudi Arabia	39
Bahrain	37
Oman	35
Qatar	30
United Arab Emirates	26
Kuwait	25

Source: Calyon Corporate and Investment Bank, Research Dept. based on World Bank and McKinsey data.

Human Development Report

Current cash flows into the GCC countries are providing huge investments in various development and real estate projects. According to some statistics, the size of investment in the GCC countries is expected to reach US$1,500 billion in the coming years, especially in infrastructure projects. Such investment is important in view of demographic pressures and expenditure from both the private and public sectors contribute to improving overall performance in the GCC countries, according to human development indices.

There is a noticeable discrepancy in the 2006 Human Development Report, issued by the United Nations Development Program (UNDP), with regard to the GCC countries. The State of Kuwait ranks 1st position among the GCC and Arab countries, while at world level it is ranked 33rd—a rise of 11 positions in one year. The Kingdom of Bahrain has succeeded in improving its ranking by four positions to 39th worldwide, and ranks 2nd position among Gulf and Arab countries. In contrast, the State of Qatar and the UAE have dropped 6 and 8 positions respectively. However, the Sultanate of Oman has realized the best progress by rising 15 positions and now ranks 56th worldwide, while the Kingdom of Saudi Arabia has moved one position to rank 76th worldwide.

The Human Development Report evaluates countries according to three major criteria: age expectancy at birth; the percentage of literate population; and per capita income (Table 9.8). The UAE has the highest rate of life expectancy at more than 78 years, followed by Kuwait with 77 years, Bahrain and Oman with 74 years, Qatar with 73 years, and finally Saudi Arabia with 72 years. In general, the rate of life expectancy in the Gulf countries is similar to that in developed countries as a result of advanced health services (Japan with 82 years has the highest rate of life expectancy in the world). However, a significant question remains unanswered—a large number of chronic diseases such as diabetes and hypertension are widespread among the old age population of the region.

As for education, the figures published show that Kuwait comes top among Gulf and Arab countries. More than 93 percent of the population in Kuwait is literate; next comes Qatar with 89 percent and then Bahrain with around 87 percent. It is noticeable that there are no figures available for education in the UAE. However, the lowest rates of literacy exist in the Kingdom of Saudi Arabia at 80 percent. This might be due to the unwillingness of some families in areas far from cities to send their daughters to study in state schools.

With regard to per capita income, GDP figures indicate that the UAE citizen has the highest per capita income among the citizens of the GCC countries, at more than US$24,000 per year based on purchasing power.

In brief, if used properly, oil surpluses could contribute to improving the performance of the GCC countries according to human development indicators. Funds could be directed into areas such as education and health, which would help improve the living conditions of citizens and residents alike.

Table 9.8

2006 Human Development Report – Statistics for the GCC

Country	Life expectancy (years)	Ratio of literate people (%)	Per capita income based on purchasing power (US$)
Kuwait	77.1	93.3	19,384
Kingdom of Bahrain	74.3	86.5	20,758
Qatar	73.0	89.0	19,844
UAE	78.3	NA	24,056
Sultanate of Oman	74.3	81.4	15,259
Saudi Arabia	72.0	79.4	13,825

Source: UNDP, 2006 Human Development Report.

Diversifying the Economy Away from Oil

Many indicators show that GCC countries are serious about reducing their oil dependency, and the following examples outline a number of attempts made in this direction.

The Dubai Strategic Plan

Dubai seems to be determined to go as far as possible in reducing oil dependency within its economic cycle. The ruler of Dubai, H.H. Sheikh Mohammed Bin Rashid Al Maktoum, disclosed in February 2007 the Dubai Strategic Plan, which covers the period 2007–2015 and is aimed at realizing an annual GDP growth of 11 percent. According to this ambitious plan, the GDP in Dubai should reach US$108 billion by 2015 in comparison to US$37 billion in 2005. It also aims to raise the per capita income from US$33,000 per year in 2005 to US$44,000 by 2015.

[237]

Five Secondary Plans

The Dubai Strategic Plan is divided into five secondary plans. These are: economic development; social development; infrastructure, land and the environment; security, justice and equality; and government.

ECONOMIC DEVELOPMENT

Dubai's economy will concentrate on certain sectors, namely tourism, transportation, trade, construction and financial services—the latter representing the strongest components of Dubai's economy.

SOCIAL DEVELOPMENT

Since expatriates form the vast majority of Dubai's population, this calls for adopting certain measures to maintain the Emirati national identity. Officials hope to encourage greater cultural movement by paying more attention to cultural activities. Moreover, the government will work on improving the quality of heath care services and the health of the population in general.

INFRASTRUCTURE, LAND AND THE ENVIRONMENT

Official departments will solve problems related to traffic congestion in Dubai. The authorities also undertake the responsibility of guaranteeing the supply of energy, electricity and water.

SECURITY, JUSTICE AND EQUALITY

Government departments will increase the number of marine patrols and improve the competence of operations. The plan also emphasizes the necessity of providing safety regulations in all areas of work and for all workers. Authorities will also work on reducing time spent on litigation and legal procedures. More importantly, authorities will secure the enforcement and implementation of decisions after they are passed.

GOVERNMENT

Emphasis will be placed on the development of the government structure, in addition to deepening the culture of accountability and transparency with regard to the practices of the government sector. There will also be an emphasis on developing competence in government offices, modernizing accounting policies and practices, as well as managing complaints electronically.

The Role of Government

Traditionally, the public sector has played a pivotal role in the economic development of Dubai and this is unlikely to change in the future. The policies of the Dubai government are also known to have contributed to enhancing the role of the private sector, which is evident in its policies dealing with the development of infrastructure and the launch of giant projects, such as Internet City and Media City. In other words, government initiatives have provided the incentive and the engine for growth and attracting investment. Therefore, it is expected that the public sector will continue to play its pivotal role in realizing major goals.

The Dubai Strategic Plan is considered a qualitative addition to the emirate's reputation at the regional level. The goals of the strategic plan will probably be realized before the deadlines set, as happened last time in 2000 when the government of Dubai announced a strategic plan to achieve certain goals for the period ending in 2010. However, the government managed to realize its economic goals in terms of GDP growth and the average per capita income by 2005—i.e. five years ahead of schedule.

Bahrain and its Reduction of Oil Dependency

The Kingdom of Bahrain is working on developing its economy away from the oil sector. This was made clear in an interview conducted by the *McKinsey Quarterly* in the first quarter of 2007 with Bahrain's Crown Prince Sheikh Salman Bin Hamad Al-Khalifa.

The Crown Prince stated that his country was facing two challenges— the demographic challenge and oil dependency. The first challenge deals with issues such as population growth and the fact that Bahraini society is very young. Population growth in the Kingdom reached 2.5 percent in

2006 (2.3 percent for the citizens and 2.7 percent for expatriates), and approximately 37 percent of the population is under 15 years of age. Thus, large sectors of the population will join the labor market in the coming years. This will constitute a challenge for the Bahraini economy, and will require expansion so that it can provide job opportunities that meet the needs of those entering the workforce.

With regard to Bahrain's oil dependency, the oil sector constitutes a significant part of the Kingdom's imports and exports and constitutes 76 percent of the actual revenues of the national budget in 2005 compared to 73 percent in 2004. Analyzed further, oil exports constituted 78 percent of the total value of exports in 2005 compared to 74 percent in 2004; while oil imports constituted 52 percent of the total value of imports in 2005 compared to about 43 percent in the preceding year.

However, when it comes to GDP the situation is different. In 2005, the financial sector was in unrivalled first position and constituted about 28 percent of GDP. Second was the government services sector, contributing less than 15 percent of GDP. Statistics show the retreat of the crude oil and natural gas sectors in Bahrain's GDP, dropping from 15.6 percent in 2003 to 13.1 percent in 2004, and then to 11.1 percent in 2005 (Table 9.9).

The Kingdom of Bahrain has proved itself to be a capital for banking services at the regional level and has consolidated its position by approving a project to build a financial hub on the site of the old port in the center of Manama. Many public and private financial institutions, such as the Central Bank and the stock exchange, are expected to move their headquarters to the financial hub (the first stage of the project was inaugurated in 2007).

According to Bahrain's Crown Prince, economic reforms in the Kingdom will be based on three major goals: to make the private sector the main engine of the local economy; turning the role of the government sector into a supporting role for the private sector instead of being the engine of the economic process; and investing in its citizens.

Table 9.9

The GDP of the Kingdom of Bahrain in Fixed Prices (2003–2005)

	2005 (million dinar)	Percentage to total %	2004 (million dinar)	Percentage to total (%)	2003 (million dinar)	Percentage to total (%)
Financial Services	966	27.6	820	25.3	580	24.2
General Administration	506	14.5	476	14.7	543	14.7
Industry	465	13.3	392	12.1	372	12.1
Trade	449	12.9	404	12.4	397	12.9
Oil & Natural Gas	388	11.1	424	13.1	479	15.6
Transportation & Communications	300	8.6	285	8.8	256	8.3
Real Estate & Business Services	296	8.5	278	8.6	276	9.0
Total Including Other Activities	3,496	100	3,243	100	3,071	100

Source: National Financial Accounts, The Audit Bureau, *Al-Wasat* newspaper.

It appears that the government is also keen to consolidate the role of the private sector, as is evidenced by the policy of removing obstacles that institutions face. For example, in February 2007 Hassan Al-Fakhro, Minister of Industry and Commerce, allowed commercial businesses the right to announce sale occasions without the need to obtain permission from any department. Therefore, the tendency is now to reduce the role of the government to that of an organizing body of trade activities rather than a participant in the production process.

Establishment of Economic Cities in the Kingdom of Saudi Arabia

Since the middle of the decade, the Kingdom of Saudi Arabia has concentrated on the establishment of economic cities to speed up the development process throughout its vast territory and eventually reduce oil dependency. The King Abdullah Economic City, north of Jeddah, was launched at a cost of about US$27 billion, and Dubai-based Emaar is in charge of developing this city. In addition, plans for another economic city – Prince Abdul Aziz bin Musa'id Economic City – have been announced and the development will be situated in Ha'el, northwest of the capital Riyadh. Spreading over 156 million square meters, the cost of the project is expected to reach US$8 billion over a ten-year period and will include six main activities: transportation and logistic services, educational services, agricultural services, industrial and mining services, recreational services, and a residential area. The transportation and logistic services plan also includes the construction of an airport. Moreover, an educational area is being constructed on ten million square kilometers and will include a number of universities, colleges, schools and research centers to cover the needs of 40,000 students in the Ha'el area.

A whole sector in this designated economic area will be allocated to agricultural production, since Ha'el is well known for this industry. Also, the natural resources of the area, such as minerals and raw materials, will be exploited with the aim of establishing new transformational industries. The plan also includes the establishment of a number of hotels and commercial complexes through investment in tourist and recreational services. Finally, it is expected that 30,000 residential units will be constructed to provide accommodation for about 140,000 people. The whole project will be funded through private sector institutions, led by Rakizah Holdings, under the supervision of the General Commission for Investment (GCI).

A Financial Center in the Capital, Riyadh

In addition to the two new economic cities, it was announced in 2006 that another project – The King Abdullah Financial District – will be established in Riyadh in accordance with the latest standards in terms of infrastructure, supplies and services.

It would appear that the financial district will be distinguished by its size, and will be established on an area of 1.6 million square meters (by comparison the area of Canary Wharf in the British capital is 345,000 square meters). In other words, the Saudi authorities would like to make the center the most important place for financial services throughout the Middle East, and also compete with international – not just regional – financial centers. Authorities also hope to open the King Abdullah Financial Academy in the heart of the King Abdullah Financial District to train young Saudis in financial services and skills, in addition to providing numerous facilities for specialized conferences. The district will also incorporate different official institutions linked to financial services, such as a financial market, stock exchange, and branches of banks and financial consultancy firms.

The King Abdullah Financial District aims to enhance the role of the financial sector in the national economy. As the Saudi monarch, HM King Abdullah bin Abdul Aziz Al-Saud stated, the establishment of the center concurs with the:

> [C]ontinuous revision and restructuring of the sector and its organizational frameworks with the aim of continued development. This is intended to meet the needs of the national economy, and to enhance its regional and international competitive potentials. The aim is also to continue to encourage the private sector to increase its contribution to economic and social development through developing an active partnership between the public and private sectors; and to complement the organizational and monitoring frameworks required for that.

Commitment to developing the banking sector, including the development of structures and regulations, is notable in the Saudi monarch's address, since development is a fundamental issue in view of rapid changes in today's world. In fact, the Saudi step to establish such a center has been relatively late, in view of the fact that the Saudi economy is the largest among the countries of the region (it accounts for half of the combined GDP of all the other GCC states). These three projects are expected to consolidate the economic potential of Saudi Arabia at the regional level.

The 2007 Saudi Budget and the Focus on Education

The 2007 budget is the largest ever in the history of Saudi Arabia, reflecting the fact that oil prices remain relatively high. The value of Saudi revenues is US$107 billion while expenses stand at US$101 billion, leaving a surplus of US$6 billion. However, the real surplus is expected to be much higher since Saudi authorities have adopted a conservative figure for the average price of oil as part of the country's financial policy and in line with other GCC countries. Oil-based income represents the foundation of Saudi general finances, accounting for three quarters of the budget's revenues.

With regard to expenditure, the government has allocated huge amounts to the implementation of development and services projects: US$26 billion for education; US$10 billion for health and development services; and US$7 billion for water, agriculture and basic services. These steps aim to enhance the position of Saudi Arabia in terms of human development. It ranked 76th on the 2006 human development indices—the worst among the GCC countries. The increase in expenditure could realize some of the goals of the eighth five-year development plan, which includes the creation of tens of thousands of jobs for its citizens, in addition to enhancing the economy's competitiveness as required by joining the World Trade Organization.

Finally, it is clear that GCC states are determined to invest oil surpluses accumulated in the period 2002–2006 to diversify their sources of income. According to the most trustworthy estimates, the combined revenue of all GCC countries rose from US$100 billion in 2002 to US$325 billion by the end of 2006. In other words, the oil sector (including crude oil, natural gas and oil products) is being used as a means to achieve economic diversity in the GCC countries. No doubt, it is an irony to see the dominating oil sector contributing to the realization of such desired economic diversity. However, once this economic diversity is achieved, it would surely be an extra credit to this vital sector, which has played a pivotal role in the development of the region's countries.

Free Trade Agreements and Economic Security in the GCC Countries

Hamad Suleiman Al-Baz'ie

A free trade zone is defined as an area in which obstacles to trade are removed by a free trade agreement between two or more countries. It is a tool of economic integration that does away with customs tariffs and allocations of mutual trade between countries that are parties to the agreement.

Many countries are keen to sign free trade agreements. Article (24) of the General Agreement on Tariffs and Trade (GATT), which is concerned with the reduction of barriers to international trade, gives countries and economic blocs the right to sign free trade agreements among themselves and permits such agreements to be an exception to the Most Favored Nation (MFN) principle. Thus, countries and economic blocs which are members of the World Trade Organization (WTO) can also enjoy this advantage.[1] Similarly, Article (5) of the General Agreement on Trade in Services (GATS) gives countries and economic blocs the same right.[2]

The number of free trade agreements between countries and regional blocs rose to 200 in 2005 and about 40 percent of world trade takes place between countries that have established some form of commercial exchange agreement.[3] This paper examines the strategy of the Gulf Cooperation Council (GCC) countries in negotiating free trade agreements and the potential effects of these agreements on the economic security of the GCC states.

The Negotiation Strategy of the GCC Countries

The GCC Economic Agreement provided for the establishment of a free trade zone. Work on this trade zone began with the foundation of the GCC and has since developed into the common Customs Union—as of the beginning of 2003. Currently the countries of the GCC are working to complete arrangements for a common market in 2007 and are also seeking to launch a unified Gulf currency in 2010.

The foundation of the Customs Union has had a positive impact on the development of trade among the countries of the GCC. Statistics indicate that commercial exchange between the GCC states in 2003 was about US$23 billion and intra-GCC trade grew by about 20 percent over 2002. This growth rate is three times greater than that achieved in the previous ten years before establishing the Customs Union. The amount of commercial exchange between the GCC countries in 2004 was about US$29 billion, reflecting an increase of 26 percent in comparison to 2003. This highlights the importance of removing obstacles to the free flow of trade.[4]

As for world trade, the EU is the most important trading partner of the GCC. The EU accounted for a 19 percent share of the total foreign trade of the countries of the GCC in 2004 and 2005, followed by Japan (15 percent), and thereafter by the countries of the Greater Arab Free Trade Area (GAFTA) with a share of 9.15 percent in 2004 and 8.71 percent in 2005. China ranked 4th with 6 percent for the same period, followed by India with nearly 3.5 percent.[5]

The nature of the economies of the GCC countries – which depend mainly on revenues generated by crude oil exports, petroleum products and associated industries – combined with fluctuations in income resulting from uncontrollable developments in global oil markets, has forced these countries to place the diversification of income sources at the top of the hierarchy of priorities stipulated in their respective development plans. Simultaneously, they continue to work towards reducing dependence on oil as a basic source of government revenue by developing other productive sectors and providing the necessary means to diversify products. As a result of the progress achieved in these sectors and the expansion of their production capacities beyond the needs of the local market, it has become necessary to search for external markets for these products. Policies that support this include trade arrangements with other economic blocs in order to open new markets for these products and ensure their unobstructed flow to external markets.

Consequently, the 21st session of the Supreme Council of the GCC, held in December 2000, approved the "long-term strategy of the relations and negotiations of the countries of the Council with regional blocs and international organizations." The aim of this strategy is to:[6]

- Achieve integration among the GCC countries in all fields, coordinate their policies and trade relations with other countries and economic regional and international blocs.

- Encourage commercial exchange and improve access for exports from the countries of the Council to global markets and increase the competitiveness of these countries.

- Encourage foreign direct investment in the countries of the Council in conformity with the objectives of the economic and industrial development of these countries.

- Protect the investments of the countries of the Council in other countries and international economic groups.

- Support and encourage industrial cooperation between economic authorities in the GCC countries and other countries and groups.

These objectives are consistent with Article (2) of the GCC Economic Agreement, which requires member states to outline collectively their policies toward, and economic relations with, other countries and regional and international blocs in order to improve the conditions and equitable aspects of international economic transactions with the GCC states. The article also advises member states to take the necessary measures to achieve this goal, including the conclusion of economic agreements collectively with trade partners. These objectives are also consistent with Article (31) of the same agreement, which stipulates that it is not permissible for a member state to grant preferential treatment to a non-member state that goes beyond what is stipulated in the agreement, or to conclude an agreement that contradicts the rules of the Economic Agreement.[7]

In its 26th session in December 2005, the Supreme Council approved the policy of unified internal trade among the GCC countries. This covers commercial and economic procedures; unifying the external trade policy of the countries of the Council regarding the outside world and international organizations; promoting commercial exchange and investment; increasing the competitiveness of GCC products; reducing customs duties to which these products are subject; and removing other constraints imposed on these products.[8]

Requirements of the GCC Customs Union and Free Trade Agreements

In its 23rd session held in December 2002, the Supreme Council approved the establishment of a Customs Union for the GCC as of the beginning of 2003.[9] The most significant tasks of the Customs Union are:

- Implementing the unified customs tariff on all foreign goods imported from outside the Customs Union while exempting a group of basic goods.
- Unifying customs and administrative procedures in all customs centers of the GCC countries via implementing a unified customs regime in all the customs departments of the member states.
- Applying a single point of entry to the GCC countries so that any land, sea or air customs port of the GCC states that is connected to the outside world is regarded as a point of entry of imported goods into any member state.
- Establishing a system to view and inspect imported goods and finalize all required customs and non-customs procedures, including paying customs excises due on imported goods.

Unifying GCC Trade Policy with the Outside World

Since the Supreme Council's issuance of the resolution to establish a Customs Union, the importance of unifying the trade policies of the GCC countries toward the outside world has been reinforced; this is especially true regarding customs exemptions. In its 26th session, the Supreme Council emphasized two points: the obligations of member states towards the principle of collective negotiation with other countries and economic blocs; and consideration of the individual bilateral trade agreements between the Gulf states and the United states as the only exception to this rule.

The GCC Negotiations Team

To organize and coordinate the efforts of the GCC states in their negotiations with other countries and economic blocs, and their negotiations with other parties with a unified voice, a negotiations team of experts from the member states was formed, based on a resolution of the 33rd session of the Ministerial Council (which comprises the Ministers of Foreign Affairs of the GCC countries) held in November 1989 under the chairmanship of the General Coordinator of Negotiations. To implement the December 2006 resolution of the Supreme Council, the 72nd meeting of the Financial and Economic Committee issued a resolution to restructure the remit of the negotiations team to support the GCC delegation in Brussels in order to cope with the expansion of negotiations between the Council and a number of countries and economic blocs.[10] The proposals stipulated that the negotiation team should be responsible for negotiations with countries and economic blocs in accordance with the long-term strategy of the GCC countries. The proposals included: giving priority to negotiations with other countries; studying agreements presented by the GCC countries and determining stances towards them; analyzing existing relations between the GCC and other countries in accordance with an action plan and a time schedule for negotiations; and forming technical negotiations teams composed of experts in member states and the Secretariat General to deal with common subjects of negotiations such as goods, services, countries of origin, government purchasing, investment, and general texts and rules.

The Priorities of the GCC Countries in Negotiations

GCC priorities in negotiations with other countries and economic blocs are influenced by either the importance of GCC trade with these other countries or blocs relative to its gross trade with the world, or on the basis of what opportunities the GCC countries expect from developing trade with these other countries and blocs. This explains the keenness of the GCC countries to begin negotiations with the EU, where trade between the GCC countries and the EU formed about 19 percent of the GCC's gross trade with the outside world in 2005, compared to its trade with Japan (15 percent) and China (6 percent). However, GCC trade with China is growing substantially.

As for the European Free Trade Association (EFTA), the GCC countries have been keen to negotiate with it because it is an extension of the EU. With regard to India, Pakistan, Turkey, Singapore and the common market of South American countries (MERCOSUR), there exist opportunities in these countries to market products from the GCC states—hence the GCC has given priority to negotiations with these states. Also, negotiations with Australia, New Zealand and South Korea are being launched.

Stages of Negotiations with certain Countries and Economic Blocs

The free trade agreements that the GCC countries are negotiating are not restricted to trade in goods but involve several sectors including; services trade, investment, government purchases, countries of origin, and other aspects associated with commercial and economic relations among countries that are parties to the agreements. In this way, agreements comprise most aspects of the GCC's trade relations with other economic parties.

In order to facilitate the trade efforts of the GCC countries, the GCC delegation in Brussels designed a 'model' agreement covering all commercial and economic aspects relevant to GCC countries' negotiations with other states. Such a model agreement helps the GCC countries initiate proposals, negotiate conditions and develop opportunities to reinforce gains for their private and public economic sectors.

Potential Impacts of Free Trade Agreements on the Economic Security of the GCC Countries

Studies indicate that the spread of free trade agreements has changed the profile of international trade. Theoretically, these agreements aim to open and deepen commercial integration with other countries by reducing customs tariffs and encouraging competition. These agreements can complement the individual efforts of a state whose aim is to liberalize its economy. Yet various studies, including the World Bank's *Global Economics Prospects 2005* report, also point out that free trade agreements can have negative impacts—namely the exclusion of non-member states from these agreements, even if these states might be more competent as sources of goods and services. However, proponents of these agreements point out that the gains still exceed the losses.

In order to maximize the returns of liberalizing trade, the World Bank report recommends adopting a three-constituent strategy:[11]

* *Self-liberalization of trade in the countries concerned*: this is related to economic reforms, including liberalizing trade vis-à-vis the world, as has recently happened in Brazil, Chile and India, which have liberalized their foreign trade policies to improve productivity in their own economies. Studies by the World Bank indicate that two-thirds (i.e. 65 percent) of the amount of reduction in average customs tariffs in the world between 1983 and 2003 (which amounts to 21 percent) was due to internal economic reform; 25 percent of the remaining amount (i.e. 35 percent) was a result of the GATT since the Uruguay

round; and 10 percent resulted from free trade agreements. The World Bank strongly advocates that tariff reduction should stem from the course of internal economic reform carried out by the country in question.

- *Liberalizing multiple parties*: this liberalization aims to reinforce the gains of internal economic reforms by increasing opportunities for access to global markets—in other words, reinforcing the agendas of the WTO. This is of particular benefit to developing countries as it leaves their sources of competent goods and services imports at preferential exchange conditions untouched. Moreover, this liberalization facilitates the import demands of developing countries with regard to goods that are important to them, especially agricultural goods. However, this undermines the progress of the Doha round of negotiations within the context of the WTO. Agreements on free trade zones ought not to be considered a preferred option to multi-party liberalization, since developing countries might lose out if they all sign individual agreements of preferential trade (free zones) with the United States, Japan and the EU.

- *Regional openness*: this option refers to the potential benefits and advantages of regional economic openness as a preparatory stage for a wider openness to the world.

With regard to the strategy of the GCC countries, certain steps have been taken within the framework of recommendations of the World Bank. Firstly, the GCC states have been keen to open up their economies, and in this respect they are considered the most liberalized in their region and in the developing world in general. In addition, their efforts in economic reform and liberalization are continual. Secondly, the GCC states have moved toward multi-party liberalization by establishing free trade zones among themselves, which have developed into a Customs Union, and work is underway to complete the Gulf Common Market. There is also the fact that they have been actively involved in the Greater Arab Free Trade

Area (GAFTA). Thirdly, they have joined the WTO and are effectively participating in negotiations taking place within the organization.

As mentioned earlier, the GCC countries are conducting intense negotiations with most of their major commercial partners – which comprise more than 60 percent of their foreign trade – and aim to conclude free trade agreements with them. It is expected that these agreements will contribute to greater trade liberalization and increased competitiveness and opportunities for the GCC countries' access to the markets of these countries.

In general, reinforcing foreign trade between the GCC states and those countries of global economic importance contributes to greater economic security for the GCC countries by deepening common interests and conducting trade according to specific, predictable rules and judgments within a framework of transparent and stable commercial policies. The efforts of the GCC countries towards economic reform (liberalizing the internal economy) and economic development are promoted by liberalizing trade and encouraging competition. Likewise, the adoption of clear and transparent acts to liberalize trade, such as effective participation in the WTO and concluding free trade agreements with major commercial partners, contribute to achieving the goals of economic reform and development. Opening more markets to exports from the GCC countries is an important goal and free trade agreements have a vital role to play. In order to achieve this aim, these agreements are required to observe the following:

- The customs tariffs for other countries remain low, which can be achieved if external customs tariffs do not exceed 5 percent.
- There are limited exemptions, either for sectors or products. By reviewing the current negotiation proposals of the GCC countries in the sectors of goods and services, we find that there are very few sectors which are exempt—and no exemptions of note are to be found in products. Rather, any sector exemptions, if found, are not absolutes and might only be for a limited period and/or pertain to a particular style of importing services.

- Countries of origin should not be limited and this is something that the GCC countries are keen to resolve in their negotiations. Exhaustive negotiations were conducted between the GCC countries and the EU on this subject, in which the former demanded greater flexibility with regard to certain EU rules deemed too rigid, and which could impede exemption of some GCC products when they enter European markets. The EU relented and showed relative flexibility in this respect.

- Investment and intellectual property rights should be accorded attention. The GCC countries pay special attention to developing investment markets and applying the Principle of National Treatment to their investments abroad. The GCC countries have committed themselves to a number of international agreements concerned with intellectual property, and the agreements being negotiated include provisions specific to investment and intellectual property rights.

The keenness of the GCC countries to open up their economic bloc to the outside world through free trade agreements embodies their concern for broader integration with the global community. This aim is commensurable with the policies and goals of the GCC countries to encourage economic growth and development—thereby raising the economic affluence of their people.

The reassurance and security that exporters and investors feel with respect to the economic and trading stability of the GCC countries is a prerequisite to motivate local production. It is commonly known that the GCC countries possess great natural resources, especially in the energy sector, that exceed the needs of the local market. Therefore the maximum trading benefit of these resources requires the existence of foreign markets to support local demand as well as transparent, clear and concise laws of commercial exchange.

On the other hand, there are lucrative opportunities for investment in the GCC countries which many investors around the world look forward to taking advantage of. Needless to say, the reassurances felt by these investors with respect to investment laws and economic policies, as well as the existence of foreign markets for these investments and products, are prerequisites to attract these investors.

The attention the GCC countries accord to the completion of the requirements for economic openness between themselves, their effective participation in the WTO, and the conclusion of important free trade agreements between the GCC countries and their partners are necessary for growth, economic development and security in the GCC countries.

Conclusion

With the implementation of the Customs Union in 2003, unifying the policies of the GCC countries toward the outside world has become a prerequisite, to which the GCC countries have committed themselves by supporting collective negotiations with other countries. As mentioned above, the quest of the GCC countries to conclude free trade agreements is complementary to their efforts to liberalize their economies and reinforce regional economic integration. It is necessary that the GCC countries continue supporting collective negotiations, and harmonize their commercial policies with the requirements of these negotiations as well as the unified trade policy of the GCC.

It is expected that the conclusion of these agreements will contribute to developing trade between the GCC countries and other economically important countries, as well as those of growing importance in the global economy. To maximize benefit, the GCC countries ought to make their agreements with other countries include greater flexibility for countries of origin, along with fewer exemptions for their products, goods or services sectors. These agreements must also take into consideration the outlook and future development direction of the GCC countries. In this way, the agreements will complement the efforts of the GCC countries to diversify their economies and achieve the goals of their future development plans. Those agreements that take into consideration these aspects will contribute to the economic security of the GCC countries.

11

Growing Asian Economic Interest in the Arabian Gulf Region

S. Narayan

Asia's growing engagement with the Arabian Gulf region, particularly the Gulf Cooperation Council (GCC) countries, is a measure of the increasing importance of the GCC region as well as its relationship with Asia. The economic, strategic and security developments of the last few years have added fresh impetus to this engagement. There has also been a paradigm shift in GCC development strategies, which has led to greater integration with other Asian economies. This chapter examines the changes in trade, economic development strategy and energy security against the backdrop of issues linked to regional security and strategy.

The GCC States: Economic Developments and Policies

Following the 1970s, which saw a substantial increase in oil prices, GCC economic developments and policies can be broadly divided into four periods:

- The oil boom period (1981–1985) when high oil prices increased export revenues and helped to build up current account surpluses that were used to finance imports and build infrastructure.
- The period up to the 1990s when the continued erosion of oil prices weakened GCC economies and resulted in external financial imbalances.

- The economic adjustment period that was disrupted by the regional crisis in Iraq.
- The current scenario of rapidly growing oil revenues and financial stability.

During the initial years, in an attempt to insulate their economies from external inflation, the GCC established a *de facto* peg with the US dollar, which led to the significant rate appreciation of their currencies. Simultaneously, there were increased expenditures on development projects, with some GCC countries actively pursuing policies to promote basic industries based on their vast hydrocarbon reserves.

Increases in expenditures in the 1980s coupled with simultaneous decreases in oil revenues affected fiscal balances. Adjustment policies that were implemented during this period included reductions in capital outlays from around 21 percent of GDP during 1981–1985 to 13 percent of GDP during 1986–1989. The external current account position shifted to a deficit of 1 percent during the same period.

The Iraqi regional crisis affected several GCC countries. The budget deficit of Kuwait exceeded 100 percent of GDP in 1990–1991 while that of Saudi Arabia increased to 17 percent of GDP, and the aggregate current account deficits of the GCC countries increased to 7 percent of their GDP. By 1994, although their stock of external debt had stabilized at about 12 percent of GDP, debt service payments had increased sharply.

It became evident in the early 1990s that high dependence on oil revenues was unlikely to lead to sustainable growth. Several experts suggested privatization and economic restructuring as survival strategies. The unwillingness of regional governments to open up in the 1990s was cited as one reason why these countries were unable to participate in the economic boom of those years. Privatization drives commenced in Saudi Arabia during the Sixth Development Plan (1995–2000), and subsequent developments have substantially increased the role of the private sector. Other GCC members have also adopted similar strategies. Current developments in Dubai are indicative of the aggressive way in which private capital is being wooed. The vision of building an alternate financial, business, entertainment and tourism hub has prompted the initiation of several mega projects in Dubai, as well as policy measures that enable greater integration with global markets and financial centers.

These remedial measures have received a major boost due to the recent increases in oil prices. GCC oil revenues have increased substantially and have helped these economies to reach a comfortable fiscal and current account surplus position. The average real GDP growth was estimated to be 6.9 percent in 2005. This strong fiscal stimulus is spurring economic activity in the region. In addition, efforts by GCC governments to diversify economies and foster private sector development have resulted in a positive investment climate.

Table 11.1

Real GDP Growth Rate in the GCC States

Country	1980	1985	1990	1995	2000	2001	2002	2003	2004	2005
Bahrain	7.5	-0.9	7.3	3.9	5.3	4.5	5.1	5.7	5.5	5.3
Kuwait	-20.4	-4.3	-26.2	1.4	1.9	0.7	-0.5	9.7	7.2	3.2
Oman	6.1	14.5	8.4	4.8	5.5	7.5	1.7	1.4	2.5	3.6
Qatar	-1.0	-13.0	-14.6	5.5	9.1	4.5	7.3	8.5	9.9	5.1
Saudi Arabia	7.9	-4.1	10.6	0.5	4.9	0.5	0.1	7.2	5.3	4.1
UAE	-1.8	-2.5	16.6	7.0	12.3	3.5	1.9	7.0	5.7	4.5

Source: IMF World Economic Outlook, 2006.

High oil revenues have transformed the government budgets and the balance of payments of the oil-producing countries. Considerable surpluses are now available for investment in economic development projects. Past lessons have been learned well and diversification away from hydrocarbons remains an important objective for these economies.

[259]

Some of these countries, most notably the United Arab Emirates, have adopted a more ambitious agenda that focuses on certain unique opportunities. Given its geographical location – midway in time zones between New York and Hong Kong – Dubai seeks to position itself as a major financial hub and hopes to offer a better alternative than Singapore. Initial efforts have included the opening of commodity trading exchanges as well as a more liberal financial markets architecture, but much remains to be done to achieve this objective. In short, it is possible to perceive that these countries are pursuing a multi-pronged strategy, which is quite different from the public expenditure-oriented development strategy that characterized the earlier oil boom period.

The increases in oil prices have had a lesser impact on the world economy than in the 1970s or the 1980s, primarily because economies have grown larger and more diversified. It is possible to assume that, given the growth of the global economy, and the emergence of high-growth countries in Asia, oil revenues are likely to be sustained over the medium term. That is to say, the GCC countries could reasonably expect the current account and revenue surpluses to continue for the next few years. It may be difficult to predict the near term volatility of oil prices, dependant as it is on several exogenous factors, including peace in the region, but it can safely be assumed that net revenues in excess of US$50 per barrel will continue to accrue to the oil-producing countries for considerable time. Therefore, the development strategy can take these opportunities into account. It is indeed a primary objective to channel revenues into the manufacturing sector, with a focus on downstream value additions based on petroleum products or petrochemicals. Availability of cheaper energy sources could direct investment towards energy intensive industries like aluminum smelting. At the same time, it is important to take note of the increasing additions to the population and the labor market. Growth must take note of job creation. The construction industry offers one such opportunity. The first phase of the boom investments went to real estate and tourism-related construction, which has helped to sustain current growth.

However, the emerging challenges for the economic management of the GCC states are several. Fiscal balances have become more structural in nature, while at the same time the GCC countries are undergoing major demographic changes characterized by a rapidly growing and younger population, with important implications for the labor market. The dominance of the public sector, restrictions in private sector development and rigidity of domestic institutions are some of the other challenges that these countries face.

There is public sector dominance in these economies ranging from 34 percent in UAE to 54 percent in Saudi Arabia. This is because in the initial years of the oil boom, in the absence of a private sector, government invested not only in public services, but across the board in industry as well. Thus the GCC countries face important policy challenges and opportunities in view of an uncertain oil market outlook.

On the fiscal front, there is a need to replenish ageing capital stock and to carry out maintenance. The additional debt-servicing cost incurred during the lean years must be taken into account. Expenditure in the social sector has increased in proportion to the growing population. Greater expenditures on education, healthcare, housing and provision of basic public amenities will continue to demand a flow of public investments. The traditional approach of absorbing large numbers of labor force entrants into public employment with guaranteed wages and extended social benefits may not be a workable strategy any longer. There is a need to review the employment strategy, putting greater reliance on private sector opportunities.

The challenge is to use the new oil wealth more wisely than before. The net assets of the OPEC member countries crashed from a level below US$160 billion to an almost negative $60 billion in 1995. It is important that the new oil revenues are conserved and put to work more efficiently. An important aspect of this strategy would be to create productive assets in the non-oil sector, which can grow and create wealth that is independent of government subsidies. In the past, political pressure on governments to spend on military items had deprived other sectors of development funds.

A major concern is the rapid population growth of the GCC states in comparison to their labor productivity. The high birth rates of the last two decades will result in the national labor force increasing by 6 percent, or an additional 7 million nationals in the labor market in the next decade. If government revenues remain stagnant, per capita incomes will shrink over the next ten years, unless there is corresponding growth in other sectors.

It is against this backdrop that diplomatic initiative and economic dialogue between Asian countries and the GCC states have been heightened over the last few years.

The GCC's Evolving Shift toward Asia

At a broader level, the GCC's evolving shift toward Asia is logical. Asia consumes 23 million barrels per day of crude oil, which is 30 percent of the world's demand. The GCC exports two-thirds of its oil output to Asia, which could more than double by 2020. Oil demand increased by 12 percent between 1998 and 2004. Nearly 30 percent of that increase came from China, whose economy grew rapidly during that period. Demand for oil grew three times as fast in 2004 as in 2003, and for the first time since the 1970s, OPEC was producing at full capacity. In 2003, the US-led war disrupted Iraqi exports, while disturbances in other oil-producing countries such as Nigeria and Venezuela increased supply anxieties and helped to boost prices by an average of 15 percent. In recent years, billions of dollars have been channeled into speculative investments in oil futures, further exacerbating the price increase.

Moreover, more than half of GCC exports go to Asian countries, while one third of GCC imports are from Asia. Together, the GCC–Asia oil and non-oil trade figure is approximately US$200 billion. This figure will certainly grow, since negotiations for free trade agreements are currently underway with China, India, Japan and Pakistan. There is also a global trade shift away from the developed countries while trade within

Asia as well as into and out of Asia is growing much more rapidly than with the developed world.

Cooperation and greater linkages between the two regional blocs in the oil sector is thus a key element to ensuring supply security for Asian consumers and demand security for GCC oil producers. The rise in energy demand by Asian countries is likely to influence the long-term political economy of the GCC countries and shape international relations in the coming decades.

Beyond the oil and trade dynamics there is the human element. Approximately 70 percent of the GCC labor force is made up of expatriates, who send home remittances amounting to nearly US$30 billion a year. Again, of the 12.5 million expatriates in the region, about 70 percent are Asians. In the initial years, this stock of manpower consisted largely of wageworkers. Over the last decade and a half, there has been a steady upgrading of the skill levels of these expatriate workers, as more and more professionals including engineers, doctors, accountants and financial experts have joined the workforce. Several entrepreneurs have taken advantage of opportunities in these regions and are making significant contributions to the GCC economies.

Apart from the increasing level of economic engagement, recent political developments in the region have sharpened awareness and interest in Asia. Events in Iraq and Iran have contributed in no small measure to heightened security concerns. In the post 9/11 period, the world views engagement with the entire region as being vital, in order to ensure that international terrorism does not spread. For Asia in particular, this region forms the backyard, and it has therefore increased diplomatic as well as strategic initiatives in the last five years.

Asian concerns and the thrust for increasing engagement with Gulf states stems from the growing energy needs over the last decade of the rapidly expanding Asian economies, most importantly China, and more recently, India.

Finally, there is also some degree of mutual rivalry between emerging Asian economies, such as China and India, and developed economies such as Japan, Korea and to a lesser extent, Singapore, all of which are vying for opportunities in the region. This new-found interest from the Asian countries stems from their dependence on oil supplies, although it is no longer restricted to energy alone.

Between 1998 and 2004, oil prices virtually tripled in current dollars. From 1999–2005, oil revenues to the OPEC countries were on average US$100 billion higher each year than in the preceding seven years.

Table 11.2
OPEC Basket Price (1998–2005)

1998	1999	2000	2001	2002	2003	2004	2005
12.28	17.47	27.60	23.12	24.36	28.10	36.05	54.26

Source: MEES and OPEC (www.opec.org/home/basket.aspx).

Supply during these years was hampered by the lack of investments in the oilfields, refineries, pipelines, ports and ships. This was partly because the low oil prices prevailing in the late 1980s and most of the 1990s, constrained the ability to invest in these sectors. The rise in oil production was 9.8 percent during this period, with OPEC contributing 7.5 percent. This was lower than the increase in demand and inventory levels fell. Increases in demand were exacerbated by the disruptions in supplies from Venezuela, Nigeria and the developments in Iraq. These uncertainties fuelled enhanced speculations on oil price futures, most importantly in the New York Mercantile Exchange (NYMEX), further adding to the volatility of the price increases. The mismatch caused prices to rise even though, on the aggregate level, overall supplies matched demand.

These price increases resulted in growing incomes for the oil exporters, as has been pointed out. Between 1998 and 2005, oil export revenues of the OPEC Gulf states rose by an estimated 200 percent. The average oil income per capita also rose significantly.

Table 11.3
Balance of Payments and Fiscal Developments (1999–2005)

Foreign Balance Effects	1990–2000 Average	2002	2003	2004 (estimate)	2005 (estimate)
Export Revenues: Bahrain, Kuwait, Oman, Saudi Arabia, UAE	109.2	152.4	195.0	262.6	276.1
Current Account Balance	-0.7	19.7	47.2	94.1	96.4
Fiscal Effects					
Fiscal Expenditures: Bahrain, Kuwait, Oman, Saudi Arabia, UAE	57.9	158.6	188.5	26.0	244.9
Fiscal Revenues	66.4	151.6	162.0	213.3	213.8

Source: *MENA Economic Developments and Prospects 2005: Oil Booms and Revenue Management,* World Bank.

The figures for the year 2005 are probably underestimated but the huge improvements in the fiscal balance over this period are evident. According to the International Monetary Fund (IMF) there was a substantial increase in savings by these countries from their export revenues, and investments in banks in the industrialized countries increased by 46 percent. Between 1999 and 2004, the Saudi Arabian Monetary Authority (SAMA) recorded an 84 percent increase in assets. Similar investments from the other oil-producing countries are also visible. Reserves in Kuwait, Qatar, the UAE, Bahrain and Oman rose by over 50 percent. An interesting phenomenon was that more funds were deposited at home rather than overseas, probably due to political as well as economic factors. Tensions with the United States precluded large-scale investments there.

Saudi Arabia has been one of the biggest beneficiaries of the oil price increases. The increase had its impact on the balance of payments, the national debt, GDP and investment. The development of the Haradh field was accelerated to increase production capacity. Government debt fell from 83 percent of GDP to 66 percent in 2004. After several years of neglect, government spending on infrastructure increased substantially. There is a strong pressure on public expenditure due to high rates of unemployment. It also faces serious security threats, including terrorism. The government is reported to have increased security spending by 50 percent in 2004. Saudi Arabia has experienced over two decades of large budget and trade deficits, but its finances are on a turnaround.

The UAE economy has also benefited from high oil prices and revenues and has accumulated large current account surpluses. The consolidated government balance improved from a deficit of 10.3 percent of GDP to a surplus of 8.1 percent of GDP. The non-oil and private sectors have responded with strong development initiatives, especially in Dubai.

Kuwait has also benefited substantially from the increases in oil revenues. Oil revenues account for about 90 percent of the country's income. Oil export revenues have doubled between 2002 and 2005, and the government budget reveals a surplus for the sixth consecutive year. There has been considerable reduction of the country's debt burden.

These energy supply-related fiscal changes have an impact on relationships with different Asian countries. On the one hand, the heightened interest in securing energy supplies brought all the major Asian countries closer to the GCC, and on the other, the GCC states perceived these developing countries in Asia as opportunities for the investment of their surpluses, an alternative that would not be linked to the fortunes of the US economy. Different Asian countries, therefore, have slightly different agendas in dealing with the Gulf countries, although the common denominator of oil security underpins all the interactions.

Developing GCC–India Economic Ties

The GCC region is the major source of crude oil supplies for India. Traditionally, Indian public sector companies have favored annual contracts either with government or government-owned entities, supplementing their requirements through spot purchases. The energy relationship has been developed and maintained at the highest level in the state-owned oil producing entities. India is convinced that for considerable time to come, the major source of supplies will continue to be the GCC region.

Energy is at the heart of the economic relationship between India and the GCC, but is not the sum of it. Bilateral non-energy trade between India and the GCC countries is also on the rise. According to some estimates, bilateral non-oil trade between India and the GCC states is now approaching US$18 billion. High oil prices and soaring revenues have boosted growth in the GCC economies, and this in turn has fed into a growing demand for imports, creating an increasingly attractive market for Indian businesses. The UAE, which also serves as a hub for Indian trade with the rest of the Arabian Gulf, Pakistan and Afghanistan, is now the destination for about nine percent of Indian exports. In fact, the UAE is one of India's ten most important trading partners. The GCC region as a whole accounted for around 12 percent of Indian exports in 2004–2005, making it India's second largest export market. Meanwhile, the Gulf is home to over 3.5 million Indian nationals who are estimated to generate between US$6–$8 billion of annual remittance flows back home.

India is also becoming an increasingly attractive destination for investors looking for a stake in its growth story. Private equity funds and institutional funds are seeking investment opportunities in the financial markets as well as the production and services sectors. The last two years have witnessed a substantial increase in investor interest. Several financial institutions are active in the secondary market. Mindful of these substantial and growing economic ties, Indian policymakers have also added the GCC countries to their list of preferred partners for Free Trade Agreements (FTAs), which may be finalized as early as 2008.

The developing GCC–India economic ties neatly dovetail with growing political and strategic ties. Counter-terrorism cooperation is a key area of mutual interest, the potential for which has only begun to be explored. In this connection, it should be noted that Saudi Arabia has significant influence over India's historic adversary Pakistan. Meanwhile, China is also deepening its ties with the region, which will impel New Delhi to do likewise. India has an early advantage in that it has more developed naval capabilities and enjoys geographic proximity. The latter aspect has already been reflected in the naval exercises that India has conducted with many Gulf states, including Saudi Arabia as well as Iran. Although India's ability to support and sustain naval operations at such long ranges is not yet fully developed, the importance of such exercises cannot be underestimated. India, like China, is emerging as a new strategic player in the Gulf. While India and China will never rival the United States with respect to its power projection capacity in the region, they may well occupy a position some day similar to that of France and the United Kingdom, introducing new realities into the strategic equation in the Gulf.

Indeed, it seems likely that some Gulf countries such as Saudi Arabia already understand this. It was clear, for example, that King Abdullah bin Abdul Aziz Al Saud's visit to New Delhi in January 2006 was intended not only to help consolidate a burgeoning commercial relationship, but also to enhance ties in other fields, as illustrated by the agreement signed on counter-terrorism cooperation. India is potentially an important strategic actor for Saudi Arabia in more than one respect. Within the region, Riyadh will be keen to balance New Delhi's growing energy relationship with Tehran, perhaps concerned that it may develop strategic dimensions. The visit in 2006 helped to reaffirm old ties and also saw several industry specific initiatives:

- Saudi Arabia's Zamil Steel Industries announced that it would establish a US$20 million factory in the Indian state of Maharashtra to design and produce pre-engineered steel buildings.
- Zamil Industrial Company, has planned to increase its investment in India to US$30 million next year in order to establish an additional manufacturing facility in the country.

- A leading Saudi investor, Fawaz A. Al-Hokair, signed a MoU with Pratap C. Reddy, Executive Chairman of Apollo Hospitals, and a leading Indian health services group. Al-Hokair said he would invest about US$100 million in building three state-of-the-art Apollo hospitals and twenty clinics in the Kingdom.
- The agreements also covered a joint investment company, a water service project, pipe manufacturing, television development, medical and healthcare services, strategic partnership on mortgage financing as well as oil and gas equipment.

While there are great opportunities for the development of strategic ties between the GCC states and India, there are also policy dilemmas— mainly for New Delhi. India will be keen to avoid having to choose between its increasingly important energy ties with the countries in the region and its rapidly developing strategic relationship with the United States. India has been careful to adopt a neutral stance, and has distanced itself from events in Iraq and Palestine.

Nonetheless, there are some potential longer-term dilemmas, including the fact that Saudi Arabia's engagement with China and India raises some interesting questions about its relationship with the United States. Both these Asian countries offer great opportunities for commercial cooperation without the political baggage that accompanies the relationship with the United States or even Europe. Neither China nor India, for example, would ever press Saudi Arabia on the pace of its internal political reform. Although neither China nor India offer a short or even medium-term strategic alternative to Saudi Arabia's relationship with the United States, a deepening of such ties may well be intended as a signal to Washington not to take its strategic partnership with Riyadh for granted.

China and the GCC: Flourishing Ties

In the initial years, China paid little attention to the Arabian Gulf region. In 1956, Egypt became the first Arab country to establish diplomatic relations with China and it was not until 1990 that Beijing established ties with all of the GCC littoral states. Saudi Arabia was the last GCC country to establish ties with China in July 1990. All of its smaller neighbors had by then exchanged diplomats with China, some much earlier.

Until recently, Sino–GCC relations could be characterized as being generally lackluster and uneventful. However, this situation has changed and in the past few years relations have flourished. Most noticeably, Beijing has rapidly widened and extended its links with the region and substantially upgraded its economic ties. Arab countries are currently China's eighth largest trading partners and the Gulf states represent a very important trading bloc. Since 1991, China–GCC trade has surged from US$1.5 billion to $20 billion in 2004. In 2005, trade skyrocketed again, climbing to $33.8 billion—36 percent more than that in the previous year. Total region-wide Sino–Arab trade stands at $36.7 billion, underscoring the GCC's dominance in this trade. At the same time, China has signed deals worth more than $100 billion with the GCC's large neighbor, Iran

At the heart of the new interest is certainly the need to secure long-term oil supplies. Although oil is not the only factor behind Beijing's thinking, the importance of energy cannot be underestimated in examining Sino–Arab relations. China is the world's second-biggest consumer and third-biggest importer of oil. China's oil consumption surpassed Japan's in 2003 and now stands at 6.5 million barrels per day, compared to 20 million barrels per day for the United States.

Chinese oil demand has been rising at an astonishing rate – increasing on average per annum by more than one million barrels per day – comprises about 40 percent of the world's increased demand and is a major influence on the record high international prices for oil. The International Energy Agency (IEA) predicts that by 2030, Chinese imports will equal US imports, impressing upon China the need to ensure a stable supply of oil.

It is estimated that by 2010, oil will represent between 51.4 to 52.6 percent of China's energy needs, up from 29.1 percent in 2000. According to the IEA, China currently imports 32 percent of its oil, but this is likely to double between now and the end of the decade. China's gas consumption is rising at an even faster pace, with imports projected to increase from zero in 2000 to 20–25 million cubic meters by 2010.

Today, 58 percent of China's oil imports come from the Middle East, mostly from the GCC states. China has adopted a strategy of geographical diversification by investing in foreign oil/gas fields in more than 20 countries, including Venezuela, Nigeria and Australia. Diversification away from the Middle East, however, has its limits. Two-thirds of proven oil reserves are located in the region, mostly in the Arabian Gulf. Similarly, many of the oil reserves in non-Middle Eastern countries are rapidly being depleted. The IEA predicts that Chinese oil imports from the Middle East will rise to at least 70 percent by 2015, underpinning the fact that the future of the Chinese economy is inextricably tied to the Middle East.

The lion's share of GCC trade lies in Chinese imports of oil and exports of cheap textiles. In 2004, China and the GCC states started negotiations on a Free Trade Agreement (FTA). These talks coincided with the new China–Arab Forum, a biannual dialogue of leaders from China and the 22 states of the Arab League (which includes the GCC states). The Chinese Ministry of Commerce expects Sino–Arab trade to reach $100 billion by 2010. At the end of 2005, Chinese investment in Arab countries stood at $5 billion, while Arab investment in China was $700 million, according to the Chinese Ministry of Commerce. Trade ties are set to grow further if free trade agreement (FTA) talks bear fruit. The third round of negotiations took place in January 2006, and the FTA was expected to be concluded in 2007.

There is a clear push for economic and trade gains as well. Located on the Dubai–Oman road is the 1.2 kilometer-long Dragon Mart complex, which houses over 4,000 Chinese businesses and covers 150,000 'square meters and aims to become the largest trading hub abroad for Chinese products. These businesses are looking at the Arabian Gulf region as a future market for their products. Trade with the GCC states has quadrupled in the last ten years. Bilateral trade with Saudi Arabia increased

30 percent between 2005 and 2006 alone. Total cross-border capital flows between the GCC and the rest of Asia are predicted to climb from $15 billion today to over $300 billion by 2020.

Cultural ties are also strengthening with the establishment of the China–Arab Forum and the launch of a dialogue between China and the Arab League. According to Chinese newspaper reports, the government has provided scholarships for students from more than 10 Middle East countries and China is planning to train hundreds of professionals in fields including agriculture and biochemistry. However, in the 2006 *International Energy Outlook Report*, the US Department of Energy (USDOE) warned that the rising dependence of China on Middle Eastern oil supplies has geo-political implications, both for relations between the two countries as well as for the oil-consuming world as a whole.

The Gulf economic boom has added impetus to China's strategy. Gulf states have launched several infrastructure projects in agriculture, education, healthcare and information technology, providing more opportunities for Chinese groups. The investment arms of Gulf governments have also been seeking investments in Asia. Gulf money has gone into Chinese Initial Public Offerings (IPO), and the Kuwait Investment Authority bought $720 million worth of shares in the Industrial and Commercial Bank of China last year. McKinsey estimates that up to $250 billion would be available in the Gulf region for investments in Asia in the next ten years, with China being the largest recipient.

Among the GCC states, it is not surprising that China has the closest relations with Saudi Arabia—the world's largest oil-producing country. Today, China is Saudi Arabia's fourth largest importer and fifth largest exporter. Saudi Arabia is China's tenth largest importer and biggest oil supplier. The Saudis now account for almost 17 percent of China's oil imports and Saudi Arabia's oil exports to China increased to some 500,000 barrels per day in 2005, up from 440,000 barrels in 2004. This is set to increase further with Saudi oil giant Aramco agreeing to provide the China Petroleum and Chemical Corporation (Sinopec) with one million barrels per day by 2010. Saudi–China relations reached their zenith in April 2006 when King Abdullah became the first head of state to visit China since the establishment of bilateral ties. This was King Abdullah's first trip outside the Middle East since assuming power officially in 2005, potentially signaling a new strategic alignment. The summit in Beijing saw the signing of five agreements, including a landmark pact for expanding cooperation in oil, natural gas and minerals, as well as in the economic, trade and technical spheres. Taxation agreements were also signed and Saudi Arabia granted China a loan to improve infrastructure in the city of Aksu in China's oil-rich Xinjiang region. Saudi Arabia has also offered Chinese companies investment opportunities in the country's enormous infrastructure sector that includes petrochemicals, gas, desalination, power generation and railways and is worth an estimated $624 billion. Prior to that, China had also been busy negotiating a series of lucrative deals in the region. In March 2005, Sinopec signed an agreement with its Saudi counterpart, Saudi Aramco, to develop natural gas resources near the Ghawar field in the country's east. Ghawar is the largest conventional oilfield in the world.

Again in 2005, Saudi Aramco signed a $3.5 billion deal with Exxon Mobil and Sinopec for a joint oil refining and chemicals venture in Fujian Province in southern China. The deal involves the expansion of the existing refinery, a petrochemical plant and a joint marketing venture to operate 600 service stations in the province. Also in Fujian, Aramco said that the two sides agreed on the establishment of two joint ventures for an ethylene plant and marketing efforts in Fujian in 2006, as well as the operation of the joint project for integrated refining and ethylene production by 2009. Also, discussions are underway with Sinopec regarding investment in a plant in the northern Chinese port of Qingdao.

China has sought to secure new energy sources and at the same time deepen relations with existing energy producers. Sinopec, China's largest oil refiner, is involved in about 120 projects in the Middle East, most of which are in the Gulf region, and is seeking more opportunities. In December 2005, China and OPEC launched an energy dialogue.

China has also sought the assistance of Saudi Arabia and Kuwait to invest in downstream infrastructure, including oil refineries and petrochemical plants to boost domestic capacity. This includes the recent agreement between Sinopec and Kuwait Petroleum Corporation to develop China's southern Guangdong Province. The deal, which is worth $5 billion, could become China's biggest foreign joint venture in the petrochemicals industry.

Kuwait has said that it is studying a number of other ventures. Kuwait currently provides China with 200,000 barrels of oil per day, which is set to double in the next few years. Similarly, China's Sinopec has a ten percent stake in an international consortium led by Chevron that is bidding for the $8.5 billion Project Kuwait.

Other GCC states have witnessed lower trade volumes compared to Saudi Arabia. Trade has tended to focus on the export of crude oil to China whereas joint projects and sharing of technical expertise has been more limited. Nevertheless, economic ties have increased substantially. Chinese goods are increasingly replacing Western goods throughout the region, as they are no longer considered poor or inferior. This trend looks set to continue in the event of the China–GCC Free Trade Agreement coming into force.

In 2002, the total volume of trade between China and Oman was $1.506 billion. By 2004, according to the International Monetary Fund, it had jumped to $4.4 billion. Oman is now China's third largest oil supplier after Saudi Arabia and Iran. The trade volume between China and the United Arab Emirates amounted to $3.895 billion, with imports from the United Arab Emirates consisting of oil and petroleum-based products.

Bilateral trade between China and Kuwait in 2002 was $727 million and has expanded rapidly since then with the series of high-profile deals discussed above. Among the Arab countries, Kuwait has had the longest relations with China and is the largest supplier of preferential official loans to China. From 1982–2001, the Kuwait Fund for Arab Economic Development had provided China with loans worth $620 million on favorable terms. In September 2006, Beijing announced an initial public offering of the Industrial and Commercial Bank of China. The Kuwait Investment Authority is reported to have invested $720 million in shares, with the Qatar Investment Authority investing a further $206 million.

Concurrently, China has sought to capitalize on rapid growth in Qatar, especially in the country's booming construction industry. Whilst the volume of trade has been relatively small, it shows an upsurge, touching $896 million in 2005, compared to just $390 million in 2004 and a minuscule $90 million in 1999. At just $110 million, the total volume of trade between Bahrain and China is the least among the GCC countries. In itself, this causes little surprise since Bahrain is the least wealthy of the GCC states due to its lack of oil resources.

China has skillfully exploited its comparative advantages. It does not carry the historical baggage of being a colonial power nor has it laid out a vision or a policy to transform the region like the United States. China also has a huge market that is very attractive to rich Gulf investors. Similarly, China has been more opportunistic and willing to engage those whom the United States has sought to isolate, including Sudan, Iran and Iraq (under Saddam Hussein). The 9/11 attacks and the subsequent difficulties that Arabs are facing in entering the United States has resulted in a sharp decline in visitors, especially from the Arabian Gulf, further tarnishing the US image and creating more opportunities for China.

China has also been strengthening its military capacity along its Middle East oil supply routes from Central Asia through to Iran. This is a direct response to the Chinese fear that the United States, as the pre-eminent power in the Middle East, could possibly impede Chinese oil imports and thus severely damage its economy. As such, the Chinese government wants to reduce the vulnerability of its Middle Eastern oil supply to US power. This need coincides with Chinese moves to modernize its navy. To date, Beijing has expressed no desire to police the

[275]

Arabian Gulf. Nevertheless, China has clear intentions to boost its presence in the South China Sea and Indian Ocean, and in keeping with its emerging power status, may one day seek to maintain a naval presence in the Middle East.

GCC Relations with other Asian Countries

Japan's New National Energy Strategy calls for increasing the ratio of Hinomaru oil (that is, oil developed and imported through domestic producers), from the current 15 percent to 40 percent by 2030. This will lead to further political involvement in the GCC states as well as in Iran. Japanese policy makers have realized that oil supply diversification has become an unachievable goal, and that the Arabian Gulf will remain a major source of supply for the foreseeable future. Energy conservation strategies have also been unable to provide an absolute alternative to Middle Eastern oil supplies. As a result, ensuring the security of energy supply from Gulf countries is imperative for Japan. Consequently, Japan will make every effort to gain priority within oil projects vis-à-vis Chinese competitors. Japan is also interested in augmenting supplies from Iran and will therefore not precipitate any action that would affect its long-term interests.

ASEAN is clearly interested in pursuing closer cooperation with the GCC. For this purpose, the ASEAN Riyadh Committee was established in 2000. The Committee consists of the seven Ambassadors of ASEAN Member Countries in Saudi Arabia (Cambodia, Laos and Myanmar do not have their embassies in Riyadh). The ASEAN Riyadh Committee would welcome increased interaction with the GCC Secretariat. Since 1990, ASEAN and the GCC have traditionally held their annual ministerial meeting in New York on the sidelines of the UN General Assembly. The last meeting discussed several interesting ideas: holding a joint trade and investment seminar; promoting inter-faith dialogue; and institutionalizing ASEAN–GCC cooperation through a MoU between the Secretariats of

ASEAN and the GCC. Another very useful process is the Asian Cooperation Dialogue (ACD) initiated in June 2002 by Thailand. All six GCC Members and the 10 ASEAN Member Countries are in the ACD. Saudi Arabia and the Russian Federation joined the ACD this year at the Fourth ACD Ministerial Meeting in Islamabad in April 2005. Qatar hosted the Fifth ACD Ministerial Meeting in 2006. Through the ACD, the Gulf states have ample opportunity to increase their interactions with ASEAN Member Countries and with East Asia. Food and energy security are the high priority issues that require increased cooperation between the two sides.

The Asia–Africa Summit has given rise to another avenue for the Gulf to cooperate with countries in Asia as well as Africa. This forum is the Asia–Africa Sub-Regional Organizations Cooperation (AASROC), in which ASEAN is the coordinator for the Asian sub-regional organizations. One can expect to hear more about AASROC in the near future as Egypt and South Africa volunteered to host the next Asia–Africa Ministerial Meeting in 2007 and the Second Asia–Africa Summit in 2009 respectively.

In addition to these inter-governmental processes, there are also parallel "track two" channels like the Boao Forum for Asia (BFA), based on China's Hainan Island, and the Asia–Middle East Dialogue (initiated by Singapore in June 2005), in which cooperation ideas can be explored and developed. Singapore is paying greater attention to investments in the GCC and an increasing number of business and government delegations have been visiting the Arabian Gulf states. While the primary interest is in the UAE, Singaporean entities are viewing other countries as well. Singapore has recognized that Dubai may develop as a rival location for tourism, as well as financial and retail services, and is therefore focusing seriously on emerging opportunities in Abu Dhabi.

The overall picture is one of increasing engagement between Asia and the GCC. On the part of the growing Asian economies, there is recognition that the Gulf will continue to remain the most stable source of oil supplies. The competing claims of different countries means that each must engage with the GCC over a wide range of issues, not necessarily related to oil. The GCC countries also view Asia as the region that is growing faster than others in the world, and proximity as well as history lends a special nature to the relationship. There are also surplus oil revenues that need to be invested, and on current considerations, returns on investments in China, India and other fast-growing Asian countries outweigh opportunities in the developed world.

There is also real concern about finding an alternative to security dependence on the United States, especially after the Iraq war. China and India are also viewing the GCC in terms of their own strategic and security needs. India in particular would like to see healthy relationships that would enable it to tackle security and terrorism-related concerns with full GCC cooperation. India has always been concerned that several groups inimical to the country have been using bases in some Gulf countries and a closer relationship can help to obviate these concerns.

These macro-level objectives need to be converted into real opportunities. A problem encountered in translating these ideas into new initiatives is the difference in approval processes in various countries. There are incidents of Gulf investors waiting interminably for investment clearances in China and many investors consider the Indian market to be slow and non-transparent. At the same time, retailers from China have yet to understand the demand patterns in Gulf markets while Indian investors in GCC financial markets miss the flexibility of regulations that the Indian market affords. There is need for a framework that can convert intentions into action, and eventually into real gains for all. This is the paradigm sought by all the actors. A possible framework can be perceived in several agreements signed between Saudi Arabia and India, which *inter alia,* include the following activities:

- Expanding and diversifying mutual trade and investments.
- Supporting entrepreneurs in both countries to harness each other's strengths.

[278]

- Cooperating in the fields of information and communication technology, agriculture, biotechnology and non-conventional energy technologies. India has agreed to assist in setting up an ICT Center of Excellence and institutes of higher learning in Saudi Arabia, involving both education and research in the field of technology. India would offer opportunities for Saudi students to pursue postgraduate and doctorate programs in Indian technical institutions, and enhance cooperation in human resource development related to telecommunications.

- Developing a joint strategic energy partnership based on complementarities and interdependence. The elements of this partnership would include:
  - ensuring reliable, stable and increased volume of crude supplies through "evergreen" long-term contracts;
  - launching cooperative and joint ventures in public and private sectors, upstream and downstream oil and gas sectors in both countries, as well as in third countries;
  - promoting Saudi investments in oil refining, marketing and storage in India; and
  - exploring joint ventures for gas-based fertilizer plants in Saudi Arabia.

This framework offers a broad guideline for a possible approach that could be adopted. Such an approach would have three main pillars:

- *Leveraging existing relationships, most importantly in energy*: For India, securing energy sources and supply is a priority, and therefore all alternatives including long-term agreements, exclusive contracts as well as joint investments could be explored.

- *Sharing India's strengths in the knowledge and services sectors*: This could be done through outreach in education and healthcare, training opportunities in information technology (IT) and software, as well as in GCC skill development programs. There should also be greater opportunities in the Indian financial markets for investors, both individuals and institutions. India should position itself, vis-à-vis China, as a provider of services, as a place to make market profits, and not necessarily as a supplier of consumer goods.

• *Setting up an institutional mechanism to help entrepreneurs and institutions:* Such an institution, working at both ends, would assist in overcoming the process hurdles that hinder smooth development. It should serve as a clearing house that could assist in obtaining host country approvals in a time-bound manner. It is interesting that there is now consensus among GCC investors that it is necessary to develop alternatives to investments in developed countries, particularly the United States, and that Asia does offer such an alternative. Many countries, especially China and India, stand to benefit, and it is in India's interest to promote its credentials as the superior investment location offering attractive opportunities for market-based returns, and to strengthen institutional ties that would herald an era of joint cooperative development between India and the GCC in both the goods and services sectors.

TERRORISM AND ORGANIZED CRIME IN THE GULF REGION

12

Terrorism: Causes of Dissemination and Methods of Combating

Fouad Allam

Terrorism has become an international phenomenon that is no longer restricted to a particular region, yet there is no coordination between states to implement a system with which to combat terrorism on the global level. In the meantime it has been observed that the causes fueling the growth of terrorist thinking are broadening and global acts of terrorism are increasing.

The destructive effects of terrorism are no longer hidden. In addition to the loss of human life, infrastructure and other such tangibles, terrorism now threatens the economic, social and political status quo of nations. These effects are no longer restricted to the countries where such crimes are committed— their destructive effects now extend to other nations.

In this chapter we will deal with the definition of terrorism and address those factors that help disseminate terrorist thought, and examine whether those factors are global or specific to some countries. Emphasis is primarily placed on terrorism that has a religious base in view of the fact that it is this form which is currently most widespread, especially in the Arab world.

The Definition of Terrorism

There have been many attempts to define terrorism and definitions have multiplied conspicuously, although they do all agree on certain elements. The problem centers round the fact that no agreed definition has been issued by any of the United Nations' (UN) agencies that all countries would be obliged to recognize. This is due to differences in opinion among countries regarding organizations that commit acts of violence—in particular the goals of these organizations. Some countries perceive organizations that resist occupation as terrorist groups, even though the UN Charter acknowledges the use of violence to resist occupation. Meanwhile, other countries consider such organizations and their actions as legitimate.

This study is inclined towards defining terrorism as "an act by an individual or a group directed against society for political purposes." Or more specifically, "the use of violence – in its material and incorporeal forms – to exercise influence on individuals, groups or governments, and create an atmosphere of instability and insecurity to affect beliefs and dominant social, economic, cultural and political conditions, which enjoy consensus in the state and represent the national interests of the country."

By employing violent methods, terrorism usually threatens innocent lives in order to intimidate the bulk of the population and spread fear—albeit by resorting to religious, social or political pretences.

Factors Abetting the Dissemination of Terrorist Thinking

In the 1960s, the world witnessed an unprecedented movement in the history of national liberation. Empires, in their conventional forms, vanished and the tempo of life and the nature of socio-economic relations changed. Consequently, political struggle acquired new forms, rules and laws. The role of political terrorism ascended and the effect of this rapid change even extended to the youth of the time. In 1968, the International Youth Movement emerged in France in the form of an anti-establishment revolt based on frequently incomprehensible motives. Its contagion spread to most countries of the world, promoting extremist movements, and ultimately terrorism became the new method for political struggle, replacing conventional war.

In the Middle East, certain fanatical religious movements were able to seize power in a number of Arab and Islamic countries, resulting in a prevailing atmosphere that helped spread terrorist thinking under the guise of religion. In addition, real disasters that afflicted Muslims in the world received little or no intervention from the world powers or the international community in general, which was felt to be exercising a form of double standards. This angered Muslims to the extent that certain individuals even volunteered to fight by the side of Islamic groups in certain parts of the world.

The escalation of terrorist operations in many countries in the world (the United States, Britain, Spain, Turkey, Saudi Arabia, Yemen, Egypt, Syria, Lebanon, Algeria, Morocco, Tunisia, Afghanistan, Pakistan, Iraq and the Philippines, among others) created an international atmosphere that encouraged individuals to believe that terrorism and terrorist crimes were the only means available to them to achieve political objectives.

Recent wars – particularly in Bosnia and Herzegovina, Afghanistan, and more recently in Iraq – attracted sympathizers to terrorist ideology and opportunities to obtain military training and acquire arms and explosive materials. In addition to this, a number of European countries continued to provide refuge to terrorist elements—be they convicted, fugitive, or wanted terrorists. Some of these countries have gone so far as to give these elements political asylum, thus helping them to continue practicing their terrorist activities and encouraging others to follow their example. Furthermore, the capacity of certain well-known terrorist leaders to avoid capture and arrest by today's international powers has added to their prestige. The most prominent examples are the leadership of the Taliban movement and the leaders of Al Qaeda – especially Osama bin Laden and Ayman Al Zawahri – whom the United States has failed to detain despite their continued appearance on global television networks. All this has emboldened leaders of terrorist organizations. Finally, the Internet has given rise to access very important and critical information. Such is the efficacy of the Internet that it is even possible to obtain information on how to manufacture explosives. Moreover, the Internet has facilitated communication between commanders and their bases and made the quick, confidential issuance of orders an easy task.

[285]

Local Factors

Local factors are divided into the areas of economy, society, politics, security and religion as follows:

Economic Causes

In the last few years the economic factor has become the focus of researchers and scholars when interpreting many aspects of human behavior—whether as individuals or groups. Economic factors are believed to have an effect on an individual's values, inclinations and personality. However, this effect is not restricted to the individual. Rather, it goes beyond this to affect the formation of social classes and determines their characteristics, distinctive features, culture and inherent conflicts or harmony with other classes. In addition, the economic factor affects inter-state relations and may entail establishing relations based on friendliness and peace; or war, hostility and exploitation. It is clear that the individual in all aspects of their personality, behavior, material and social life is affected by class position, which is determined by economic status. Hence, the character of a professional is different from that of a worker or an impoverished farmer.

Human relationships can become richer and purer if they are not subjected to the burdens of poverty and deprivation and are supported by material assets that help them flourish. Hence, it is not surprising that the question of development heads the list of international problems. The greater part of modern economic studies, in the East and the West, now accords more importance to the question of socio-economic development—a factor now picked up on by politicians, religious leaders, UN experts and UN-affiliated international organizations. Based on this, the economic system generally plays a significant role in determining character type and can have a decisive effect. Here I would like to refer to two important aspects relating to the economic factor and its effect on character development.

The first aspect relates to the interaction between economic effects and other factors, as the relationship between the two is dialectical. The economic factor is affected by an individual's ambition, class, and dominant values and attitudes. From this, it affects the emotional balance of the individual and his relationship with his social milieu. Thus, we realize the importance of the economic effect on the social condition of an individual and any inclination, or not, towards extremist views.

The second aspect pertains to the fact that the income of the individual is not merely an amount. This income might be sufficient to satisfy the basic needs of the individual, such as a home and clothes to wear, yet it might not realize a state of psychological and social contentment. Therefore, modern-day reformers warn against great wealth disparity within a society. However, reform is not only about raising living standards for the working class and reducing wealth disparity. It also seeks to realize emotional balance, limit conflicts that might arise from such situations, reduce psychological pressures and suppress tendencies toward religious extremism.

Evidence shows that good economic conditions help create normal, integrated, productive and religiously tolerant personalities. It has also been observed that a high percentage of extremists were born into difficult economic conditions. Those who grew up in deteriorating economic conditions found in religion a safe haven and a means of convincing themselves that religion would compensate them for their lost chances in life. Many such adherents embrace the kind of fanatical ideas that drive them toward terrorist behavior in order to realize their goals. In addition, the financial aid offered by extremist groups, whether inside the country or abroad, is often sufficient reason to join the cause of extremism.

Moreover, poverty, deprivation and low social status may lead these extremists to reject peaceful, constructive dialog with the state, and instead employ violence and force to realize their purposes. In other words, we find that this brand of extremist cannot interact with society, cope with rapid and bewildering development, solve ordinary day-to-day problems, or even find opportunities to develop talents and skills. Hence, the only recourse for expression is through extremism.

Further to the economic condition of extremists, is the economic condition of the state itself. The policy of receiving aid to satisfy the needs of society, and its attendant economic subordination to a wealthier country or bloc, makes this category of extremist feel that the state is subject to an external economic system. This fuels resentment against the regime and drives extremists towards overthrowing it.

The economic state of the country, and any prevailing crises that the country might face, facilitate the process of filling naïve and uneducated minds with ideas that are advocated by extremists, which find acceptance in the face of daily suffering and the need to vent pent-up aggression. In this regard, the issue of unemployment is one of the most significant economic problems plaguing the developing world, and one that might provide an excuse to reject the status quo and resort to extremism.

In light of this, we can conclude that the state has an obligation to promote the welfare of all its citizens within the principles of equal opportunity, the rule of law and access to justice and employment. If the state succeeds in fulfilling this, the citizens' commitment to the state will be achieved and consequently the phenomenon of extremism will be constrained.

Social Causes

A discussion about social causes of extremism must include discussion of the role of the family and the education system. The family unit is part of the social system and consists of vital interlocking and overlapping relationships surrounded by social norms that guide and facilitate its operation. The family is also tied into scholastic, religious and economic systems. The major responsibility for preventing extremism falls on the family. Parents must not fail in their role and need to act on the signs of extremism in their sons and daughters. Parents must provide their children with a good example to emulate.

The education system also shoulders significant responsibility in this respect. Schools must inspire adolescents with a desire to learn that suits their natural talents; deal with their social and emotional characters; and instill knowledge and religious virtue. This requires skill and concern on the part of teachers in monitoring excessive or unusual behavior in students inside or outside the classroom and in their relations with friends and peers.

The school has all the characteristics of a self-contained community where individuals are divided into various groups in terms of age and scholarly ability. The school as a small community has its norms and goals and a relatively permanent "togetherness" that gives students a sense of belonging. Schools also have their own systems of social control through the actions of the principals and their staff, which have defined limits with regard to authority and control. Hence, the school is the larger family and guides the path of its pupils. Those in charge of youth affairs and education believe that the current curricula of religious education and teaching methods actually assists youths to gravitate toward extremism in religious practices. Religious education needs to be overhauled and teachers properly qualified in order to instill sensitive, humane and civilized values in students to help create balanced personalities imbued with correct Islamic principles.

Religious Causes

In reality religious extremism is a complex and sophisticated phenomenon. Its causes are varied and overlapping; some are direct while others are indirect; some are visible and some lie at great depths.

One of the reasons behind religious extremism is an impoverished knowledge and vision of the role of religion and its teachings, and a failure to understand its true spirit. Those who only possess a little religious knowledge often imagine themselves to be great scholars, while in fact they are ignorant of a great part of it. Their knowledge is incoherent, unable to link the parts to the whole, and promotes assumptions over facts.

The Imam Abu Ishaq Al Shatbi demonstrably draws attention to this fact in his book *Al I'tsam* (Adherence). He considers that the first cause of heresy and conflict, leading to the division of Islam into factions that ruthlessly engage in fighting one another, is when one believes that one is a scholar qualified to interpret religion in a new light. This is also true of someone who is believed by others to be such a scholar. In this case, although the person concerned is not qualified, he espouses new interpretations, gives supremacy to his view and considers that he is different from other scholars. Sometimes this occurs within a branch of a religion, and at other times it totally contradicts religious fundamentals and is thus heretical.

Conflict management in Islam has its own protocol. A scholar who follows a certain doctrine believes it to be right and others wrong. Extremist groups are not committed to the principle of consensus and when they are convinced of a doctrine or a view on a particular issue, they never question it or accept to discuss it—and expect others to comply with their view.

Extremist Muslim groups have often accused others of apostasy. This has resulted in conferring legitimacy on spilling blood and confiscating the wealth of Muslim people on the pretext that they are apostates or originally non-Muslims. This is extremism par excellence; the kind of extremism which *Al Khawarij* created (Islamic dissidents during the reign of Ali, the Fourth Caliph). In addition to this, we find that a major focus of extremist thinking in religion is preoccupation with ancillary questions instead of major ones. This accords importance to partial and subordinate matters at the expense of major issues relating to the existence and identity of Islam.

The fact that youths ignore religious scholars is one of the most important reasons for this unfortunate level of extremism in religion. This aversion stems from their lack of confidence in religious leaders that are close to rulers. Experience has proven that intellectual dialog helps to reform extremists by exposing the religious and cultural shallowness of the leaders of extremist groups; repairs the bridges of confidence between scholars and the younger generation; and convinces them of the true concepts of Islam, especially with respect to regulating the style of *Da'wa* (call to Islam) and the avoidance of violence.

Political Causes

The religious motive is one of the most potent on which extremist movements depend when it comes to changing the political status quo. No doubt, unstable political conditions in the state and a corrupt system of governance make citizens lose confidence in the regime and leave them in a constant state of doubt and anxiety. From this grows a sense of resentment that prepares the stage for turmoil, which leads to anarchy and the emergence of various extremist ideas and theories that permeate the state and enable extremists to seize power.

Islamist political movements, like the Al Tahrir (liberation) party and the Muslim Brotherhood movement, came into being in the first half of the 20th century. A review of modern political history since the time of the French campaign in Egypt shows that the European colonial conquest of Islamic countries targeted the domains of politics, economics, thought and culture. It could be maintained that Western thought, in the form of political and social theories and jurisprudence, was not sown in Egypt until the late 19th century by schools closely tied to the colonialist powers.

This conquest led to the emergence of secular thinking that spearheaded national movements and depended on Western civilization for political and theoretical inspiration. The Ottoman Islamic Caliphate in Turkey was annulled, causing the loss of the identity of the Islamic political institution and the partition of Muslim countries into chunks shared among European powers. In these historical circumstances, Islamist political movements emerged as a reaction and a means of rallying nations anew. However, they took an extreme form in terms of concepts, ideas and style of work using the charge of apostasy against society and its rulers as a rationale for forming their Islamist agenda.

[291]

Hence, they used violence and coercion as a means of realizing their desired objective,

Studies and experience have proved that the democratic system helps constrain the dissemination of terrorist ideas. Sustaining freedom of opinion and the peaceful exchange of power are factors that help to prevent the promotion of terrorist beliefs. Contrary to this, dictatorial regimes that prevent the public from voicing opinion and attaining power peacefully drives many to clandestine action in the form of terrorist organizations. Unfortunately, there are a considerable number of Arab countries whose rulers still do not believe in democracy and thus make this region more exposed to the spread of terrorist ideas than others.

One should not overlook the fact that the international community is witnessing US military unilateralism and current US foreign policy is often at loggerheads with the hopes and demands of Arab nations. Some Arab governments are forced to comply with US demands, thus contradicting the deep-rooted sentiments of their people. This has bred a sort of popular fury against their rulers and some believe that there are opposition forces growing against these ruling regimes, which could rapidly turn into terrorist organizations.

Security Causes

Undoubtedly the police, as a law enforcement agency, play an essential role in tackling the negative aspects of religious practices, the destructive effects of which are reflected in various aspects of day-to-day life. Security-related causes of religious extremism include neglecting to confront this detestable phenomenon and failure to take all appropriate security measures to arrest the leaders of such organizations, reveal their hiding places and confiscate their weapons, documents, leaflets and associated tools.

In spite of the efforts exerted in this regard, difficulties surround such measures, including the speed of action of the authorities concerned – where confrontation of these extremist elements must be executed without delay – and exposing the intentions of these extremist groups. Also, the

[292]

amount of information available to the security services to combat terrorism might be insufficient to create adequate security plans to confront extremist factions. Lack of information is due to the strict confidentiality under which extremists operate and communicate.

Security-related reasons for the spread of religious extremism also include the failure to use efficient approaches in confronting the phenomenon, such as resorting to violence and torture, which do not prevent extremism but generate it. This is clearly demonstrated by the fact that some extremist organizations have been founded inside prisons.

Such a confrontational style by the security services drives extremists to accuse rulers of apostasy and even to accuse fellow Muslims of the same, their justification being that that those who agree with rulers that do not rule according to the word of Allah are apostates because "accepting apostasy is blasphemy." From this, the wave of accusation of apostasy spreads and encourages extremism. One of the most common security-related errors that has contributed to the spread of extremist ideology is perpetrated by prison officials who keep terrorist detainees together in close proximity. This has resulted in fostering ties between them and often encouraging the formation of new organizations inside prisons. This issue necessitates coordination among the different security services of Arab countries. However, in spite of the fact that the conference of Arab Ministers of the Interior is convened annually, coordination between the security services concerned has not yet reached the required level.

Combating Terrorism

Terrorism has become an international phenomenon. Terrorist ideology is disseminated via the Internet and other means of communication, and international cooperation to facilitate the confrontation of terrorist organizations in an efficient manner has become an urgent necessity. Although international and regional efforts have been exerted towards realizing this goal, these efforts have not achieved the desired outcome of eradicating terrorism. On the contrary, terrorist crimes are increasing and spreading through different parts of the world. Hence, I will review some international and regional efforts and make some proposals that might contribute to solving this problem.

International Efforts

Terrorist activity has spread beyond national borders to become a global, universal reality. This makes terrorist activity an international crime affecting the vital interests of nations, the security and safety of humanity, and basic individual rights and freedoms.

At the international level, terrorism has become an effective tool in the process of making political decisions and a method employed by states to coerce opponents into political submission. Now there is international consensus on criminalizing a number of acts that jeopardize international security and classifying them as international crimes; these include war crimes, crimes against humanity, crimes against peace, and crimes of international terrorism.

The spread of terrorism over the last few years has led to the development of innovative means with which to eliminate this dangerous phenomenon. Hence, various international agreements have been published and efforts exerted by the UN in this regard. These are summarized as follows:

International Charters on Terrorism

There are several international agreements and protocols regarding terrorism. These include:

- The 1937 Geneva Convention for the Prevention and Punishment of Terrorism.
- The European Convention on the Suppression of Terrorism, Strasbourg, 1977.

- Convention to Prevent and Punish the Acts of Terrorism Taking the Form of Crimes against Persons and Related Extortion that are of International Significance, Washington, DC, 1971.
- Convention on the Prevention and Punishment of Crimes against Internationally Protected Persons, including Diplomatic Agents, New York, 1973.
- International Convention against the Taking of Hostages, New York, 1979.
- Convention on Offences and Certain Other Acts Committed on board Aircraft, Tokyo, 1963.
- Convention for the Suppression of Unlawful Seizure of Aircraft, The Hague, 1970.
- Convention for the Suppression of Unlawful Acts against the Safety of Civil Aviation, Montreal, 1971.
- Convention on the Physical Protection of Nuclear Material, Vienna, 1979.
- Protocol for the Suppression of Unlawful Acts of Violence at Airports Serving International Civil Aviation, Montreal, 1988.
- Convention for the Suppression of Unlawful Acts against the Safety of Maritime Navigation, Rome, 1988.
- Protocol for the Prevention of Unlawful Acts against the Safety of Fixed Platforms Located on the Continental Shelf, Rome, 1988.
- Convention on the Marking of Plastic Explosives for the Purpose of Detection, Montreal, 1991.
- Convention on the Safety of United Nations and Associated Personnel adopted by the UN General Assembly in December 1994.

United Nations Efforts in Combating Terrorism

As terrorist crimes have become more widespread, the UN has issued several decrees relating to this phenomenon. However, not all of these decrees would seem to be fit for their purpose. This fact necessitates the organization of an international conference under the aegis of the UN to discuss the phenomenon of terrorism and the causes of its dissemination, provided that this is done with absolute transparency and the conference issues specific decrees that the global community is obliged to implement.

The UN General Assembly issued decree no. 3034 in 1972 on forming a special committee to face terrorism. The committee was asked to submit a report to the General Assembly including recommendations for methods of international cooperation to eliminate the phenomenon of terrorism. The committee formed three sub-committees: the first one to work out a definition of terrorism, the second to study the causes of the dissemination of terrorism, and the third to discuss arrangements for the prevention of terrorism. These committees convened to undertake their tasks, but unfortunately there was disagreement among the parties on common concepts relating to terrorism and major differences on the definition of terrorism. Hence, whenever a report by the committee was raised to the General Assembly, it would issue a decree authorizing the committee to continue its work. The committee is still continuing its work in accordance with the decrees of the General Assembly. So far, the committee has not accomplished a universal plan for combating terrorism due to intransigent views between countries over the legal aspects of international terrorism. There is also disagreement over what constitutes terrorism, and the desire of world powers, especially the United States, to issue a specific definition of terrorism that protects its policies – especially after the invasion of Afghanistan and Iraq – and protects Israel against the consequences of its deeds in the occupied Palestinian territories.

Local Efforts in the Arab Countries

As mentioned earlier, the problem of terrorism is a complex issue with overlapping political, social, economic, security, and cultural dimensions. Therefore, confronting terrorism requires thorough academic study to determine the causes of its dissemination and create a universal, integrated system to deal with these causes. Hence, the responsibility of confronting the phenomenon of terrorism lies with society as a whole (political parties, educated elites, religious leaders, security services, ministries of culture and information, etc). Efforts exerted so far include:

Security Efforts

Although it is now agreed that security measures alone are not enough to confront terrorism, it should also be noted that such security measures should be the last stage in the process of confronting terrorism. Care must be taken to ensure that methods of confronting the phenomenon of terrorism should not lead to an escalation of the problem. Hence, the police services must be supported and empowered appropriately considering the scale of the challenge involved. The necessity of rationalizing the security methods of terrorist confrontation must be emphasized and the security services must be availed of all assistance in order to enable them to perform their role with greater efficiency and competency. The following are some proposals which might assist the security services in confronting terrorism:

- Increase security awareness and training through improved educational courses at the various police institutes.
- Those security officials dealing with terrorist organizations must be aware of the intellectual mindset of the terrorists and able to discuss their doctrinal beliefs and demonstrate their fallaciousness. Those who confront religious extremism must be knowledgeable about religious detail in order to recognize extremist thinking and thus be able to deal effectively with religious extremism.
- Avoid security personnel performing the same repetitive security functions for extended periods of time in order to prevent lack of attention and consequent lapses in security.
- Ensure practical training of different security forces involving realistic exercises to combat terrorist activities.
- Security strategies should focus on the necessity of dealing with *anticipated* danger based on reliable factual information.
- Increase security protection either by expanding surveillance in general or raising the level of security periodically in accordance with intelligence received.

- Decrease security services' dependence on all other support services.
- Establish closed circuit surveillance of all major roads, public areas and facilities, operated from one central command station, enabling information to be supplied to security agencies in real time.
- Encourage greater security awareness among the public to prevent crime.
- Improve the training levels of security personnel of all ranks.

Confronting Terrorism via Religion

Religious dialog is one of the basic methods of confronting the problem of terrorism. Terrorism uses Islam as a camouflage for its desire to polarize youth through erroneous religious interpretation. Sharia law's position on acts of violence is unequivocally clear and ideas and practices pertaining to violence run counter to correct Islamic behavior. In spite of this, extremist ideas find their way into the minds of many. However, an experiment conducted in Egypt proved that when extremist ideas were confronted and debated by specialized scholars from Al Azhar, the outcome was positive. The frames of reference alleged by extremists were taken to task and through dialog the extremists were shown to have had committed grave mistakes in their interpretation.

Legislative Confrontation

Legislative policy is considered one of the most important methods of confronting terrorism. Hence, all countries that have suffered from terrorism have resorted to enacting specific laws to enable them to confront this phenomenon. Enacting terrorism-specific laws has become necessary in order to achieve a balance between society's need for security and stability and the rights and freedoms of its citizens.

Confrontation via the Media

The media plays an important and essential role in confronting terrorism owing to its ability to reach citizens directly and its ability to shape public opinion and societal behavior. Of course, there are various roles media can play – especially television – to confront the problem of terrorism by disseminating well-founded opinions, raising basic issues related to terrorism, and involving the citizen as an essential tool in confronting the phenomenon. Media involvement requires several essential elements, which are summarized as follows:

- The existence of an on-going media policy of confronting terrorism.
- Recognizing the true scale of terrorism in order to create a balance between the degree of media concern with terrorism and the level of danger to society. Underrating the dangers of terrorism is as counter-productive as exaggerating it and deters the search for ways to confront the problem.
- Media channels of all types – written, audio and visual – must differentiate between extremism and terrorism and treat each of them in the appropriate manner.
- Media confrontation must combine direct and mass media. Studies have revealed the necessity of achieving an integrated approach when confronting major problems such as terrorism.
- Media confrontation cannot achieve its goal of defeating terrorism unless there is effective citizen participation. To realize this, it is necessary to stir an interest in the issue and a link must be established between the problem and the public by highlighting the danger terrorism poses to their lives, interests and freedoms.
- Media integrity is a substantive prerequisite. Media integrity is subject to certain conditions, namely the rapid release of information and the highest level of objectivity in the media coverage of terrorist events.
- Concern with the suitability of broadcast and published materials in relation to the prevailing religious and moral values of society.
- Media confrontation must be based on sound planning that benefits from all advancements in appropriate disciplines. For any media plan to succeed, the following factors must be available: a good choice of presenter – i.e. the person performing media work – and a competent media message that projects the required information to the intended audience.

[299]

Proposals to Confront Terrorism

To confront terrorism in the Arab world, the following is proposed:

- Establishing research centers to conduct studies on the dissemination of terrorist ideology and the ideal methods of confronting it.
- Establishing a center for combating terrorism, which is affiliated to the Council of Arab Ministers of the Interior, and which is able to execute plans to confront terrorism in the region.
- Exchanging information on all terrorist organizations between different Arab countries.
- Agreement on extraditing wanted persons by any Arab country, especially those charged with terrorism.
- Agreement on approving legislation on combating terrorism which is acceptable to all Arab countries.
- Intellectual confrontation via conducting debates that expose and correct mistakes of interpretation committed by terrorist organizations.
- Media and cultural confrontation via an agreed, integrated program set up by the proposed center for combating terrorism.
- Encouraging the role of religious institutions to confront terrorism masquerading as religious thought, as well as upgrading the abilities of Dou'at (Islamic missionaries) to make them capable of intellectual confrontation.

13

The Impact of Terrorism on our Societies and Methods to Combat it

Ali bin Fayiz Al-Jahni

Just like many other countries in the world, Gulf societies and Arab societies in general face many challenges and are undergoing rapid developments in all areas of life. Among the challenges that have emerged in recent years are the phenomena of terrorism and extremism, which mark a departure from moderation and tolerance.

Efforts must be made to search for the causes of this pestilence and find suitable solutions to it. This paper explores the impacts of terrorism on the security of our societies, specifies means of combating it, and emphasizes the role of institutions in Arab societies in reinforcing moderation, thus bolstering security and immunity to intellectual and behavioral aberrations.

Naturally, terrorism exposes nations to security threats, obstructs the progress of their institutions, frustrates development, and undermines the standing of states. It also prompts migration from capitals, discourages foreign investment and creates fertile ground for the growth of other serious criminal behavior. What is more, its effects can place severe strains on national unity. In addition to all this, it has economic repercussions, owing to the high cost of operating the judicial system (including the security apparatus, courts, prisons, etc). Intellectual security, and its relationship with national security within states, attracts great attention from those concerned with security as a whole. This is especially true since the communications, transport and information boom and the emergence of groups that call for inhuman violence, killing without justification, the undermining of authority, and terrorist acts in the name of Islam. Therefore, we must adopt comprehensive methodologies to combat the phenomenon of terrorism, which has endangered the discourse of reform, moderation, dialogue and tolerance. This in itself illustrates the significance of this issue and its discussion in the framework of both social systems and overall security.

Linguistic and Terminological Definitions of Terrorism

The term *terror* has several meanings, and for example could refer literally to fear and fright. In the Holy Koran Allah says, "Said Moses: 'Throw ye (first).' So when they threw, they bewitched the eyes of the people and struck terror into them, and they displayed a great magic" (*Al-A'raf*, 7, 116). Allah also says, "… to terrify the enemy of Allah and your enemy…" (*Al-Anfal*, 8, 60). In Arabic language dictionaries the common denominator between the related forms of the word 'frighten' are fear, intimidation and fright.

It is difficult for specialists to reach a consensus on a unified definition of the term *terrorism*. However, the approach adopted by the Arab countries in reaching a widely accepted definition has been well-received. They unanimously agreed on a unified definition of terrorism in the Arab Convention for the Suppression of Terrorism, which was concluded by the Council of Arab Ministers of Justice in 1998. The Convention defined terrorism as "Any act or threat of violence, whatever its motives or purposes, that occurs in the advancement of an individual or collective criminal agenda and seeking to sow panic among people, causing fear by harming them, or placing their lives, liberty or security in danger, or seeking to cause damage to the environment or to public or private installations or property or to occupying or seizing them, or seeking to jeopardize a national resource."[1]

The Attitude of the Ulema
(Muslim Scholars) toward Terrorism

Islam and terrorism are irreconcilable, since the former forbids extremism, deviant thought or behavior, prohibits killing and aggression of all kinds, rejects all forms of anarchy and divisionism, and encourages people to cooperate, become brothers, and embrace love and peace.

The *Ulema*, authorities, councils and Islamic organizations at all levels in the Arab and Islamic countries have clearly condemned and rejected acts of violence and terrorism in all forms, regardless of the motive. This is illustrated by the decisions issued by the Academy of Islamic Jurisprudence in the Kingdom of Saudi Arabia regarding the phenomena of terrorism and extremism, and the importance of combating them. These decisions included:

* The categorization of unjust killing as a form of *haraba* (highway robbery in Islam); (issued in 1395 Hijri/1975).
* The decision to define bombing, hijacking and arson, etc. as contemporary forms of *haraba* (Decision no. 148 of 1409 Hijri/1988).
* The decision to regard bombings in certain Arab cities and the resultant death, destruction and terror to be declared criminal acts, rejected by *Shari'a* law (1417 Hijri/1996).

In addition to this, decisions have also been issued by the Muslim World League, the Organization of the Islamic Conference (OIC), and a number of jurisprudence councils and Arab, Islamic and international conferences. In the light of this, the phenomena of extremism and violence should be confronted by focusing on the following issues:

* The *Shari'a* is just; it acknowledges the principle of tolerance of non-Muslims; tolerance in *Shari'a* is a principle applied by Muslims to all others.
* Islam accords great importance to international pacts and charters; this attests to the fact that *Shari'a* rejects violence and terror.

[303]

- Islam prohibits the spilling of human blood, whether the slain is a Muslim or non-Muslim. Allah says, "... whoever slays a soul, unless it be in retaliation for murder or for spreading mischief in the land, it would be as if he had killed all of mankind; and whoever saves a life, it would be as if he saved the lives of all mankind ..." (*Al Maeda*, 5, 32). In one interpretation, the Prophet, peace of Allah be upon him, says, "A believer is at one with his religion if he does not spill blood unlawfully" (*Al Bukhari*).

- Islam seeks to create a community where love prevails, class distinctions disappear, and all the motives for violence become extinct. Allah Most High says, "O people! be careful of [your duty] to your Lord, who created you from a single being and created its mate of the same [kind] and spread from these two many men and women" (*An Nisa*, 1).

- Emphasizing the importance of mercy, love and solidarity between members of society. Allah Most High says, "We sent thee not, but as a mercy for all creatures" (*Al Anbiya*, 107).

- Through its aims, principles and values, Islam seeks to achieve peace, security, stability, social justice, and to fight poverty, disease, unemployment, corruption and authoritarianism.

- The *Ulama*, *Dou'at* (Muslim missionaries), media personnel, teachers, and all social activists bear the great responsibility of calling for a discourse of moderation, tolerance, and avoidance of extremism, fanaticism and narrow-mindedness.

- Intellectual deviation, extremism and terrorism should be confronted universally via a strategy that examines the true causes of these phenomena. Terrorism is like a malignant disease that must be studied in a scientific way to determine its causes and the appropriate treatment.

- Efforts should be made to confront the problems of development – be they educational, economic, social, moral, psychological, or intellectual in nature – with confidence, capability and high morale.[2]

[304]

Terrorist organizations and groups that claim to be "Islamic" should not be labeled as such. If we are to refer to "Islamic" terrorism, Catholic, Protestant, Buddhist and other extremists should also been named after their religious persuasions. For example, Timothy McVeigh, the member of a right-wing Protestant group who bombed the Federal Building in Oklahoma in 1995, killing 168 people and wounding hundreds more. Or, indeed, David Koresh, the man who claimed that he was Jesus and was besieged with his group on his Waco farm in 1993. When he refused to surrender, the besieging troops assaulted the farm and 75 of his followers were killed, including women and children. In 1978 an extremist American group committed a collective suicide involving 775 Americans who were followers of the Temple of the People sect. This sect isolated itself from American society. There was also the Japanese *Aum Shinrikyo* (The Religion of Truth) group, which released Sarin gas in the subway in Tokyo, killing 12 and injuring 5,500. Indeed, they had planned to kill 40,000 subway passengers in 1995.

The Effects of Terrorism on Gulf and Arab Societies

Security Effects

The effects of terrorist acts are many and multifarious. At the forefront of these effects are those which relate to the security of Gulf and Arab societies. The gravity of these effects and their resultant damage increases as terrorist cells multiply in a fissional pattern to form affiliate cells, each spitting its own individual venom without recourse to the mother organization.

Security is the pillar of every development effort and a precondition of stability and the building of societies. The most prominent security effects are represented by acts of violence, the terrorizing of citizens, spreading fear, targeting critical installations, and attempting to undermine confidence in the security services.

[305]

Political Effects

The political effects of terrorism surface when these groups attempt to target countries of the region which seek to improve their relations with the great powers. They allege that these relations indicate weakness and allegiance to Western countries in general and the United States in particular. Consequently, they incite the public in the region against governments and convince them to demonstrate and to participate in acts of sabotage.

Religious Effects

Perhaps the most prominent religious effect of terrorist operations in our societies appears to be the restriction of Islamic missionary work, which was active before 9/11 in many communities across the world.

Islamic centers used to play an effective role in spreading Islamic *da'ouwa* (call to Islam) and *do'aat* (missionaries), moving with complete freedom from one community to another without restrictions or control. However, after 9/11 everything changed. Islamic centers have been constrained and the movement of missionaries has been obstructed and controlled. Moreover, hatred and hostile feelings towards Muslims have spread and some Muslim youths have become confused and led astray.

Social Effects

These criminal and destructive acts also have negative impacts on the social and humanitarian situation in the affected countries. Numerous public and private interests have been damaged as a result of terrorism. Every public statement released by terrorist groups levels the charge of apostasy at myriad religious groups across the Islamic World. Since the social structure of our societies in particular is composed of several social categories with different doctrinal allegiances, these statements have religious–doctrinal implications and ignite sectarianism.

Economic Effects

Terrorism affects the economy and development of states in several ways, the most important of which is the financial strain involved in combating terrorism, and in supporting economic recovery in the aftermath of terrorist acts. The required funds would otherwise have been used to fuel development. Among the most severe effects is the damage to installations and property and the resultant downturns in investor confidence. This leads to reduced local and foreign investment as funds are channeled to other places and projects. Furthermore, increased security measures also have negative effects on business.

The Effects on Tourism

Tourism is the sector that is most directly affected by the level of security in any country. Security is the first priority of the tourist anywhere in the world. Statistics provided by the World Travel and Tourism Council (WTTC) indicate that the effects of 9/11 have led to a reduction in international demand for tourism and consequently a semi-complete recession in the tourism sector and its related activities. 9/11 has also led to the unemployment of more than 10 million people worldwide in the tourism sector.[3]

In view of the terrorist activities in our societies in recent years, the Middle East was classified as one of the most dangerous regions in the world and some countries warn their citizens not to travel to the area. The countries of the region have now doubled their security efforts to protect foreigners living in their territories. Protection is not only limited to resident foreigners; but also extended to cover the citizens of the region. Extreme security measures at tourist sites and growing entry restrictions have prompted some to refrain from visiting these places. Ultimately, the most significant effect of terrorism on the tourism sector has been low tourism returns, and in some cases the complete cessation of tourism altogether, which takes its toll on national income.

Methods of Combating Terrorism

Terrorism not only undermines security and stability, it also negatively affects the religious, social, political, psychological, ethical and media spheres. Societies use both traditional and varied means of combating terrorism. The most prominent of these are penal laws, security and judicial intervention and punitive reform. Although these methods are useful, they have not stopped the growth of the phenomenon of terrorism.[4] Indeed, they have been criticized for their dependence on the security services, the deterrent effect of punishments, and the adoption of strategies based on official decisions rather than realistic studies.

The fact that traditional methods for protecting against terrorism and preventing its dissemination in these societies have faltered, fuels demands for a shift in strategy towards one that does not rely on the security solution alone.[5] This shift in methodology involves devising preventive policies based on facts and concepts provided by the social, humanitarian and strategic sciences. Using such a strategy provides a more realistic method of confronting terrorism, supported by scientific accomplishments which provide novel and innovative techniques.[6] Such methods prevent societies from becoming isolated from contemporary developments in strategies combating crime, including terrorism and intellectual and behavioral deviation. The attention accorded to this matter has manifested itself in knowledge centers via:[7]

- An institutional orientation that aims to create a pillar of protection against terrorism and all other crimes.
- Preventive strategic planning to combat criminality via a universal strategy with specific objectives, methods and mechanisms, which conforms with global opinions yet does not contradict traditional norms.
- Developing an overall, universally accepted view of security – economic, political, cultural, penal and intellectual – and recognizing the role of public and private institutions and the necessity of societal

involvement in taking responsibility for security—we are all in the same boat and security is therefore our collective responsibility.

- Adopting a general reformative approach, while instantly correcting the acts and reasoning of those who err.

Statistics from the Arab world confirm a general increase in crime rates and the emergence of new patterns in crime owing to both technological, economic, social and political advances and the gradual deterioration of living conditions. Studies have also proven that the central factors associated with crime – i.e. which create conditions favorable to criminality – are poverty, unemployment, limited education, lack of suitable residence, poor health services, the rapid shift to urbanization, population increases and family disintegration, etc. These discoveries make viewing security through an all-encompassing prism that accommodates all these factors inevitable.

The factors which are most likely to produce the character of a terrorist comprise: family disintegration; social, economic and personal factors; lenient local institutions of social control; and international conditions that are charged with crisis and tension. In the face of all these factors, we must focus on combating terrorism on several levels including:

The Official State Level

- Rejecting, condemning and confronting terrorism at all levels.
- Encouraging perpetrators to face their errors and advancing rehabilitation via reasoned, scientific discussion.
- Avoiding ineffective methods by moving away from exhortation and intimidation towards arguments from the *Koran* and *Sunna*.
- Punishment of those who undermine security and stability.
- Use of media channels to warn against terrorists who want to damage society and its members by interpreting the verses of Allah incorrectly and issuing *Fatwas* (Islamic juridical views) without having the appropriate knowledge or authority.

[309]

- Distinguishing between intellectual deviation that is not conducive to action and that which is conducive.[8]
- Increased development of methodologies of political, economic, social, and developmental reform.
- Promotion of solidarity among all members of society and in their support of efforts to combat terrorism and any other crimes that threaten their security and stability.

The Educational Level[9]

This comprises instilling the right concepts in the minds of youths in order to provide them with intellectual immunity from extremism; preserve authentic cultural constituents and legacies in the face of extraneous, cultural influences; preserve normative behavior; and ensure that students avoid falling into the ideological traps of terrorists. This can be achieved if both families and schools teach sound socialization based on:

- Emulating and imitating righteous values and deepening allegiance and belonging.
- Commitment to traditional values and age-old beliefs, as well as traditions stemming from pure Islamic teachings.
- Enabling students to develop self-appreciation that is based on interaction with others.
- Appreciating the opinions and viewpoints of students without ridiculing them or simply imposing the views and ideas of teachers and educators.
- Including information in the curricula about security in its universal sense and implanting respect for security staff and figures of authority.
- Opening channels of dialogue and communication with students and providing them with opportunities to express themselves and voice their ideas.
- Enlightening young people with respect to the dangers surrounding them such as wars, disasters or the intellectual and cultural conquest

of their traditions, and assisting them to develop their abilities to resist and protect themselves from such events.

- Encouraging and motivating students to read and to develop a passion for work in a manner that contributes to expanding their cultural horizons.

Based on the above, the future role of education systems must be to reform the essential factors of the learning process – the student, the teacher and the curriculum – in order to prevent deviation and the spread of terrorist ideology.

The Religious Level

The most significant aspects of the role which the religious system can play in the lives of young people can be summarized in four points. Intellectual security is considered to be of the utmost importance in modern Arab societies, and using a tolerant religious system is the only way to combat the spread of terrorism. This can be achieved via the following:

- Immunizing the minds of the younger generation against being led astray by extremists, and warning them of the dangers of falling under the influence of terrorist groups. This can be achieved through a number of mechanisms: Friday prayer sermons; guided religious debates, lectures, televised programs and dialogues; scientific books; and basing arguments on balanced, traditional Islamic views.
- Selecting men of *Da'awa* and guidance from among those who are versed in *Shari'a* disciplines to become role models for the young instead of allowing them to be influenced by those who encourage them to embrace extremism.
- Directing orators, *Do'aat*, and preachers to focus on security awareness and illustrate the dangers associated with extremism and terrorism.
- Reinforcing moderate Islam and spreading the spirit of tolerance and acceptance of others, thereby avoiding extremism and accusations of apostasy against others.

[311]

The Economic Level

One of the most urgent issues in this context is the need to produce qualified young workers to suit the requirements of the labor market and help the younger generation to find jobs. Work is essential in instilling a sense of belonging and worth in one's homeland.[10] It is also necessary to fight poverty and unemployment, reduce economic obstacles and benefit from international experience in this regard. Ultimately, combating the phenomenon of terrorism must involve the following:

- Religious therapy that serves to nurture and reform adolescents throughout the different stages of their education.
- Supporting the family institution and preserving family ties.
- Taking responsibility for dealing with the concerns of the younger generation.
- Guiding the media discourse to project an accurate picture of Islam and highlighting the dangers of terrorism.
- Confronting terrorism via concerted security efforts.

Security Cooperation in Combating Terrorism

Today's world is characterized by improved mobility between countries, closer inter-state relations, and the impacts of global events on state security—be they negative or positive. Hence, it is imperative that security be supported and reinforced and that cooperation and understanding be achieved in combating criminality, including the phenomenon of terrorism. The need for such cooperation is highlighted by the following factors:

- The world has become increasingly interconnected; moving closer to a "global village" owing to the presence of modern means of communication, advanced technology, economic blocs and mutual interdependence.

- If criminals can commit crimes in one country and take refuge in another, this will have serious ramifications with respect to state security.
- If the present global age is one based on exchanging benefits and interests between nations, why then cannot security cooperation and coordination between nations be the basis for further cooperation?
- States should benefit from the experiences of others in the fields of security, legislation, and security systems and techniques. The necessity of such dissemination of knowledge and experience is dictated by the modern reality of Arab societies and made inevitable by common interests of Arab states.[11]
- Arab security cooperation has improved dramatically in recent years and Arabs everywhere realize that such pan-Arab cooperation can only be of benefit to the Arab world.

The GCC countries share firm and clear attitudes towards terrorism. They have highlighted the danger posed by terrorism and the necessity of facing it and confronting its source. These clear-cut attitudes are manifested by the following facts:

- All the GCC states have signed the Arab Convention for the Suppression of Terrorism, along with a number of other similar agreements.
- All the GCC countries have concluded relevant international and regional agreements.
- The security strategy of the GCC countries has been universally approved and so too the security strategy of combating extremism and terrorism.
- The Muscat Declaration on Terrorism, issued by the 21st meeting of the Ministers of Interior of the GCC countries.
- The decisions, press statements and communiqués of the Supreme Council of the Gulf Cooperation Council and its ministerial committees all emphatically condemn criminal and terrorist acts.

[313]

- Issues and groups that disturb security and stability have been confronted.
- Conferences, symposia and forums on terrorism are regularly convened and issue important recommendations pertinent to combating terrorism. The most important of these events was the Counter-Terrorism International conference ("Riyadh Declaration"), which was convened in Riyadh, Saudi Arabia, in 2005.

Obstacles to International Cooperation in Combating Terrorism

Although arrangements on combating terrorism have been made globally within the framework of international conventions, if obstacles to international cooperation are not overcome, the effect of these conventions will remain limited. Such obstacles include:

- The problem of defining *terrorism*, which hinders international cooperation to combat the phenomenon.
- Conflicting laws among parties, which make the extradition of terrorists difficult.
- The use of terror to influence international relations.
- Disagreements over the methods of addressing the causes of terrorism, identifying priorities in this regard, and the willingness of some countries – such as the United States and the United Kingdom – to resort to collective punishment.

Conclusion

Diagnosing the true causes of terrorism entails viewing the phenomenon from a multi-dimensional perspective. This is necessary as some causes are linked to socialization, education, culture and values. Others are linked to prevailing religious, political, economic and social conditions. Still others relate to the shortcomings of civil society institutions. International events can also be catalysts, as can security and judicial conduct in countries of residence. Combinations of these causes exist in differing forms depending on the environment and society inhabited by the terrorist or movement concerned.

Our governments now have an historic opportunity to implement universal and qualitative reforms in their structures, institutions and procedures – especially in the domains of education, economy and politics – and to surpass the constraints of backwardness by exerting strong political will. The effects of terrorism are immeasurably dangerous and terrorism centers must be combated by focusing on intellectual confrontation via public and higher education institutions, *Ulama* (Muslim scholars), *Dou'at*, imams, media channels and all the institutions of civil society.

The truth of the matter is that the most effective solution for stemming the flow of these terrorist groups depends on Muslim scholars and other relevant authorities playing their roles effectively. The security solution should only be a last resort in protecting societies.

14

Internal and Cross-Border Organized Crime in the Gulf

Ali bin Abdul Rahman Al-Du'aij

Organized crime is no longer an isolated problem which a state can deal with domestically. Instead, organized crime has become a phenomenon that transcends national borders and is now a subject of international concern.

Cross-country, or cross-border organized crime represents a direct threat to national and international security and stability. It even challenges the authority of the state itself by weakening social and economic institutions, causing a loss of confidence in the functioning of the state, and even limits personal freedoms. Cross-border organized crime can also create imbalances in economic development, deflecting prosperity from its proper recipients and so disadvantages an entire population. This crime poses a global threat from which the Arabian Gulf region is not immune, and since this region plays an important and effective part in the global economy, the GCC states could well be targeted by organized criminal groups. Shedding light on this phenomenon of organized crime as it relates to the region enables one to grasp its reality, scale and dimension in order to find the appropriate means of combating it.

This study endeavors to review the concept of cross-border organized crime and the efforts exerted by the United Nations in combating it, identify the reality of organized crime in the Gulf region, and finally present a proposal for preventing cross-border organized crime in the Arabian Gulf.

[317]

Defining Cross-Border Organized Crime

It is worth mentioning from the outset that there appears to be a lack of a definition that clearly describes organized crime and cross-border organized crime. This is because the latter is not totally independent of the former, but is considered a variation of the former in view of its spatial scope—i.e., cross-border organized crime is simply organized crime when it moves outside the domain of one country and into another, whether in terms of planning, execution or effect.

However, some researchers consider organized crime to be similar to terrorism in terms of having no precise definition, or at least one which is widely agreed upon. What can be said is that it is a criminal enterprise with an organizational structure that operates in total secrecy, with an internal law regulating operations and imposing punishments on members who attempt to go against its designs in order to guarantee its continuity. Sometimes in order to increase its camouflage, some organized crime gangs operate under legitimate signboards.

Standing[1] points out that the first person to speak of organized crime was the American President Herbert Hover in 1929. Prior to the study of criminal organizations there was no official term to describe organized criminal gangs until they became the subject of discussion and research, after which identifying those criminal activities as 'organized' became a necessary label.

The General Assembly of Interpol defined organized crime in 1988 as: "a continuous unlawful activity executed by an organized entity which seeks to realize its criminal goals even by transcending its national borders." In a second definition – submitted by Colombia during the discussion by the UN General Assembly of the bill on the UN Convention Against Transnational Crime, Vienna, March 8–12, 1999 – organized crime is described as: "an illegitimate activity practiced by two or more persons bound by hierarchical or personal relations, whether permanent or not, with the intention of reaping economic gains via violence, terrorism, corruption, or any other means."

[318]

A third definition of organized crime attempts to consolidate this further as "a criminal activity or behavior engaged in by a group of persons in a regular form, enabling them to agree and plan to commit a criminal act by using illegitimate means [sic] like violence, threats, deception, and corruption in order to achieve financial or other material gains."[2]

Such definitions have implicitly included the basic elements that characterize organized crime, and any one of these definitions is appropriate in itself to indicate the intent of the crime—at least from a legal point of view. But criticism has been directed towards past definitions because they neglect to provide for the existence of criminal penalties in one form or another for these illegitimate acts, and that the interconnection of crime and punishment has been ignored. No definition of organized crime enjoys global acceptance. Modern definitions lack vision and consensus because of their focus on the activities of organized crime and not the constituent characteristics of criminal organizations.[3]

In an attempt to find a solution to the problems for those who study organized crime, Liddick[4] compiled academic and governmental definitions of organized crime to deduce the elements common in organized criminal gangs. He found that they share: a continuous pyramidal organization; make reasonable profits by committing crimes and using violence and threats; a connection between their activities and corrupt officials; the existence of a demand for the services they provide; control and monopoly of illegitimate markets; restricted membership; specialization in operation tasks; master planning; and the fact that they are non-ideological organizations.

Many definitions were forged in the early 1970s and hence it has become necessary for the United Nations to adopt a definition which is more appropriate to countries all over the world, which led to the United Nations Convention against Transnational Organized Crime in Palermo, Italy in 2000. In article 2a the Convention defines an "organized criminal group" as a "structured group of three or more persons, existing for a period of time and acting in concert with the aim of committing one or more serious crimes."[5] Crime can also have a transnational aspect to it and conforms to the definition of serious crime as outlined in article 3/1b of the same Convention—"where the offence is transnational in nature and involves an organized criminal group." We can conclude from the UN Convention mentioned that organized crime is now characterized by the following:

- Organized crime is dangerous and very often it employs violence to realize its ends.
- These are not individual crimes, but crimes perpetrated by organized criminal groups; i.e., these groups possess an organizational structure.
- The goal of committing organized crime is primarily to achieve financial benefits or obtain other material gains; organized crime is based on profit/loss calculations since it always operates in places where money is found and where there is minimal security.
- It is characterized by supreme resilience and the ability to go beyond state borders, recruiting operatives in more than one country and organizing criminal networks operating at the national and international levels.

This definition, which is characterized by excessive generalization, is preferred rather than creating an infinite list of the most common organized crimes. Hence one finds that the aforementioned characteristics and traits apply to drug trafficking, trade in arms, trade in persons, trade in stolen cars, corruption and bribes, money laundering, forgery, products piracy, trade mark theft, violation of intellectual property rights, informatic crimes associated with cyber space such as accessing, stealing and forging bank account and credit card details, and other hi-tech crimes that informatics have brought to the fore.[6]

The General Characteristics
of Cross-Border Organized Crime

Historical Overview

Many organized criminal groups have emerged in modern history in several regions of the world. The Italian Mafia is one of the oldest and most effective of these groups, and it has laid down the fundamentals of the modern concept of organized criminality. The history of the Italian Mafia stems from the 13th century when the French conquest of the island of Sicily took place in 1282. A secret organization had formed to resist the French invaders, whose slogan was "Death to the French is Italy's Cry" (*Morte Alla Francia Italia Anela*), hence the word *mafia* which represents the first letter of each word in the slogan.[7]

The early Italian Mafia took the form of small gangs committing highway robbery, burglary and levying illegitimate taxes. Its nucleus began to form in the backstreets of Italian cities and notably Palermo on the island of Sicily. Smuggling tobacco, manufacturing and smuggling liquor, as well as the familiar activities of levying tributes and burglary, were the main sources of huge amounts of money for the Mafia. Later it moved into other activities such as trafficking in pharmaceuticals, narcotics, etc.

Other groups include the American Mafia, which was inspired to a great extent by the Italian Mafia, and was chiefly active in drug-smuggling operations[8]; the Chinese triad gangs whose activities involve extortion, trafficking drugs, prostitution and gambling through an extensive international network; the infamous Japanese organized crime group *Yakuza* whose criminal activities involve trade in firearms and narcotics, gambling, deception, money laundering and the sex industry; and the Colombian drug cartels that work chiefly in the narcotics trade and conceal illegal gains through legal businesses in order to discourage suspicion and criminal investigation.[9]

Currently, the most infamous organized crime group is the Russian Mafia. After the disintegration of the Soviet Union and the subsequent political turmoil in the Eastern Bloc, accompanied by economic collapse and social disintegration, organized criminal activities flourished. One activity particular to the Russian Mafia was the exportation of girls for sex to the Middle East and Europe in what is known as the "white slave trade." Russian organized crime is multi-faceted and is made up of nearly 3,000–4,000 criminal groups that are involved in narcotics, political assassinations, firearms, nuclear materials, and trade in human organs; and operate within the framework of weak local laws and various close ties between members of the Russian Mafia and former officials.[10]

After a closer look at the spatial range of activity of today's organized criminal groups, it becomes clear that their actions have gone beyond the borders of one state and into a wider domain—transnational organized crime. Moreover, these groups have invented many techniques to disguise their criminal activities, including frequent attempts to confer legality on illegitimate gains in order to put off any judicial follow-up—a process known as "money laundering." The activities of the gangs of organized crime now represent a tangible reality in most countries of the world after having been restricted to a limited number of states previously. The United Nations estimates that the economic scale of activity of these gangs is in the region of US$1 trillion.

The Characteristics of Organized Crime

Organized crime, whether transnational or not and in contrast to other crimes, is characterized by:

- *Organization*: The most important distinctive feature that sets organized crime apart from other crimes is organization. The criminal organization conducts its activities via a clear structure that takes the form of a pyramid and is characterized by coherence and efficacy. Criminal organizations are graded in terms of power in accordance with the competence of their organization and efficacy.

- *Professionalism*: Operatives in criminal organizations commit illegal acts that may amount to specialization. Hence the attributes of bravery and inclination to risk-taking are no longer sufficient to practice organized criminal activities. Studies point out that managing organized criminal activities has become a complex process, which requires from those who engage in it high managerial skills such as job analysis, supervision of operations, following up the execution of orders, etc.

- *Specialization*: The number of criminal organizations is on the increase and therefore heightens competition among them, which drives some to specialize in particular illegal activities, such as stealing cars or forging currencies.

- *Profit-making management*: Criminal organizations are managed and administered in ways that target the achievement of rapid profit with the least possible effort.

- *Continuity*: Criminal organizations develop as a structure whose purpose is continuity in illegal operations, and evidence today highlights the continuity of many criminal organizations for long periods of time despite the fact some of their leaders may have been arrested or have disappeared. This fact demonstrates that there are those within such groups taking the initiative to continue operations. The best examples of the continuity of criminal organizations are those that take the form of family where its members inherit the management of criminal activities—as is the case in Italy and the United States.

- *Secrecy*: Criminal organizations practice their activities in utter secrecy, which is strictly enforced, and such is the concern with secrecy that the severest punishments are imposed for disclosure— usually execution, which is carried out with no exceptions.[11]

The Difference between Cross-Border Organized Crime and Locally Organized Crime

The scope of operations of organized crime has two forms that conform to the domain of its activities. The first is locally (or nationally) organized crime, where the crime committed by the criminal organization is within the regional borders of the state, and is subject to the state's legal scrutiny in accordance with the principle of regional jurisdiction of criminal law, or "the principle of regionalism" as it is known.

The principle of regionalism indicates the effectiveness of the state criminal law on every crime committed within its borders irrespective of the nationality of the perpetrator. Most punitive legislation in Arab countries, including the Egyptian Penal Code (article 1) and the Jordanian Penal Code (article 7/1) and the Libyan Penal Code (article 4/1) have provided for this principle.

The second form of organized crime is trans-country organized crime, which is commonly referred to in UN documents as "transnational organized crime," or as it is termed by some researchers "cross-border organized crime." All terms denote a crime committed by a criminal organization that involves several countries. In light of the links between cross-border/country organized crime and locally organized crime, we can say that the former is characterized by distinctive qualities and raises several legal problems that set it apart from locally organized crime, which will be examined in detail below.

The Distinctive Characteristics of Cross-Border Organized Crime

Research and studies continue to identify the distinctive characteristics of both locally organized crime and cross-border organized crime and how to distinguish between them. Nevertheless, there is a consensus on a group of characteristics that set cross-border organized crime apart. Harasymiw[12] says methods of studying organized crime are as multiple as the multiplicity of the interests of the researchers. This relates to the major characteristics of the phenomenon of organized crime—these include organization, criminal activities, conspiracy, violence and political relations. This enables us to summarize the distinctive characteristics of cross-border organized crime in the following way:

Operating on the international level: The activities of cross-border organized crime are characterized by the fact that they are not only restricted to the domain of a single state, but surpass this to include the domains of several countries. As for locally organized crime, its activities are practiced within the internal domain of a single state.

Having a graded pyramidal organization: An international or cross-border criminal organization is composed of levels of authority where tasks and responsibilities are distributed appropriately, provided that each member respects this hierarchy and implements his/her responsibilities accurately and specifically. This form of organization is characterized by the order of its levels and its chain of leadership, as well as unity of purpose and total commitment by its members. Thus, an organized crime group is well structured and is characterized by its robustness and continuity of activity.[13]

Achieving large profits: Cross-border organized crime realizes massive profits in comparison with the gains reaped by the activities of locally organized crime. This corresponds to the greater market and demand for cross-border organized criminal activities found outside the state, as well as its mobilization of a larger number of members to assist in realizing its goals of obtaining maximum profit.

Resilience and ability to adjust: Resilience is the most important characteristic of cross-border organized crime, giving it the ability to adjust to the various efforts of legal authorities that seek to combat it. If cross-border criminal organizations find themselves subject to pressures from law-enforcement authorities, they resort to the ability to transfer their activities to other countries where laws are weaker and law-enforcement authorities are less strict. Resilience does not only bestow on cross-border criminal organizations the ability to cope with law and law-enforcement agencies only, but also gives them the ability to respond to different opportunities that arise in order to achieve their criminal goals.

Focusing on strategic coalitions: Practicing their activities in regions of other countries may make criminal organizations collide with other cross-border criminal organizations that wholly or partly control the

[325]

markets in these regions, or make them collide with local criminal organizations that practice their activities there. This conflict of interests might lead to rivalry and even violence between them. To avoid this outcome, cross-border criminal organizations resort to establishing coalitions with other local (national) and cross-border (transnational) criminal organizations. These kind of coalitions contribute to increasing the chances for success of criminal operations, and also distribute the consequences of being discovered by the legal establishment.

Legal Problems Raised by Cross-Border Organized Crime

Locally (nationally) organized crime is an internal crime, which is subject to criminal law and does not cause legal problems associated with investigation, interrogation, trial or enforceable law between countries. On the other hand, cross-border organized crime, owing to the fact that its activities take place in more than one state, creates several legal problems; the most important of which are:

- The country in which a cross-border organized crime is committed finds it difficult to conduct investigations or interrogations in a solo manner unless other countries, where the criminal activity or their consequences have also occurred, provide it with the necessary information.
- It is difficult to specify the appropriate enforceable law from the differing criminal legislation of the countries where organized crime is committed. Because the activities of cross-border organized crime occur in more than one state, it raises the legal problem of choosing and enforcing the appropriate criminal law for these crimes.
- The fact that the perpetrator or perpetrators flee to a foreign country or countries after committing criminal activities raises the question of extradition. To which country (of the ones demanding extradition) are the perpetrators going to be extradited? What are the conditions of

[326]

extradition? The fact that most signed extradition treaties are bilateral, and not international, complicates the question of extraditing criminals.

• The confidentiality of bank transactions and account numbers in certain countries, such as Switzerland, constitutes a barrier to controlling and appropriating illegal funds.

Despite the legal problems raised by cross-border organized crime, the international community is exerting great efforts in reinforcing cooperation between countries in order to combat this type of crime and block the attempts of perpetrators to escape punishment.

The Factors and Dangers of the Spread of Cross-Border Organized Crime

In this regard there are two aspects: First, the investigation of the spread of cross-border organized crime. Second, the investigation of the dangers of the spread of cross-border organized crime.

Factors in the Spread of Cross-Border Organized Crime

The emergence of organized crime at the international level and the fact that it possesses great capabilities in terms of its pattern of activity and massive funds, are a result of several factors that have contributed to the expansion of the geographical domain of its activities. Foremost among these is the rapidity of international transport and the growth and ease of international trade. This has facilitated the movement of people and materials from one country to another. Criminal organizations have exploited this to spread the influence of their criminal activities across borders in order to achieve maximum profit and have been able, as a result, to promote their illegal goods and services in other countries, thereby internationalizing the activities of organized crime.

Migration is an additional factor, which has played a significant role in spreading organized crime trans-nationally. Criminal organizations have become active in smuggling emigrants to several countries that have shortages in their labor force, through travel document forgery and bribery of officials. This also extends to exploiting the illegal immigrants themselves, especially women for the sex industry, who are forced to repay the debts they have accrued in the process of smuggling themselves abroad. In addition, internal conflicts within some countries have helped contribute to the spread of trans-national organized crime and provided an opportunity for illegal trading in firearms.

Economic necessity has meant some countries require direct foreign capital investment for economic development, and do so by encouraging such investments through easy and attractive terms and conditions. Frequently this is done without background checks on the sources of these capital investments, and so providing opportunities for criminal organizations to launder the proceeds of their criminal activities by depositing them in the banks of these countries and investing them later in legal projects that yield huge profits. Such "money laundering" allows criminal organizations to conceal the origins of their illegal financial gains.

Perhaps the most important factor utilized by criminal organizations to expand the perimeter of their criminal activities in the sphere of money laundering is electronic communications. Due to the rapid development of electronic payment systems in the banking and financial sectors, it has become possible to transfer huge amounts of cash around the world with great speed—allowing criminal organizations to launder the proceeds of their criminal activities with ever greater efficiency.

The Dangers of Cross-Border Organized Crime

Cross-border organized crime constitutes a danger to state sovereignty because it infiltrates regional borders and practices criminal activities in other countries, making use of today's advances in technology, global trade and financial systems. Cross-border organized crime also represents a danger to national stability and state control, especially in countries where criminal organizations are wide-spread such as Italy and Colombia. For instance, the Sicilian Mafia resorts to employing methods of corruption and violence to perpetuate its activities, including establishing relations with ruling political parties, and has been able to infiltrate and influence state institutions at the highest echelons. It has also resorted to using violence to liquidate its adversaries, including judges, policemen, politicians, public employees and trade unionists. A case in point is the murder of Giovanni Falcone in 1992.

The danger of cross-border organized crime to society and its values becomes clear when it targets the very elements of coherence in a society, tearing the social fabric through criminal activities such as trafficking narcotics, and establishes its own values that run counter to the values and ethics of a society. Cross-border organized crime not only affects democratic fundamentals but also obstructs democracy through corruption of law-enforcement agencies. It is self-evident that cross-border organized crime poses great dangers to developing countries, since such states do not possess sufficient resources and the necessary expertise to confront the activities of cross-border organized crime. Countries that do allocate part of their scarce resources to confront these activities undermine their own development efforts by diverting funds to organized crime investigation.

Cross-border organized crime also represents a danger to financial institutions where corruption of employees may turn these institutions into a stage for money-laundering activities, which in turn can cause corruption to spread still further in a workforce. If discovered, the natural outcome of this will be these institutions losing their financial reputation – which is the basis of dealing with them – the consequence of which is the loss of public confidence in them and threats to their survival.

Sometimes cross-border organized crime causes great harm to the environment. The fact that some criminal organizations undertake the disposal of nuclear waste in an illegal manner inflicts devastating harm on water sources and agricultural lands, in addition to human settlements.

Finally, cross-border organized crime constitutes a danger to individuals who are the direct victims of its activities, thus violating their rights and basic freedoms that are preserved in international charters and treaties—an example of which is the white slave trade. Individuals caught up in this illegal activity are treated like economic products without the slightest regard for their humanity, rights or freedoms.

The Crime of Money Laundering

The emergence of organized crime and spread of criminal gangs has been accompanied by the establishment of large-scale illegal economic activities in order to obtain large amounts of money. Since gaining money through criminal activities is illegal, countries where such activities occur resort to tracking down and combating criminal gangs to prevent the continuity of their activities. In order for these gangs to escape the hunt, especially those investigations that enable a state to appropriate the funds of these gangs and freeze their assets, they resort to transferring money gained from illegal activities to locations outside of a state, where it is invested in projects and economic utilities. The state receiving this economic investment usually does not know the source of the funds since concealment is an essential element in the process. Thus the action of "laundering dirty money" is described as "a process capable of hiding the illegal source of the funds" (Al Baz, 2006).

The huge technological development in mass communications has facilitated such money-laundering activities due to fast electronic transfers of funds via different financial channels and banking systems. This is achieved via several complex financial processes involving illegal funds that hide their source and project them as "clean," then invest them in legal projects, after which they are reused in illegal schemes. Since this operation is based on utter secrecy, criminal gangs have found that banks are the most appropriate places for laundering ill-gotten money. Banks maintain privacy and discretion regarding deposits made and refuse to provide statements or disclose account numbers involved in transactions. This encourages criminal gangs to deposit funds in global banks in the form of saving trusts and realizing profits on fixed interests.

What this highlights is that money coming from illegal sources changes from "dirty" money into "clean" money once it enters the cycle of operations approved by law. Estimates indicate that half of the total of these transactions comes from trade in narcotics. The other half has diverse sources such as deception, forgery, car theft and arms smuggling. Despite increasing coordination between world security services specialized in combating such organized crime, these services do not possess a complete map of the movement of dirty funds, which are thought to be in massive figures. Statistics and preliminary estimates indicate that the amount of dirty funds that go through the process of laundering is in the region of US$100 billion within the United States and US$300 billion in the rest of the world. Other economics experts estimate that the amount of dirty money in circulation in the world now is closer to US$600 billion.

What has stirred the concern of the world in the last two decades of the 20th century is the sheer volume of funds resulting from the process of money laundering, which are in turn used to strengthen and support the institutions of organized crime. The damage from this process is not restricted to the economic domain, but has crossed to the political and social spheres. Hence, searching for and taking record of these funds, as well as taking legal procedures to freeze and appropriate them, has become a necessity.

The difficulty of uncovering the work of cross-border organized crime groups increases in light of the fact that these groups tend to use legitimate companies – import and export, services sector, or even multinational financial institutions – as a cover for their activities. Sometimes the criminal organization itself hides within a large company or actually controls such a company. Hence, the dividing line between acts constituting financial crime, or crimes relating to managing companies, and acts constituting international organized crime is quite often blurred. From this, it follows that there are three basic kinds of company associated with crime, namely: illegal commercial companies such as drug cartels; legal companies such as banks that commit financial crimes; and legal companies established wholly or partly by funds from organized crime.

The International Position towards Money Laundering

Laundering money by investing illegal funds in legitimate projects is the sort of economic crime that is met with opposition from all states. This kind of criminal deception has started to diversify globally due to the technological progress found in advanced banking systems around the world. Moreover, this type of crime is no longer specific to a particular state; rather, it is a global issue resulting from the movement of crime across countries in pursuit of effective camouflage and good profits, thus distancing itself from the possibilities of checks and appropriation. Such crime movements make use of existing gaps in current legislation and the legal procedures used to enforce it.

As a result, the collective will of states and desire to cooperate internationally are necessary to combat this type of crime, and there is a growing consensus in the world that is emphatically pushing towards taking quick steps to tackle this problem. Attempts to combat cross-border organized crime have taken legal and economic forms, especially in developing countries which are the point of focus for gangs to launder ill-gotten funds. Developing countries, whose economies are in a stage of transition and transformation, provide ample opportunities to launder money by investing it in various projects in these developing economies. This inevitably requires those states affected to create legislation and enact laws that criminalize those engaged in money laundering within their borders. In addition, this requires passing acts that permit disclosing the names of the owners of funds deposited in their banks if the source of this capital is suspicious.

In order to increase international cooperation in the sphere of investigation, mutual legal assistance, extraditing criminals, tracking down funds emerging from the process of money laundering and appropriating it, concerned states have coordinated the necessary legal and economic arrangements to hunt down money launderers. Various conferences and signed agreements have taken place including the European Convention on Laundering, Search, Seizure and Confiscation of the Proceeds from Crime, 1990; and the International Conference on Preventing and Controlling Money Laundering and the Use of the Proceeds of Crime, held in Italy 18–20 June, 1994. The latter was organized by the International Consultation and Technical Council in cooperation with the Italian government and the sponsorship of the United Nations Center for International Crime Prevention.

No doubt intensifying international efforts to constrain the use of the banking system for money laundering processes represents an effective weapon in the face of organized crime groups. This is best attested to by the recommendations of the task force concerned with financial procedures, proposed by the G-7 group of countries, which are also the states most affected by such crimes. The following is a summary of their proposals:

- Incriminating money laundering acts and determining deterrent penalties for them.
- Determining the criminal responsibility of banks and companies on the basis that they are legal personalities (*legales hominos*), in addition to the fact that their employees incur criminal responsibility as accomplices.
- Keeping records of the identities of clients and their transactions, and reporting cases of suspicious sources of money.
- Taking necessary measures to carry out investigations of owners of institutions and firms that do not practice commercial activity in the country where they are registered.

- Investigating big operations and unfamiliar patterns of transactions with no specific economic objective.
- Intensifying monitoring on funds coming into banks in every state, and obtaining knowledge about the sources of the funds of those opening accounts with banks, especially if the deposited amount is large and there is suspicion about its legality.

International Efforts in Combating Cross-Border Organized Crime

Today, human fears are not restricted to the hazards of war but also other dangers, such as organized crime, that affect spheres of human development including the economy, society and politics. Consequently, organized crime undermines both the foundations of the state's existence and the drivers of national prosperity. Thus, we find that the Charter of the United Nations has provided for the necessity of exerting all efforts to prevent and combat crime and stem its effects, which extend across the borders of states.

In preventing and combating crime, the United Nations depends on a number of authorities, the most important of which is the Commission on Crime Prevention and Criminal Justice, which is affiliated to the Economic and Social Council. This Commission is set the task of making decisions specific to the activities of the United Nations in the sphere of crime and justice, referring these decisions to the international congresses of the United Nations or the Economic and Social Council, and preparing for the United Nations' conferences on crime prevention. There is also the Center for International Crime Convention and Criminal Justice in the Center for Social Development and Human Affairs in Vienna, which is considered the sole professional and specialized agency responsible for the United Nations' program of preventing crime and promoting criminal justice. It is responsible for implementing and coordinating the activities of the United Nations in this field in addition to its day-to-day planning and coordination of preventing and combating crime, including providing technical assistance that is urgently needed by developing countries.

Other agencies concerned with crime include the United Nations regional and provincial institutes for combating crime and treatment of offenders, which are set the task of technical training and research into criminology, in addition to their work in the sphere of developing criminal laws and training judges and members of public prosecution. There is also the United Nations Crime and Justice Information Network (UNCJIN).[14]

In addition to the activities of the agencies affiliated to the United Nations in the field of preventing and combating crime, and as a result of a desire by the international organization itself to confront all issues relating to preventing and combating crime and the treatment of offenders, international conferences have been successively held since 1950. These conferences take the form of forums that investigate new developments in criminology in terms of quantity, quality and effect. The consistent expression of concern by certain UN members about the progressive and observable development of organized crime, especially when it traverses borders, has prompted the United Nations to make the discussion of cross-border organized crime part of the agenda of UN congresses that have convened of late.

These congresses include the Fifth Congress on the Prevention of Crime and the Treatment of Offenders (Geneva, 1975), which illustrated the need to combat crime on the national and transnational levels; the Sixth Congress on the Prevention of Crime and the Treatment of Offenders (Caracas, 1980), which addressed organized crime as a form of abusing power; the Seventh Congress on the Prevention of Crime and the Treatment of Offenders (Milan, 1985), which tackled new dimensions of criminal acts by putting crime in the context of development and future challenges and issued several decisions relating to cross-country organized crime; the Eighth Congress on the Prevention of Crime and the Treatment of Offenders (Havana, 1990), which addressed procedures of combating economic crime that is organized on national and transnational levels; and the Ninth Congress on the Prevention of Crime and the Treatment of Offenders (Cairo, 1995), which called for the establishment of an international organization concerned with cross-border organized crime, provided that the common domains of cooperation, assistance, information exchange, and judicial pursuit are made available.[15]

It is worth mentioning that the focus on cross-border organized crime came to prominence for the first time in the Fifth Congress in 1975, which was convened in Geneva. Interest in organized crime centered round the realization that it was a dangerous activity threatening the entity of nations. Since this date is relatively recent, one is inclined to say that the international community had largely ignored the danger of this kind of crime until now.

It is to be noted that some of the UN congresses have accorded importance to cross-border organized crime in terms of it being linked to other issues, such as a form of power abuse, or linking it to development and future challenges, or even terrorism—as happened at the Seventh Congress in Milan in 1985.[16] The efforts of the United Nations in combating cross-border organized crime via such congresses have paved the way for many member states to sign an accord whose aim is to put in place procedures to prevent and combat this criminal activity. This took place at the United Nations Convention against Transnational Organized Crime in Palermo, Italy, 12–15 December, 2000, and was signed by 148 nations.

From this accord, governments are committed to criminalizing money-laundering processes, corruption and obstruction of justice. Also, the provision on the confidentiality of banking was very clear in the accord—"states should not refuse to cooperate ... because of bank confidentiality." This article might be the most efficacious element in the Palermo accord since organized crime loses much of its attraction if beneficiaries fail to keep their profits safe.

The new accord also provides a framework for confiscation and seizure of proceeds of organized crime and properties and equipment used in criminal acts. It also comprises special rules for international cooperation in this sphere. This is an important tool for recovering funds stolen via corruption and deposited abroad. The longest article of the accord is devoted to matters of mutual legal assistance and deals with a large group of practical methods through which states can cooperate. In addition to this, it also covers matters pertinent to investigations and special investigative techniques through separate articles in the accord.

Organized Crime in the Gulf Region

Although the Gulf region in particular, and the Arab world in general, has not experienced organized crime in the same capacity as other regions of the world, it can also be a victim. The amount of money exchanged in the region has tempted organized crime groups to transfer some aspects of their activities to the Gulf. It is worth mentioning that there is no single or separate law to combat organized crime in GCC states, but there are articles in penal codes, such as bank acts and others, that regulate combating organized crime and the confiscation of the illegal proceeds accrued.

Factors Contributing to the Spread of Organized Crime in the Gulf

Although Arab societies, including Gulf societies, are conservative ones, which take pride in their religion and values, like all societies in the world they are affected by social, economic and political circumstances and variables. What follows is a review of the factors that might promote the spread of the phenomenon of organized crime in the Arab Gulf region.

Geographical Location

The Gulf region is characterized by its geographical location and lies at the crossroads of the major economic powers of the world. In addition, Arab Gulf countries enjoy strong economic growth and prosperity and a high demand for goods and services that has prompted many global institutions and firms to set up branches in the Gulf region in order to benefit from the facilities offered to them, to come closer to the local market, and to reduce transport and communication expenses.[17]

[337]

The Gulf region lies midway between East Asia and the West. The origin of most of the products of organized crime come from East Asia, including the growing and production of narcotics in the region known as the "Golden Triangle," Asian girls transported for the sex industry, child prostitution and trade in human organs (which traverse the Gulf region to reach consumers in Western Europe and the United States).

Criminals in this form are effectively traders. Since an investor always searches for a market to sell his goods, it is therefore natural to say that whenever these criminal gangs find prosperous markets and investors in the Gulf region, marketing in this particular area becomes preferred to the hazard and risk of delivering their commodities to Europe and the United States.

Openness to the Outside World

The Gulf region is part of the international community. Gulf states have adopted the principle of economic freedom and opened their markets to foreign investment. Their economies depend to a large extent on exporting oil and in return they import most of their needs from different countries across the world. The danger here lies in gangs of organized crime exploiting this openness to set up fictitious corporations and firms in order to establish a footing in these countries and consequently carry out their illegal activity with an air of legitimacy.

Legislative Inadequacy and Legal Gaps

The international community suffers from legislative inadequacy in the sphere of organized crime, and the Arab Gulf states particularly so. In fact, legislative inadequacy in the Gulf is so apparent that it is regarded as a big problem, reducing the efficacy of strategies to combat organized crime laid down by the Arab League and its councils specialized in this field.

This inadequacy stems from a lack of experience on the part of those in charge of combating organized crime, since it is still a relatively new

[338]

phenomenon to Arab societies in general and Gulf societies in particular. Causes of inadequacy also include lack of flexibility in legislative amendments and updating laws, thus making legislation incapable of keeping abreast of current developments in the world of crime. Consequently, gaps appear in the existing legislation, which attracts those wishing to benefit from them. Moreover, legislation prohibiting intentional sabotage of information saved in computers, or legislation prohibiting trade in human organs, or preventing burying nuclear waste, or money laundering are all matters lacking detailed provision in most Arab legal systems.

The High Percentage of the Migrant Labor Force

The development of a foreign labor force in Gulf states coincided with the discovery of oil. From that time onwards these countries began developing modern economies that included advances in all spheres of life. In light of the shortage of an appropriate labor force in the Gulf states, which is linked to their scant populations, the inclination was to import foreign labor as a necessary measure to support the labor market and the growing development at a time when the Gulf citizen lacked sufficient experience and readiness to meet this task.

As the economy of the Gulf countries continued to grow rapidly, the need for this foreign labor force increased until it led to an imbalance in the demographics of these countries. For example, the migrant labor force constitutes 82.4 percent of the population of the United Arab Emirates (UAE), and most of this labor force is from the Indian subcontinent. This foreign labor force has a significant effect on the social, economic, security, and political spheres of life. Socially, the negative effect is manifested in the structure and identity of society, where the ideals and ethics of a society recede and may acquire social values that do not deter people from committing crimes. In summary, organized crime finds in this loose, uncontrolled structure a golden chance to start illegal operations and form a nucleus for its criminal gangs.

Low Taxes and Charges

The taxes and charges levied in the Gulf states represent some of the lowest by international standards. This is primarily due to the dependence on income from oil revenues and their desire to encourage individuals to operate businesses and invest without obstacles or constraints. This situation has certainly encouraged many investors to head toward the Gulf region to invest and benefit from these fiscal regime. However, this calls for caution to prevent gangs of organized crime exploiting these facilities and moving fictitious institutions and firms into the region in order to obtain a foothold to launch their operations.

Inadequate Security Experience

The Gulf security experience is generally limited and inadequate in so far as organized crime is concerned, mainly because the activities of organized crime have until recently occurred away from the Arab region. With the exception of smuggling drugs, there are no tangible practices of these gangs in most Arab countries. In view of these circumstances the need to accord attention to preventing and combating methods, and their requirements, has only recently become imperative.

There is currently an urgent need to have Arab security services activate their efforts to lay down a strategy to prevent, combat and anticipate such dangers. Perhaps one of the priorities is the rapid preparation and training of special units to deal with organized crime, and adopt the concept of specialization in this field in order to guarantee minimal acceptable levels of success. The Secretary General of the Council of Arab Ministers of the Interior has proposed forming a standing committee within the Secretariat General to be called the committee of "Combating Organized Crime." The proposal envisaged the constitution of this committee, its specializations and methods of work. The proposal called for entrusting the committee with the responsibility of oversight and coordination between all the authorities concerned in the field of organized crime in the member states.

The Reality of Organized Crime in the Gulf

Although the author attempted to investigate the reality of organized crime in the Gulf region, data on criminal organizations was not available in general. This is especially true of criminal organizations of Gulf origin. However, there are obvious premonitions of the possibility of the emergence of such organizations in the region. Those who probe criminal organizations and examine their characteristics, techniques and methods of work, realize that the Gulf region will not remain safe from contagion by such organizations unless preparations are made to confront these criminal phenomena. This should be done by making the environment of the Gulf region unsuitable for the emergence of criminal organizations whether of Gulf, Arab or foreign origin.

A report by the Gulf Center for Strategic Studies claims that GCC states face security challenges of an economic nature in the domain of narcotics and money-laundering operations. The report included the GCC states in the countries attracting these operations in accordance with international indicators. The Center's report also pointed out that the GCC countries have begun to be included within those countries attractive to those involved in money laundering as indicated by the Financial Action Task Force (FATF), which operates a scale giving countries with greater attraction a higher number of points. According to the FATF, the Kingdom of Bahrain, the State of Qatar, and the UAE came in the middle of the list with 150–190 points, while the Sultanate of Oman, the State of Kuwait and the Kingdom of Saudi Arabia ranged from 50–99 points. Although the report demonstrated that these scores are far less than other countries such as Luxemburg, which comes at the top of this list with 686 points, the USA with 634 points, and Switzerland with 617 points, the fact that the Gulf countries are even mentioned in this list at all represents a challenge in itself. The report adds that this matter underscores the importance of moving quickly to deter money-laundering gangs and promulgating legislation to combat these crimes, even though they are on a much smaller scale when viewed globally, especially compared to

Southeast Asian countries, in terms of the scale of money-laundering operations.

The same report pointed out that the biggest case of narcotics smuggling in the Gulf was the one discovered in the UAE in 2006 when an Asian gang tried to smuggle a quarter of a ton of hashish. Although the amount was huge, it was not the only case. Prior to it two tons of hashish were seized in the Sultanate of Oman. The report revealed that a study conducted in Kuwait pointed out that the amount of drugs seized in 2001 was 466,671 kilograms of hashish, 22,252 kilograms of opium, 6,808 kilograms of heroin and 1,512 kilograms of marijuana. The study also demonstrated that deaths caused by using drugs alone increased during a five-year period from nine to 45 deaths in 2001. Meanwhile, the number of those who commit drug-induced crime increased from 432 to 807 individuals during the same period.

The report concluded that the Gulf region is one of the locations likely to be targeted by global money-laundering gangs for a number of reasons, including its noted geographical location as a link between drug-production centers in places such as Pakistan, Afghanistan, Thailand and Iran, and drug-consumer countries in Europe and the United States. The report added that what increases the targeting of the GCC states by money-laundering gangs is the fact these countries enjoy extensive coasts that facilitate smuggling. In addition, these countries also have an advanced transport infrastructure which allows easy movement of goods within or outside the country. Moreover, administrative procedures and checks in customs departments, ports and airports of some of these countries are minimal.

The report confirmed that the presence of massive numbers of migrant workers, exceeding 9 million in the GCC, are mostly from Asia and makes them a source for money-laundering operations, and especially so when most of these workers come from drug-producing countries in Asia. Some of them, who have experience and are active, form gangs to practice organized crime in the Gulf.

A Proposed Program to Prevent
Cross-Border Crime in the Gulf Region

This research presents an ambitious scheme through which cross-border crime can be confronted in Arab Gulf countries. The scheme depends on expanding the scope of approaches to combat cross-border crime, since this kind of criminal activity requires consolidated efforts to ensure success. The scheme here incorporates noble goals, firm pivots and effective programs.

The Goals of the Scheme

This scheme seeks to realize several goals. The importance of specifying goals stems from the fact that this outlines the expected outcomes, determines approaches and therefore decides the remaining elements of the scheme. The goals of the scheme are:

- Raising the awareness of the Gulf community with respect to the danger of modern crimes and their effects.
- Unifying the efforts of official institutions in order to combat modern crimes.
- Taking preventive measures to thwart the spread of this type of crime.
- Reinforcing communal participation to support official efforts in combating crime.
- Upgrading the efficiency of legal systems in order to deter criminal activities.
- Immunizing members of society against this aberrant behavior, reinforcing community integrity, and upgrading the kind self-censure that prevents individuals from engaging in crime-related activities.
- Inventing appropriate solutions and creative methods of combating different criminal activities related to cross-border crimes.

The Pivots of the Scheme

Pivots denote the system of supporting foundations on which the scheme is built. They are employed to serve the realization of the desired goals.

Good goals are those that take into consideration the constituents of their environment so that these goals become characterized by realism, acceptance and clarity. These pivots comprise the following:

The Pivot of Creed

Religion is the greatest influence on the behavior of individuals and groups. Gulf society embraces Islam, which combats crime in all forms, conventional and novel, and plays a major role in controlling the actions of individuals and groups in this life. Moreover, firm faith as well as the increase in religious consciousness in the Gulf countries, affirms the adherence of Gulf societies to Islamic teaching.

The Socio-Cultural Pivot

Gulf nations are distinguished by societal values and cultural paradigms that contribute to ties and coherence between individuals. Furthermore, the customs and traditions of the Gulf community come second after religion as regards protecting individuals against crime. Social customs and traditions of the Gulf community are characterized by cohesion and family unity. Social customs and traditions shun and combat crime, and individuals avoid crime lest society ostracize them.

The Techno-Economic Pivot

Gulf countries enjoy strong economies and huge surplus budgets, enabling them to develop manpower, finance anti-criminal activities and procure modern technology that helps to uncover crimes before they are committed.

The Security Pivot

It goes without saying that progress and growth in any society requires that the society enjoys the necessary security to enable individuals to achieve and contribute to their country's development. Gulf countries enjoy the existence of security and the availability of training institutions in the form of colleges and police institutes that train security personnel and maintain the development of their capabilities and skills. These services enjoy official and communal support and encouragement.

The Legal Pivot

The Holy Koran and the *Sunna* are the source for legislation in the Gulf countries. Constitutions and regimes that are compatible with the Holy Koran and the Sunna have been devised at the same time to meet the prerequisites of the age and keep up with changes. Gulf countries enjoy legislative institutions, specialized cadres in *Shari'a* and law, which are capable of stipulating effective legislation to take into account new developments.

The Media Pivot

The media contributes greatly to the education and awareness of societies and to enhancing their values and beliefs. The Media in the Gulf countries enjoys a high level of proficiency, which is reflected in its diversity (press, radio and television), the integrity of its orientation, its creative potential, the capabilities of those in charge of it, and the confidence of society in its credibility.

The Scientific and Informatics Pivot

In the last few decades the Gulf countries have devoted much attention to the creation of institutions of higher education and research centers, databases and empowering researchers—all of which is reflective of the importance of research in development plans in GCC states. This has effectively contributed to developing qualitatively and quantitatively the capabilities of specialized personnel in the domain of scientific research.

Programs and Implementing Bodies

Programs are operational plans incorporating a group of activities that seek to utilize pivots and translate goals into practical realities. Programs are characterized by detail and are subject to development and change in a manner that guarantees consistency with circumstances and new developments that are faced by societies. Hence, programs are often characterized by clarity of scope and detailed objectives and should satisfy the following criteria:

- Contribution to achieving one or more of the goals of the schemes, either directly or indirectly.
- Utilizing available pivots with a high degree of efficiency.
- Incorporating an accurate specification of activities and the necessary methods of implementation.
- Specifying the bodies that implement the activities of the program.
- Characterized by realism via conformity with available capabilities.
- Activities of programs should be linked to a specific timetable.
- Programs should be designed in a scientific manner that guarantees integration and avoidance of contradiction with other programs, as well as the presence of a performance criteria that are open to observation and measurement and demonstrate levels of acceptable achievement.

What follows here are the proposed programs and relevant implementing bodies:

First Program

Reinforcing Citizenship and Protecting Adolescents from Crime via School Curricula

Program Description

Incorporating subjects pertinent to protection against crime in existing curricula in the primary, intermediate and secondary stages of education conforming to the age of the pupil, level of his/her maturity and grade. Thus, the study of such subjects can be encouraged at university level and developed with reference to relevant Arab and world experiences, provided that a specialized group of instructors, security personnel and specialists in *Shari'a* and jurisprudence participate in preparing the subjects.

Implementing Bodies

Ministries of Education/Higher Education, Arab Departments of Education.

Second Program

Developing Programs to Prepare and Train Security Personnel and Incorporate Modern and relevant Materials in Study Syllabuses

Program Description

Police colleges in the GCC states should contribute to a better preparation of security personnel in such a manner that guarantees a minimal level of knowledge and skills that are relevant to modern crimes. In addition, specialized training sessions should be designed for those security personnel whose jobs require the confrontation of innovative and cross-border crimes.

Implementing Bodies

Security and Police colleges, institutes and centers for security training.

Third Program

Unifying Legal Frameworks and Deterrent Penalties for Cross-border Crimes

Program Description

The program consists of revising current legislation in the GCC states and working on their preparation for integration. In addition, unifying financial procedures between banks to limit economic crimes and combat those involved in organized crime by denying access to suspect funds that might help in financing such criminal groups.

Implementing Bodies

Ministries of Justice, legal institutions, punitive institutions and correction centers.

Fourth Program

Designing Media Programs to Educate Gulf Communities about Criminal Methods and Clarify the Role Expected from them in Prevention and Deterrence

Program Description

Creating radio broadcasts, visual programs and documentary films to illustrate organized crime in its various forms, and allocate space in newspapers and magazines to raise awareness in Gulf society and demonstrate the expected role of individuals whether in the domain of prevention or deterrence.

Implementing Bodies

Ministries of Information, security institutions and journalists' associations in the Gulf.

Fifth Program

Founding Research Centers and Databases Catering for the Study of Criminal Phenomena in the Gulf Region

Program Description

Founding a regional center for security research for the GCC states, with branches in each Gulf state, in order to prepare Gulf criminal statistical studies on general and cross-border crime, as well as monitoring international variables and their relation to cross-border organized crime, and devising methods to utilize the positive and limit the negative aspects of these variables. Needless to say, research centers, in spite of their diversity, cannot work in the absence of integrated databases. Hence it is necessary to build relevant databases to allow for the exchange of information between specialized authorities in each Gulf state, provided that information exchange is restricted to experts in the fields of law and crime.

Implementing Bodies

Ministries of Interior, crime research centers and government departments concerned with organized crime in the GCC states.

Sixth Program

Promoting A National Sense of Belonging

Program Description

This program is concerned with reinforcing the role of societal institutions by promoting the national sense of belonging among members of Gulf society and employing the theories of crime prevention that demonstrate the integrative relationship between social and security institutions. In addition, it is concerned with promoting the social values derived from *Shari'a* and projecting the importance of social integration that Islam upholds to guarantee the security of both individuals and society; and spreading religious consciousness among all members of society in order to promote strong moral values and awareness in society as a whole.

Implementing Bodies

Mosques during Friday sermons, guided religious debates, lectures, programs and dialogue.

Outlook for the Future

The prevailing policy of openness adopted by the majority of the member states of the global community will mean that international relations will become more intricate and involve more complex international overlaps than ever before. In light of international security shortcomings with respect to combating cross-border organized crime, this will provide a suitably fertile environment for such criminal activities. The implication of this is: firstly, an increase in the current activity of organized criminal groups; and secondly the emergence of new groups of organized crime that engage in criminal acts with transnational effects.

The relations between criminal groups may be consolidated in an attempt to gain individual benefit by supporting each other's criminal activities. Instances of this include the intimate relations between terrorism, the arms trade and the trafficking of narcotics. In this process, terrorist groups hope to obtain a share in these financial gains by virtue of the role they performed on behalf of criminal groups.[18]

Future cross-border organized crime will encompass several spheres:

- A spatial sphere that encompasses almost all the member states of the international community.
- A qualitative sphere represented in the multiplicity of criminal activities, current and future, as long as there is the potential for massive profits that are safe from the attention of security services.
- A sphere where the management of criminal acts is conducted by complex organizational methods that are difficult to penetrate, and a conscious study of developments on the international stage which can be exploited for the satisfaction of criminal objectives.[19]

Perhaps this rapid and extremely dangerous development of cross-border organized crime calls for a re-examination of current international variables that affect more familiar crimes in the sphere of a single state on the basis that, "any change in the modes of living as a result of a change in the surrounding circumstances necessitates new concepts and a kind of thinking that conforms to the new situation, and hence different methods of handling [it],"[20] i.e., we cannot examine the positive effects of these variables only, but must also examine the negative effects in order to work out appropriate solutions. From this perspective, cross-border organized crime has also been subject to change, whether in terms of how it is spread, how it is committed and executed, or in its negative effects. Hence, a deeper study is required in order to expose legislative, judicial and security gaps through which its perpetrators escape and avoid punishment. This must be carried out in preparation for a new, conscious phase of international cooperation, the goal of which is to implement suitable solutions that conform to the rules of the United Nations Convention against Transnational Organized Crime.

Technological advances in communications and transport, the growth of mutual commercial and economic dependence between states, and the increase in international commercial activity, as well as the globalization of financial markets, has played a major role in creating the "global village." This has been accompanied by a changing environment within which organized crime works on the international level, and has witnessed the emergence of dangerous criminal organizations that forge alliances with other organizations in order to impose their hegemony and spread their influence in all countries. Therefore, the danger of organized crime in its new form is of concern to all countries.

The danger posed by criminal organizations is not only restricted to the results of their criminal activities, but also extends to their ability to corrupt the public apparatus of the state. The issue of cross-border organized crime will be one of great concern to policy makers in the 21st century. No domain of international affairs will escape its consequences when the economic fabric and the political and financial regimes of countries collapse under the rising influence of the organizations of international organized crime.

Section 5

DEMOGRAPHIC CHALLENGES FACING THE GULF COUNTRIES

15

Migrant Labor Force and the Security Situation in the Gulf Region

Mohammed Ibrahim Dito

The phenomenon of migrant labor in the GCC states constitutes a unique case in the context of global labor force migration. The unique nature of this phenomenon in the Gulf region stems from both its controversy and its continuity over several decades, despite numerous efforts and attempts on the part of the GCC states to limit its flow and effects. The main obstacle to dealing with this phenomenon lies in the fact that the majority of proposed solutions seek to strike a balance between often conflicting economic, social and political requirements, which makes the issue difficult to solve via solutions based on any single policy.

The challenge of labor force migration in the world today poses a prominent global challenge which can no longer be confronted by adopting absolutist policies such as simply closing or opening borders to migration. The outcomes of the experiences of several countries in addressing the problem of labor migration have proven that ignoring the facts of the phenomenon will not lead to satisfactory results; indeed, it often aggravates the problem. Hence, it is not surprising that a new global approach to this issue has developed in recent years, characterized by efforts to re-examine the realities of labor migration while maintaining a positive developmental perspective linked to an integrated method of formulating relevant policies that take into account the interests of the different parties concerned. This coincides with an expansion of the parties participating in the dialogue on migration, owing to the growing activity of local and global civil society organizations.

There is a growing tendency among the different actors in the process of labor migration towards developing a multi-lateral international framework based on an integrated group of principles and universal values in order to govern migration. This has resulted in a number of agreements and international guidelines protecting the rights of migrant labor forces, agreed upon within the International Labor Organization (ILO) and other United Nations (UN) agencies. The most prominent of these is the Plan of Action for Migrant Workers, which was approved by the international labor conference in its 92nd session in June 2004. The action plan recommended the development of a "non-binding multilateral framework for a rights-based approach to labor migration which takes account of labor market needs, proposing guidelines and principles for policies based on best practices and international standards."[1]

This effort has achieved significant progress in recent years. However, it still faces several obstacles. These include the challenge of balancing the requirements of economic growth and the integration of emerging markets into the world economy on the one hand, and the need to protect the social gains and further develop them in accordance with the objective of sustained human development on the other. The roots of this challenge are manifested throughout the social, economic and political aspects of the societies concerned.

Migrant Labor in the GCC States: Reaching a Framework of Common Understanding

In the case of the GCC states, the most prominent manifestation of this challenge is the clear need to develop a new strategy to shape the course of dependence on migrant labor and the necessary policies to achieve integration of their economic, political and social policies in this field. The most important prerequisite in modernizing this vision is to come to terms with the role of migrant labor in these states and formulate policies that can lead to efficient and constructive integration in the international community rather than international isolation.

The correct approach to achieving efficient modernization of this strategy is to develop a two-dimensional social dialogue on the policies dealing with migrant labor. The first dimension of such a dialogue involves conducting a separate balanced socio-economic dialogue inside each state, whilst the second comprises the launch of a regional and international social dialogue between all the different actors involved (governments, employers, workers, etc.). Such efforts would be complementary; the first dimension would reinforce the position of the state in the regional and international context, and the second would affect the content and course of the internal social dialogue.

Social dialogue, as an effective tool in meeting the challenges of migration, is not being fully utilized in the GCC states. Although there have been notable improvements in this regard in recent years, both the depth of dialogue – in terms of identifying the basic causes of the problem of migrant labor – and the expansiveness of dialogue – encompassing all the spheres of management of migrant labor (employment, recruitment, protection, etc.) – have been disproportionate to the scale of the challenges facing these states.

A major question is: how do we reach a common understanding of the phenomenon of migrant labor in the GCC states that can act as a basis for policies capable of benefiting all (both sending and receiving countries) and which encourage sustained development? In this context, I believe that it is time for the GCC states to launch this dialogue at the local, regional and global levels.

Two fundamental aspects of migrant labor movement place the phenomenon at the top of the list of concerns both in terms of public opinion and local and international decision making. The first relates to the size and rate of the flow of migrant labor, while the second relates to the emergence of new principles that protect the rights of this labor force and establish criteria with which to deal with the phenomenon.

Regarding the first aspect, we find that during the period 1990–2005, the GCC countries "were responsible for nearly 57 percent of the total increase in migrant labor force in the Arab world."[2] While "the size of the migrant labor force increased from 4 million in 1990 to 7 million in 2005 in the *al-Mashriq*[*] Arab region, this number increased from 9 million in 1990 to 13 million in 2005 in the GCC countries."[3]

This increase in the volume of migrant labor led to a rise in its percentage of total population, greatly surpassing the global average. "The percentage of foreigners in total population varies between 24.4 percent in the Sultanate of Oman and 78.3 percent in the State of Qatar." Migrant labor accounts for not more than 3 percent of total world population.[4] The migrant labor force in the GCC countries is growing at a substantial rate; "in five years (2000–2005) the rate of increase of migrant labor force in the UAE alone was 6.8 percent annually, i.e. nearly six times the global rate, which is 1.5 percent" (see tables 15.1 and 15.2 and figure 15.1).[5]

The interconnectivity of the three basic characteristics of the flow of migrant labor force into the GCC countries – large size, high percentage of total population and annual rate of growth – lead to the emergence of complex challenges. The large flow of male laborers affects the demographic structure of the population, as well as the population of the labor market. The increase in the proportion of foreigners to nationals has led to the emergence of challenges relating to cultural identity and the development of a hidden struggle based on the "estrangement of nationals" and a general fear of "naturalizing expatriates." In the public and official consciousness, the rapid growth in the flow of migrant labor is most associated with its impact on the job opportunities of nationals.

---

[*] As apposed to *al Maghareb* (occident). This includes Syria, Lebanon, Palestine, Jordan and Iraq.

Table 15.1
Growth Rate of Migrants (Percentage)

Country	1990–1995	1995–2000	2000–2005
Bahrain	4.7	3	3
Kuwait	-8.9	6.6	3.7
Oman	4.8	1.1	0.7
Qatar	1.9	2.5	6.5
Saudi Arabia	-0.6	2.2	4.3
United Arab Emirates	5.1	5.7	6.8
World	1.3	1.4	1.5

Source: UN, Department of Economic and Social Affairs. *World Migrant Stock: The 2005 Revision*, Populations Database (http://esa.un.org/migration/index.asp?panel=2).

Table 15.2
International Migrants as a Percentage of the Population
of the GCC States and the World

Country	1990	1995	2000	2005
Bahrain	35.1	37.5	37.8	40.7
Kuwait	72.4	58.7	62.2	62.1
Oman	24.5	26.3	24.8	24.4
Qatar	79.1	77.2	76	78.3
Saudi Arabia	29	24.7	23.9	25.9
United Arab Emirates	71.2	70.5	70.4	71.4
World	2.9	2.9	2.9	3.0

Source: UN, Department of Economic and Social Affairs. World Migrant Stock: The 2005 Revision, Populations Database (http://esa.un.org/migration/index.asp?panel=2).

[359]

Figure 15.1

Percentage of Migrants in Total Population (2005)

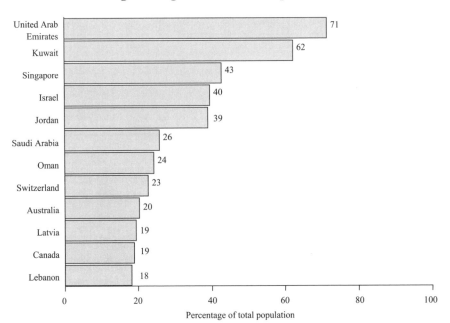

In studying the state of migrant labor forces, the figures are not as important as the constant movement of humans they represent. The fact that this movement relates to human beings should be reflected in the way the issue is approached, together with economic, political, social, or cultural considerations. These aspects often conflict, creating obstacles to the correct treatment of global labor migration, especially in the GCC countries. The integration of these considerations, which operate in accordance with different systems, is vital in formulating a framework of common understanding with which to view and deal with this phenomenon. I believe the basis of such a framework must be rights, which accommodate both the flexibility required by labor markets in the era of globalization and the requisite social protection for migrants. The current economic climate in the GCC states – despite increased economic efficiency and increasingly diversified sources of income – provides demand for the type of professions occupied by migrant laborers, especially in sectors of weak productivity.

The importation of migrant labor has yielded contradictory effects; some positive, some negative. Often the negative effects outweigh the positive ones. Thus, this matter must be re-examined, taking into consideration its root causes. Most importantly, the efficacy of current recruitment policies must be assessed and the migrants themselves should not be blamed for failed policies or the negative effects of general labor migration.

It is impossible to consider the Gulf region's modern renaissance without appreciating the positive role played by millions of migrant workers (Arabs and non-Arabs). This is especially true in terms of providing a new skill base and having access to the labor demanded by large-scale development projects in the region. However, this has also bred negative results. The "oil boom" and the "human boom" have grown exponentially and dependence on a male-dominated, low-skilled, low-qualified labor force – as well as abuse of the "sponsorship" system – has spurred a transformation of the socio-economic structure. This success fuels the need for foreign labor in increasing numbers and in a pattern that provokes greater anxiety among nationals. Furthermore, the influx of foreign labor has frustrated attempts to absorb and integrate thousands of Gulf youth into the labor market for the first time. Thus, while the UAE benefits in some respects, it is negatively affected in others.

Despite the short-term benefits of employing a largely migrant labor force, this has not provided social benefits to citizens in the long term, leading to growing dissatisfaction among Gulf youth. This is especially so in light of the fact that the salaries offered to young Gulf nationals in the private sector do not equate to the standard of living and social protectionism enjoyed by their fathers in the public sector and the big joint companies operating in the oil and manufacturing industries. From the 1950s the status in terms of wages and levels of social protectionism of generations of nationals in the Gulf region steadily improved. Much of this transition occurred either in emerging public sectors or in large companies in the oil and gas, or manufacturing sectors—jointly owned by the public and private sectors. The present generation faces a contrary situation. Understandably, observers relate the increasing numbers of unemployed nationals to the growing numbers of migrant laborers.

The theme of this chapter is not to examine the phenomenon of unemployment among Gulf youth or analyze its causes. However, it is necessary to point out the fact that the potential security repercussions of unemployment are closely linked to the growing proportion of migrant labor. This is especially so with regard to low-skilled laborers and those who have a competitive advantage in the labor force over their national counterparts. Dissatisfaction – owing to ignorance of the true causes of the situation – could lead to the evolution of a kind of xenophobia, which in some cases might result in aggressive behavior toward foreigners. There is also the possibility of aggressive behavior against nationals if there is discrimination in the allocation of rights and wages based on nationality. Both the importance of redefining the dangers this may pose to security, and possible strategies to curb the development of such dangers will be discussed later in this study.

Another important aspect of the security dimension associated with the migrant labor force in the GCC states is linked to the working conditions of this force and some of the abnormal practices to which some laborers are subjected, especially in the construction and domestic service sectors. Concern among the international community with regard to these practices has escalated in recent years—specifically human rights organizations and those who specialize in labor and migration. Furthermore, this issue has become increasingly important in negotiations with the World Trade Organization (WTO), as well as in the emerging debate on labor conditions, which indicates growing global concern regarding the future status of migrant labor forces and their working conditions. Rather than simply reacting politically, or through the media, it is important that some of the core issues of concern held by international civil society

[362]

organizations are dealt with. This issue is both important and sensitive; it ought to be accorded serious attention and used as an incentive for developing policies and programs to protect rights.

Security of Society and the Labor Force

The rapid flow of high quantities of migrant labor to the Gulf over the past few decades has raised anxiety among the peoples of the region, state authorities and those who study the affairs of the Gulf. There is a common fear among these parties that this issue will have severe ramifications on the political, social, economic and security situation in Gulf societies. In spite of the persistent efforts of state services to control the flow of migrant labor, results on the ground are limited. Despite the high-profile public discourse calling for limits on the number of migrant workers, the policies or radical measures taken thus far (for example, attempts to increase the fees levied on companies importing workers to the Kingdom of Bahrain) have met with strong opposition from those sectors that rely on the migrant labor force.

In this situation lies a paradox: although GCC nationals fear migrant "hegemony" in the region, the Gulf is seemingly unable to break its dependence on migrant workers. Such contradictions highlight fundamental flaws in the assumptions and prejudgments that govern debate on this issue and its consequences, frustrating efforts to tackle current problems and future challenges. This necessitates a frank and critical review of the policies concerning the region's migrant labor force.

In tackling this problem, it is important to confront the denigrating "xenophobia" which prevails in our perspective of this phenomenon, and to analyze it by adopting a rational methodology based on developmental and humanitarian values. Hence, what follows is an attempt to shed light on some of the fundamental aspects of the presence of migrant workers in the GCC that affect security. This comprises two levels: the first pertains to the general framework for understanding any potential repercussions of the presence of large numbers of migrant laborers in the GCC states. The second seeks to redefine the concept of "security threats" and identify them in a manner that enables us to combat them effectively. There is an interactive relationship between these two levels, therefore the perspective that determines our understanding of the first level will help us in dealing with the second in the long term. Also, the nature of the challenges we meet on the second level affect the quality of our understanding of the first level. Put simply, the first level relates to the strategic vision of our societies and countries regarding demand for migrant labor, policies of recruitment, and procedures of entry. The second level relates to confronting potential security threats after the recruitment, entry and residence of the migrant labor force.

Generally, the movement of labor in great numbers leads to rapid population increases in recipient societies. Such increases in any contemporary society carries with it the possibility of the emergence of security threats, irrespective of whether this increase is a result of external migration or a natural expansion of the native population, as the threats of social marginalization increase. Marginalization of groups within society constitutes an ideal environment for the spread of crime and other negative phenomena. This occurs in societies irrespective of the percentage of migrants, however the likelihood social marginalization is much higher in those which have a high proportion of migrants. The treatment of migrant labor forces is generally proportional to their duration of stay in host countries, whether they are advanced or developing, as is illustrated in Figure 15.2:

Figure 15.2
Migrant Labor and Receiving Countries: A Theoretical Framework

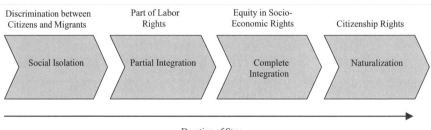

Duration of Stay

People move between different regions and countries for different reasons and for various durations. Sometimes the movement is voluntary while at other times it to escape prevailing conditions such as war, famine, or natural disasters. There is also a relationship between the motivation for migration and the length of stay in the receiving country. If the motivation is temporary or circumstantial, i.e. with a specific end-date or goal, the stay in the host country is temporary. However, if the motivation for migration is a result of a radical situation, the end of which is difficult to predict, the stay in the host country is longer.

There are also cases where the initial motivation for the movement is temporary but becomes permanent for different political or economic reasons. Groups of the population may be forced to migrate temporarily to neighboring countries owing to armed conflict or war, but often their stay in the host country becomes semi-permanent because of unsuccessful attempts to resolve these conflicts. In such cases, a state of "temporary continuity" arises. Perhaps the situations of refugees in the regions of the Middle East, Africa and Southeast Asia embody such a state. It would not be an overstatement to equate this to the labor forces in the GCC, which were attracted by the "temporary" need for migrant laborers in the mid-1970s and became "semi-permanent" in terms of their duration of stay.

The fundamental problems associated with the co-existence of opposites in a society (i.e., the transient and the permanent) relate to the political, social and economic rights bestowed upon the transient according to length of stay in the host country as well as the potential repercussions of their presence on the security of the host state and society.

Movement of labor of this proportion and quality can take one of three common forms:

- *Temporary movement for a short period (less than one year) in order to complete contracts or projects.* Often this labor force is socially semi-isolated from other citizens and is characterized by discrepancies between their rights and the rights of nationals.

- *Movement to work for a semi-temporary period (2–5 years) in accordance with programs specified by the host country.* Entry requirements vary for nationals of different countries (EU countries, OECD countries, the GCC countries, etc.). Often national labor laws applied to migrant laborers result in varying degrees of integration into the host societies in accordance with the prevailing level of political, economic and social rights bestowed. Integration can be partial and depends on these economic and social (and sometimes political) rights.

- *Movement to work permanently with the aim of final settlement.* The majority of such programs are found in advanced industrial countries, especially those depending on migration to satisfy a shortage of workers resulting from demographic issues. In such cases, migrants are naturalized and are considered citizens who are equal to the native population in terms of their rights and duties. These migrants face several challenges relating to the efficacy of the policies and procedures governing integration.

It is important to understand the role played by integration in the treatment of migrant labor forces by host societies. This requires a review of immigrants' duration of stay and the political, social and economic consequences of that duration. The failure of migration policies is often a result of states' inability or unwillingness to deal with these consequences when migrants reach the point where they qualify for residence and equality in political, economic and social terms. This kind of risk can be avoided when harmony is achieved between recruitment and integration policies, in a manner that reflects both the needs of migrants and states. These needs exist in both short-term and long-term migration. In determining the requirements for migrant labor, only the essential needs should be considered—be they temporary/short-term or permanent/long-term. These needs will depend on the economic, social and political growth of recipient societies, which will differ from one stage to another.

Table 15.3
Non-Bahraini Residents (15 years +) based on Nationality and Duration of Stay (2001)

Nationality Groups	Duration of Stay in Years			
	< 2 years	2–5	> 6	Total
Arabs of the GCC States	1,519	1,695	3,609	6,823
Other Arabs	4,340	7,228	8,482	20,050
Asians	46,658	68,832	90,136	205,626
Africans	909	1,673	342	2,924
Europeans, Americans & Oceanasians	3,162	3,408	2,944	9,514
Total	**56,588**	**82,836**	**105,513**	**244,937**

Note: the number of foreigners who have stayed for more than six years is 105,113, i.e. 43.1 percent of the total population.

Sources: Central Information Office, Kingdom of Bahrain, *Population Census 2001*, Table 1202.01 (http://www.vio.bh).

The degree of integration of migrant laborers in the societies of the GCC states varies from one country to another. Despite the existence of legislation that guarantees the rights of this labor force, employers' observance of such legislation is still less than satisfactory. In many cases, employers fail to provide necessary protection to migrant workers. A large percentage of the unskilled migrant labor force is composed of single male workers, often living in collective complexes isolated from the residential areas where nationals live. Such segregation for long periods has negative consequences. This is true for both the migrants and the society where they dwell, especially since the duration of stay of 40 percent of the labor force in countries like Bahrain, the UAE and Qatar is at least six years (see tables 15.3, 15.4 and 15.5).

Table 15.4
Length of Service Duration of Non-Qataris (2005)

Service Duration (in years)	Qatari	Non-Qatari	Total	Percentage
< 2	8,593	20,644	29,237	71
3–9	14,161	20,217	34,378	59
> 10	15,255	12,866	28,121	46

Source: Ministry of Planning, Qatar, *Population Census 2005*, Table 24.

[367]

Table 15.5
Length of Stay of Migrants in the UAE (1995)

Years of Stay	Females	Males	Total	Percentage
< 1	95,036	236,612	331,648	18.19
2–5	169,744	444,837	614,581	33.70
> 6	249,187	628,295	877,482	48.11
Total	513,967	1,309,744	1,823,711	100

Source: UAE Ministry of Planning, *Population Census 1995*.

The author has been unable to obtain data illustrating developments since the mid-1990s in the UAE and the Kingdom of Bahrain. However, the data presented above indicates that the potential consequences of migrant workers' isolation from the local community for lengthy periods could be extremely grave. If this situation persists, we may witness a new system of "ghettoization," which will worsen if its rapid growth is neglected.

Therefore, it is not only necessary to focus on controlling the entry of migrant laborers, but also to manage efficiently the post-entry stage. I believe there is a gap in current policy in this regard between those directed toward controlling the processes of entry – whether via the management of work permits or entry visas – and those policies meant for managing the situation of the migrant labor force after entering the country. The latter are meant to be directed toward providing the necessary protection to the labor force and combating all potential forms of exploitation. An efficient link between the two stages would reduce the potential dangers of the flow of large numbers of laborers, and ease their situation in the longer term. One of the current problems in dealing with a migrant labor force in the GCC states lies in the limitedness and narrow scope of the political options available in dealing with it. To achieve success on the ground we must determine what is permanent and what is transient. In order to harmonize what is permanent with the desired identity of our societies, it is necessary to formulate and implement specific integration policies to curb potential social marginalization.

Treating the entire labor force as one and in a stereotypical manner is not conducive to improving the current situation and will postpone any decisive settlement of the issue. The notion that the migrant labor force can be dispensed of or reduced before raising the percentage of nationals in the population is an illusion (in light of the natural rates of growth of nationals). It is also not possible economically, as the structure of demand in some economic sectors is based on the availability of a migrant labor force. Instead of repeating slogans that gain popular acceptance but fail politically and economically to achieve practical results, we must move towards "rationalizing" the long-term dependence on migrant labor. This requires two important processes: a restructuring of those economic sectors with a high demand for unskilled labor to reduce recruitment, and the implementation of an integration plan within a socio-economic framework to manage the skilled foreign labor force.

The Necessity of Redefining Security Threats

Central to the issue of the security repercussions of the presence of migrant labor forces in GCC societies is the need to develop an understanding of the relationship between the growth of labor forces and increases in crime rates. The widely held belief is that increased foreign labor has led to increased crime. However, an analysis of the data available on three Gulf states – Bahrain, Kuwait and Oman – shows that the facts do not confirm these prejudgments. Statistical sources available in the countries above (no comparative data was available on the rest of the GCC countries) show that the issue of crime in the GCC states is too complex to be attributed to a specific nationality, or indeed to either migrants or nationals.

Figure 15.3 shows that the number of Bahraini suspects in criminal cases is consistently higher than that of non-Arab migrants in the period 1996–2004. In the case of Kuwait, the number of Kuwaiti suspects is similar to the number of suspects of other nationalities (see

[369]

Figure 15.4). The number of Omani suspects is greater than that of other nationalities according to 2005 statistics. It is necessary to point out that these statistics differ from one period to another in accordance with the official categorization of crimes and security-related offences. Hence, we can depend on them to reflect the reality of the situation, but they can only be used as indicators showing certain aspects of the prevailing security situation.

Figure 15.3

Bahrain: Offenders in Criminal Cases by Nationality (1996–2004)

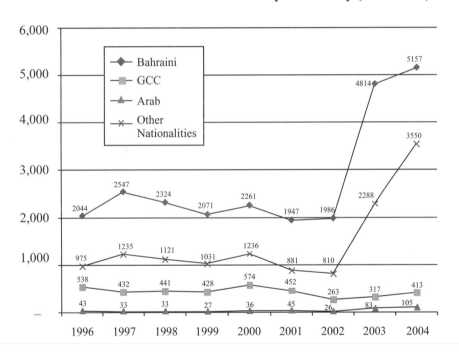

Source: Information taken from the annual statistics book of Bahrain, 1996–2004, website of the Central Statistics Office (http://www.cio.gov.bh).

Figure 15.4
Felons by Nationality in Kuwait

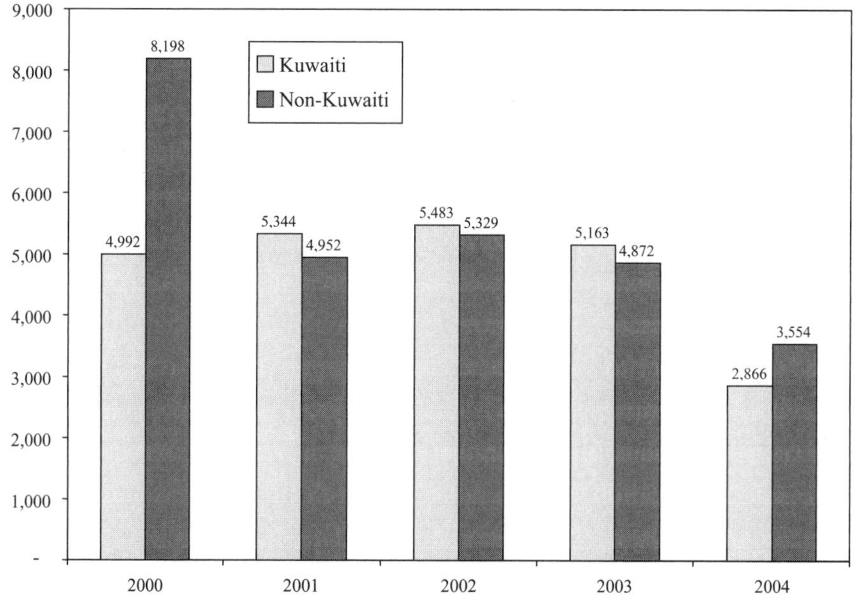

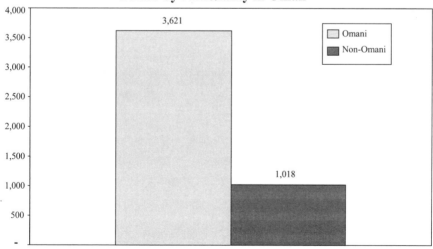

Source: Ministry of Planning, Kuwait, Annual Statistical Group, 2005.

Figure 15.5
Felons by Nationality in Oman

Source: The Sultanate of Oman, *Annual Statistical Book*, 2005.

[371]

For a better understanding of the potential effects of migrant labor forces on security, any study that aims to encompass overall "security threats," rather than just traditional crimes – as in the above statistics – must include two important elements. The first is the "hidden" exploitation of migrant labor forces, especially relating to the "visa trade" or any criminal practices linked to human trafficking. The second relates to the security consequences resulting from violating the rights of the labor force through non-payment of wages and poor health and occupational safety conditions.

Regarding the first element, it is important to understand that just because such practices are not openly practiced, this does not make them any less of a threat. Such practices can lead to unrest because of mounting tension among those targeted. In recent years, these hidden forms of exploitation have come to light; the most significant of which are those connected with the exploitation of the sponsorship system which is still used in the GCC states. One study pointed out that the visa trade in the GCC states is worth around US$1 billion.[6] The surveys conducted by a research center in India showed the extent of the suffering endured by many workers who shoulder severe debts to obtain entry visas to the Arab Gulf states.[7] This does not end on their arrival in the Gulf. Besides the visa trade, there are other illegal commercial practices in the GCC states that remain largely hidden from public view. However, such practices have become "norms" and are considered socially acceptable—with revenue accruing as a result of these activities viewed as normal "business activity."

The majority of forms of exploitation that certain segments of the migrant labor force are subjected to stem from the sponsorship system, which gives the employer power over the migrant worker, outside the authority regulated by the labor law. One of the worst aspects that migrants are subjected to – especially women – is the enforcement of compulsory labor via the employer holding the worker's passport or travel documents. In spite of the lack of clear evidence for the prevalence of these forms of exploitation from official quarters, international human rights organizations often cite them in their reports and studies of the region. These forms of hidden exploitation of the migrant labor force are a global reality. Such practices include human trafficking and forced labor. These detestable practices are found in different countries irrespective of their level of economic, social and political development. The secrecy that surrounds these practices increases their danger and harm to society. It is not shameful to disclose facts if they are true—this is more beneficial for the security of our nations than simply refusing to acknowledge the existence of practices that abuse the sponsorship system.

The second element pertaining to security threats – alienating the rights of the labor force – is being confronted by intensive efforts on the part of the GCC states, specifically via preventative policies and measures implemented by Labor Ministries. The continued practice of non-payment of wages and the deteriorating conditions of occupational health and safety in several facilities that employ migrant laborers should not be viewed only as labor-related issues. Acute dissatisfaction caused by such practices can lead to protests that will not always be peaceful. However, granting rights to migrant laborers must not be driven by fears of unrest but by the positive gains of such actions, such as contributing to the efforts of official authorities in the field of commitment to upholding labor laws and preventing detestable exploitation of the sponsorship system.

The dialectical relationship between the security of our societies and the security of the migrants who live among us can be successful if based on basic rights and duties. The rights of the labor force are not a burden but a humanitarian duty and a politico-economic necessity. No country or economy has suffered as a consequence of granting rights to its labor force.

Our security will continue to depend to a great extent on the security of those who live in our countries and work in our markets. This, however, does not mean that the political, social and economic security of our citizens should be overlooked. Rather, it means that we should seek to broaden our understanding of the interconnected dimensions of these security challenges and endeavor to guarantee the sustained security of our people. Redefining our concept of "security threats" requires developing and modernizing information systems and statistics relevant to this issue. Security policy, like other policies, must be based on evidence not conjecture and fear. This requires developing information systems in two important realms: labor market information and criminal statistics. Since the first is the prerequisite of labor market policies, the reality of the situation in the GCC states indicates an on-going "impasse" in recording the quantitative and qualitative dimensions of the presence of migrant labor, despite substantial efforts in recent years.

The poor quality of information stems from the institutional partitioning of its sources. The lack of integration within a unified system at the state or regional level in the GCC countries makes the efficient recording of the reality of migrant labor force a difficult task for any researcher in this field, let alone decision-makers. Simply modernizing the systems and software used by different authorities concerned with the affairs of migrant labor is not enough. This information must be interconnected and integrated with statistics and periodic surveys that reveal the qualitative aspects of laborers and their working conditions. This information can help us identify potential dangers with security dimensions, such as the paying of wages, conditions of occupational safety and health, and others.

The other area where information and data is required is that of criminal statistics. This is meant to denote "the process of collecting crime data and turning them into digits in order to determine the scale of violence and label it in accordance with place, pattern, style and motives. This facilitates identifying the relations between them and different social, cultural, economic and developmental variables."[8] The source of criminal statistics is data from prisons, the Judiciary and the Police.[9] These statistics greatly contribute to the monitoring of crime of all forms in society.

The study of the current situation of migrant labor in the GCC states indicates that the repercussions of its presence on the security situation of the countries of the region and its societies depend on a complex group of factors and policies. It is important to review the policies of labor markets that regulate recruitment of migrant laborers, specifically by joining policies of recruitment and integration, tailoring them to the developmental orientation of each country of the GCC individually. Since we are in an era characterized by numerous variables affecting labor force demand, and stronger interconnectivity of labor policies with human rights than in any past era, such developments should not be feared. Rather, we must take this opportunity to develop our policies of dependence on migrant labor and integrate them with the policies of substituting nationals for expatriates. We must also attempt to integrate Gulf youth into the job market and benefit from the creative abilities of Gulf women in the market, as increasing the participation of women is a vital element of any strategy to reduce dependency on foreign labor.

The issue of how to combat potential security threats associated with the presence of migrant labor in the GCC states is possible to solve if the root causes are dealt with instead of simply treating the superficial symptoms. This will require the integration of policies concerning the labor force and a modernization of the institutional framework concerned with recruitment. It also requires harmonizing regional policies between the GCC states and effective international cooperation aimed at widening the scope for social dialogue to include countries and civil society organizations in both sending and receiving countries. The member states of the GCC can also apply the agenda of "decent work" on the basis of the obligations agreed upon at the 14th Asian regional meeting of the International Labor Organization (ILO) in Busan, Republic of Korea, in 2006. The conference committed itself to "an Asian Decent Work Decade – for the period up to 2015 – during which we will make a concerted and sustained effort to realize decent work in all countries of our diverse continent."[10]

The concept of decent work that is advocated by the ILO represents, in my belief, the correct and most efficient basis to tackle the "migrant–national" issue in labor market policies and the dichotomy between "us" and "the others" in terms of identity in our societies. What is more important is that it represents the first step toward a new solidarity, the driving principle of which is "our security is complemented by the security of other nations."

16

Migrant Labor Force in the Gulf Region: A New Approach

Shafiq Al-Ghabra

The migrant labor force in the Arabian Gulf represents a huge challenge to the countries of the region. The incomes generated by these states, which have resulted from large-scale growth in the second half of the 20th century up to the present day, have led to large-scale development that has required the importation of labor from various nations. This in turn has led to nationals of the Arab Gulf countries becoming minorities, dependent on migrant workers.

It is unlikely that this need for migrant labor will diminish in the medium term. Most Gulf societies are characterized by limited national population density. Consequently, maintaining standards of services and their rate of growth requires dependence, in varying degrees, on foreign and expatriate Arab labor forces. However, this dependence in itself constitutes a constant challenge because it gives rise to a number of problems related to identity in the GCC states, specifically:

* local identity vis-à-vis non-local identity.
* Arab identity vis-à-vis non-Arab identity.
* Islamic identity vis-à-vis non-Islamic identity.

Oil production increases and the resultant rises in income, coupled with limited population size and an absence of infrastructure, have created a situation different to any other in the history of the Gulf region. In the mid-20th century, Gulf elites began working toward populating the desert of the Arabian Peninsula. Hence the Gulf has changed from a region with a sparse population, far-removed from wars, conflicts, and the pull of strategic interests, to the most important region in global politics with the highest rate of population growth and the largest volume of immigration.

In a short period of time, the population of the six littoral societies of the Gulf (Saudi Arabia, Kuwait, the United Arab Emirates, Oman, Qatar and Bahrain) has grown from 4 million people in 1950 to more than 35 million people, 12 million of whom are migrants.

While nationals represent 63 percent of the total population of the Gulf region, migrant labor forces form majority populations in states like Qatar, the UAE and Kuwait. In the UAE, the migrant labor force represents 80 percent of its population of 4 million; in Kuwait it represents 65 percent of a population of 3 million, and in Qatar it accounts for 70 percent of a population of 750,000. In the Kingdom of Bahrain the migrant labor force represents 38 percent of a population of 750,000 and it represents 20 percent of the population of Oman which is 3 million. Finally, in Saudi Arabia the migrant labor force represents 27 percent of a population of 22 million.

The challenge posed by migrant labor forces in the Gulf region cannot be summed up in simple terms. There are two main models for dealing with the issue of labor forces. The first is the US model – also adopted by Canada and Australia – which naturalizes the labor force coming into the country and, in doing so, encourages immigrants to take on and adjust to the indigenous language, lifestyle and culture. The second model, which is widespread in Europe and many other countries throughout the world, avoids naturalization and instead is based on labor contracts and the rights and liabilities they bestow upon migrants. This model is also followed in the Gulf region. The first model transforms migrant workers into citizens with equal rights and duties, and contributes to building a state of harmony in the long term. The second, on the other hand, makes migrants temporary residents until the need for their service comes to an end.

Naturally, no system is perfect, and both models suffer from short-comings and generate their own challenges.

Although the model followed in the Gulf region is not based on open naturalization, the countries of the region have naturalized hundreds of thousands of migrants, as naturalization occurs with the passage of time. For instance, one third of the citizens of Kuwait have gained Kuwaiti nationality after having migrated to the country in the second half of the 20th century. However, the issue remains: what is to be done with all the other nationalities which create settlements in cities that simply reflect their original homelands in, say, India or other Arab countries?

The chosen model in the Gulf region involves a number of consequences. There are hundreds of thousands of second and third generation migrants who have become part of Gulf communities by virtue of the long years they have spent in the region, but are nonetheless unable to enjoy the rights attached to citizenship. Hence these migrants live contradictory lives, torn between commitments to their countries of ethnic origin and the countries in which they were born and raised.

In time, these communities, which are composed of both Arab and non-Arab migrants, will eventually vent their frustration through acts of protest. They want to "belong," but are unable to under the laws applied in the Gulf countries. Furthermore, migrants from Asia and other regions are reluctant to forsake their original cultures. Naturally, different degrees of *Arabization** exist within non-Arab migrant communities. Over time these communities have come to represent part of the national social map, despite not being naturalized. These issues will surface more frequently in the future and will be difficult to confront in the absence of solutions that are consistent with human rights on the one hand, and the natural desire of national communities to preserve their identity on the other.

---

* (ECSSR Translator's Note) There is a consensus among modern linguists to use the term *Arabization* to denote 'ethno-cultural assimilation' and retain the term *Arabicization* to denote the 'process of introducing words of foreign origin in the Arabic language and using Arabic as a medium of instruction and acquisition of knowledge in *Academia.*'

This issue poses greater problems for Arab migrants than it does for migrants of other nationalities because many Arab migrants only speak Arabic and are thus not easily integrated into the wider migrant communities in the Gulf whose common language is often English. Also, discrimination between national and migrant workforces in institutions and firms breeds a state of competition, dissatisfaction and bloc-creation in professional environments, the outcome of which is, naturally, detrimental to the institutions themselves. This situation might even provide a foundation for foreign intervention when problems relating to migrant work forces occur. In some situations, this may also open the door to political bargaining and intervention by human rights organizations.

The issue of migrant labor requires innovative solutions, since conventional ones are no longer useful. Openness under globalization provides a more educated and professional migrant labor force, but also facilitates the influx of unskilled workers. This adds to pressures on the Gulf countries to enforce human rights and to naturalize some of their migrant labor forces—especially those skilled workers who have lived in the Gulf for decades. Also, institutions will be forced to treat all workers equally in order to create a healthy working atmosphere and boost production.

One of the greatest concerns centers on the treatment of the migrant labor force as a threat, when reliance on such labor forces is increasing. Increasing national dependence on a migrant labor force, which feels unwelcome but which carries out many functions that are essential to the national economy, further aggravates the existing state of alienation and tension.

The situation is worsened by daily official and media discourse in many of the Gulf countries which is antagonistic to migrant labor forces, leading to unnecessary tensions. It is difficult to expect peaceful coexistence with a labor force which is told everyday that it must depart with haste; that it constitutes a threat to the demographic structure of the region; that it exploits and plunders the wealth of the region; and that it is a threat to the customs and societies of the host nations. Such treatment is devoid of sensitivity. Even if laws only allow a person to stay for one week, that person must feel welcome and appreciated for what he/she does during this period. Talk of expelling migrant workforces – while reality dictates increasing dependence on them – creates major problems for institutions, firms and markets, as well as for relations between migrants and nationals.

Remedying this situation requires innovation and a new strategy to provide Gulf societies with the opportunity to preserve their Islamic–historical identity. There must also be room for the assimilation of different nationalities. This entails conforming to fundamental aspects of human rights, appreciating the professionalism and competence of migrant workers, and considering a suitable time span as a prerequisite to offering permanent or conditional rights of stay.

The situation regarding the relationship between migrant and national labor forces calls for the development of professional competence in the Gulf, and motivation for male and female Gulf nationals to work in different spheres. This requires educational, social, economic and political reforms to motivate competition and production. The tendency of Gulf youth to confine themselves to working in the public sector increases the magnitude of the problems involving foreign labor forces and limits the ability of national labor forces to reach their full potential.

The Costs of the Past

It is difficult to argue that recruiting labor forces, both uniformly and randomly, over the last fifty years has not affected the countries of the region. Migrant labor forces – be they skilled or unskilled, specialized or non-specialized, Arab or non-Arab, Muslim or non-Muslim – have become part of the diverse population of the Gulf region, and have brought developments in the realms of economics, health and education. In fact, some of these labor forces no longer meet the universal definition of a "foreign labor force." Many have become an integral part of the social map of the Gulf states. Indeed, how can someone who has lived in the Gulf for 50 years be a foreigner? Calls for naturalization among migrants are to be expected, but there is little known about such movements as data concerning labor forces in the region is based only on basic figures of population size and nationality.

Over time, obstacles to the integration of second and third generation migrants in Gulf communities creates massive alienation. The *Bidoun* (those without nationality) in the state of Kuwait, and other similar communities in other countries in the Gulf region will remain an integral part of this issue. This alienation is especially acute among foreign nationals who do not have strong roots in their original communities because they have been born and raised in the Gulf. In such cases, groups of migrants are created that are composed of people who feel more at home in their new country of residence than their original homelands but do not possess the legitimacy to stay indefinitely. This is a problem faced by a large proportion of the migrant labor force, and especially by Arab migrants.

In spite of the system whereby the sponsor of an employee can control their change of job; the existence of permanent resolutions to reduce the numbers of incoming migrants; the refusal to allow entry of certain nationalities; hasty decisions in implementing administrative deportation (deportation without a court decree); and violations of the human rights of migrant laborers, the number of incoming migrants has not dropped. Everyone who investigates the issue of migrant labor since the 1980s notes that the problem of increased immigration has worsened over the years. Even Kuwait, which was the most cautious state in the region in this regard – after having lost about 90 percent of its migrant labor force in the wake of the Gulf War in 1990/1991 – has replenished its migrant labor force in the post-war years, albeit with different nationalities to those who were resident before the war.

The ever-expanding free economy of the Gulf region, spurred on by foreign investment and ongoing improvements in infrastructure, plays its role in this reality. Many migrant workers remain in the Gulf States after the expiry of their contracts. Gulf businessmen still prefer non-local workers because they are easy to deal with—there is less pressure on employers to provide promotions or end-of-service payments, meaning they cost less, and they are not reluctant to take up jobs that require a psychological readiness to work for long hours in the private sector. As capital and development increases, so does the need for larger labor forces and the construction of new cities and infrastructure to accommodate both nationals and migrant workers.

However, if oil prices were to drop in the future due to alternative energy sources becoming more widespread in the next ten to fifteen years, Gulf societies would be left to deal with a labor force of millions that has lost connections with their original countries of origin and aspire to remain in the Gulf states. The resulting struggle for survival will be influenced by numerous actors including human rights groups, major powers, regional states, local forces and private sectors striving for profit, quality, competition and stability. Furthermore, a clash might occur between local Arab identity and Asian identity, as has happened in the past between Gulf identity and broader Arab identity. Such issues will evoke sleepless nights for the governments of the Gulf, especially with the emergence of India and other Asian countries as major economic powers in the coming decade. The process of democratic transformation will see migrant communities demanding representation in the highest authorities of the states which they inhabit. This situation will be similar to that of cosmopolitan European cities that have become mixed by virtue of market forces and modern mobility.

The Gulf states have become dependant on imported migrant labor forces. This situation is an unavoidable consequence of the social, political, professional and economic system of the region. In fact this system is the root of the predicament. Government recruitment practices, limitations placed on female workers, and the lack of competence in certain government institutions and their affiliated authorities have led to the emergence of unemployment and dwindling motivation among Gulf youth. In taking steps to indigenize workforces, governments have succeeded in localizing the public sector, but the representation of nationals in the private sector has remained between 18 and 30 percent in the GCC countries. Overall participation of national labor forces in local labor markets has also remained small, averaging not more than 30 percent in the public and private sectors combined.

However, as the percentage of non-local labor in the Gulf countries increases, so does the number of national youths. For instance, 61 percent of the nationals of Saudi Arabia are under 25 years of age, compared to 60 percent in Kuwait, 50 percent in India, 39 percent in China and 30 percent in Europe.[1] The energy of youth can be of great benefit if harnessed to liberalize the economy and the growth of the private sector. However, it will only hinder progress if national youth remain wholly dependant on the aid and services of the state.

The task of providing jobs for citizens in the Gulf region represents a major challenge. The private sector in the region has provided nearly 55,000 jobs annually during the last ten years. However, to absorb Gulf youth – both male and female – who have general secondary school certificates and university degrees, this figure must rise to 300,000 jobs per year. Thus, the question is how will such a dramatic increase be achieved? And who will succeed in realizing the kind of universal reform required for job expansion?[2]

How might we deal with the absence of Gulf youth in the private sector? And how can we guide young nationals toward competition, exerting effort and working hard? Must we change the very nature of our states and the society of affluence which we have built? Are we seeking the liberalization of our markets and greater motivation for innovation? How can we reform education programs?

The most strategically significant challenge facing the Gulf social system is the need to enhance the role of women. In Saudi Arabia female participation in the labor market is not more than 10 percent and young women are pressured to work only in education, irrespective of their ambitions. There are many restrictions placed on women in the workplace, in education, when traveling, and when developing their aspirations. Such restrictions deprive Gulf nations of a great productive energy that must be set free and exploited. Academic programs should be established and real incentives provided based on the kind of psychological foundation that makes citizens more effective competitors without resorting to nepotism and government hand-outs. Building the capabilities of Gulf citizens is essential to developing more healthy and competitive societies.

The resulting divisions between the migrant and the citizen has created a relationship that is pervaded by a spirit of dominance. This has created a state of negativity in Gulf communities, which is reflected by the atmosphere in institutions and firms and among workers in general—a situation that further complicates the goal of applying fundamental values such as equality and non-discrimination.

Furthermore, in view of the low wages of many workers in the region and the introduction of laws which seek to limit the importation of migrant labor, a common feature of a large sector of the migrant workforce is the absence of resident families, which has led to the emergence of bachelor communities. Such communities are inherently more conducive to serious social and security-related problems.

The Forthcoming Struggle for competence

While struggling to define the migrant and the local labor force, the severity of the global struggle for competence increases. There is an ongoing international struggle to attract skilled workers to the countries of the advanced world and to multinational companies, irrespective of nationality, sex or color. Under globalization and market liberalization, deals are struck whereby companies with local capitals change into companies with foreign ones. For example, a Qatari company might be established in Kuwait or vise versa, but the new company may arrive with its own administrative cadres that rely on inherent skills and competition.

The questions facing us today which require universal answers are: how does the narrow view of the struggle over national and non-national labor forces apply when attempting to confront the issue of competence? How can the Gulf countries attract serious investors who are capable of indigenizing science and skills in the region? Do the Gulf states possess the intellectual capacities and policies to deal with this situation? Will the Gulf region provide a platform and an historical opportunity to transfer the intellectual and scientific capabilities of the West to the East in preparation for an era when oil is depleted? Should the Gulf countries frame their strategic thought within the duality of national and foreign labor forces, or must they incorporate extra dimensions?

The Future

The success of any new approach will require the acceptance of the emergence of mixed cities where nationals and semi-permanent residents – as well as temporary ones – live together. They will be bound by the common interests of success in work and the transformation of the region from dependence on oil revenues to reliance on diversified sources of income, based on production and the role of the private sector as much as generating wealth via work and innovation. In other words, it is not a prerequisite that a collision must occur between Arab and non-Arab identity, or between national and non-national identity in the Gulf countries. It is possible to build integration via government policies that encourage investment, construction and economic openness. However, such policies must also defend the nexus of authority–security–stability in a turbulent regional and international environment. The government must not compromise the rights of the inhabitants of the country – those who carry its authentic nationality – and their role in controlling the basis of political authority. Gulf societies can promote competition while transforming the region into a cosmopolitan one, the survival and power of which transcends the presence of oil or its depletion.

This will require a review of the Gulf countries' approach to their respective labor forces by adopting a strategy that values competence – thereby attracting a higher quality labor force – and establishing the private sector as the main pillar of their respective economies. The Gulf states could also liberalize their economies by establishing a common market and improving the mobility of their labor forces, allowing them to move from location to location and from sector to sector. Governments could then act as general regulators of quality instead of business owners, engaged in collecting taxes while the labor force moves freely and competitively. Furthermore, the Gulf countries could establish and enforce controls regulating the standard of the labor force, the countries from which it is imported, and other vital issues.

Such a strategy would require competition and principles based on justice to be applied across the board for all workers – be they local or migrant – in a manner that guarantees achievement, competence, legitimate ambition and competition among Gulf youth. Today, the Gulf system remains part of a closed circle, which weakens competition between nationals and propels them toward more dependence on new migrants. This system is unsustainable.

The Gulf countries must work towards building a diversified economy and empowering the private sector to the extent that allows surplus value to be exported internationally. Without this surplus value, the issue of the foreign labor force will be aggravated because it implies a structural weakness in Gulf society. The nature of the tribal and individual system, as well as the patriarchal system, which does not develop national powers through global achievement and competition, will preserve limited local capabilities.

In order to deal with the labor force in a context that is free from fear, and to avoid re-building barricades around Gulf cities and obstructing development, it is necessary to change the social system that depends on nepotism, favoritism and exception, since these are practices that undermine motivation. Also, nationalization of the labor force as a result of government policies to employ more national graduates in the public sector will not help to encourage Gulf citizens to accept the kind of work that foreigners are willing to undertake. What incentive is there for citizens to move to the private sector if the public sector is a breeding ground for absenteeism and laziness?

In other words, it will not be possible to overcome all these difficulties in the absence of a broader and more forward-looking vision of a modern society and modern relations that foster professionalism and celebrate achievement. In this respect, encouraging an educational renaissance is vital to the process of change and increased self-reliance.

At the same time, naturalization of the qualified and skilled sons of migrant laborers is of great importance, but a prerequisite for naturalization must be legitimacy. What makes Western countries that are different in terms of religion, culture, race and history welcome Arab doctors, engineers, scholars and students, and provide them with indefinite leave to remain and nationality rights in return for their experience and investment? Can this be possible because Western regimes subject citizenship to taxes and socio-economic responsibility? How does the West benefit from those who have worked and studied in Arab societies for two or three generations and then left to settle in the United States, Canada or Australia, leaving the Arab world behind? What is more interesting is that some of them return to the region after becoming foreign experts in the West, and therefore receive very different treatment to that which they experienced before they gave up their Arab nationalities.

By virtue of oil and its ongoing development, the Gulf region has become an attractive option for migrants. A prerequisite for dealing with the question of the migrant labor force in the Gulf is a universal strategy based on good administration, legislative development, increased human rights and the search for competence amid intensive investment in the competitive capabilities of youth in the Gulf region.

17

The Imbalance in the Population Structure and its Impact on the States of the Region

Maitha Al Shamsi

The imbalance in the population structure of the GCC states is one of the most important issues to evolve during the process of socio-economic development witnessed by the GCC over the last few decades. Although this issue has been accorded great importance in the policies of these states, the imbalance, embodied in the high ratio of expatriates to nationals, has not been dealt with successfully. This imbalance entails socio-economic, political and security pressures.

The process of development embarked on by the Arabian Gulf societies is a factor that has spurred the rising waves of migration since the 1970s. The Gulf countries represent a major destination for migrant workers. Between 1990 and 2005, the estimated number of migrants to the GCC states was 8.6–12.8 million. In addition, the sources and patterns of migration have diversified—today there are more than 140 nationalities of migrants in the GCC states.[1]

For more than 25 years, no issue has been subject to more controversy than the question of migrant labor in the GCC. If the economic impact of this labor force has caused heated debate in the past, then this has refocused in the last few years on the potential demographic, social, cultural and security dangers of migrant labor. Such fears are reinforced by demographic projections, which indicate that the rate of increase of the migrant labor force will be greater than the rate of growth of the indigenous population, and that demand for foreign labor in the Gulf will remain high.[2]

No doubt the societal cost of migrant labor – particularly of the current large numbers and demographic make-up – is very high indeed, especially when the causes of certain migrant flows are due to the kind of socio-economic activities that have a negative influence on the region and its future generations. For these reasons, dealing with the current imbalance in the population structure is an urgent necessity.[3]

This study addresses the current and future challenges and problems imposed by the demographic situation in the Arabian Gulf states. This presupposes studying population realities and proposing policies and strategies to stem the negative consequences of imbalance in the population structure. The study not only refers to the most important challenges posed by foreign migration but also reviews the efforts of the GCC in redressing the demographic imbalance.

The Population Situation and the Labor Force in the GCC States

Demographic transformations in the GCC states are taking place at a rapid rate when compared to other countries. This is expected to continue in the future at the current rate or faster. One of the most important causes of this demographic change is the fact that the GCC countries are rapidly opening up to the world and making substantial progress in the fields of health, education and housing services. In addition, these countries have adopted models of economic development that encourage more openness and investment, and therefore advance trade prospects. All these factors create challenges for GCC countries in terms of a population growth that is not linked to questions of fertility, as is the case in other countries. Rather, they relate to the massive inflow of foreign labor that has created an abnormal population imbalance between migrants and nationals.

This study attempts to deal, firstly, with the size of the population, its characteristics and the size of the labor force in order to illustrate the severity of the issue. Secondly, the study confronts the question of migration as a major and direct factor in the imbalance of the population structure.

Size and Rate of Growth of the Population

Since the discovery of oil, the states of the Gulf region have become modern countries. This transformation has been accompanied by rapid population growth. Over the past 50 years, the population of the six GCC states has increased ten-fold, rising from 4 million in 1950 to 40 million in 2006. This is one of the highest rates of population growth in the world. However, the increase was not the result of any natural fecundity of the local inhabitants, but rather because of the immigration of foreign workers.

Owing to increasing oil wealth and the change in economic conditions, the populations of these countries have doubled every 15 years since 1960, when the population of the GCC was estimated to be around 5 million. In 1975 it reached 9.6 million and from 1975–1990 nearly 11.7 million had been added to the population. By 1995 the population of the Gulf countries stood at 26.213 million, with the number expected to rise to 45.360 million in 2010 and 79.617 million in 2025.[4]

In the aftermath of the first oil boom in the early 1970s, great numbers of workers from Arab, Asian and other countries migrated to the Gulf to find work. By 1975, the population of the GCC states had reached almost 10 million, of which 26 percent were migrants, while its labor force comprised 2.9 million of which 45 percent were migrants. In 1980, after the second oil boom, the population rose to 12 million with a labor force of 4 million workers, of whom 54.5 percent were migrants; and by 2001 the population in the GCC states had risen to 32 million of which 34.9 percent were migrants, and included a labor force of 10.7 million workers of whom two thirds (65 percent) were migrants.[5]

The population of the Kingdom of Saudi Arabia makes up 70.8 percent of the total population of the GCC states; while the UAE population represents 10.4 percent; Oman, 7.7 percent; Kuwait, 7.2 percent; and Qatar and the Kingdom of Bahrain nearly 2 percent. In 2000, Omani nationals constituted 74 percent of the Sultanate's population, whereas nationals constituted 73 percent in Saudi Arabia. In 2001, nationals constituted 62.3 percent, 38.1 percent, 28.9 percent and 22 percent of the populations of the Kingdom of Bahrain, Kuwait, Qatar and the UAE respectively.[6]

[391]

Table 17.1

Total GCC Population and Gender Percentage in 2005

Country	Total Population (1,000)	Male (1,000)	Female (1,000)	Percentage of Male to Total %
UAE	4,496	3,448	1,048	76.69
Bahrain	727	419	308	57.63
Saudi Arabia	24,574	13,356	11,218	54.35
Oman	2,567	1,354	1,213	52.75
Kuwait	2,688	1,685	1,003	62.69
Qatar	813	590	223	72.57
Total GCC	35,865	20,852	15,013	58.14

Source: United Nations, *World Population Prospects*, The 2004 Revision (New York, NY: UN, 2005).

Table 17.2

Number and Percentage of Nationals and Expatriates in GCC from 2001–2002

	Nationals (1,000)	%	Expatriates (1,000)	%	Total (1,000)
Bahrain	410	60	280	40	690
Kuwait	885	37	1,475	63	2,360
Oman	1,790	74	630	26	2,420
Qatar	165	28	420	72	585
Saudi Arabia	16,000	70	7,000	30	23,000
Emirates	622	20	2,488	80	3,110
Total GCC	20,000	61.5	12,500	38.5	32,500

Sources: GCC SG, Annual Report. July 27, 2002 concerning Bahrain, Oman, Qatar, and Saudi Arabia; in addition to countries economic reports from mid 2002; Concerning Saudi Arabia, reports from different Saudi ministries were also used; concerning Kuwait, reference is made to Ministry of Planning data.

The continuity of population increase in the GCC states is noteworthy. In 2005, the GCC population rose to 35.865 million as shown by the data in Table 17.1, with the UAE registering a population increase to 4.496 million; Bahrain rose to 727,000; Saudi Arabia rose to 24.574 million; Oman rose to 2.567 million, Kuwait rose to 2.688 million; and Qatar rose to 813,000. It is also noticeable that the percentage of non-nationals has been consistently high in the GCC population for decades. By 2002 the population in these states was 32.5 million of whom 12.5 million were expatriates, representing 38.5 percent of the total population (see Table 17.2). In Qatar, the UAE and Kuwait, migrants constitute a majority—as much as 80 percent in the case of the UAE. In Saudi Arabia, Oman and Bahrain they represent a sizeable section of the total population with percentages varying from 26–40 percent.[7]

Of course, this massive increase in the population is not due to natural growth. Rather, it is due to the unprecedented migration to the Gulf states during the oil boom. In 1975 the nationals of these countries represented the majority, occupying some four-fifths of the total population at that time. After twenty years, i.e. by 1995, this percentage had dropped to around 64 percent.[8] Table 17.3 shows comparative rates and estimates of the population of the Gulf region by 2015. It indicates that the total number of nationals in that year will be 33.946 million and the number of migrants is estimated at 20.84 million, i.e. the total number of nationals and migrants will rise to 54.786 million.[9] Average population growth in the GCC states during the period 1991–2000 was nearly 3.3 percent, with regional variations ranging from 4.6 percent in the UAE, 4.3 percent in Kuwait, 2.9 percent in Saudi Arabia, 2.7 percent in Qatar and 2 percent in both Oman and Bahrain.

United Nations estimates[10] indicate that the next twenty-five years will witness a clear decline in the rates of population growth in all the countries of the Economic and Social Commission for Western Asia (ESCWA), including the GCC states. However, this decline varies among countries in accordance with the prevailing levels of fertility. It is expected that the fertility rate will be approximately 1 percent in the UAE, Kuwait, Qatar and Bahrain, 2 percent in Saudi Arabia, and 3 percent in Oman. (The fertility rate for each woman during the period 1990–2000 was 6.2 percent in Saudi Arabia, 5.9 percent in Oman, 3.7 percent in Qatar, 3.2 percent in the UAE, 2.9 percent in Kuwait and 2.6 percent in Bahrain.)[11]

[393]

Table 17.3

Population in GCC Countries (in thousands)

Country	2000			2005			2010			2015		
	Nationals	Expatriates	Total	Nationals	Expatriates	Total	Nationals	Expatriates	Total	Nationals	Expatriates	Total
Emirates	748	2,163	2,911	882	2,632	3,514	10,048	3,051	4,099	1,246	3,452	4,698
Bahrain	430	296	726	494	348	842	563	393	956	639	435	1,074
Kuwait	829	1,174	2,003	967	1,429	2,396	1,109	1,656	2,765	1,264	1,864	3,138
Saudi Arabia	16,096	7,273	23,369	19,180	9,282	28,462	22,897	11,024	33,921	27,264	12,657	39,921
Oman	1,882	859	2,741	2,258	1,123	3,381	2,730	1,270	4,000	3,279	1,402	4,681
Qatar	159	614	773	188	765	953	218	909	1,127	254	1,028	1,282
Total	20,114	12,379	32,523	23,969	15,579	39,548	28,565	18,303	46,868	33,786	20,84	54,694

Source: Abdul Razzaq Faris Al-Faris: Indicators of Quantitative Education Growth in the Light of Population and Economic Projections in the Next Two Decades in the Member countries (Riyadh, GCC Education Council, 1988), 93–94.

Table 17.4

Percentage of Population According to Age Groups (%)

Country	1975			1990			2002		
	0–14 yrs	15–64 yrs	+65 yrs	0–14 yrs	15–64 yrs	+65 yrs	0–14 yrs	15–64 yrs	+65 yrs
Emirates	28.4	69.4	2.2	30.8	67.7	1.5	*25.2	*73.8	*1.0
Bahrain	43.0	54.8	2.2	31.8	65.8	2.4	**28.8	**68.4	**2.8
Saudi Arabia	44.3	52.7	3.0	40.8	56.7	2.5	37.1	59.9	3.0
Oman	44.4	52.9	2.7	46.4	51.2	2.4	42.3	55.0	2.7
Kuwait	44.3	53.1	2.6				*15.8	*82.6	*1.6
Qatar	33.3	64.9	1.8	28.7	70.5	0.8	**26.8	**71.8	**1.4

* 2004 data

** 2001 data

Source: Arab Fund et al, The Unified Arab Economic Report (Abu Dhabi, Arab fund, September 2005), Appendix 2/8.

As for age composition, Table 17.4 indicates that the percentage of nationals of working age (15–64 years old) increased during the period 1975–1990 and then again in 2002. The UAE witnessed an increase from 69.4 percent in 1975 to 73.8 percent in 2002; in Bahrain it increased from 54.8 percent in 1975 to 65.8 percent in 1990 and then to 68.4 percent in 2000; in Saudi Arabia it increased from 52.7 percent in 1975 to 59.9 percent in 2002; in Oman it increased from 52.9 percent in 1975 to 55 percent in 2002; in Kuwait it increased from 53.1 percent in 1975 to 82.6 percent in 2002; and in Qatar it increased from 64.9 percent in 1975 to 71.8 percent in 2002. This category (working age) outweighs all other age groups.

Table 17.5

Population Estimates According to Wider Age Groups in GCC in 2005

Country	Total (1,000)	Age Groups			
		0–14 yrs	15–24 yrs	25–64 yrs	>65 yrs
UAE Total	4,496	988	783	2,677	48
%	100	22.0	17.4	59.5	1.1
Bahrain Total	727	197	110	398	22
%	100	27.1	15.1	54.7	3.0
Saudi Arabia Total	24,574	9,161	4,548	10,147	718
%	100	37.3	18.5	41.3	2.9
Oman Total	2,567	885	538	1,078	66
%	100	34.5	21.0	42.0	2.6
Kuwait Total	2,688	653	415	1,572	48
%	100	24.3	15.4	58.5	1.8
Qatar Total	813	177	112	514	10
%	100	21.8	13.8	63.2	1.2

Source: UN, World Population Prospects, 2004 Review (New York, NY: UN Publications, 2005).

The data in Table 17.5 also illustrates the age distribution of the total population of the GCC states in 2005. This data confirms the fact that GCC societies are relatively young and that the majority of the population is in the working age category. The percentage of the elderly (65 years and above) is obviously very low, representing only 22.5 percent of the population, whereas those who are less than 14 years old – i.e. those who are dependent in absolute terms – represent 35 percent. Generally, the size of this category (those less than 14 years old) is large when compared to other countries of the world, which stood globally at 31.5 percent in 1995, and even lower in advanced countries—for example, the United States is 21.9 percent.[12]

It is expected that this age structure – dominated by the youth – will guarantee that the absolute number of births remains high even if the total fertility rate drops. Moreover, the increase in the population of the working age group will lead to huge pressures on the labor market and will limit employment.[13] As for the age structure of non-nationals, it is noticeable that GCC states have witnessed similar patterns. In the early stages of development during the 1970s, migrant males of working age characterized migration. For example, in 1975 the percentage of the UAE's migrant population in the age group 15–59 years was 80.3 percent. In Kuwait, this figure was 58.7 percent in the same year, and more than 74 percent in Bahrain in 1971.[14]

With the continuation of social and economic development in the Gulf countries, two important changes occurred in the structure of migrant populations. The first was an increase in the migration of females to these countries, either as part of families or in the form of a specific female labor force following demand in the services sector (education, health, public services, etc.) and the domestic sector. The second change was the gradual transformation of the age structure of non-nationals, which began to reflect that of nationals. The main reason for this is the expansion of family migration and the high rate of fertility in migrant families. Referring back to Table 17.1, Saudi Arabia has the largest migrant population, some 6–9 times that of the UAE and Oman. Gender imbalance in favor of males in 2005 saw the UAE, Qatar and Kuwait record the highest percentages (76.6 percent, 72.5 percent and 62.6 percent, respectively) whereas Saudi Arabia recorded 54.3 percent. Generally, this is due to the phenomenon of selective migration as well as the fact that some migrant employees leave their wives in their countries of origin.

It is difficult to foresee future population trends in the GCC states. This is due to the presence of a large number of migrants whose numbers increase or decrease rapidly in accordance with national policies pertaining to migration or importation of foreign labor. There is also the impact on the economies of these countries from volatile oil revenues.[15] Despite this difficulty, Gulf demographic estimates for the period 1950–2050 indicate that the total population of the Gulf countries will rise to 111.67 million. By comparison, the population of Iran will reach 100.2 million and that of Iraq will become 56.4 million in the same year (see Table 17.6).

There is another demographic estimate which predicts that if the population of these countries continues to increase at the present rates, or even at growth rates lower than the present ones, the total population will reach 166.8 million in 2050, based on the annual growth rate of 4.23 percent witnessed in the period 1985–1995. If the annual rate is 3 percent, the population will reach 86.8 million in 2050. This total estimate is less than that projected by the US Statistics Bureau. However, it illustrates the danger of future population trends in the GCC states.[16]

As for the educational make-up of the population, firstly it is necessary to confirm that development, in its general definition, is more than a sheer increase in the national income per capita. The economist Amartya Sen, who won the Nobel Prize for Economics in 1998, perceives social justice as indicative – in one of its senses – of development, and implies that the freedoms enjoyed through social justice lead to a more valued life. Of these freedoms, Sen mentions the ability to read and write and to contribute effectively to the cultural life of one's society. As Ali Abdul Qadir Ali maintains, this broader meaning of development points to education as a human right.[17]

Table 17.6

The Demography of the Gulf Region 1950–2050 (Population in millions)

Country	1950	1960	1970	1980	1990	1995	2000	2010	2020	2030	2040	2050
UAE	0.07	0.1	0.25	1	2	2.2	2.4	2.8	3.1	3.4	3.5	3.7
Bahrain	0.11	0.16	0.22	0.35	0.5	0.57	0.63	0.74	0.83	0.9	0.95	0.97
Saudi Arabia	3.7	4.7	6.1	9.9	15.8	18.6	22	30.5	41.9	55.8	72.3	91.1
Oman	0.49	0.6	0.78	1.2	1.8	2.1	2.5	3.5	4.7	5.9	7.2	8.3
Qatar	0.03	0.05	0.11	0.23	0.48	0.61	0.74	0.97	1.1	1.2	1.2	1.2
Kuwait	0.15	0.29	0.75	1.4	2.1	1.6	2	2.8	3.7	4.6	5.5	6.4
Iran	16.4	21.6	28.9	39.3	55.7	61.5	65.6	73.8	84.2	91.5	96.9	100.2
Iraq	5.2	6.8	9.4	13.2	18.1	19.6	22.7	29.7	36.9	43.9	50.5	56.4

Source: Estimates of the US Statistics Bureau, quoted from the Gulf Strategic Report, Political Data and Statistics Table (Al-Sharjah: Al-Khaleej House for Journalism and Publishing, 2002), 298.

Unlike the nationals who found in education a means of attaining a higher social position in the local hierarchy (and perhaps an advanced economic position), education for migrant groups to the Gulf region (especially Arab migrants) is a means to negotiate a better position in the local labor market. Comparing the educational positions of nationals and migrant groups reveals the supremacy of the latter in this field. In 1975, the percentage of illiterate migrants was 29 percent of the total foreign labor force in Kuwait, whereas the percentage of illiterates among Kuwaiti nationals was 45 percent. However, this percentage dropped in Kuwait, as in other Gulf countries, to around 17.8 percent by 1985. By the early 1990s, the illiteracy rate was 15.2 percent among Kuwaitis and 18.4 percent among non-Kuwaitis.

It might be wrong to generalize about all Gulf countries. The nature of the demographic, social and economic structure of the migrant community in each Gulf state differs, for example in states where the Asian labor force has professional and educational levels that are low. The UAE population census of 1975 shows that 68.4 percent of the labor force had not received any formal education and 41.2 percent were illiterate. The remaining 27.2 percent were proficient in reading and writing. By 1980 there was a relative improvement, with those who did not receive formal education dropping to 52.1 percent and the percentage of university degree holders rising from 5.8 percent in 1975 to 9 percent in 1980. This might also be true to some extent of the labor force in Qatar and Oman. In Bahrain, statistics then showed that the level of illiteracy among Bahrainis was higher than that of non-Bahrainis. However, it dropped for both groups from 31.3 percent in 1981 to 17.4 percent in 1991, and to less than 10 percent by the end of the 1990s in the case of Bahrainis. Similarly, it dropped among non-Bahrainis from 20.2 percent to 9.4 percent in the same years.[18]

It is important to point out that the level of illiteracy among non-Arab migrant groups, especially Asians, is higher than that of the Arab migrant population. For instance, the illiteracy rate of the Arab population in Kuwait was 28.7 percent in 1970 whereas for the non-Arab population it was 46.3 percent. Although the population statistics of 1975, 1980 and 1985 do not give detailed data on this point, it is possible to say that the increase in importing Arab and foreign migrants with minimal professional levels during the last three decades has helped raise the illiteracy percentage rate of the migrant labor force, especially for Asians.[19]

Foreign Migrants in the GCC States

The phenomenon of migration to the Gulf differs greatly from other contemporary migrations worldwide. Within a few decades, the Gulf region witnessed radical changes in its population structure and labor force, and in some of these countries, non-nationals now form the majority of the population. These migrants came to the region from various parts of the world and belonged to many professions. Modern migration relating to oil started in the Gulf region with Bahrain and Kuwait in the 1940s, and then extended to the rest of the region, with Oman being the last Gulf state to become a destination for migrant labor (in the past it was regarded as a labor-exporting country). Opening the doors of the labor market of certain Gulf states (Bahrain, Kuwait, Qatar and the UAE) to the world was the only means for economic progress as a result of surplus capital and an acute shortage of skills in the national labor force.[20]

Migration to the Gulf Arab states is, therefore, an old phenomenon. It has continued in a manner that has created several obvious economic and social imbalances, especially the direct impact on the demographic structure of the population. The migration and movement factor has a profound effect on rates of growth of the labor force and the professional make-up of the workers. It also affects age and gender distribution and especially the level of female participation in the labor force.[21]

Migration to the Arabian Gulf: Its Nature and Stages

International migration of labor to the Arabian Peninsula began in the aftermath of World War II. It grew with the increase in oil revenues and the development of the economies of the Gulf Arab countries. Foreign labor migration to these countries can be divided into four or five stages in accordance with the flow of oil revenues.[22]

The first stage extended from the beginning of the 1940s to the early 1950s when the commercial investment of Arab oil and its economic effects began. Foreign labor was used to assist modernization projects and the expansion of public services. India and Iran were the major sources of migrant workers.

The second stage extended from the beginning of the 1950s to the beginning of the 1970s—until 1973, to be exact. This period was characterized by the reorganization of administration and the opening of schools, hospitals and roads. Arab migration from Egypt, Palestine, Sudan and Jordan outnumbered migration from India and Iran, which also coincided with the era of Arab nationalism.

The third stage began during the autumn of 1973 in the wake of rising oil prices and ended with the oil price collapse in 1983. Then, the price of oil rose from US$3 in 1973 to US$10 in 1974 and US$28 by 1980. In 1982 the price rose to US$34—the highest price recorded in that period. The oil price rise was accompanied by an increase in the amount of oil produced by Arab countries, from 14.7 million barrels per day in 1970 to 18.8 million barrels per day in 1973, and 22.3 million barrels per day in 1979. Thus, Arab oil revenues rose from US$4,543 million in 1970 to US$78,300 million in 1978, and US$213,600 million in 1980. The increase in oil revenues was also accompanied by an expansion in development projects and forced the GCC countries to open their doors to Arab and foreign migrant workers as a result of the lack of an adequate national labor force.

The fourth stage of foreign labor migration started in the early 1980s and coincided with the collapse of the oil price and subsequent revenues, resulting in a reduction of the migrant worker migration rate, which averaged 8 percent for the period 1980–1985.[23] The migration rate continued to slow and averaged 3.3 percent from 1985–1990 and 3 percent in the period 1990–2000.

When considering the period after the first Gulf War (1991) the fifth stage remains a controversial one. However, the war did not change the characteristics of the fourth stage but merely accelerated the rate of Asian dominance in the Gulf labor market. In Kuwait, hundreds of thousands left for their home countries during the Iraqi occupation and the Kuwaiti government deported the remaining Palestinians (who numbered around 300,000 before the invasion) after its return to power in 1991. A number of migrants of other nationalities did return to Kuwait after its liberation and there is evidence that they largely consisted of Asians. The total number of migrants by the end of 1990 was a little less than before the invasion. However, the flow of migrant labor started anew during the 1990s and onwards.[24]

The Scale of Migration to the Countries of the Region

To understand the present levels of migrants, it is necessary to examine the development of migration to the GCC states over the last three decades. Historically, there has been an increase in the population percentage of international migrants compared to the number of nationals. In the UAE the migrant percentage rose from 2.4 percent in 1960 to 58.9 percent in 1975, and to 70.5 percent and 71.4 percent in 1995 and 2005 respectively. In Qatar, the percentage rose from 32 percent in 1960 to 69.6 percent in 1975 and 77.2 percent in 1995 to 78.3 percent in 2005. The UAE and Qatar are exceptional cases because of the increasing numbers of migrants and the clear dominance of the migrant population over the native population. Oman represents a case where the state has been less affected by the percentage of migrants in its population. Its percentage rose to 5.6 percent in 1960, 8.2 percent in 1975, 26.3 percent in 1995 and then down to 24.4 percent in 2005.[25]

The migrant share of the GCC states is modest on the global level—just 6.7 percent of the total number of migrants in the world. Yet the peculiarity of the Gulf situation lies in the fact that its ratio to the total population of the GCC states exceeds global levels significantly and makes this a unique case in the history of human migration. As for the percentage of female migrants in the foreign labor force, the levels in all GCC states is significantly less than the world average due to the dependence on female migrants for domestic work only, as confirmed by the data in Table 17.7.[26]

Table 17.7

Statistics of World Migration: The 2005 Revision, Population Database

Indicator	Population in Mid Year (1,000)						Percentage of International Migrants to Population (%)						Percentage of Females from the Total of International Migrants (%)					
Country	1980	1985	1990	1995	2000	2005	1980	1985	1990	1995	2000	2005	1980	1985	1990	1995	2000	2005
UAE	1015	1410	1868	2435	3247	4496	70.8	71.5	71.2	70.5	70.4	71.4	24.4	28.7	28.5	28.2	28.0	27.8
Saudi Arabia	9604	12880	16379	18682	21484	24573	20.0	26.4	29.0	24.7	23.9	25.9	32.0	31.0	30.0	31.0	32.8	30.1
Kuwait	1375	1720	2143	1696	2230	2687	69.6	71.1	72.4	58.7	62.2	62.1	37.5	40.9	39.0	31.0	31.0	31.0
Qatar	229	361	467	526	606	813	72.2	78.2	79.1	77.2	76.0	78.3	25.8	25.8	25.8	25.8	25.8	25.8
Bahrain	347	413	493	584	672	727	29.8	33.1	35.1	37.5	37.8	40.7	24.9	26.2	28.5	30.9	30.9	30.9
Oman	1187	1527	1843	2177	2442	2567	15.2	21.4	24.5	26.3	24.8	24.4	20.9	20.9	20.9	20.9	20.9	20.9
Egypt	43860	49612	55673	61225	67285	74033	0.4	0.4	0.3	0.3	0.3	0.2	47.3	47.2	47.1	47.0	46.8	46.7
Syria	8978	10836	12843	14755	16813	19043	6.1	5.7	5.5	5.4	5.4	5.2	48.5	48.6	48.7	48.8	48.8	48.9
Lebanon	2698	2793	2741	3177	3398	3577	8.8	12.3	19.0	18.7	18.5	18.4	57.5	57.5	57.5	57.5	57.5	57.5
Jordan	2225	2706	3254	4288	4972	5703	36.4	34.8	35.2	37.7	39.1	39.0	48.6	48.7	48.8	48.9	49.0	49.1

Source: United Nations, Population Division, *World Migrant stock: the 2005 Revision* (http://esa.un.org/migration).

The first wave of mostly Arab migration to the region started in the late 1960s and the early 1970s, with migrants from south and Southeast Asia constituting 19.8 percent while Americans and Europeans made up 2 percent, with the remainder coming from Iran, Turkey and Africa. Although some construction projects were completed by 1975, the labor market continued to attract new foreign workers for a variety of reasons including the movement of some Iranians and Iraqis back to their home countries in order to work on new developments there; the growth of private and industrial services; and the failure of the main labor-exporting countries (Egypt, Jordan and Yemen) to meet the growing requirements of the labor market in the Gulf countries. As a result, the Gulf countries started to import workers from outside the Arab world, primarily from Asia.

After the first drop in the oil price in the late 1970s, a new factor emerged that reinforced the trend to favor Asian migrant workers—the preparedness to accept low wages. Thus the percentage of Arab migrants dropped to 30.1 percent from 65 percent from 1975–1985 whereas that of migrants from South Asia (India, Pakistan, Bangladesh and Sri Lanka) and East Asia (the Philippines, Thailand, Indonesia and others) rose to 43 percent and 20.3 percent[27], respectively. According to the estimates in the *Regional Report on Migration in the Arab Region*, and on 2004 data from the International Labor Organization, the total number of migrants from South Asia in the Gulf countries was 7.5 million and the percentage of Asians in the labor force was 65 percent.[28]

It is difficult to estimate the size of migrant communities in the GCC states because officials do not release the relevant information. However, the available information tends to suggest that there were 12.5 million migrants living in the GCC states in 2002. Of these nearly 3.5 million were Arabs, 3.2 million Indians, 1.7 million Pakistanis, approximately 1 million Bangladeshis, more than 700,000 Philippinos, and more than 700,000 Sri Lankans (see Table 17.8). Thus the number of Asians is more than double that of non-Gulf Arabs, who comprise mostly Egyptians (more than 1.5 million), Yemenis (1 million), Palestinians/ Jordanians (500,000) and Syrians (300,000).[29]

[405]

Table 17.8

Main Expatriate Communities in GCC Countries
(2002 Estimates in thousands)

	Bahrain	Kuwait	Oman	Qatar	Saudi Arabia	UAE	Total
Indians	100	295	300	100	1,400	1,000	3,200
Pakistanis	50	100	70	70	1,000	450	1,740
Egyptians		275	15	35	1,000	130	1,455
Yemenis					1,000	35	1,035
Bengalis		160	110		450	100	820
Sri Lankan		160		35	350	160	705
Filipinos		60		50	500	120	730
Jordanians/ Palestinians		50		50	270	110	480
Syrians		95			170		265
Iranians	45	80		20		40	145
Indonesians					250		250
Sudanese					250		250
Kuwaitis					120		
Turkish					100		
Bedouins		70					70
Total	**280**	**1,475**	**630**	**420**	**7,000**	**2,488**	

Source: Andrezej Kapiszewski, "Arab Labour Migration to the GCC States," The Regional Conference on Arab Migration in a Globalized World, the Arab League and the International Migration Organization, Cairo September 2–4, 2003

Note: The table includes figures relating to main expatriate communities only in each GCC country. Due to this limitation, the total column cannot be calculated.

The Size and Characteristics of the Labor Force

What characterizes the labor force in the GCC states is the predominance of migrants in the total population. By the end of 2001, there were 8–8.5 million expatriates in the GCC, out of the 12–13 million that constitute the total labor force, and expatriates also constituted the majority of the labor force in most of the GCC states; for example 70 percent on average in Qatar, 72 percent in Kuwait and 80–90 percent in the UAE. The smallest percentage was in Bahrain and Saudi Arabia, but even in these countries migrants represent 60 percent of the labor force. These rates have also varied little of late, which implies the percentage of foreign labor has stabilized for the time being in the GCC states.[30]

The migrant labor force has increased in Kuwait during the last two decades, rising from 1.2 million workers in 1985 to 1.6 million in 2005. However, the numbers did drop to less than 1 million in the early 1990s due to the Iraqi invasion and its ramifications. In addition, the number of migrant families dropped in Kuwait from 39 percent in 1990 to 31 percent in 2005, although this percentage remained unchanged during the same period in the rest of the GCC states. Meanwhile, the migrant labor force nearly doubled in Saudi Arabia during the same period, rising from 3.4 million in 1985 to 6.3 million in 2005. The total migrant labor force doubled in all the GCC states during the same period, rising from 6.3 million in 1985 to 12.8 million in 2005, with a three-fold increase in the UAE, rising from 1 million to 3.2 million in 2005. This labor force is mainly male. Females constituted 29 percent of migrants in 2005, with numbers of females headed towards the GCC states since the late 1970s to take up jobs such as nursing, teaching and domestic service.[31]

Irrespective of the reasons to employ migrant workers, it is noticeable that numbers have risen significantly and this workforce is primarily relied upon to power the pace of development in GCC states. As statistics indicate, the percentage of this migrant labor force varies, as Table 17.9 shows, between 46 percent and 90 percent. It represents 46 percent of the labor force in Oman, 70 percent in Qatar and Saudi Arabia, 77 percent in Kuwait, and 90 percent in the UAE.

[407]

Table 17.9

Percentage of Expatriate Workforce to Total Workforce in the GCC States in the First Half of 1990s

Country	Source	Size of National Workforce	Size of Expatriate Workforce	Percentage of Expatriate to National Workforce
Bahrain	1991 Census (7th Census)	90,662	135,786	60%
Kuwait	1992 Survey	140,246	467,462	77%
Oman	1993 Census (First Census)	470,000	400,000	46%
Qatar	1993 (Ali Khalifah Al-Kwari	30,195	274,805	90%
Saudi Arabia	1992 (The Last Census)	2,308,800	3,463,200	60%
UAE	1992 (Workforce Survey)	73,350	660,150	90%

Source: Maitha Al Shamsi, "Labour Migration in the GCC States" (in Arabic), a study presented to the Arab Conference on Implementing the Action Plan of the International Conference on Population and Development, ESCWA, Beirut, September 22–25, 1998, The Statistical Appendix.

Table 17.10

Workforce in the Government Sector in GCC States, Years 1991, 1996, 2001

Country	Year	National Workforce (%)	Expatriate Workforce (%)	Total Workforce
UAE	1991	36.8	63.2	50,313
	1996	39.9	60.1	56,414
	2001	44.5	55.5	56,386
Bahrain	1991	82.9	17.1	28,641
	1996	87.8	12.2	30,454
	2001	90.7	9.3	32,078
Saudi Arabia	1991	75.0	25.0	529,974
	1996	82.2	17.8	616,291
	2001	88.8	11.2	710,859
Sultanate of Oman	1991	65.1	34.9	72,493
	1996	67.8	32.2	78,277
	2001	78.1	21.9	87,652
Qatar	1991	43.9	56.1	37,028
	1996	43.9	56.1	46,355
	2001	66.1	33.9	34,380
Kuwait	1991	77.6	22.4	105,258
	1996	71.1	28.9	147,010
	2001	76.0	24.0	161,147
GCC Total	1991	71.0	29.0	823,707
	1996	75.3	24.7	974,801
	2001	83.0	17.0	1,082,502

Source: Ahmad bin Sulaiman bin Obeid, "Unemployment in the Gulf society and Potential Employment" (in Arabic), The Population Policies of the GCC symposium, Qatar, April 19–20, 2004, 7.

The public sector is a major employer of the national labor force in the GCC states, accounting for 83 percent in 2001. Statistics show that the percentage of the national labor force in the public sector increased in the period 1991–2001 and indicates the tendency of the public sector in the GCC States to employ nationals to replace the migrant labor force in this sector. This tendency is quite apparent in all the GCC states except Kuwait, because of the conditions at the time of liberation and the need of the country to employ a migrant labor force in the public sector (see Table 17.10).

The fact that the governments of the GCC states are replacing expatriates with nationals is attested to by the fact that the numbers of migrant workers in the public sector has dropped in both Saudi Arabia and Bahrain during the period 1991–2001. Numbers also dropped in the rest of the GCC states by the end of this period. In parallel, there is a noticeable rise in the numbers of employees from the national labor force in all the GCC states during the whole of this period. The public sector in the GCC states employed 11 percent of the total labor force and 26.5 percent of the total national labor force during 1999. The public sector percentage employing nationals is similar in the GCC states except the UAE where the contribution of the public sector to employing the national and migrant labor force is less at 2.7 percent.[33]

While Oman and Qatar depend on the public sector to offer employment to nationals, three other states, and the UAE in particular, depend to a lesser degree on the public sector for national employment due to their large private sector. Moreover, the private sector in these countries employs relatively large numbers of nationals. In the late 1990s the number of the nationals employed in the private sector in Bahrain was three times that employed in the public sector; likewise in Saudi Arabia, and more than five times in the UAE. In parallel to this, the percentage of nationals employed by the private sector in Qatar, Oman and Kuwait was less than in the public sector. This discrepancy naturally raises questions regarding the reasons why.[34]

As for the professional structure of the expatriate labor force in the GCC states, it is strongly linked to the stages of economic growth through which these countries have passed during the second half of the 20th century after the discovery of oil. A study by the World Bank revealed that the percentage of skilled and semi-skilled migrant workers at the beginning of the economic boom was approximately 70 percent. Those who held professional jobs were approximately 17 percent of the total migrant labor force.[35]

As for the kind of professions practiced by nationals and migrants, of the 2.1 million employed nationals, nearly one fifth work in office jobs and one third work in technology, technical, administrative, organizational and business jobs. Hence, nearly 53.4 percent are considered white collar workers who earn larger salaries, while 72.9 percent of expatriates work in low-wage jobs.[36] As for the professions in which both nationals and migrants participate, the percentage of employed nationals and expatriates is 28.6 percent and 71.4 percent of the labor force respectively. In spite of this, the percentage of nationals occupying administrative and organizational positions is approximately 54.9 percent, of which 62.2 percent are in government jobs and 42 percent in the business sector. Nationals represent only 12.5 percent in the major productive sectors and 27.8 percent in the services sectors. It is also worth mentioning that there is a growing tendency in the GCC states to select expatriates in favor of a skilled and specialized labor force.[37]

It is generally agreed that education plays an important role in the participation of women in the economy, as shown by statistical data in most communities. The participation of women in the economy of the UAE has increased along with the rise in their educational standards – a reality demonstrated in all Gulf societies – and is reflected in the workforce accordingly, with educated women working in the professions and services sector, although the majority work in the education system.

Migrant Labor Force and Productivity

There has been no in-depth economic study of the productivity of the migrant labor force in terms of nationality, education, gender, etc.

However, some data can offer relevant assumptions. Available data on productivity in three Gulf States (Saudi Arabia, Kuwait and the UAE), which are the countries that employ most of the Asian labor force, show that productivity rose from the mid 1970s until the 1980s, and then fell after that. From this, can one assume that the drop in work productivity was related to the replacement of Arab workers by an Asian labor force.[38] Productivity in 1981 rose to 113 percent, in comparison to 1975. It then started to drop constantly to 81.6 percent in 1983, 58.2 percent in 1987, and 49.9 percent in 1993. The value added by the migrant worker dropped by a half throughout the whole period—from US$45,000 to US$20,000.[39]

There is a temporal relationship between the increase in the Asian labor force and the drop in the productivity of the migrant worker. This raises some important questions. Is this drop due to the growth of the Asian labor force or to other factors relating to the pattern of development in the Gulf, especially the dominant pattern of production and consumption? It is worth mentioning that data also indicates the Asian labor force is concentrated in the services sector, especially the domestic sector. It is therefore difficult to calculate its productivity, since the data only indicates, for instance, that there is on average one woman working in the domestic services sector (housemaid) for every three Gulf nationals and two women for every three persons in wealthy families.[40] Moreover, the private sector has created an informal market for migrant labor by exploiting the "sponsorship" system to make profit by importing workers. The supply of cheap Asian labor therefore increased because of the low cost of moving them to the Gulf and their readiness to undertake unskilled work for modest wages.

The Asian social network – organized or not – plays a vital role in sourcing jobs for relatives. A study conducted in 1996 on a sample of 800 skilled and unskilled Asian migrants in Kuwait showed that 34 percent were assisted by social and family networks in order to migrate legally to Kuwait. 56 percent of Pakistanis in the sample also admitted that they had received strong support from social networks when looking to migrate. This networking is not available to the Arab labor force.[41]

The Continuity of Demand for a Migrant Labor Force

Demand for foreign labor in the Gulf countries in the coming years depends on several factors. The most important of these are:

- The number of young nationals who join the labor market.
- The impact of localizing the labor markets (primarily resulting from government-led initiatives).
- The ability of the economy to create new job opportunities.
- Training the national labor force to meet market requirements.
- The readiness of nationals to perform low level work.
- The competition with foreign workers, especially Asians.
- Political and security considerations.[42]

The Gulf region attracts the largest foreign labor force in the world. Research sources, including the Gulf Authority for Industrial Consultations, expect a rise of 66 percent in the Gulf's demand for migrant labor by 2010 compared to 1995, due to the expansion of development projects. Mackenzie International Co. expects that the average rate of increase for migrant labor in the GCC states will be 92 percent during the coming decade. All this means that the Gulf's demand for foreign labor force will remain high, especially in a number of economic sectors. It should also be noted that the large number of migrant workers in some countries does not necessarily imply demographic dominance. For example, the number of Indians in Saudi Arabia is 1.4 million, but their ratio to the population is much less than that of the UAE.[43] Moreover, there are problems with the workings of the labor market itself.[44] These problems include:

- The lack of planning in foreign worker recruitment in the public and private sector, which leads to over supply, low productivity and ineffective employment.
- The division of the labor force in terms of nationality, religion, language and culture. This can lead to competition and friction and negatively affect work and productivity.

[413]

- The skills categories of workers needs better definition. If the region is undergoing a stage of growth and needs a skilled labor force, there is no justification for importing unskilled migrants in large numbers.

Migration Policies

In reality, there have been no declared migration policies in the GCC states since the marked increase in migrant flows in the mid 1970s. What migration policies exist are reflected in a number of legislative acts to create the legal framework for importing migrants for a specific labor force. As the GCC states have developed, and in the light of regional and global socio-political developments, this legislation has undergone revision. However, none of this revision was conducted within a comprehensive vision based on research and planning. Hence, this has created various shortcomings when dealing with the issues of migrant labor. Despite this, these regulations and legislation have kept abreast of the flow of migrant labor force and created a sort of balance in supply and demand, and allowed the national labor force to develop. Points of note expressed by these regulations and acts are as follows:[45]

- There are strong controls imposed by the Gulf countries on the inward flow of foreign labor. The Ministries of the Interior (via visit visas, residency rules and deportation) and the Ministries of Labor and Social Affairs (via work permits and work identity cards) engage in this dual control.
- The desire of the Gulf countries to replace the migrant labor force with a national labor force is certain. However, several factors hinder this, including lack of human resources, the educational and training deficit, refusing manual jobs, and access to a reasonable income through citizenship alone.
- The Gulf countries share the absence of accurate information about the labor market. Collecting, processing and exchanging such information can provide control over the movement of migrant labor and preempt potential problems.

It is worth mentioning that the GCC states have increasingly introduced policies to limit the numbers of migrants in their populations. For instance, after the first Gulf War Kuwait established policies to prevent ministries from re-employing more than 35 percent of their former foreign labor force. Its Ministry of Planning also proposed diversifying as much as possible the nationalities of the labor force in order to avoid the dominance of one nationality over the labor market. Other policies included limits on support for expatriates and giving priority in employment to the nationals of other GCC states and Arab countries.[46]

In 2002 Saudi Arabia announced a plan to be implemented in 10 years that would limit the percentage of expatriates and their families in the Kingdom to 20 percent.[47] In other efforts to localize the labor force, the Kingdom announced limiting certain professions to Saudi nationals only, such as taxi drivers, workers in goldsmiths shops, employees in the offices for *Haj* and *Umrah,* salespersons in showrooms of cars and public relations officials.[48] Saudi Arabia is also continuing to establish rules to diversify the nationality breakdown of foreign workers.[49]

In addition to the introduction of such constraints, the GCC states began to pay greater attention to the skill levels of migrant workers and their training. In 2002, the UAE announced its intention to cut 240,000 workers in the private sector who did not have suitable educational qualifications.[50] Similarly, Saudi Arabia announced a plan to test technicians to verify that they have the required qualifications to do the jobs they aspire to keep.[51]

Migration Policies and the Labor Market

No doubt these policies were essentially focused on creating a balance between supply and demand in the GCC labor market. Although these regulations did not provide decisive solutions to the problem of the demographic imbalance, they at least contributed to creating opportunities for the national labor force by controlling migrant inflows. For this reason migrant worker policies were built on two pillars: the desire of the Gulf countries to control the flow of migrants according to the needs of the labor market; and the inflow of migrant workers to be managed at the lowest possible cost.[52]

As for managing the flow of the labor force, the governments of the Gulf countries do not interfere directly in the process of selecting foreign workers in order to maintain the free economic system. Until very recently, these countries did not tie themselves into agreements with other states regarding workers. Moreover, the administrative authorities leave the matter of recruiting workers to the private sector, which selects foreign workers and determines their wages according to managerial requirements. However, the process of formally moving migrants into the country is subject to the permission of the public authorities. In addition, a migrant does not have the right to change his sponsor unless the latter agrees. If his contract expires and is not renewed, he has to return to his home country unless he is able to obtain a contract from another sponsor. This system permits different sponsors to benefit from the skills and experience of workers available in the country whose contracts expire. Public authorities help limit national unemployment by administrative and legal measures.[53] These include returning migrants to their home countries after their contracts expire as well as refusing any possibility of gaining citizenship.

The entrance of the GCC states to the global market and their growing strategic importance poses problems. GCC governments need to review their population, economic and development policies to establish comprehensive strategies to deal with the imbalances in their populations and labor forces. Gulf countries have traveled a long way in the process of localizing their labor forces, yet they still face several obstacles that require economic restructuring in order to provide opportunities for future generations to work in the public and private sectors.

The Challenges and Impacts of the Imbalance in the Population Structure

Undoubtedly, all Gulf officials and citizens feel the danger of the presence of a foreign labor force in their countries, of which the majority are Asians and whose financial transfers out of the Gulf stand at US$25 billion annually. There are other negative effects created by the foreign labor force in the Gulf's social fabric. It affects the Arab-Islamic cultural identity, social values, population structure and demographic development. It also has a negative effect on the economic, political and security situations—in particular the presence of illegal migrants, which is expected to increase due to difficult economic conditions in those countries near the Gulf. However, observers of Gulf affairs clearly realize that it is difficult to get rid of the foreign labor force at the present time, due to the reluctance of nationals to undertake certain forms of work such as manual labor, and the general fact that the foreign labor force is essential to the movement of the economy.

The Challenges of the Imbalance in the Population Structure

What follows is a review of the challenges posed by the imbalance in the population structure of GCC countries.

1. The Political and Security Challenge

Gulf countries' fears over the high percentage of their foreign labor force are growing. There is also the possibility of pressures by international organizations on Gulf governments to naturalize migrant workers if their labor relationship with the GCC countries is not clearly defined. Certain researchers maintain that the danger lies in the increasing numbers of migrant Asian workers, which could lead to several security challenges for GCC countries.[54] These challenges include regional political differences and views held by migrant workers with regard to international conflicts, in particular those that affect their countries of origin.

A foreign labor force could also result in negative political effects that might threaten internal stability if used by its countries of origin to destabilize Gulf countries through the encouragement of violence, disorder and sabotage. Moreover, migrant workers could be used by their countries of origin as a bargaining chip when dealing with Gulf countries, not forgetting the dangers pertaining to any loss of national identity. One study of a sample composed of nationals and migrants in the UAE pointed out that 69.5 percent of nationals believe that the loyalty of foreigners would be to their original countries even if they were given UAE nationality. On the other hand, 30.4 percent of the migrants in the sample maintained that loyalty to their home country or the UAE would depend on circumstances at the time; whereas 10 percent of the migrants did not express a view either way on the issue. Of the sample, 11.4 percent said that their loyalty would be to the UAE while 26.6 percent said that their loyalty would be torn between their original countries and the UAE.[55]

Some opinions point to fears concerning the transformation of the migrant labor force into a power exercising a political role that could threaten political stability. Proponents of this also argue that the migrant labor force could probably be used by foreign powers to create tensions and instability within the state, and maintain that the discordant population mix is a factor that could lead to the disintegration of the political structure if certain circumstances arise. Moreover, they mention the possibility that this force might demand the "right of self-determination," when generations of migrants feel that through the passage of time they transform from residents into indigenous inhabitants. Such migrant groups could develop political movements, which express their thoughts, aspirations and demands. Naturally, any movement of this sort will receive the sympathy and support of the governments of their indigenous countries and various human rights groups around the world.[56]

2. The Challenge of an Increasing Dependence on a Migrant Labor Force

Certain studies indicate that in spite of programs for replacing migrant workers with nationals and the successes achieved by some countries, especially Bahrain, Gulf countries will continue to depend on a migrant labor force for years to come. This will be the case even if such governments managed to employ all their citizens since the labor market requirements continue to outpace the local population. A study issued by the Institute of Public Administration in Riyadh pointed out that the Kingdom of Saudi Arabia will continue to host migrant workers for several decades to come even with the program of "Saudizing" jobs in the private sector. The study added that projection statistics confirm that even if all of the Saudi labor force were employed in the private sector, they would use no more than 40 percent of the capacity of the labor market. Hence, nearly 59 percent of the capacity in the Saudi private sector needs to recruit foreign labor. A Kuwaiti study mentioned that the program of replacing foreign workers with Kuwaitis is not a strategic option to solve the problem of recruitment and the labor force in Kuwait. However, it currently remains an available option to solve the problem in stages. This means that Gulf countries have plans to restructure the labor sectors, yet they must not neglect the role of foreign labor as a primary supply of their workforce. All this requires a clear-cut strategy to deal with the issue.[57]

3. The Challenge of the Labor Market Imbalance

Imbalances in the Gulf labor markets now include:

- A large increase in the percentage of migrants in the labor force compared to nationals, especially in the private sector.
- The national labor force is largely found in the public sector and little represented in productive sectors such as oil, gas and other commercial industries.
- There is an imbalance between supply and demand in the labor market.

Presently, the number of migrants working in the GCC countries is estimated at 7.5 million while the number of unemployed nationals varies between 420,000 and 475,000. This figure is almost 7 percent of the total labor force. Employing migrants also leads to unemployment among nationals and is a major socio-economic problem faced by the GCC countries that has worsened in the few past years. A study of future demands for foreign labor (following the current trends) predicts that demand for foreigners will increase from 6,143,000 in 1995 to 10,799,000 in 2010. Likewise, demand for nationals in the labor force will increase from 2,857,000 in 1995 to 5,013,000 in 2010. In addition, population increases will result in higher unemployment among nationals, from nearly 4.4 percent in 1995 to nearly 13.7 percent in 2010.[58]

In addition to the problems discussed, the ease of importing skilled, qualified and expert migrant workers on request, compared to the expensive and time-consuming investment in developing the local labor force, reinforces the attraction of employing foreigners by the business community. Although governments emphasize the importance of employing citizens, the private sector has taken few measures in this regard. With the exclusion of administrative and office jobs, only a limited number of nationals work in this sector, which is also pervaded by complaints regarding the fact that wage differences and training costs far exceed the cost of employing well-trained foreigners. In addition to this, it is difficult to get rid of unproductive nationals. Often, trained nationals leave for other jobs thus squandering investment in their training. The challenge facing the governments of the GCC countries centers around the need to reduce the numbers of foreigners working in these countries and their dependence on them, especially in the private sector. Although the policy of "localization" has been easily implemented in the public sector, it is difficult to impose a similar policy in the private sector, which is characterized by the ability to compete.

The national labor force is flawed; especially in the public sector where supply can exceed demand. This flaw is due to the rapid increase in the number of Gulf graduates from universities and other institutions of education. However, governments do seem serious about change, by replacing foreigners with Gulf nationals in the labor force of the GCC countries[59]—despite a lack of any comprehensive plan for the labor force.

4. The Challenge of Unemployment

The phenomenon of unemployment has emerged in the past few years irrespective of the concern and attention of some GCC governments to employing nationals entering the labor market. This is done either by creating new job opportunities for nationals, or by replacing migrant workers with nationals. Despite this, there is still rising unemployment, especially among young people in the GCC countries.

The Economic and Social Commission for Western Asia (ESCWA) reported that more than 50 percent of the population of the GCC is below 15 years of age, which can be attributed to the rapid growth of the population over the last two decades. As a result, the rate of unemployment increases (estimated at 15 percent in 2002) unless new job opportunities are created. It is estimated that there are close to 500,000 unemployed nationals in the GCC countries and this is expected to increase by 210,000 annually.[60] The deputy chairperson of the Labor Force Council estimated in December 2002 that the rate of unemployment among Saudi youth was nearly 14 percent. Others mentioned a rate of 20 percent or higher. The estimates from the Saudi-American Bank show that there are 30,000 jobs annually for Saudi citizens. However, the number of Saudis who join the labor market annually is 100,000, of which high school graduates constitute 63 percent.[61]

The causes of unemployment – especially among the young – lie in three factors: the demographic factor, the policies of employment in the public sector, and the poor ability of the national worker to compete with the migrant worker. The high rates of fertility and subsequent population growth, especially in Saudi Arabia, Oman and to a certain extent Bahrain, have led to an increase in those entering the labor market.

Unemployment in the GCC countries can be divided into "frictional unemployment" and "structural unemployment." Frictional unemployment in the GCC countries emerges from the fact that unemployed youth often wait to obtain a lucrative government job, despite the availability of information on other jobs in the labor market. Structural unemployment occurs primarily because of differences in the rates of productivity and levels of skills required for a large number of jobs in the private sector, which are taken up by the migrant labor force. Young nationals entering the labor market do not satisfy the requirements of a large number of jobs in the private sector, hence the emergence of structural unemployment in the Gulf labor market.[62]

[421]

5. The Challenge of Empowering Youth

Youth represents huge potential and is a basic pillar of a country's development. Some population projections refer to two important events by 2010 with respect to the Gulf labor force. The first event is the average age of total population in Saudi Arabia and Oman will be 23 and 22 years old, respectively; between 31 and 33 years old in Kuwait, the UAE and Qatar; and 36 years old in Bahrain.[63] Therefore, the GCC countries will witness a great increase in the numbers of those reaching working age, and its potential benefits require formulating an alternative development policy to prepare human capital in terms of knowledge and skills. It also requires expanding the opportunities for nationals to participate in the labor force and not be hindered by the need to support family members. Otherwise, this opportunity will be wasted and dependence on migrant workers will remain and even increase.[64]

Improving the quality of the national labor force represents a major challenge, since it entails creating individuals capable of contributing positively to development. Raising the quality of the national labor force begins by re-examining the educational system and revising its strategy, and goals, redesigning its programs and improving its content to meet the actual present and future needs of society.[65]

There is a need for the presence of an effective policy to encourage a national labor force in all sectors of the economy. This policy must feature incentives and create opportunities for the national labor force to take up employment. Yet, employing youth is problematic mainly for the fact that the pubic sector, which is the traditional employer of nationals, has failed to take on as many new staff due to a growing deficit in its budgets. Opportunities to work in the public sector are restricted to the replacement of retired employees. Moreover, the public sector is shrinking and therefore there is a rising pressure to employ nationals in the private sector. However, nationals wishing to find jobs in this sector have to compete with a foreign labor force that accepts lower wages and has higher skills.[66]

In spite of the impressive quantitative growth in the level of education, the opportunities of finding jobs are a great concern for nationals. There is a growing number of graduates who experience difficulty in obtaining jobs in the private sector because they lack essential labor skills, which can be attributed to a longstanding attitude that there is guaranteed employment in government institutions irrespective of certificates, specializations, degrees, and other such achievements. In the state of Kuwait the total number of students who graduate annually from its institutions of education is nearly 10,000. In the past, the public sector used to absorb most of these new graduates, but this sector is presently satiated and there are plans to reduce it by privatization. Possibilities to create jobs lie in the private sector where foreigners now constitute more than 90 percent of the labor force. Arrangements to encourage employment of nationals in the private sector, which are encouraged by the governments of the GCC countries, are met with strong opposition from business circles, which point out that the majority of national graduates lack the necessary skills to compete effectively with the foreign labor force. In addition, nationals refuse a varied and expansive group of available jobs on the pretext that they are not socially appropriate, entail great hardship, or give wages and fringe benefits less than those offered by the public sector.[67]

The outcome is that such attitudes toward work – and a lack of commitment to do hard jobs and acquire a competitive edge – are encouraged by the system of social care and the existence of an educational system that depends on obsolete educational curricula and will continue to severely limit the replacement of foreign workers by nationals. The private sector finds difficulty in meeting the governments' desire for employment of nationals because the overwhelming majority of nationals seeking jobs are school leavers with limited experience and skills. This might seem an apparent contradiction in view of the fact that the private sector in the GCC countries is often labor-intensive and offers low-wage jobs that require few skills. Yet it still requires experienced workers, who are productive and committed to work hard and have self-

[423]

motivation. The fact remains that the national labor force still asks for higher wages despite the lack of appropriate labor skills, which local training institutions and programs fail to provide.[68]

The problem of employing nationals in the private sector is a matter of great significance for regional economies and society as a whole. Few countries in the world suffer from the dominance of foreigners over its private sector as the UAE, and although it is true that foreigners will remain in the private sector for decades to come and will continue to play an important role in the national economy, the continuous growth of the private sector and employment of non-nationals without redress is unacceptable. Even if we assume accelerating rates of employment in the public sector, a large number of Gulf nationals will not find jobs in government departments and must turn to the private sector, which now provides three times the jobs available in the public sector. Moreover, these private-sector jobs are occupied by the migrant labor force at the rate of 98 percent.[69] It seems that the private sector will not take upon itself the initiative of providing jobs for nationals seeking work. However, young Gulf nationals seeking jobs will not find the sort of opportunities they desire in a competitive market with little or no practical experience.

All countries that receive migrant labor have laws that do not permit foreigners to take up jobs unless there are no qualified citizens available. The laws of the GCC countries provide for this, yet the application of such laws is not an easy business in countries where the migrant labor force is the rule and not the exception. It must be clear that this does not mean that the issue of a foreign labor force is insurmountable. On the contrary, avoiding the issue of migrant workers could have a negative effect on development in general and the development of national manpower in particular.[70]

6. The Challenge Posed by Workers' Remittances from GCC Countries

The study prepared by the GCC Secretariat General in 2004 showed that the total amount of remittances made by foreign workers in the GCC countries currently stands at US$24 billion per annum. Saudi Arabia accounts for 63 percent of this amount, the UAE for 15 percent and the remainder comes from the other GCC countries. The study also showed an upward trend in the size of remittances in the six GCC countries during the period examined (1975–2000). Remittances jumped from US$1.6 billion in 1975 to US$24 billion by the end of 2000.[71]

According to the study, these remittances have a direct and negative impact on the GCC countries in terms of a sizeable, lost source of financial investment opportunity. Without adequate investment tools for absorbing the funds that are transferred out of the local economies of the GCC countries, the resultant loss is equal to more than one third of actual investment. It is noted that there are no adequate policies to encourage expatriate workers to invest part of their remittances inside local economies as savings and deposits. In fact, new measures have been devised to encourage facilitate sending funds abroad, which constitute a drawback in the performance of local finance markets and a deficit in the growth of funds available.

Finally, remittances by expatriate workers leave negative impacts on the balance of payments of the GCC countries as well as the balance of foreign cash in these countries. Changes in the current accounts of the GCC countries reached 166 percent on average in the period 1979–2000.[72]

7. The Challenge imposed by Expatriates' Overstay

Expatriate workers might stay in the country for long periods, and this could lead to numerous problems from a national point of view. These include:

- Creating undesirable political, social and cultural trends.
- The presence of a highly experienced foreign workforce (such as company executives, specialists and their assistants, clerical jobs etc.) for long periods could jeopardize nationals' chances to work and succeed in sought-after jobs.
- Long-staying expatriates could hinder employers' opportunities to gain new migrant workers with better qualifications in terms of technical and professional knowledge and expertise.

Naturally, there is a need for certain distinguished expertise at all levels of employment. However, the challenge lies in deciding policies that would help strike a balance between retaining necessary foreign expertise and injecting new blood into the workforce.[73]

Impacts of Imbalance in the Demographic Structure of the Region's Countries

The GCC countries face an increasing imbalance in their demographic structure, and this will be reflected on their societies both directly and indirectly. Such impacts on these societies are noted as follows:

Economic Impact

There are two major issues with the economic impact of international immigration: first, the impact of migrant workers on wages and employment opportunities for nationals; second, the net financial balance of immigration, due to increases in public spending on health, education and other public services.

According to the neo-classical economic theory, immigration, through continued manpower supply, puts pressure on wages and could lead to an increase in unemployment rates among nationals, provided the number of jobs inside the countries concerned is constant. However, the skills of some international migrants are different from those of nationals. Instead of competing with nationals, migrants complement them in the labor market. Low-skilled migrant workers tend to work in areas that do not attract nationals, at least for the wages offered. This happens with manual jobs in agriculture, mining and construction as well as a variety of low-paid jobs in the services sector such as domestic work, care for the elderly, cleaning and catering etc.[74]

In addition to the repercussions on economic activity, a large expatriate workforce could lead to the loss of a significant amount of savings and investment opportunities, which are crucial for encouraging development, through remittances to their home countries. For example, Indian workers alone in GCC countries transferred about US\$17 billion in 2000. In addition, a growing percentage of these remittances goes to non-Arab countries. Previously, remittances to Arab countries had effectively contributed to reducing poverty in those states and provided significant facilities for development and stability. The amount of remittances by Indians mentioned is equal to remittances made by all Arab workers in the Gulf countries.[75]

Finally, the presence of an expatriate workforce in the Gulf countries has contributed to certain negative phenomena among these countries' citizens that could harm economic activities. For example, some citizens tend to show laziness in performing their part of jobs which they share with expatriates. They also show lack of enthusiasm in acquiring required knowledge and skills for simple jobs. This situation would entail an increase in the size of workforce on the one hand; and would not facilitate using available local workforce on the other hand.

Impacts on Values and Culture

There are concerns that the growing numbers in the expatriate workforce and their long-term settlement are negatively affecting the knowledge and mastery of the Arabic language among nationals. For example, certain Indian dialects are widespread and are used more commonly than the Arabic language in some areas of the Gulf. Those concerned cite examples of Asian "ghettos," which serve the Indian community only. Certain old districts in these countries and some housing projects for low-income people have been turned into pockets populated mainly by Asians. Numeric supremacy of the expatriate workforce, and the increase in areas where they collect, pose risks which, as some see it, will deepen cultural alienation in this part of the Arab World.

This negative impact is not limited to language only. It goes further to influence the nature of child upbringing due to the presence of large numbers of foreign domestic carers. According to some studies, the intensive employment of Asian child carers in the Gulf countries has contributed to the spread of some undesirable social values, has weakened the fabric of families and has provided the children with a non-Arab culture.[76]

Asian carers unwittingly create a serious impact on the psychological make-up of children in the Gulf countries. Such an impact is not restricted to knowledge of the Arabic language; it goes further and imbues new generations with values, customs and traditions which are alien to the Arab World. Eventually, certain individuals from among these affected generations will take up leading positions in their countries, yet they will lack an Arab identity, affiliation, personality and the knowledge of the language. Children are often more exposed to "cultural uprooting" than adults, and the time they spend with servants is much more than the time they spend with their family members. What else other than psychological and educational confusion could be expected from a child who finds himself forced to communicate in a language that is different from his mother tongue?

Another relevant issue is the phenomenon of marriages between nationals and foreigners, especially with Asian women. Official statistics indicate that the percentage of nationals who have married expatriates is no less than 30 percent in some Gulf countries, for example the UAE.[77]

The presence of an expatriate workforce also affects the pattern of social relations in Gulf societies. According to a study on social relations between nationals and expatriate workers, 52.7 percent of nationals surveyed said their relations were poor, 47.3 percent said their relations were not bad, while only 10 percent said their relations with expatriate workers were good. In addition, work ethics are also negatively affected by a large migrant workforce, since their domination of low-skilled jobs deepens the negative approach to such employment and discourages citizens from engaging in such jobs.[78]

The Arab countries of the Gulf are witnessing a cultural conflict between the indigenous culture of the nationals and the values, customs and traditions that it represents; and the incoming culture of expatriates with different values and customs. This culture clash places a heavy burden on nationals who need to acquire medium and high-level knowledge and skills to be able to compete with expatriates and replace them at various levels.[79]

Social Impacts

Migrant worker immigration has also brought various crimes to Gulf societies. There is a widespread belief among Gulf nationals that migrant workers, in particular Asians, are associated with various forms of criminality. Such beliefs stem from the perception that Asians from certain countries live in environments favorable to crime and indecent behavior. There is a fear that such patterns of behavior could be imitated in Gulf countries, resulting in the formation of gangs, etc.

Various crimes have spread because of the arbitrary method of recruiting and using foreign labor. Workforce requirements have never been studied thoroughly to ascertain exactly what the needs are in every sector. Except for those who arrive in the Gulf countries on employment contracts to work in companies or as domestic maids, jobseekers simply arrive in these countries and start looking for employment. Such a situation leads to over-employment and job insecurity for expatriate workers, as well as a whole host of other problems, not helped by the chaotic situation involving sponsors and guarantors.[80]

There is a need to regulate and control this phenomenon within a comprehensive plan for employment and the use of migrant workers. However, this does not mean that the negative impact of the expatriate workforce in the Gulf countries is restricted only to Asian workers. Arab migrant workers as well as those from other nationalities also play a part in this.

Health Impacts

One negative impact of the influx of expatriate workers, especially Asians, is the spread of endemic diseases. Some of these workers come from densely populated countries with low levels of medical services and a study of the history of diseases in the Gulf region shows that a number of communicable diseases have spread in the region, particularly in the past twenty years following Asian migration, and such diseases have been transmitted to nationals. It is true that any person who takes up employment must undergo a medical examination, yet many diseases cannot be detected by a routine medical check-up. In addition, a medical examination of applicants is carried out only once before a migrant starts working. However, the same worker would travel from time to time to visit their home country and return to the region. Although pronounced clear from any disease or infection at the beginning, a migrant worker could become a carrier later during home visits.[81] What supports this argument is that certain communicable diseases are widespread in the Indian subcontinent and in some Asian countries, and these diseases have become prevalent in the Arabian peninsula, where previously they were unknown.

Medical specialists confirm that the health risks posed by Asian workers are various, including malaria, typhoid, leprosy, tuberculosis, parasitical diseases and sexually transmitted diseases (STDs). The most widespread disease is tuberculosis, which is associated with the unhealthy conditions of large numbers of workers living together.

The health of expatriate workers can also be affected by migration itself. A geographical change of residence can make migrant workers more susceptible to epidemic risks present in the area to which they move. Moreover, those migrant workers who are concentrated in difficult, manual jobs are more susceptible to the risks of injury or death. Workers can also be more predisposed to injury and accident through inexperience of the working conditions in their new destination and language barriers. In many countries receiving migrant workers, the percentage of work injuries is much higher among foreign workers than the indigenous workforce.[82] In addition, having to live in shared accommodation for long periods far from their families, expatriate workers become more prone to engage in indecent behavior that increases the possibilities of catching contagious diseases.[83]

An especially alarming issue is the risk of abuse to female workers. Housemaids are subject to exploitation because of their isolation and dependence on their employers and reports about the mistreatment and abuse of female housemaids are abundant. There are also concerns about the health conditions of female migrants who work in entertainment industries and could become victims of human trafficking.

For receiver countries, expatriate workers are usually considered potential carriers of communicable diseases, especially HIV, and the policy in this respect is to ban those migrants who are HIV positive from entering the country. A survey conducted in 144 countries from 1999–2002 shows that 104 countries have imposed some kind of travel restriction related to HIV, mostly for visitors who intend to stay longer than three months.[84] Yet, these measures have failed to limit the spread of contagious diseases internationally. Usually tourists and returning expatriates are not required to undergo medical examination, even though contagious diseases are often transmitted by them.

Another cause for concern is the cost of medical care for migrant workers, especially when they are in breach of the law. Certain countries have restricted the provision of medical care for new arrivals, especially those who do not have leave to stay. However, such policies are debatable. Restricting health care might not result in reducing costs if the country concerned has to spend more on emergency treatment because of inadequacy in spending on preventative care.[85]

Efforts of GCC Countries to Minimize the Negative Impacts of the Demographic Imbalance

Since the early 1990s, the GCC countries have realized the negative impacts of their dependence on an expatriate workforce and the risks involved in their continued presence in large numbers. These countries have started to tackle this issue by adopting policies that would lead to replacing expatriates with nationals. Efforts have been made by all governments of the GCC as well as by the GCC Supreme Council which, at its 15th meeting (Bahrain, December 1994), decided that all departments and public and private companies should take necessary measures to limit migrant workers and replace them with GCC nationals.[86] The GCC Council of Ministers of Labor and Social Affairs issued a number of resolutions at the end of their meeting, which included a recommendation to the Supreme Council to put a ceiling on the stay of expatriate workers in the GCC countries of no more than six years. The recommendation excluded certain specializations that cannot be filled by nationals.

At its 26th meeting (Abu Dhabi, December 2005) the Supreme Council approved the regulations and procedures to deal with the impact of the expatriate workforce on the demography of the GCC countries. However, the issue of putting a ceiling on the stay of expatriate workers was excluded. This matter was referred back to the Council of Ministers of Labor and Social Affairs for further study.[87]

The "localization" policy derives its legitimacy from the desire for national independence and the citizens' right to have an opportunity to contribute to the development of their countries. The policy also shows awareness of various economic, social, cultural and security issues that are connected to the presence of a large number of expatriates in the country.

However, this issue is often dealt with merely in terms of a quantitative replacement of expatriate workers with nationals without considering other relevant issues. For example, what category of the migrant workforce is to be replaced by nationals? Are they qualified or just marginal workers? Are they Arabs, Gulf citizens or foreigners? Does replacement involve people or technology? What is the timetable for substitution? Should it be a quick or a gradual substitution? Should the replacement take place: in the public or the private sector; in regulated or unregulated areas; and how is it going to take place? [88]

Furthermore, the GCC governments have implemented various measures aimed at giving more weight to the national workforce in their bid to fight unemployment among their citizens. Such measures include legislation that demands employing nationals in all sectors, and yet such measures have proved ineffective in fighting unemployment. At the 21st

GCC Summit Conference in December 2000, it was decided to introduce a gradual cut in the number of foreign employees in order to create a demographic balance. Although no quantitative goals were set, it was agreed to set quotas for expatriate workers and to increase the fees levied for their recruitment in a bid to discourage dependence on foreign workers. Although these measures could improve nationals' employment chances, the impact on their competitiveness would remain minimal. Replacement of migrant workers could affect the competitiveness of the product or services concerned, if it was based on nationality and not on the basis of skills and competence. It could even be harmful within the context of a globalized economy, which depends on ease of movement and on competitiveness. [89]

Future Vision and Strategies Proposed to Redress the Demographic Imbalance

So far we have reviewed the nature of the demographic imbalance in the GCC countries, and the extent of the challenges and problems it poses. Governments need to limit the negative impacts on Gulf society, be they social, economic or political. Here we shall tackle a number of issues by creating strategies to reach specific solutions that protect Gulf societies from any social or economic threat, providing such a strategy is aimed at tackling the issues of population and the labor market together.

The main aim of any such strategy should be to raise the social productivity of the GCC population. This would lead to a high level of social well-being in a society that would also maintain its identity and values. Such a strategy should also be linked to the development of human resources in compliance with a comprehensive approach to development.

In general, to reach an informed strategic perspective in any area, a detailed and accurate knowledge of the issue in question is required— especially the tools required for change. In this respect, the data available regarding population and human resources in the Gulf is not adequate to develop a realistic strategy. Although defining the required studies accurately implies a specific strategy, the following general issues can be included: demographic studies; social studies (measuring productivity in various areas of social and economic activity and social limitations to productivity); quality of education and training (i.e. accurate measurement of knowledge and capabilities that graduates gain from various areas of the educational system); compatibility of education with the requirements of a desirable pattern of development; and the size and nature of unemployment.[90]

In every Gulf country there is more than one department concerned with drawing up policies for various areas related to human development. It is, therefore, imperative that parties concerned coordinate and cooperate among themselves to mobilize all efforts and to secure the highest level of effectiveness in the area of sustained human development strategy.

The situation is more complicated when it comes to drawing up a strategy for human development for the GCC countries as a single entity. Here arises the possibility of overlap and contradiction between the countries of the GCC as a whole. Even if there is consensus, disparity as to the availability of mechanisms for drawing up and implementing a Gulf-wide strategy for human development is an issue. [91]

A viable strategy for human development requires a review of priorities by the region's countries in terms of goals—and the means for implementing such goals. Sometimes it is not easy to make a distinction between the goals and means of development. However, it suffices here to refer to the conclusion of a study of the oil-producing Arab countries that bring in migrant workers, whose development efforts pivot around "a strategy that aims for oil and gas-based economic industrialization." It must be mentioned here that one of the declared objectives of economic industrialization in oil-producing Arab countries is to avoid dependency on one single finite source, i.e. oil. Therefore, some believe that these oil-dependant industries are in fact perpetuating a migrant worker situation that they are meant to avoid. However, it is preferable to review priorities from time to time to realize the desired development with as little foreign employment as possible.[92]

It is currently imperative to devise a long-term strategy for economic, social and cultural development. A demographic imbalance can only be viewed through its overall impact on economic growth and within a long-term strategy for development. Therefore, dealing with the demographic imbalance and its economic and social impact on the GCC countries would require redirecting and mobilizing all official efforts to draw and implement appropriate, reasonable and targeted policies first. The next step should be to make all possible attempts to strengthen the concept of "localization."[93] However, according to the information available, despite all efforts to encourage localization there are some obstacles that still hinder success. Such obstacles include the reluctance of some Gulf citizens to work in certain professions, such as manual jobs or the services sector.

Communications technology, learning opportunities, information and the spread of knowledge brought about by globalization have provided the Gulf countries with opportunities for intensive and continued training in the light of joint investments and international projects.[94] To overcome the main obstacle facing localization, Arab Gulf integration is put forward as the most suitable scenario for creating competitiveness in the Gulf countries. This requires preparing the young qualitatively and in terms of professional awareness in order to release their potential. Once mobilized, these potentials could provide a competitive edge at the regional level and would allow for a more flexible professional workforce.

Elements of Human Development Strategy in the Gulf

A strategy of human development for the GCC countries should concentrate on objectives and measures that create individuals capable of taking up jobs efficiently and effectively. Thus, a strategy of human development in the GCC countries should focus on a number of important issues. These include:

Education

First priority should be given to the education system. Although all GCC governments provide free education, their education systems do not meet market and globalization needs. The problem lies not in access to education but in its quality. Growing unemployment and the increase in non-productive jobs both in the private and public sectors serve as proof of this statement. Higher education has raised hopes and expectations that the labor market has not been able to realize. There is a need to promote vocational and technical training and to raise language skills. Also, there should be more focus on basic sciences. Social studies in universities should be limited. In the academic year 1998/1999 about 60 percent of graduates from GCC universities majored in education and arts including Islamic studies and social sciences. Graduates of engineering accounted for 14.4 percent and sciences only 10.3 percent out of the total number of graduates. This inclination toward humanities does not correspond to market needs.

The education system should also focus on creative thinking, collective work, and the acquisition of modern skills.[95] There is also a need to encourage vocational training and work among young citizens. A positive outcome from developing education and training systems could take some time to materialize. However, such development would leave a deep impression on the future success of national employment.

Despite the relatively high amounts spent on developing education in the GCC countries, the quality of education attained does not match expenditure. Education systems in the GCC countries face various problems that chip away at their quality. Such problems include the high percentage of drop-outs and low success rates (which means longer periods at different stages of education); education methods are mostly teacher-led, and involve memorization on the part of students; self-discipline methods are rare; teachers suffer from low social status; the financial return of the job is low compared to the work involved, which does not encourage excellence; large numbers of students prefer joining departments of humanities; there is an imbalance between education output and higher education requirements; and

[436]

there is incompatibility between education output and development requirements. These problems require effective solutions to raise the quality of human resources in the Gulf.

Despite difficulty in measuring the contribution of human resources to economic growth, there is no dispute about the basic components of economic and social development. Moreover, high rates of economic development cannot be achieved unless certain factors are present. Most important among these are the expansion of the vocational skills of the workforce and improving management and organization.

Improving Productivity

Productivity and its development is definitely one of the most important issues related to the future of human development in the GCC countries. In addition, it is a pivotal issue in the general approach toward human development.

We are aware that the GCC countries are going through a transformational period at present. It follows a stage where plentiful oil revenues have been used to set up appropriate infrastructure that is compatible with the competition-based age of globalization. This transformation involves changing job categories, increasing skill levels, and the role of public and private sectors in the economy. However, the medium-term impact of these changes on nationals' employment is not clear. If the governments of these countries hope to enable their citizens to play their part in the economy, they have to pay attention to making plans for the development of human resources. This should be done in the light of increased capabilities of the workforce in terms of skills and knowledge in order to increase productivity.[96]

It is the author's opinion that the issue of studying and raising productivity does not enjoy the necessary attention from the GCC countries. Data about this basic phenomenon is so scarce that it hampers the possibility of conducting a precise scientific analysis. Therefore, increasing productivity requires maximizing workers' capabilities, and a

[437]

match between a person's job and his capabilities. If this is not feasible, the reason lies in the imbalance between the education system on the one hand and the labor market's needs on the other. Therefore, the final solution to this problem should be based on a re-harmonization between education and the future needs of employment through effective planning.

In the short term, two means should be adopted: first, reintroducing an element of balance between the potential workforce available and the labor market's needs. This could be achieved by transferring workers from their current areas of work to other areas where they could use their capabilities to better effect. Secondly, additional training could be introduced to enable workers to carry out their current jobs more effectively if finding appropriate job opportunities for them proves to be difficult.

Increasing productivity continuously requires comprehensive attention in various areas, starting from the structure and nature of employment and ending with the pattern of incentives in society. In the area of employment, the "job for life" should be discontinued, irrespective of performance and appointments, promotions and job security should be based on merit according to objective and transparent evaluation standards. The financial reward of a job should be defined by the skills required to qualify for it, the workload it involves, and the need for it in the labor market.[97]

Developing the Gulf Workforce

Needless to say, priority should be given to serious efforts aimed at developing the local workforce and thus facing the problems that hinder an active role for nationals. This should, in fact, become one of the most important local issues for the Arabian Gulf states. It is frequently emphasized that education policies should be created with the aim of realizing the objectives of human development. In addition, there are certain work sectors where the local workforce in the GCC countries should be maximized by:

[438]

- Redistributing the local workforce among various economic sectors where it can be more productive instead of concentrating it in limited areas, such as the government sector, which has limited productivity.[98]

- Changing nationals' attitude toward work. GCC citizens must adapt to the needs of jobs required by the new globalized economy. They should also be prepared for the removal of all unnecessary benefits that discourage the free movement of workers as a result of generous employment plans implemented by the government.

- People's perceptions of artistic work and attitudes toward women in the workplace should change. This applies especially to young nationals who form the majority of new entrants to the labor market, and those who will try to join the private sector and compete with skilled foreign manpower. Unless the nationals' preference for certain job categories is discouraged and instead replaced with incentives that increase productivity, any effort to limit dependence on expatriates will be in vain. Labor laws should also be more flexible toward the hiring and firing of nationals and salaries should be performance related.[99]

- Building a national job database. Every GCC country should have a database that shows the status of the current and projected workforce in every sector, in addition to salary structures. Such databases would facilitate studying and evaluating the needs of the market, and would allow for planned developments in the national labor market by adopting policies based on accurate data. Moreover, such databases would help develop suitable labor regulations and employment laws. The need for these kind of databases is a priority due to the large numbers of young people entering the labor market and the expected increase in female employment.[100]

Requirements for Redressing the Demographic Imbalance

The current demographic imbalance is due to the size and composition of the expatriate workforce, which has been recruited in response to so-called labor needs. As discussed earlier, some of these needs are unnecessary while others are a result of poor exploitation of the workforce available. Moreover, the current composition of the migrant workforce in terms of education and skills, as well as its cultural composition, have been the result of overlooking quality and focusing on quantity without giving due consideration to the cost to society.

An analysis of the characteristics of the current workforce and its huge social, cultural, political and economic cost to society makes it imperative to search for a solution that will restore demographic balance and stabilize society in the long term. Such a solution is possible. It should begin with encouraging nationals to return to the labor market and thus restrict the expatriate labor force to necessary positions only. In addition, the source and quality of the expatriate workforce should be addressed and better organizational and administrative structures used. This will need to involve:[101]

Creating the Will for Change

The will for change, both socially and politically, is the first and most basic condition for streamlining every country's workforce needs. Social and administrative customs that govern the current demand for a migrant workforce make it difficult to consider any approach to decreasing demand for this workforce.

Creating the will for change is not impossible if we consider the dimensions of the demographic problem and its repercussions on the vital existence of all nationals and decision makers. The social, cultural, political and economic cost involved can no longer be justified vis-à-vis the need for an expatriate workforce. This is true even if we consider its benefits for socio-economic development and the political stability of the country concerned. The cost is too high by any standard, and this calls for action to crystallize a minimum degree of social and political will required to streamline the country's need for an expatriate workforce by limiting its number, improving its quality and changing its current composition. [102]

Drawing up a Demographic Policy

A demographic policy represents the basis for regulating migration. This policy requires a political decision that is backed up socially. It should be drawn up in light of regional Arab integration; be based on the needs of real and comprehensive development; and should be limited by society's ability to absorb new immigrants without destroying the harmony of its social and cultural fabric or its political stability. A demographic policy should aim at determining the country's ideal demographic size in the long term with reference to considerations that are vital to society's well-being. The other consideration is to maintain a society's identity and social coherence. It should also be linked to social policies.

Under such a demographic policy, there should be a distinction between the need for a permanent and a temporary workforce. The desired demographic increase, its quality and composition could then be determined accordingly. The demographic policy should also deal specifically with qualifications required from expatriate workers and set the conditions by which society would absorb the numbers of workers in line with its long-term needs. The other consideration should be creating an acceptable degree of cordial cultural relations between nationals and expatriates. Finally, the policy should provide for measures that guarantee the return of temporary expatriate workers to their country after finishing their employment.[103]

The demographic imbalance is at the heart of the demographic policies of the GCC countries and is the catalyst for drawing up demographic policies to counter negative consequences arising from the workforce imbalance, namely the unemployment of nationals.[104]

In brief, stemming the flow of immigrant workers requires a well-defined demographic policy with clear targets. This requires realistic and logical reasoning that would lead to reducing the local need for an expatriate workforce.

In view of the importance of devising a demographic policy, reference should be made to efforts already exerted by the GCC countries in this respect. Some GCC members have announced a demographic policy, such as Kuwait, and others are working on drawing up such a policy, such as Oman and Qatar. However, the majority of the GCC countries have so far concentrated on demographic programs adopted by certain government departments within GCC countries, which will become policies when implemented. The magnitude of the difficulties and challenges facing these countries demands serious attention. For many years now, the GCC countries have faced problems that run contrary to the future of their desired economic and social development. There is an urgent need to draw up demographic policies that contribute to confronting those difficulties.

Demographic policies will also preserve rights and promote gender equality and full access to a universal education that befits the needs of modern times, thus allowing every national to participate in public life. [105]

The national population growth rate is not sufficient. Lowering or raising fertility or employment rates is only one of a number of elements that act and interact together to bring progress to society, develop individual and collective potential and combat poverty. This was reiterated in the work plan of the Cairo Population and Development Conference of 1994. It adopted a new approach to population policies, considering them a mechanism and a dynamic that basically aims to improve the quality of individuals' lives and to eradicate disease, ignorance and poverty. There was a consensus on these issues among the 183 countries that attended the conference.

Many of the participating counties reviewed their policies and programs. Others, which did not have clear population policies, were keen to draw up such policies with the proviso confirming that there were practical plans to implement such policies.[106]

Measures to Reduce the Size of the Expatriate Workforce

To move away from the current demographic imbalance to one of equilibrium in the long term, the country concerned needs to practice control over the influx of expatriate workers instead of letting the influx itself be the determining factor. The cost this influx brings to the society of the host country and the country from which workers come, as well as its long-term consequences, were never taken into consideration. What follows are examples of mechanisms that could reduce the size of the expatriate workforce.[107]

Review of Immigration Regulations

The details and enforcement of immigration regulations influence the size of the expatriate workforce and its composition. Despite the apparent rigidity of immigration regulations, which are sometimes described as unfair, these regulations have been unable to stop the influx of expatriates and have been inadequate in redressing the demographic imbalance and the problems arising thereof. The ineffectiveness of current immigration regulations is due to the fact that administrative regulations are unstable in the first place. The attraction of the region have rendered these regulations ineffective since loopholes have been exploited, putting continuous pressure on immigration authorities. Moreover, these regulations are not based on a thorough and realistic study of the causes of the expatriate influx, neither are they based on a clearly defined demographic policy. In addition, these regulations are not geared towards realizing specific qualitative and quantitative goals. Therefore, immigration regulations should be tightened gradually to control the influx of the expatiate workforce. This should be carried out according to each country's potential to absorb more people, and on the basis of the cost to society vis-à-vis potential benefits. Immigration regulations can be incorporated in demographic policies as well legal and administrative restrictions, in addition to local incentives that can lead to a drop in the need for expatriate labor. The actual financial cost of importing foreign labor should be calculated and charged to the employer directly. [108]

A Transitional Plan to Reduce the Size of the Migrant Labor Force

A transitional plan could be proposed to reduce the need for migrant labor. Such a proposal involves translating available measures for reducing labor and improving its composition into a quantitative action plan. The next step would be to determine the direction of policies and the quality of measures required to realize goals.

[443]

However, what are the possible solutions to the phenomenon of expatriate labor? It seems there are not any fast and practical solutions to face this issue in the short and medium term. It is possible, though, to face the phenomenon through concise and long-term plans. Important measures to realize this goal include providing high quality training for the national workforce in order to ready them to replace the expatriate workforce, especially in sectors where there is no specific need for expatriate labor.

According to available research, it is not possible for the Gulf countries to do without the Asian labor force. It is possible, however, to reduce the size of the Asian labor force through the introduction of more laws that streamline employment and promote awareness and cooperation with the private sector in the manner employed by the ministries of labor in Saudi Arabia and Bahrain. The research explains that part of the problem is that about 80 percent of the Asian labor force is employed in domestic jobs, which require little or no skill. Yet, these jobs are necessary and cannot be discarded or replaced with local labor because of their nature. Moreover, the financial return is poor and unattractive.

This implies that other economic and specialized sectors, such as advanced technology, petroleum, the Internet and IT, can start replacing expatriate labor with local labor. However, it is noticeable that plans to reduce dependency on expatriate labor constitute a source of concern for many businessmen, as they believe their businesses would be affected negatively.[109]

Use of Advanced Techniques

No doubt, using advanced techniques is one of the most important means of reducing labor dependency in development plans. Therefore, adopting more advanced techniques should be among the main methods to help reduce the size of the expatriate workforce required to implement development plans.[110]

Coordination between Countries Importing Labor

The similarities between the region's countries make their respective labor markets competitive. A majority of these countries suffer from qualitative and quantitative shortages in the national workforce, and they depend to a large extent on a migrant workforce from the same exporting countries. Moreover, the same migrant attraction factors apply in each of these countries. This situation requires coordination between the GCC states. For example, an initiative for a common labor market in the Gulf could contribute to the creation of suitable solutions to some of the problems arising from this competitive situation. However, this also requires continued coordination not only in the development of local human resources, but also in attempting to realize economic integration between the GCC countries. Perhaps putting an end to the repetition of similar projects and focusing on those that could serve the same purpose in one or more of these countries, such as universities, could be an effective means of reducing expatriate labor. [111]

Maximizing the National Workforce

No doubt there is great potential for exploiting the national workforce. One of the main approaches of a policy of lessening the influx of expatriates should be to remove incentives that marginalize the national workforce. Incorrect incentives and policies that affect the quality of their education, vocational training, and continuing professional development should be addressed. This could bring about a real change that would benefit the national workforce and indeed is tantamount to a pressing national obligation.[112]

In principle, expatriate labor should complement and not replace national labor. Exploiting national labor could be looked at from a quantitative as well as qualitative perspective. This could be achieved through efficient mobilization, preparation and provision of incentives. Perhaps the continued need for expatriate labor is due to the ineffectiveness of the policies of mobilizing, replacing and directing the national workforce. The structural weakness in policies that are supposed to benefit the national workforce have accumulated through complicated social, political, economic and cultural circumstances. The situation has intensified and its negative impacts have been exacerbated by the economic financial surpluses enjoyed by GCC states and the manner of policies that control these surpluses and their allocation.[113]

Reforms in Economy, Management and the Labor Market

Economic liberalism does not mean in any way giving full freedom to a private sector controlled by expatriates to impose patterns of growth that could negatively affect the country's economy in the long term. There should be a clear definition of those economic sectors that are compatible with the requirements and interests of the national economy. These are the sectors that depend greatly on advanced technology and on capital, not labor. Necessary reforms in this area include:[114]

- Revising the concept of substitution to include: [115]
    - Substituting technical illiteracy with efficiency (wrongly referred to as education), and increasing human capital.
    - Replacing expatriate workers with nationals or Gulf workers (in an economical and practical way).
    - Substituting low-value human resources (both local and expatriate) with technological resources in view of the low level of human skills required for certain work.
    - Allowing the private sector to replace public employment.
- Broadening data on the labor market and making it available to various parties, including:
    - Macro-managers of human resources.
    - Employers.
    - Local job providers.
    - Students of secondary schools and upwards for the sake of educational and vocational guidance.

- Liberating wage structures and making them economical.
- Moving toward non-oil exports, i.e. competitiveness that would create job opportunities in high value-added, high human capital, and highly technical markets.
- Abandoning the concept of quantitative balance (traditional manpower planning) and moving toward modern employment strategies and policies.
- Supporting the employment of women: certain cultural factors and social concerns may not allow the employment of women in specific sectors and positions. However, exploiting female human resources is very important; it is a vital factor for economic development and for the success of plans to replace the expatriate workforce with a national workforce. However, intervention policies to improve employment opportunities for women in the private sector require a great deal of support to succeed. [116]
- Providing institutionalized support to nationals trying to set up private businesses. Without such support young citizens who are willing to – and capable of – entering the private sector will face significant difficulty under current circumstances, which allows for unfair competition. Unequal opportunities are a result of – among other things – close relations among expatriate communities on the one hand, and between them and foreign exporters on the other. Moreover, the margin of profit only provides for a standard of living deemed suitable by expatriates who come from countries with low standards of living.
- Promoting scientific research and increasing investment in research and development in a manner that develops the economy and creates value-added job opportunities.

H.H. LT. GENERAL SHEIKH SAIF BIN ZAYED AL NAHYAN is the Minister of the Interior of the United Arab Emirates. Prior to his ministerial appointment in October 2004, His Highness occupied several leadership positions. He was the Deputy Director of the Abu Dhabi Police in 1994–1995 before becoming its Director General in October 1995. In December 1997 His Highness was appointed Under Secretary of the Ministry of the Interior, retaining this post until his appointment as Minister of the Interior.

In December 2004 he was promoted to the rank of Lieutenant General and was re-selected as Minister of the Interior in the Government formed by H.H. Sheikh Mohammed bin Rashid Al Maktoum, Vice-President and Prime Minister of the UAE and Ruler of Dubai, following the death of Sheikh Maktoum bin Rashid Al Maktoum.

H.H Lt. General Sheikh Saif bin Zayed Al Nahyan is a pioneer of development in police work and his mark is evident in many achievements realized in recent years. Characterized by an openness of mind, he provides support for federal matters without overlooking local concerns. He believes in the importance of developing ancillary roles for the police and is convinced about the need to engage the youth of the state.

His achievement in the realms of Police and Security includes launching the Community Police Project in 2003; founding the Ministry of the Interior's centers for rehabilitating individuals with special needs in 2002; and the Social Support Center in 2004. He also directed the five-year plan for the strategic development of the Abu Dhabi Police (2004–2008), the five-year plan for the Ministry of the Interior and oversaw the restructuring of the Abu Dhabi Police. Moreover, he sought a permanent solution to the problem of child jockeys in camel races and initiated a number of practical security measures to counter this problem. He also launched the "iris scan" project – which has succeeded in preventing more than 114,000 migrants from returning to the UAE since the project was implemented nationwide – and launched the project of the Emirates Identity Authority.

His Highness has participated in various training events, including the special training session for paratroopers in 1991. He has received a number of medals and honors, including the Order of Merit for Dedicated Service in 2000, the Red Crescent Charitable medal, and the Order of Merit of the International Civil Defense Organization (Commander Rank).

His Highness obtained a BSc in Political Science (with a specialization in Political and Administrative Sciences) from the United Arab Emirates University in Al Ain. After graduation, he joined the Police College in the second foundation session for graduates in 1990.

H.E. ABDULRAHMAN BIN HAMAD AL-ATTIYAH is currently Minister of State for the State of Qatar, and has been the Secretary-General of the Gulf Cooperation Council (GCC) since 2002. He has held several positions in the past, including Undersecretary of the Foreign Affairs Ministry (1998–2002), Ambassador Extraordinary (non-resident) of Qatar to Greece (1986–1992), Ambassador Extraordinary to Italy (1985–1991), and Qatar Alternate Governor to the International Fund for Agricultural Development (IFAD) (1985–1992).

He was the General Coordinator for the 9th Islamic Summit Conference held in Doha in November 2000, and also the Deputy Chairman of the Permanent Qatari–Palestinian Committee to Support Jerusalem, as well as a member of the Arab Thought Forum (Amman), and an Associate Member of the Strategic Studies Center in Khartoum.

H.E. Abdulrahman Al-Attiyah has participated in several regional and international meetings and conferences, the latest of which were the 17th Arab Summit (Algeria, March 2005), the Arab–South American Summit (Brasilia, May 2005), the World Economic Forum "Davos Forum" (Amman, June 2003), and the US–Arab Economic Forum (Detroit, 2003). He also headed the delegation of the General Secretariat of the GCC that attended the sessions of the UN General Assembly which convened during the period 2002–2005.

[450]

H.E. Abdulrahman Al-Attiyah has received a number of honors, including Commander of the Legion of Honor (Ordre Royale de la Légion d'Honneur) – the premier order of the French Republic (1985); the Order of Merit (as Grand Officer) of the Italian Republic (1992); the Commander of the "National Cedar" Order of the Republic of Lebanon (2004); and the Order of Independence – First Class, of the United Arab Emirates (2005). He received a BA in Political Science and Geography from Miami University, Florida, in 1972.

H.R.H. PRINCE TURKI AL-FAISAL BIN ABDULAZIZ AL SAUD is Chairman of the Board of Directors of the King Faisal Center for Research and Islamic Studies in Riyadh, and was formerly the Ambassador of the Kingdom of Saudi Arabia to the United States.

Prince Turki was appointed as an Advisor to the Royal Court in 1973. From 1977–2001, he served as the Director General of the General Intelligence Directorate (GID)—the Kingdom's main foreign intelligence service. In 2002, he was appointed Ambassador to the United Kingdom by the Custodian of the Two Holy Mosques, King Fahd bin Abdulaziz Al Saud. In July 2005, Prince Turki was appointed Ambassador to the United States and retained this post until the end of 2006.

His Royal Highness is involved in a number of cultural and social activities, is one of the founders of the King Faisal Foundation and is the Chairman of the King Faisal Center for Research and Islamic Studies in Riyadh. He is also co-chair of the C100 Group, which has been affiliated with the World Economic Forum since 2003. He is a member of the Council for Combating Terrorism, which is affiliated to the Institute of International and Strategic Studies in Washington, DC; the Trustee Board of the Oxford Islamic Center in the UK; and the Consultative Council of the Center of Contemporary Arab Studies at Georgetown University, Washington, DC.

His Royal Highness graduated from the Lawrenceville School in Lawrenceville, New Jersey, and he subsequently pursued his undergraduate studies at Georgetown University in Washington, DC, where he obtained a bachelor's degree.

[451]

H.E. MR. TERJE RØD-LARSEN has been the President of the International Peace Academy since January 2005. He is also the Special Envoy of the United Nations (UN) Secretary General for the Implementation of Security Council Resolution 1559 of 2004.

Mr. Rød-Larsen began his career as an academic teaching sociology, political science and philosophy at the universities of Bergen and Oslo, before establishing the Fafo Institute for Applied Social Sciences in Oslo in 1981. As Director of Fafo, Mr. Rød-Larsen initiated a research project into the living conditions of Palestinians in the West Bank and Gaza Strip. This led to a request by the Palestine Liberation Organization (PLO) in 1992 for his help in establishing a secret negotiation channel between the PLO and the Israeli government. The subsequent Israeli–Palestinian talks culminated in the Oslo Accords and the Declaration of Principles signed at the White House on September 13, 1993.

In 1993, Mr. Rød-Larsen was appointed Ambassador and Special Adviser for the Middle East Peace Process to the Norwegian Foreign Minister. In mid-1994, he was appointed UN Special Coordinator in the Occupied Territories with the rank of Under Secretary General. In 1996, Mr. Rød-Larsen became the Norwegian Deputy Prime Minister and the Minister for Planning and Cooperation, before re-joining the United Nations. From 1999 to December 2004, he served as UN Special Coordinator for the Middle East Peace Process and Personal Representative of the Secretary General to the PLO and the Palestinian Authority, with the rank of Under Secretary General.

H.E. LT. GENERAL FAHAD AHMAD AL-AMIR is Chief of Staff of the Kuwait Armed Forces, a position he has held since 2003. He joined the military service in 1965 and became a Lieutenant in 1967. He has held several positions in the armed forces, including as Assistant Commander (Lightning Squadron), Commander (Mirage Squadron), and as Commander of the Ali Al-Salem Air Base. He was later promoted to the position of Director of Air Force Operations, and then to Acting Assistant Chief of General Staff for Administration and Manpower. In 1993 he was promoted to Major General and appointed Deputy Chief of Staff. After signing various Defense Cooperation Agreements, he was also appointed Chairman of the Higher Committee for Defense Cooperation.

Lt. Gen. Al-Amir has taken several prestigious courses, beginning with the 19th Cadet course in Kuwait, and including courses at Aviation Ground School and Aviation Medical School in the United Kingdom; a Basic Flying course (Jet Provost aircraft); an Advanced Flying course (Hawker Hunter) in Kuwait; a Fighter Transition course (BAC Lightning aircraft) in Kuwait; a Pilot Instructor course (Lightning aircraft) in Britain; a Fighter Transition course (Mirage F-1 aircraft) in France; and Pilot Instructor (Mirage F-1 aircraft) and Advanced Flying courses (Mirage F-3 and F-5) in Pakistan. Lt. Gen. Al-Amir also attended the Air Command and Staff College and Air War College in the United States.

He has received the Bronze, Silver and Gold Medals in Kuwait, as well as several other awards including: Order of Military Duty (first rank); Order of Military Duty (high rank); the Kuwaiti Liberation Medal; and the Medal of the International Military Sports Council (Conseil International du Sport Militaire—CISM) in Belgium.

ANTHONY CORDESMAN holds the Arleigh A. Burke Chair in Strategic Affairs at the Center for Strategic and International Studies (CSIS), United States. He is also a National Security Analyst for ABC News. During his tenure at CSIS, he was Director of the Gulf Net Assessment Project and the Gulf in Transition Study, and principal investigator of the CSIS Homeland Defense Project. He supervised a number of studies in national missile defense affairs, asymmetrical war, weapons of mass destruction, and protection of critical infrastructure. He also acted as Co-Director of the CSIS Strategic Energy Initiative, which was sponsored by the Center. He has authored over 40 books, including a four-volume series on the lessons of modern war.

Professor Cordesman has formerly served as National Security Assistant to Senator John McCain of the Senate Armed Services Committee; as Director of Intelligence Assessment in the Office of the

Secretary of Defense; and as Civilian Assistant to the Deputy Secretary of Defense. He directed the analysis of the October War for the Secretary of Defense in 1974, and coordinated the military, intelligence and civil analytical studies of this conflict. He has served in other government positions, including the State Department and the NATO International Staff. Professor Cordesman was also Director of Policy and Planning for Resource Applications in the Department of Energy, with postings in Lebanon, Egypt and Iran and has also worked extensively in Saudi Arabia and the Gulf. Professor Cordesman was awarded the Department of Defense Distinguished Service medal; is a former Adjunct Professor of National Security Studies at Georgetown University; and has twice been a Wilson Fellow at the Woodrow Wilson Center for Scholars at the Smithsonian Institution.

DR. MAHMOOD SARIOLGHALAM is Associate Professor of International Relations in the Faculty of Economics and Political Science at Shahid Beheshti (National) University of Iran in Tehran. He is also the Director of the Middle East Strategic Center in Tehran, where he is the Editor-in-Chief of *Discourse: An Iranian Quarterly* (English) and *Middle East Quarterly* (Farsi). Dr. Sariolghalam specializes in international politics of the Middle East, Iranian foreign policy, and political culture.

Dr. Sariolghalam has published nine books and over one hundred articles in Farsi, English and Arabic. His published works include: *Iran and Globalization* (Tehran: Center for Strategic Research, 2005); "Iran's Emerging Regional Security Doctrine: Domestic Sources and the Role of International Constraints," in *The Gulf: Challenges of the Future* (The Emirates Center for Strategic Studies and Research, 2005); "Understanding Iran: Getting Past Stereotypes and Mythology," in *Washington Quarterly* (Autumn 2003); *Rationality and the Future of Iranian Development* (Tehran, 2002); "International Relations in Iran: Achievements and Limitations," in Arlene Tickner and Ole Waever (eds), *The World of International Relations Scholarship: Geo-cultural Epistemologies* (St. Martin's Press, forthcoming, 2008).

Dr. Sariolghalam is a member of the International Studies Association (United States) and the C-100 Group of the World Economic Forum (Switzerland). He has given lectures and participated in conferences in more than one hundred countries. Dr. Sairolghalam has a Ph.D and an MA in International Relations from the University of Southern California (in 1987 and 1982). He also holds a BA degree in Political Science from the California State University (1980), and completed a post-doctorate program at the Ohio State University.

DR. ABDULLAH AL-SHAIJI is a Professor of International Relations and Political Science and the Chairman of the American Studies Unit at Kuwait University.

Dr. Al-Shaiji gained his Ph.D from the University of Texas in Austin, United States, and is a specialist in Gulf and US foreign policy in the Arab world. He served as a Special Advisor to the Speaker of the Kuwaiti Parliament and to the Foreign Relations Committee (1992–1996) and acted as Counselor and Head of the Kuwaiti Information Bureau at the Kuwaiti Embassy in Beirut, Lebanon (2001–2004).

Dr. Al-Shaiji has attended and presented papers at over 50 conferences worldwide on subjects such as Kuwaiti security, democratization, Gulf security, US foreign policy, GCC–Iran relations, GCC–Iraq relations, and on NATO and its future role in the Middle East. He is the author of *Kuwait Under Siege: The Endless Struggle of a Vulnerable Country's Quest for Survival*, and has published over 15 refereed articles which have appeared in Arabic and English journals and books, focusing on Gulf Security, Kuwait–Iraq relations, GCC relations with Iran, democratization and the Kuwaiti parliamentary experience.

Dr. Al-Shaiji's views and comments have appeared in many publications and on news outlets and satellite TV networks including CNN, BBC, Al-Jazeera, Al-Arabiya and on many Arab TV channels. He is also a columnist for Kuwaiti, GCC and pan-Arab newspapers.

DR. GARETH STANSFIELD is Associate Professor of Middle East Politics at the Institute of Arab and Islamic Studies at the University of Exeter, UK, where he is a member of the Gulf Studies Program. He is also an Associate Fellow of the Middle East Program at Chatham House (the Royal Institute for International Affairs), London.

Dr. Stansfield has authored several publications on Iraqi policies including *Iraqi Kurdistan: Political Development and Emergent Democracy* (2003); *The Future of Iraq: Dictatorship, Democracy, or Division?* (co-authored with Liam Anderson, New York: Palgrave, 2005); *Iraq: People, History, Politics* (Cambridge: Polity Press, 2007). In addition to his work on Iraq, Professor Stansfield has also published research on Yemen's regional relations, military–civilian relations in the Middle East, federalism, and ethno-politics.

Dr. Stansfield obtained his Ph.D in Political Science at the University of Durham in 2001, where he also received his Bachelor's and Master's degrees.

DAVID MACK has, since July 1998, served as Vice-President of the Middle East Institute (MEI), an educational organization headquartered in Washington, DC. His main focus is on public policy and scholarly programs.

During his 30 years in the US Foreign Service, he has served in Jerusalem, Iraq, Jordan, Lebanon, Libya, Tunisia, Saudi Arabia and the UAE. As a business consultant and an educator, he has continued to be involved in Middle East matters since leaving the Service in 1995. He is Chairman of the US–Libya Business Association and a member of the board of the Sultan Qaboos Cultural Center. He was US Ambassador to the United Arab Emirates from 1986–1989.

As Deputy Assistant Secretary of State for Near Eastern Affairs (1990–1993), Ambassador Mack directed the conduct of relations between the United States and twelve other governments, including Iran, Iraq, Saudi Arabia and Syria. He provided political support for *Operation Desert Shield* and *Operation Desert Storm*, and was the principal, high-level US contact for the Iraqi opposition from 1991 to 1993. At the request of the State Department, David Mack developed the concept of – and managed – the Future of Iraq Program in the spring of 2002. He also served as an Advisor to the congressionally mandated bipartisan Iraq Study Group.

DR. JOHANNES REISSNER is a Senior Research Associate at the Middle East and Africa research unit at the Research Institute for International Affairs (Stiftung Wissenschaft und Politik [SWP]) in Berlin. His research activity is primarily focused on the affairs of Iran, Central Asia and the Gulf.

Dr. Reissner spent several years during the 1970s in Lebanon, Syria and the Kingdom of Saudi Arabia. Before joining the Institute of International and Security Affairs in 1982, he worked for the special research project "Tübinger Atlas des Vorderen Orients" (TAVO) at the University of Tübingen, preparing maps on the history of the Arabian Peninsula in the nineteenth and twentieth centuries. In 1995, he served as an observer at the Organization for Security and Cooperation in Europe (OSCE) mission in Dushanbe, Tajikistan. Dr. Reissner was also a Working Group Core Participant for the German Marshall Fund-sponsored Transatlantic Foreign Policy Discourse (TFPD) project entitled: "Iran and its Neighbours: Diverging Views on a Strategic Region" (2003–2005).

He has published several works on Iran, Central Asia, the Arabian Peninsula and regional socio-cultural developments, including: "Iran: Autokratischer Islamo-Nationalismus mit Erdölpolster" (Iran: Autocratic Islamo-Nationalism with an Oil Platform) in Enno Harks and Friedemann Müller (eds.), *Petrostaaten – Außenpolitik im Zeichen von Erdöl* (2007); "EU–Iran relations: Options for Future Dialogue" in Walter Posch (ed.) *Iranian Challenges*, (Chaillot Paper 89, 2006); Editor with Eugene Whitlock of *Iran and Its Neighbors: Diverging Views on a Strategic Region* (vol. II) working paper (2004); "Iran und seine Nachbarn Konkurrenz, Pragmatismus und der Ruf nach Kooperation" (Iran and its Neighbors: Competition, Pragmatism and the Call for Cooperation) in Jens van Scherpenberg and Peter Schmidt (eds) *Stabilität und*

Kooperation: Aufgaben Internationaler Ordnungspolitik (2000); "Europe and Iran: Critical Dialogue" in Richard N. Haass and Meghan L. O'Sullivan (eds) *Honey and Vinegar: Incentives, Sanctions and Foreign Policy* (2000). He holds a Ph.D in Islamic Studies from the Free University of Berlin.

DR. J.E. PETERSON is a historian and political analyst focusing on the Arabian Peninsula and Gulf. He has taught at various US universities and has been associated with the Foreign Policy Research Institute; the Middle East Institute; the Center for Strategic and International Studies; the International Institute for Strategic Studies; and is affiliated with the Center for Middle Eastern Studies at the University of Arizona. He has also served as the Historian of the Sultan's Armed Forces in the Office of the Deputy Prime Minister for Security and Defense in Oman.

Author of more than a dozen books, Dr. Peterson's work includes *Oman in the Twentieth Century* (1978); *Yemen: the Search for a Modern State* (1982); *Arab Gulf States; Steps Towards Political Participation* (1988); *Saudi Arabia and the Illusion of Gulf Security* (2002); *Historical Dictionary of Saudi Arabia* (revised, 2003); *Defense and Regional Security in the Arabian Peninsula and Gulf, 1973–2004: An Annotated Bibliography* (2006); and *Historical Muscat: An Illustrated Guide and Gazetteer* (2007). His forthcoming books include *Oman's Insurgencies: The Sultanate's Search for Supremacy* (2007); *Oman since 1970: Political and Economic Change*; and *Defending Oman: A History of the Sultan's Armed Forces*.

Dr. Peterson has published around four dozen articles in prestigious journals and annuals including *American Historical Review*; *Encyclopedia Britannica*; *Middle East Journal*; *Middle East Policy* and *Washington Quarterly*. He has also made over twenty contributions to edited works. A more recent article is "Qatar and the World: Branding for a Micro-State," *Middle East Journal* (2006). Forthcoming essays include "The Promise and Reality of Bahraini Reforms," in *Political Liberalization in the Gulf*; and "Britain and the Gulf: At the Periphery of Empire," in *The Persian*

Gulf in History. His other research and publication projects include a modern history of the Arabian Peninsula and a comparative study of state-building in all the states of the Arabian Peninsula.

FREDERIC SICRE is Executive Director of Abraaj Capital, UAE. He has over 16 years of experience in global issues, regional development agendas and community building. In the early 1990s, he established the activities of the World Economic Forum (WEF) in Africa and the Middle East. He then managed the Forum's Center for Regional Strategies and was promoted to WEF Managing Director in June 2000.

In June 2003, Mr. Sicre was responsible for the Extraordinary Annual Meeting in Jordan following the war in Iraq, and initiated dialogue and reconciliation initiatives during South Africa's transition to democracy and between Palestinians and Israelis. He has also initiated the first Africa and Arab World Competitiveness reports. Mr. Sicre is a founding member of the Arab Business Council and Editor of *South Africa at Ten*—a book celebrating the ten years of democracy in the country.

Mr. Sicre holds an MBA from the International Institute for Management Development (IMD), Switzerland; a Bachelor of Arts and Sciences from Villanova University, Philadelphia, United States; and is a Fellow of Stanford University, Palo Alto, United States.

DR. JASSEM HUSSAIN ALI has been the Head of the Economic Research Unit at the University of Bahrain since 2005, where he started teaching at the University's College of Business Administration in 1988. He is a prominent GCC economic analyst and writes weekly articles on the performance of the GCC economies in the Saudi newspaper *Al-Eqtisadiah*, and the UAE's English daily, *Gulf News*. Dr. Jassem Hussain Ali also writes articles regularly in the economic supplement of Bahrain's *Al-Wasat* newspaper, and produces economic articles on a monthly basis in publications such as Kuwait's *Investors* magazine and the *Oman Economic Review*.

Dr. Jassem Hussain Ali has participated in many analytical research studies for a number of international institutions, primarily the UK-based *Economist*. Moreover, he has taken part in many programs on Arab satellite TV channels, tackling economic developments in the Middle East and the world. He received his BA, MA, and Ph.D degrees in Business Administration from universities in the United States in 1984, 1986 and 1995 respectively.

H.E. DR. HAMAD AL-BAZ'IE has been Deputy Finance Minister for Economic Affairs in the Kingdom of Saudi Arabia since 1999. Since 2005, Dr. Al-Baz'ie has been the General Coordinator responsible for GCC negotiations in the GCC Secretariat-General. He is the Governing Board Representative for the Kingdom of Saudi Arabia in the OPEC Fund for International Development, and a member of the Board of Directors of the Gulf International Bank and the Southern Province Cement Company. He is also a member of the negotiating team responsible for Saudi Arabia's entry into the World Trade Organization (WTO), and was an Associate Professor in the Department of Economics at King Saud University in Riyadh.

Dr. Al-Baz'ie has participated in several debates and scientific conferences both inside and outside the Kingdom and published over 20 research studies in specialized journals, besides articles in newspapers and magazines. He also participates in many radio and television programs.

Dr. Al-Baz'ie obtained a Bachelor's degree in Administrative Sciences (with a specialization in Economics) from the College of Administrative Sciences at King Saud University in 1981. He earned an MSc degree in Economics (1991) and a Ph.D in Economics (1995) from the College of Liberal Arts at the Colorado State University, United States.

DR. S. NARAYAN is currently a Visiting Senior Research Fellow at the Institute of South Asian Studies at the National University of Singapore (NUS), and an advisor to think tanks in India, including the Observer Research Foundation in New Delhi. Dr. Narayan has been in public service for nearly four decades (1965–2004) in the State and Central Governments of India. As Economic Adviser to the Prime Minister (2003–2004), he monitored the special economic agenda of the Cabinet and was responsible for the economic policy implementation of over 30 ministries. His international experience includes consultancy assignments for UN agencies, including the Food and Agriculture Organization (FAO) and the Economic and Social Commission for Asia and the Pacific (ESCAP).

Dr. Narayan's most recent books are: *Growth Opportunities in Indian States* (Marshall Cavendish, Singapore, 2005); and *Documenting Reforms: Case Studies from India* (ed.) (Macmillan India, 2006).

Dr. Narayan has an MSc in Physics from the University of Madras (Madras Christian College); a Masters in Business Management (Finance) from the University of Adelaide, South Australia; an M.Phil in Development Economics from the University of Cambridge, UK; and a Ph.D from the Indian Institute of Technology.

GENERAL (RETD.) FOUAD ALLAM is currently a lecturer at the Police Academy and the National Center for Criminal and Social Research in Cairo (Egypt), and at the Naif Arab University for Security Sciences in Riyadh (Kingdom of Saudi Arabia).

Before his retirement, General Allam was Deputy Director of Egypt's State Security Police, specialized in combating riots and terrorist activities—especially those of the Muslim Brotherhood and other political Islamic groups. He has taken part in many local and international conferences focusing on fighting terrorism and crime. General (retd.) Allam graduated from the Police Academy in Cairo in 1957, when he also obtained a BA degree in Law from Ain Shams University.

DR. ALI BIN FAYIZ AL-JAHNI is the Dean of the Faculty of Training at the Naif Arab Academy for Security Sciences in Riyadh, and an Associate Professor at the Faculty of Higher Studies at the same university.

Dr. Al-Jahni has devised and supervised numerous training courses and seminars and participated in a number of Arab and international conferences. His research interests focus on comprehensive national security, human rights, security information, intellectual security, contemporary political systems and strategic studies. He has published a number of books on these topics, including: *Terrorism: Imposed Understanding of Rejected Terrorism* and *Security Information and Protection from Crime*, both published in 2000 by the Naif Arab Academy for Security Sciences in Riyadh. He has also produced a number of research works which have appeared in specialized periodicals such as "The Function of the Family in Promoting Intellectual Security," *Al Fikr Al Shurti* [Police Thought], volume 12, no. 48 (2004).

He obtained a Ph.D in Political Science from George Washington University in 1989, a Master's degree in Political Science from the same university in 1986, a Master's degree in Information from the Imam Mohammed Bin Saud Islamic University in 1979, and a Bachelor's degree in Security Sciences from the King Fahd Security College in Riyadh, 1976.

ALI BIN ABDUL RAHMAN AL DU'AIJ is currently the Under-Secretary of the Department of Criminal Sciences at King Fahd Security College in Riyadh. He is a member of several educational committees both inside and outside the college, including the criminal sciences curriculum development committee in the college. He also undertakes other academic tasks such as reviewing scientific research, refereeing research techniques, and assessing postgraduate theses.

Dr. Al Du'aij has participated in several conferences and debates such as the Congress on Crime Prevention, organized by the United Nations in Vienna in 2001; the Conference on Criminal Evidence and its Role in Uncovering Crime, Cardiff, United Kingdom in 2002; and the debate entitled "Together Against Terrorism," held in the Kingdom of Saudi Arabia in 2005. In addition to this, he has also participated in discussions and seminars held at the Center for Research and Studies at the King Fahd Security College.

He has authored a number of research studies and books including *Al Mawso'a fi 'Ilm Al Adila Al Jan'iyya* (The Encyclopedia of Criminal

Evidence), a university textbook entitled *Tahqiq al Shakhsia Bil Al Musharka* (Realizing Character via Participation) and a forthcoming book on case procedures in Saudi Arabian courts.

Dr. Al Du'aij gained a Ph.D in Law from the University of Huddersfield, UK, in 2004, and a Master's degree from the Naif Arab University for Security Sciences in 1999. He has two Bachelor degrees; the first from the King Fahd Security College and the second in *Shari'a* from the College of *Shari'a* at the Imam Islamic University in Riyadh in 1991.

MOHAMMED IBRAHIM DITO is Policy Development Manger at the Bahrain Labor Market Regulatory Authority, where he is currently involved in policy advice.

From 1989–1996 Mr. Dito held several management positions within the private sector. In 1996 he became Superintendent of the Employment Service Bureau (ESB) of the Ministry of Labor, and in 1998 became head of the Employment Service Bureau of the Ministry, a post he held until 2005 when he joined the Bahrain Labor Market Regulatory Authority.

Mr. Dito participated in a wide range of conferences, symposia and seminars organized by the International Labor Organization (ILO). He was a member of the committee reviewing the ILO's conventions on child labor in 1999; a speaker in the ILO sub-regional seminar on employment promotion of nationals in the GCC states in 2003; and a trainer assigned by the ILO to conduct a training course for Jordanian officials in 2006. He has authored and co-authored several articles and research papers on employment issues in the EU, the GCC states and Arab countries.

Mr. Dito received an MSc in Economics from the Bruno Leuschner University in Berlin in 1988. He speaks English and German in addition to his native Arabic.

DR. SHAFIQ AL-GHABRA is the Founder and Chief Executive Officer of Jusoor Arabiya, a training and consultancy center focused on leadership development and reform in the Arab public and private sector. He is the Founding President of the American University of Kuwait (2003–2006), and was Director of the Center for Strategic and Futuristic Studies at

Kuwait University (2002–2003). Dr. Al-Ghabra was the Director of the Kuwait Information Office in Washington, DC, (1998–2002), and served as the Editor-in-Chief of the *Journal of Social Sciences* at Kuwait University (1996–1999), where his columns are syndicated in several regional newspapers.

Dr. Al-Ghabra began teaching as an Assistant Professor at Kuwait University in 1987, rising to the rank of Professor of Political Science in 1997. He was also a Visiting Professor at the College of William and Mary and a visiting scholar at George Mason University. He writes weekly columns for *Al Ra'y Al A'am*, and contributes regularly to the London-based *Al Hayat*. Since October 2006, Dr. Al-Ghabra has hosted a weekly talk show on Kuwait TV (*Diwaniya*) and has lectured in many universities, think-tanks and societies.

He has published four books including: *Israel and the Arabs: From the Conflict of Issues to the Peace of Interests* (1997); *Kuwait: A Study of the Mechanisms of State, Power and Society* (1995); *Palestinians in Kuwait: The Family and the Politics of Survival* (named by "Choice" as the Outstanding Academic Book of 1989). Two of Dr. Al-Ghabra's studies appeared in *Crisis in the Contemporary Persian Gulf* (2002) and in *Radicals and Reformers: Islamist Movements of the Middle East* (2003). His updated study "Kuwait and the United States" appears in *The Middle East and the United States* (2007).

Dr. Al-Ghabra has received Kuwait's highest award for scientific research in humanities and social sciences from the Kuwait Foundation for the Advancement of Sciences. He gained his Ph.D in Government from the University of Texas at Austin, United States, in May 1987; Master's degree in Political Science from Purdue University, Indiana, United States; and his Bachelor's degree in Government from Georgetown University, Washington, DC, United States, in 1975.

DR. MAITHA AL-SHAMSI is currently Assistant Provost for Research at UAE University, where she is also Chair of the Scientific Research Council, Director of the Center for Externally Funded Research Activities (eFORS), and a Member of the Council of Scientific and Educational Affairs. Dr. Al-Shamsi is also involved in a number of local, regional and international social, educational and cultural institutions. She is Advisor to the President of the Family Development Foundation in the United Arab Emirates; Member of the Board of Directors of the Paris–Sorbonne University (PSU) Abu Dhabi; Member of the Consulting Committee of the Harvard Medical School Dubai Center (HMSDC) Institute for Postgraduate Education and Research; a member of the team of science and technology experts working with the UN Economic and Social Commission for Western Asia (ESCWA); and a Member of the UN Educational, Scientific and Cultural Organization (UNESCO).

Dr. Maitha Al-Shamsi has participated in many regional and international conferences where she has presented scientific papers, and has also completed studies and research in the form of published books, including: *The Occupational Realities for Gulf Women* (2003); *The Changing Role of Women in the United Arab Emirates* (2001); and *The Impact of the Inflow of Foreign Migration on National Workforce Development: A Field Study of the UAE Services Sector* (1999). Dr. Al-Shamsi has won several awards and certificates of recognition, including the Distinguished (Female) Arab Manager Award 2002, from the H.H. Sheikh Mohammed bin Rashid Al Maktoum Awards for Arab Management; one of "The Two Thousand Outstanding Scholars of the Twenty-First Century," selected by the International Bibliographic Center in Cambridge, UK (2002); a certificate of recognition from Qatar's Center for Futuristic Studies; and a Certificate of Recognition from the Arab League (1999).

Dr. Al-Shamsi holds a Ph.D in Sociology from Ain Shams University, Cairo (1992); a Masters in Sociology from Alexandria University, Egypt (1988); and a Bachelor's degree in Sociology from King Saud University, KSA (1980).

Chapter 2

1. Robert Jervis, *Perception and Misperception in International Politics* (Princeton, NJ: Princeton University Press, 1976) 28.

2. See James E. Sheridan, *China in Disintegration* (New York, NY: The Free Press, 1975) and Strobe Talbott, *The Russia Hand* (New York, NY: Random House, 2002).

3. Jervis, op. cit., 221.

4. Jervis, op. cit., 222.

5. Jervis, op. cit., 313.

6. See Mahmood Sariolghalam, presentation at the *Council on Foreign Relations*, New York, April 5, 2006.

7. See Mahmood Sariolghalam, "The Foreign Policy of the Islamic Republic of Iran: Theoretical Renewal and a Search for Paradigm," *Discourse: An Iranian Quarterly*, vol. 3, nos 3 and 4 (Winter 2000): 267–285 and (Spring 2002): 29–65. See also Sariolghalam, "Globalization and Iran's National Sovereignty: Challenges of Compatibility," *Discourse: An Iranian Quarterly*, vol. 5, nos 2 and 3 (Fall 2003): 31–63 and (Winter 2004): 19–49.

8. See Jonathan Garner, *The Rise of the Chinese Consumer* (Princeton, New Jersey: John Wiley & Sons, Ltd., 2006), 7–12, 19–30 and 61–72.

9. Fareed Zakaria, *The Future of Freedom* (New York, NY: W. W. Norton & Company, 2003), 29–58.

10. Milton Friedman, *Capitalism and Freedom* (Chicago, IL: University of Chicago Press, 1982), 16.

11. Vali Nasr, *The Shia Revival* (New York, NY: W. W. Norton & Company, 2006), 71–71.

12. See *The Shia Revival* by Vali Nasr reviewed by Mahmood Sariolghalam, published in *The Journal of International Affairs,* University of Columbia (Spring 2007).

13. Henry Kissinger, *Does America Need a Foreign Policy?* (New York, NY: Simon & Shuster, 2001), 196.

14. Mahmood Sariolghalam, "How Domestic Politics is Linked to Iran's Foreign Policy," *La Vanguardia*, May 7, 2007.

Chapter 4

1. I recognise that other domestic problems also exist within Arab Gulf states, namely relating to the status of expatriate workers and the demographic pressures that continue to grow in terms of expanding young populations, employment and government legitimacy. However, for the purposes of this chapter, it is more appropriate to remain focused upon the issues pertaining directly to the instability wrought by regime change in Iraq.

2. Keith Krause, "State-making and region-building: the interplay of domestic and regional security in the Middle East," *Journal of Strategic Studies*, vol. 26, no. 3 (September 2003): 101–2.

3. Krause, op. cit., 99.

4. Barry Buzan and Ole Wæver, *Regions and Powers: The Structure of International Security* (Cambridge: Cambridge University Press, 2003). For a critique of Buzan and Wæver's model, with reference to the Gulf, see Arshin Adib-Moghaddam, "Regional Security Complex

Theory: A Critical Examination," *International Studies Journal*, vol. 3, no. 1 (Summer 2006): 25–40.

5. Michael Kraig, "Gulf Security in a Globalizing World: Going Beyond US Hegemony," *Yale Global Online*, 29 June, 2004.

6. For an overview of the causes and consequences of the Iran–Iraq War, see Hussein Sirriyeh, "Development of the Iraqi-Iranian Dispute, 1847–1975," *Journal of Contemporary History*, vol. 20, no. 3, 1985, 483–92; Shahram Chubin and Charles Tripp, *Iran and Iraq at War* (Boulder, CO: Westview Press, 1991); and Gareth Stansfield, *Iraq: People, History, Politics* (Cambridge: Polity Press, 2007), especially Chapter 5: "Iraq at War, 1979–1989."

7. Stansfield, op. cit., 118–119.

8. See M. Mohamedou, *Iraq and the Second Gulf War: State Building and Regime Security* (Bethesda, MD: Austin & Winfield, 1997); and Dilip Hiro, *Neighbours, Not Friends: Iraq and Iran after the Gulf Wars* (London: Routledge, 2001).

9. For a comprehensive account of the sanctions regime on Iraq, see Sarah Graham-Brown, *Sanctioning Saddam: The Politics of Intervention in Iraq* (London: I.B. Tauris, 1999); and Tim Niblock, *'Pariah States' and Sanctions in the Middle East: Iraq, Libya, Sudan* (London: Lynne Reinner, 2001).

10. See, for example, President Bush's speech on 20 December 2006, reported by Sheryl Stolberg and John Holusha, "Bush: Iraq victory still possible," *International Herald Tribune*, December 20, 2006.

11. Yitzhak Nakash, *Reaching for Power: The Shi'a in the Modern Arab World* (Princeton, NJ: Princeton University Press, 2006).

12. Vali Nasr, "Regional Implications of Shi'a Revival in Iraq," *The Washington Quarterly*, vol. 27, no. 3, 2004, 7.

13. Ibid.

Chapter 6

1. Michael Ryan Kraig, "Forging a New Security Order for the Persian Gulf," in *Middle East Policy*, vol 13, no. 1 (Spring 2006): 85.

2. Kraig, op. cit., 86.

3. Kraig, op. cit., 88.

4. Ibid.

5. Peter Rudolf, "Entschlossenheit nach Außen, schwindende Unterstützung im Inneren: Amerikanische Irakpolitik am Ende der Ära Bush," in Muriel Asseburg (ed.), *Regionale (Neu)Ordnung im Nahen und Mittleren Osten und die Rolle externer Akteure* (Berlin: Stiftung Wissenschaft und Politik, 2007), 45.

6. Michael Ryan Kraig, "Assessing Alternative Security Frameworks for the Persian Gulf," in *Middle East Policy*, vol. 11, no. 3 (Fall 2004), 148.

7. Henner Fürtig, "The Potential for Collective Security in the Gulf Region: The Role of GCC–EU Collaboration," in Christian Koch and Felix Neugart (eds) *A Window of Opportunity: Europe, Gulf Security and the Aftermath of the Iraq War* (Dubai: Gulf Research Center, 2005), 103.

8. Kraig, "Assessing Alternative Security Frameworks," 143, [see note 6], quoting Janne E. Nolan (ed.) *Global Engagement: Cooperation and Security in the 21st Century* (Washington DC: Brookings Institution Press, 1994).

9. Giacomo Luciani and Felix Neugart (eds), *The EU and the GCC – A New Partnership* (Munich: CAP, updated February 2005), 17.

10. Vali Nasr, *The Shia Revival. How Conflicts within Islam will Shape the Future* (New York & London: Norton, 2006).

11. Barah Mikail, "Entre Mythes et Réalité: Considérations autour d'un 'Croissant Chiite,'" in *Maghreb–Machrek*, no. 190 (Hiver 2006–2007): 127.

12. See Morten Valbjørn and André Bank, "Signs of a New Arab Cold War: The 2006 Lebanon War and the Sunni–Shi`i Divide," in *Middle East Report*, no. 242 (Spring 2007): 8–11.

13. See Ayellet Yehiav, "The Anti-Iranian Front: Egypt, Saudi Arabia, and Jordan," in *MERIA*, vol. 11, no. 1 (March 2007) (http://meria.idc.ac.il/journal/2007/issue1/jv11no1a2.html); Mark A. Heller, "The Iranian–Saudi Summit. A Microcosm of Middle Eastern Contradictions," in *INSS–Insight*, no. 13 (March 18, 2007).

14. Ángeles Espinosa, "Ahmadineyad visita Arabia Saudí, rival regional de Irán y aliado de Washington," in *El País*, March 2, 2007.

15. Speech of H.R.H. Prince Turki Al-Faisal at the 12th ECSSR Annual Conference, March 7, 2007 (http://www.ecssr.ac.ae/CDA/en/StaticContent/ShowStaticContentActivities/0,1626,40-00,00.html).

16. Christoph Moosbauer, "Relations with the Persian Gulf States," in Volker Perthes (ed.) *Germany and the Middle East* (Berlin: Heinrich-Böll-Stiftung/Stiftung Wissenschaft und Politik, 2002), 121.

17. See Steffen Hertog, "Renewing an Old Geo-economic Axis," in *Gulf Asia Research Bulletin* no. 1 (January 2007): 7.

18. For the European Union see *EU Bilateral Trade and Trade with the Gulf Cooperation Council*, Tradoc, 15 September 2006 (http://trade.ec.europa.eu/doclib/docs/2006/september/tradoc_113482.pdf); for the United States see National US–Arab Chamber of Commerce (ed.), *2007 Outlook: US Exports on Track to Reach $45 Billion: A Special Report from the National US–Arab Chamber of Commerce*, March 2007 (http://www.nusacc.org/tradeline/trdln0107e.pdf).

19. M. K. Bhadrakumar, "China's Middle East Journey via Jerusalem," in *Asia Times Online*, January 13, 2007 (www.atimes.com/atimes/ Middle _ East / IA13Ak02.html).

20. Christine Fair, "Indo–Iranian Ties: Thicker Than Oil," in *MERIA*, vol. 11, no.1 (March 2007): 41–58.

21. Fair, op. cit., 49.

22. Christian Wagner, "Indien und Westasien: Die vorsichtige Balance," in Muriel Asseburg (ed.) *Regionale (Neu)Ordnung im Nahen und Mittleren Osten und die Rolle externer Akteure* (Berlin: Stiftung Wissenschaft und Politik, March 2007), 33–36.

23. "Russia, Saudi Arabia energy partners, not rivals—Putin," *RIA- Novosti*, February 12, 2007 (http://en.rian.ru/russia/ 20070212/60580105. html).

24. See Olivier Roy, *Globalized Islam: The Search for a New Ummah* (New York, NY: Columbia University Press, 2004).

25. Friedemann Müller, *Energie-Außenpolitik. Anforderungen veränderter Weltmarktkonstellationen an die internationale Politik* (Berlin: Stiftung Wissenschaft und Politik, November 2006), 9 and 13, Table 2.

26. Christoph Moosbauer, "Relations with the Persian Gulf States," in Volker Perthes (ed.) *Germany and the Middle East* (Berlin: Heinrich- Böll-Stiftung/Stiftung Wissenschaft und Politik, 2002), 108–128.

27. Johannes Reissner, "Europe's 'Critical Dialogue' with Iran," in Richard N. Haass and Meghan L. O'Sullivan (eds) *Honey and Vinegar: Incentives, Sanctions, and Foreign Policy* (Washington, DC: Brookings Institution Press, 2000), 47–71.

28. European Commission, *EU Strategic Partnership with the Mediterranean and the Middle East*, Brussels 2004 (EUROMED Report No. 78), (http://ec.europa.eu/comm/external_relations/euromed/

publication/2004/euromed_report_78_en.pdf); For its previous history see Gerd Nonneman, "EU–GCC Relations: Dynamics, Patterns and Perspectives," in *The International Spectator* 41 (July–September 2006): 3, 59–74.

29. Luciani and Neugart, op. cit., 22 [See note 9].

30. *"A Secure Europe in a Better World"— EU Security Strategy*, Brussels, December 12, 2003 (http://www.consilium.europa.eu/ uedocs /cmsUpload/78367.pdf).

31. The others mentioned by Luciani and Neugart are comprehensiveness, flexibility and separation. See Luciani and Neugart, op. cit., 24 [see note 9].

32. Christian Koch and Felix Neugart, "Introduction," in Koch and Neugart (eds) *A Window of Opportunity. Europe, Gulf Security and the Aftermath of the Iraq War* (Dubai: Gulf Research Center, 2005), 13.

33. Walter Posch, "A CSCE-like process for the Gulf Region? – Neither Integration nor Isolation: Case-by-Case Cooperation," in *Der Orient* 47 (2006): 4, 539.

34. Roberto Aliboni, "Europe's Role in the Gulf: A Transatlantic Perspective," in *The International Spectator* vol. 41, no. 2 (April–June 2006): 37.

35. For an assessment of the ICI see Aliboni, op. cit., 41–44.

36. Kraig, (2006) op. cit., [see note 1], 96; Katja Niethammer and Guido Steinberg, "A Multilateral Security Architecture for the Persian Gulf," in Volker Perthes and Stefan Mair (eds) *European Foreign and Security Policy. Challenges and Opportunities for the German EU Presidency* (Berlin: Stiftung Wissenschaft und Politik, RP 10, October 2006), 37–40. The same idea was formulated by the former Iranian Deputy Minister for Europe, Mahmoud Vaezi. See Mahmoud Vaezi, "tartibât-e amniyat-e khalij-e fars," in *Rahbord*, 40 (16/05/1385): 34.

37. Kraig, (2006) op. cit., [see note 1], 96.

38. Ibid.

39. Posch, op. cit., [see note 33].

Chapter 7

1. Robert E. Harkavy, "Thinking About Basing," *Naval War College Review*, vol. 58, no. 3 (Summer 2005): 18. See also J.E. Peterson, "The Historical Pattern of Gulf Security," in Lawrence G. Potter and Gary G. Sick (eds) *Security in the Persian Gulf: Origins, Obstacles and the Search for Consensus* (New York, NY: Palgrave, 2001), 7–31.

2. Alexander Cooley, "Base Politics," *Foreign Affairs* vol. 84, no. 6 (November–December 2005), accessed online.

3. C.T. Sandars, *America's Overseas Garrisons: The Leasehold Empire* (Oxford: Oxford University Press, 2000).

4. A. Mark Weisburd, in the *Use of Force: The Practice of States Since World War II* (University Park, PA: Pennsylvania State University Press, 1997), categorizes foreign military interventions as follows: classic invasions (United Kingdom, France and Israel against Egypt; Iraq against Kuwait in 1990–991), wars for the independence of European colonies (Britain and South Yemen in 1963–1967), post-imperial wars (India and Pakistan in 1947–1948, Israel and Arab states in 1948–1949, Korean War in 1950–1953), continuation wars (United States and Vietnam in 1961–1975, Arab–Israeli wars in 1967 and 1973), civil wars with international elements (Yemen in 1962–1970, Oman's Dhufar province in 1961–1975), maintenance of spheres of influence (Soviet Union and Hungary in 1956, United States and Grenada, 1983), neo-colonial wars (Western Sahara in 1973–1991), and limited uses of force (the two Yemens in 1972 and 1979, Israel and Iraq in 1981, the United States and Libya in 1986).

5. Harkavy (1989), op. cit., 73.

6. Harkavy, op. cit., 27.

7. These points are based on the United States and are drawn from Harkavy (2005) op. cit., 19–25. See also Lawrence Freedman, "International Security: Changing Targets," *Foreign Policy* (Spring 1998): 48–63.

8. Harkavy (2005), op. cit., 20–21.

9. Harkavy, (2005), op. cit., 24.

10. Michael O'Hanlon, "Can High Technology Bring US Troops Home?" *Foreign Policy* (Winter 1998–1999): 72–86.

11. Robert E. Harkavy, *Bases Abroad: The Global Foreign Military Presence* (Oxford: Oxford University Press, 1989), 5.

12. "U.S. scientific prowess has become the deep foundation of U.S. military hegemony. U.S. weapons systems currently dominate the conventional battlefield because they incorporate powerful technologies available only from scientifically dominant U.S. weapons laboratories … The key to this revolution in military affairs (RMA) has been the application of modern science and engineering – particularly in fields such as physics, chemistry, and information technology (IT) – to weapons design and use. It is the international dominance of the United States in these fields of science and technology that has made possible U.S. military dominance on the conventional battlefield." Robert L. Paarlberg, "Knowledge as Power: Science, Military Dominance and US Security," *International Security* vol. 29, no. 1 (Summer 2004): 122, 125.

13. Barry R. Posen, "Command of the Commons: The Military Foundation of US Hegemony," *International Security* vol. 28, no. 1 (Summer 2003): 5–46. "Command of the commons is the key military enabler of the US global power position. It allows the United States to

exploit more fully other sources of power, including its own economic and military might as well as the economic and military might of its allies. Command of the commons also helps the United States to weaken its adversaries, by restricting their access to economic, military, and political assistance. Command of the commons has permitted the United States to wage war on short notice even where it has had little permanent military presence. This was true of the 1991 Persian Gulf War, the 1993 intervention in Somalia, and the 2001 action in Afghanistan. Command of the commons provides the United States with more useful military potential for a hegemonic foreign policy than any other offshore power has ever had." Posen, op. cit., 8–9.

14. Robert E. Harkavy (2005), op. cit., 25–26. This conceptualization had antecedents in the Secretary of Defense's annual reports to the President and Congress through the 1990s, which revealed a new emphasis on access agreements and stockpiling in the Middle East where permanent basing was broadly opposed. In 1995, "the Annual Report indicated that pre-positioning was now accepted policy worldwide. 'Strong deterrence,' it said, 'requires us to maintain pre-positioned equipment in the Persian Gulf, the Indian Ocean, Korea and Europe.' The new approach was also underlined by the 1998 report which listed permanently stationed forces as only one element amongst eight designed 'to maintain a robust overseas presence.' The other seven included temporarily deployed forces, combined exercises, security assistance activities, and pre-positioning of military equipment and supplies." Sandars, op. cit., 301.

15. Harkavy (2005), op. cit., 26.

16. See Ariel Levite, Bruce W. Jentleson and Larry Berman (eds) *Foreign Military Intervention: The Dynamics of Protracted Conflict* (New York, NY: Columbia University Press, 1992).

17. Edward A. Kolodziej and Robert E. Harkavy, "Introduction," in Koldziej and Harkavy (eds) *Security Policies of Developing Countries* (Lexington, MA: Lexington Books, 1982), 13.

18. "Though it is not really a form of FMP as such, it is important to note that various forms of FMP provide the basis for coercive diplomacy, otherwise referred to – as reflected in the most well-known work on the subject – as 'politics without force.' This subject has been comprehensively canvassed in the works of Barry Blechman and Stephen Kaplan, who have produced two volumes – one for the USA and the other for the USSR – in an attempt to conceptualize, measure, and assess this difficult subject. Needless to say, in line with the vivid meaning attached to 'gunboat diplomacy,' naval forces have played a large role in coercive diplomacy, even if it is no longer as routine or formalized as in the days when, for instance, the United States had 'station fleets' routinely patrolling the Caribbean as a latently coercive force." Harkavy (1989), 63.

19. Cooley (2005), op. cit., accessed online.

20. Desirous of using the Karshi–Khanabad air base in southern Uzbekistan to support operations in Afghanistan, the United States ignored the lack of democratization and human rights abuses. When Uzbek security forces attacked massive demonstrations in Andijan in May 2004, the United States gingerly criticized the régime, which reacted with restrictions almost immediately. The government in Tashkent ordered the base to be closed within 180 days. The United States faced similar problems in Kyrgyzstan. Cooley (2005), op. cit., accessed online.

21. "Increasingly, indeed, the USA has found it difficult to persuade many of its erstwhile clients that their security interests are convergent with its own. The result in many cases has been a move towards decoupling, resulting variously in full denial of access, the imposition of more restrictive terms of access or, in combination, the imposition of higher costs in the form of rent, increased security assistance and economic aid, political quid pro quo, and so on." Harkavy (1989), 4.

22. Posen, op. cit., 23-24.

23. US Department of Defense, *Quadrennial Defense Review Report* (February 6, 2006): v.

24. US Department of Defense, op. cit., 53.

25. Cooley, op. cit., accessed online.

26. Ilan Berman, "The New Battleground: Central Asia and the Caucasus," *Washington Quarterly* vol. 28, no. 1 (Winter 2004–2005): 60–61, 61–62.

27. Michael T. Klare, "Imperial Reach: The Pentagon's New Basing Strategy," *The Nation*, April 25, 2005, 16.

28. Kurt M. Campbell and Celeste Johnson Ward, "New Battle Stations?" *Foreign Affairs* (September/October 2003), accessed online. As Secretary of Defense, Donald Rumsfeld was seen as the architect of much of this new emphasis. With his departure from office, additional questions were raised as to the conception's viability.

29. The literature on Gulf security has been exhaustively surveyed in J.E. Peterson, *Defense and Regional Security in the Arabian Peninsula and Gulf States, 1973–2004: An Annotated Bibliography* (Dubai: Gulf Research Center, 2006).

30. Tom Engelhardt, "Can You Say 'Permanent Bases'?" *The Nation*, March 27, 2006, 28–29. For a brief history of US and European bases in the region, see W. Andrew Terrill, *Regional Fears of Western Primacy and the Future of US Middle Eastern Basing Policy* (Carlisle, PA: US Army War College, Strategic Studies Institute, December 2006).

31. See, for example, Joseph McMillan, Richard Sokolsky, and Andrew C. Winner, "Toward a New Regional Security Architecture," *Washington Quarterly* vol. 26, no. 3 (Summer 2003): 161–175.

32. "During the Cold War, however, the critical issue of Persian Gulf oil became inextricably linked to basing access. American bases along oil-

tanker sea-lanes to Asia and North America came to be viewed in the context of a possible Soviet effort (from bases in Angola, Guinea, Somalia, South Yemen, etc.) to interdict them in case of war. In the late 1980s, with the 'reflagging' operation on behalf of Kuwait, the United States established new points of access in the Persian Gulf. Today, as is heavily reflected in Defense Department and Congressional Budget Office publications, overseas bases are seen in connection with potential struggles over oil resources, not only in and around the Persian Gulf but in Azerbaijan, Libya, Algeria, Gabon, Angola, Equatorial Guinea, etc. Economics, then, in the form of access to oil, has crept back into basing access and global presence." Harkavy (2005), op. cit., 17.

33. Robert A. Pape, in "Soft Balancing against the United States," *International Security* vol. 30, no.1 (Summer 2005): 10, discerns that other major powers are beginning to adopt 'soft-balancing' measures: "actions that do not directly challenge U.S. military preponderance but that use non-military tools to delay, frustrate, and undermine aggressive unilateral U.S. military policies. Soft balancing, using international institutions, economic statecraft and diplomatic arrangements has already been a prominent feature of the international opposition to the U.S. war against Iraq."

34. "A unipolar world, however, is a balance of power system, not a hegemonic one. Powerful as it may be, a unipolar leader is still not altogether immune to the possibility of balancing by most or all of the second-ranked powers acting in concert. To escape balancing altogether, the leading state in the system would need to be stronger than all second-ranked powers acting as members of a counterbalancing coalition seeking to contain the unipolar leader. The term 'global hegemon' is appropriate for a state that enjoys this further increase in power, because it could act virtually without constraint by any collection of other states anywhere in the world." Pape, op.cit, 11.

35. "After 1975, several US military analysts diagnosed the fatal assumptions of what one has called the 'Army Concept,' which allowed tactics and operational successes (employing lavish firepower and the unique mobility that helicopters afforded) to dominate and ultimately define grand strategy – an approach ignoring that there was, at best, only a scant relationship between technology and the outcome of ground combat. Military writers have even cogently criticized the hallowed official presumption that political success would follow from military victory. But however valid such censure, the war the United States fought in Vietnam remained essentially a predictable phase in the inexorable escalation in technology and firepower that has repeatedly defined the nature of warfare everywhere since World War I, irresistibly making civilians and their societies increasingly significant military objectives. Vietnam was the most extreme example of this pattern only because the United States had far greater resources to do what many other industrial nations had earlier also attempted." Gabriel Kolko, *The Age of War: The United States Confronts the World* (Boulder, CO: Lynne Rienner, 2006), 19–20.

36. "Foreign suspicion of US intentions is exacerbated by the politics of oil. Conquering Iraq puts the United States in a strategic position to control virtually all of the Persian Gulf's vast oil reserves, potentially increasing its power to manipulate supply for political and even military advantage against Europe and Asia. This power could be used broadly by withdrawing Persian Gulf oil from the world market, or selectively by imposing a strategic embargo on a specific major power rival." Pape, op.cit., 30.

37. Despite the Bush administration's excesses in this department, it would be a mistake to regard the aggressive attitude against the world as a Bush innovation. As one scholar puts it, "When George W. Bush became president in January 2001 he inherited a vast legacy of contradictions and errors, but he did not create these dilemmas. Anyone who looks at the 1990s closely will recognize all of Bush's conundrums and his responses. The unilateral direction he took had

already been set by his predecessors, who were far more diplomatic in expressing it but were after the same goals. All of his foreign policy statements, and certainly the doctrine of preemption, were very much a part of the history of US foreign policy dating back to World War II. Still, the administration's unique, blunt style created an image of wild irresponsibility – which it deserved." Kolko, op. cit., 95.

38. "1. The United States should treat basing rights and democratization as issues that must be balanced and rationalized. 2. The United States should not seek long-term military facilities in Iraq, unless strongly implored by a wide spectrum of the Iraqi leadership to do so. The United States should conduct future strategic planning on the assumption that U.S. bases in Iraq will be turned over to the Iraqis in the medium-term future. 3. The United States must make a serious effort to heal the rift between itself and the Arab World by privately and publicly treating friendly Arab states as our security partners and not our clients. 4. The United States now has what amounts to a special relationship with Qatar that needs to be continuously nurtured despite differences over Al Jazeera satellite television. 5. The leadership of the United States must make a strong effort to understand how its actions may be placed into the context of Middle Eastern history. 6. To the extent that both parties desire it, the United States needs to strengthen its military and counterterrorism relations with friendly Arab governments. 7. The United States, and especially the U.S. military, needs to reduce and remove bureaucratic obstacles to bringing allied Arab officers to the United States to receive military training and education. 8. The United States must recognize that small Gulf powers have good reasons to seek U.S. bases on their soil, but these states will also be reluctant to antagonize regional powers such as Iran. 9. The United States needs to avoid mistreating its allies needlessly as occurred as a result of the cancellation of the Dubai Ports World agreement with the United Arab Emirates. 10. The United States should continue to work with the Bahraini government to ensure a continued U.S. presence in that country. The United States also should continue to encourage ongoing Bahraini efforts at reform and a government that is inclusive of Shi'ites." Terrill (2006), op. cit., 78–84.

39. Quoted from a summary of Robinson and Gallagher's thesis in "The Imperialism of Free Trade," *Economic History Review,* Second Series vol. 6, no. 1 (1953), by Charles Kupchan in Levite et al. (eds) (1992), op. cit. 259–260.

Chapter 10

1. See the provision of article (24) of the *General Agreement on Tariffs and Trade* (GATT 94).

2. See the provision of article (5) of the *General Agreement on Trade in Services* (GATS).

3. International Monetary Fund, *Direction of Trade Statistics*, IMF Yearbook, December 2006.

4. Resolutions of the Supreme Council of GCC, 21st session, December 2000, see the official website of the GCC (http://www.gcc-sg.org).

5. Articles 2 and 31 of the Economic Agreement of the GCC countries, 26th session, December 2005. See the official website of the GCC (http://www.gcc-sg.org).

6. Resolutions of the Supreme Council of GCC, 21st session, December 2000, see official website of the GCC (http://www.gcc-sg.org).

7. Articles 2 and 31 of the Economic Agreement of the GCC countries, 26th session, December 2005. See the official website of the GCC (http://www.gcc-sg.org).

8. Resolutions of the Supreme Council of GCC, 26th session, December 2005, see official website of the GCC (http://www.gcc-sg.org).

9. Resolutions of the Supreme Council of GCC, 23rd session, December 2002, see official website of the GCC (http://www.gcc-sg.org).

10. Resolutions of the 33rd Ministerial Council, November 1989, and the 72nd meeting of the Financial and Economics Committee, 2006, see official website of the GCC (http://www.gcc-sg.org).

11. The International Bank for Reconstruction and Development, Report on *Global Economic Prospects, 2005: Trade, Regionalism and Development* (New York, NY: World Bank Publications, November 2004).

Chapter 13

1. The Arab League, the Arab Convention for the Suppression of Terrorism, issued by the Councils of Arab Ministers of Interior and Arab Ministers of Justice, 1998.

2. Yusuf Al Qaradawi, al Sahwas al Islamiyya bain al Jimoud wa al Tataruf (Beirut: Muasasat Al Risala lil al Tiba'a was al Nashr was al Tawzi', 1419 Hihri/1998).

3. Sultan al-Thaqafi, "Obstacles to Tourist Security and Methods of Overcoming Them," a research study presented to the symposium entitled Tourist Security, Naif Arab University for Security Sciences, Riyadh, 1424 Hirji/2003.

4. Saeed Misfir al Wadai', "al Amn al Fikri al Islami," Majalat al Amn wa al Hayat no. 187 (Naif Arab University for Security Sciences, 1418 Hijri/1997).

5. Abdullah Yusuf, "Al Sahbab wa al Inhiraf," Majalat al Fikr al Sharti, vol. 13, no. 15 (Al Shariah: 2004).

6. Ahmed Falah Al 'Amoush, "Asbab Intishar Zahirat al Irhab," a research study presented in Terrorism and Globalization (Riyadh: Naif University for Security Sciences, 1425 Hijri/2004).

7. Al Junhi, 1425 Hijri.

8. Mustafa Mosa, "Al Inhiraf al Fikri wa al Irhab", unpublished research paper presented in the coordination meeting of the Directors of the Research, Criminal Justice and Combating crime (Riyadh: Naif University for Seurity Sciences, 1425 Hijri/2004).

9. Mohammad al-Thaqafi, "The Role of Civil Organizations in Resisting Terror Crimes," a research study presented to the symposium Security and Society, King Fahd Security College, Riyadh.

10. Al Yusuf, op. cit.

11. Ahmed Jalal Iz Al Dean, Al Irahab wa al Ounf al Siyasi (Cairo: Dar al Huriya, 1986).

Chapter 14

1. André Standing, *Rival Views of Organized Crime*, ISS monograph, No. 77 (2003), (http://www.iss.co.za/Pubs/Monographs/No77/ Content.htm)

2. Abdul Samad Sokar, "Mahiyat al Jarima al Dowalia", majalat *al Amn al 'Aam*, no. 159 (October 1997).

3. Irv Marucelj, *Mature Peacekeeping Operations as Facilitators of Organized Crime* (Institute for Research on Public Policy, Working Paper Series no. 2005–1, 2005).

4. Donald R. Liddick, "An Empirical, Theoretical, and Historical Overview of Organized Crime," *Criminology Studies* no. 6 (Lewiston, NY: Edwin Mellen Press, 1999).

5. The United Nations Convention Against Transnational Organized Crime was approved and presented for signing by its membership in conformance with the resolution of the UN General Assembly no. 25, 55th session, 15th November 2000, UN document no. A/RES/55/25.

6. Counter Terrorism International Conference, Riyadh, February 5–8, 2005.

7. Hank Messick, *The Mobs and the Mafia: The Illustrated History of Organized* Crime (New York, NY: Ballantine Books, 1972).

8. Dennis Kenney and James Finckenauer, *Organized crime in America (Criminal Justice)* (New York, NY: Wadsworth Publishing, 1994).

9. Ahmed bin Mohammed al-'Omari, *Jarimat ghasiyl al Amwal, Nazra li Jawanibiha al-Ijtima'iya w ail-Iqtasdiya* (al-Riyadh: Kitaab al-Riyadh, 2000).

10. Kenney and Finckenauer, op.cit.

11. Ziyab al-Badaina, "al-Taqniya wa al Jariaim al Monzama," *al Fikr al Shurti*, vol. 7, no. 4 (1999).

12. Bohdan Harasymiw, "Putting Organized Crime in its Place . . . within Political Science," *Canadian Political Science Association Annual Meetings*, 2003 (http://www.cpsa-acsp.ca/paper-2003/harasymiw.pdf)

13. Abdul Kareem Dirwish, "al Jarima al Monazama 'Abr al Hidoud wa al Qarat," *al Aman wa al Qanoun*, third year, no. 2 (1995).

14. Mohammed Niyazi Hatata, *Mokafahat al Jarima wa Mo'amalat al Mujrimeen* (Cairo: 1995).

15. Op.cit., and Abdula Kareem Dirwish, "Tenth United Nations Congress on the Prevention of Crime and the Treatment of Offenders, Vienna, April 10–17, 2000," majalat *a Amn al 'Aam*, no. 168, (January 2000).

16. Mohammed al Shamrani, *al Jarima al Monazama wa Siyasat al Mokafaha fir al Tashri' al Islami wa al Qanoun al Jina'iy*, MA thesis (Riyadh: Naif Arab University for Security Sciences, 2001); and Sanaa Khalil, "al Jarima al Monzama wa al 'Abr Wataniya- al Jihoud al Douwaliya wa Moshkilat al Molahaqa al Qaddiya," *al Majala al Jinaiyya al Qawmiya* (July 1996).

17. Mohammed al Shamrani, op. cit.

18. Yusuf Sharara, *Moshkilat al Qarn al Wahid wa al 'Ishrin wa al 'Aalaqat al Douwaliya* (Cario: al Hai'a al Misriya al 'Aama lil al Kitab, 1997).

19. Mahmoud Abdul al-Nabi, "al Jamrima al Monazama 'Abr al Wataniya bain Jihoud Monazamat al Oumam al Motahida fi al Mokafahat wa Ta'theer al Motaghairat al Douwaliya," a research paper presented to the debate on *Security and Society* held at King Abdul Fahd Security College, Riyadh, 2001.

20. Yusuf Sharara, op. cit.

Chapter 15

1. International Labor Organization (ILO), *Decent Work in Asia: Reporting on Results 2001–2005* (Geneva: ILO, 2006), 78.

2. Vladimira Kantorova, "International Migration in the Arab Region," *Expert Meeting on International Migration and Development in the Arab World: Challenges and Opportunities*, Population Division, Department of Economic and Social Affairs, United Nations, Beirut, May 15–17, 2006.

3. Ibid.

4. UN Population Division, *World Migrant Stock: The 2005 Revision Population Database* (http://www.esa.un.org/migration/).

5. Ibid.

6. John Willoughby, "Ambivalent Anxieties of the South Asian-Gulf Arab Labor Exchange," American University Working Paper Series, March 2005 (http://www.american.edu/academic.depts/cas/econ/workingpapers/2005-02.pdf).

7. Based on K.C Zachariah, E.T Mathew and S.I. Rajan, "Migration in Kerala State, India: Dimensions, Determinants and Consequences,"

Working Paper 1 (Thiruvanthapuram: Center for Development Studies, 1999).

8. Akram Abdul Razaq Jassem al-Mashhadani, "Criminal Statistics: The Use of Criminal Statistics in the Arab World" (in Arabic), published on the Arab Institute for Training and Statistical Research website (http://www.aitrs.org/fasc/research.htm).

9. Ibid., 9.

10. "Realizing Decent Work in Asia," AsRM/XIV/D.7, conclusions of the International Labor Organization (ILO) 14th Asian Regional Meeting, Busan, Republic of Korea, August 29–September 1, 2006.

Chapter 16

1. See, Kito de Boer and John M. Turner, "Beyond Oil: Reappraising the Gulf States," *The McKinsey Quarterly* (January 31, 2007): 3.

2. Ibid., 3.

Chapter 17*

1. The United Nations (Department of Economic and Social Affairs), *World Population Monitoring with Emphasis on Migration and Development* (New York, NY: UN Publications, 2006), 16.

2. Salman Al-Dosari, "Desired and Feared Labour Force; Will 14 million migrant workers in the Gulf threaten the region and its demographic balance?" (in Arabic) *Ashraq al-Awsat*, London, no. 9943, December 17, 2006.

---

* Titles of books, articles and studies published in Arabic have been translated into English.

3. Ali Khalifa Al Kawari, "Towards a better understanding of the population imbalance," (in Arabic) *Majalat Dirasat Al Khaleej wa al Jazeera al 'Arabiyya*, no. 10 (1983), 44.

4. Maitha Al-Shamsi, "Assessing Migration Policies in the GCC Countries: Future Lessons" (in Arabic), *The Meeting of a Team of Experts on the challenges and Opportunities of International Migration in the Arab Countries,* the Economic and Social Commission for Western Asia (ESCWA), Beirut, 15–17 May, 2006, 10.

5. ESCWA, *Report on Population and Development, The Demographic Window an Opportunity for Development in Arab Countries*, no. 2 (New York, NY: UN Publications, 2005), 51.

6. Ahmed bin Sulaiman bin Obeid, "Unemployment in the Gulf Society and Potential Employment" (in Arabic), *The Population Policies of the GCC* symposium, Qatar, April 19–20, 2004, 3.

7. Andrezej Kapiszewski, "Arab Labour Migration to the GCC states," *The Regional conference on Arab Migration in a Globalized World*, the Arab League and the International Migration Organization, Cairo, September 2–4, 2003, 3.

8. Maitha Al Shamsi, "Assessing Migration Policies", op. cit., 10.

9. Mustafa Abdul Aziz Mosa, "Migration and the Population Structure of the GCC Countries and the Repercussions of Globalization: a Futuristic Vision" (in Arabic), *Shioun Arabiya* (Arab Affairs), no. 116 (2003), 140.

10. Ahmed Sulaiman Obeid, op. cit., 3.

11. Op. cit.

12. Al Shamsi, op. cit., 11.

13. Hiba Nasar, "Demographic Transformation, Employment and Labour Migration in the *Mashriq* (Orient) Countries" (in Arabic), *The*

Meeting of a Team of Experts on the challenges and Opportunities of International Migration in the Arab Countries, op. cit., 11.

14. Maitha Al Shamsi, "Labour Migration in the GCC states" (in Arabic), a study presented to the *Arab conference on Implementing the Action Plan of the International Conference on Population and Development*, ESCWA, Beirut, September 22–25, 1998, 10.

15. Mosa, op. cit., 134.

16. Ibid., 136.

17. See, Ali Abdel Gadir, "Building Huan Capital for Economic Development in the Arab Countries," a paper presented at the conference on *Employment and Unemployment in Egypt*, held by the ECES in Cairo on January 13–14, 2002, 2.

18. Baqir Salman Al Najar, *The Dream of Migration for Wealth* (Beirut: Markaz Dirasast Al Wihda al Arabiya, 2001), 144.

19. Ibid., 145.

20. Abbas Abdal Karim, "Internationalization of the Gulf Labour Markets: Changing Patterns and Contradictory Effects," *Gulf Economic Report 2004–2005* (Al Sharjah: Dar Al Khaleej lil Sahafa wa al Tiba'a wa al Nashr, February 2005), 31.

21. Maitha Al Shamsi, "Foreign Migration and Developing the Labour Force: a Study of the Service Sectors in the UAE Society," (in Arabic) (Dubai, Culture and Science Symposium, 1996), 31.

22. Ibid., 81.

23. Abdal Karim, op. cit., 80.

24. Al Shamsi, "Assessing Migration Policies...", op. cit., 4.

25. Ibid., 5.

26. Mohammed Dito, "Managing Migrant Labour in the GCC states: Risk and Opportunities," *The Meeting of a Team of Experts on the challenges and Opportunities of International Migration in the Arab Countries*, op. cit., 12.

27. Abdal Karim, op. cit., 81.

28. The Secretariat General of the Arab League, the Population Policies and Migration Department, *The Regional Report on Arab Labour Migration* (Cairo: Secretariat General of the Arab League, 2006), 66.

29. Kapiszewski, op. cit., 10.

30. Ibid., 5

31. UN, *World Population Monitoring with Emphasis on Migration and Development*, op. cit., 107.

32. Maitha Al Shamsi, "Labour Migration in the GCC states," op. cit., 11.

33. Ahmed bin Obeid bin Sulaiman, op. cit., p. 11.

34. Maitha Al Shamsi, "Assessing Migration Policies," op. cit., 13.

35. Othman Al Hassan Nour, *The General Framework of Building a Population Strategy for the GCC* (in Arabic) (Riyadh: the Secretariat General of the GCC, 1416 Hijri), 38.

36. Maitha Al Shamsi, "Labour Migration in the GCC states," op. cit., 15.

37. The Secretariat General of the Arab League, the Population Policies and Migration Department, *The Regional Report on Arab Labour Migration*, op. cit., 102.

38. Ibid., 104.

39. See, Maurice Girgis, "Would Nationals and Asians Replace Arab Workers in the GCC?" Fourth Mediterranean Development Forum, Amman, Jordan, October 2002.

40. The Secretariat General of the Arab League, the Population Policies and Migration Department, *The Regional Report on Arab Labour Migration*, op. cit., 68.

41. Ibid., 101

42. The Arab League and the International Migration Organization, *The Regional Conference on Arab Migration in a Globalized World*, Cairo, September 2–4, 2003, 15

43. Salman Al Dousri, "Desired and Feared Labour Force" op. cit.

44. Abdul Maalik Khalaf Al Tamimi, *Foreign Settlement in the Arab World*, (in Arabic) 'Alam al Ma'rifa (Kuwait:, the National Council for Culture, Arts and Letters, 1983), 225.

45. Maitha Al Shamsi, "Assessing Migration Policies" op. cit., 24.

46. Nasrat Shah, "Arab Migration Patterns in the Gulf," *The Regional Report on Arab Labour Migration in a Globalized World*, op. cit., 9.

47. See, *Arab News*, Saudi Arabia, February 3, 2002.

48. See, *Arab News*, Saudi Arabia, July 10, 2002.

49. See, *Arab News*, Saudi Arabia, September 26, 2002.

50. See, *The Gulf News*, UAE, December 30, 2002.

51. See, *Arab News*, Saudi Arabia, October 28, 2002.

52. ESCWA, *International Migration in the Arab World*, (New York, NY: UN Publications, 1985), 93.

53. Ibid., 95.

54. The Gulf Center for Strategic Studies, "Arab Labour Force and the Difficult Options" (in Arabic), *Kurasat istratigiyya khleejiya* (Gulf Strategic Notes) series (Cairo: 1997), 12.

55. Ibid., 13.

56. Ibid., 14.

57. Ibid., 3.

58. ESCAW, *Globalization and Labour Markets*, op. cit., 54.

59. Ibid., 56.

60. Maitha Al Shamsi, "Substituting Nationals for Migrants in the GCC states"(in Arabic), the *Fourth Forum of Human Resources*, the Chamber of Commerce and Industry, Riyadh, 2006, 22

61. ESCWA, *Globalization and Labour Markets*, op. cit., 56

62. Maitha Al Shamsi, "Substituting Nationals for ...", op. cit. 31.

63. The Secretariat General of the Arab League, *The Regional Report on Arab Labour Migration*, op. cit., 75.

64. Ibid., 75.

65. The Secretariat General of the Arab League, *The Regional Report on Arab Labour Migration*, op. cit., 113

66. Maitha Al Shamsi, "Substituting Nationals for ...", op. cit. 29.

67. ESCWA, *Globalization and Labour Markets*, op. cit., 57.

68. Ibid., 49.

69. Maitha Al Shamsi, "Substituting Nationals for ...", op. cit. 29.

70. Nadir Farjani, "The Labour Markets in the GCC states: the Reality and the Future" (in Arabic), *Al Mustaqbal al Arabi*, no. 216 (1997), 66.

71. The GCC Secretariat General, *Remittances by Expatriate Workforce in the GCC Countries: Their Limitations and Economic Impact* (Riyadh:

Department of Studies and Economic Integration at the Secretariat General, 2004), 127–128. ⁄

72. Ibid., 18–19.

73. Abdul Karim, op. cit., 99.

74. United Nations, "World Population Monitoring …" op. cit., 29.

75. Al-Wuhaishi, op. cit., 22.

76. Al-Najjar, "The Dream of Migrating for Wealth," op. cit., 124.

77. Maitha Al-Shamsi, "Foreign Migration and Developing the Labour Force," op. cit., 261.

78. Al-Wuhaishi, op. cit., 22.

79. Maitha Al-Shamsi, "Foreign Migration and Developing the Labour Force," op. cit., 266.

80. Op. cit., 262.

81. Op. cit., 264.

82. United Nations, "World Population Monitoring …" op cit., 27.

83. Op cit., 27.

84. Op cit., 28.

85. Op cit., 28.

86. (http://www.gcc-org.archieve.html).

87. (http://www.gcc-sg.org/archieve/chptr18-html).

88. Mohammad Adnan Wadie, "Human Resources Development," GCC Seminar on Demographic Policies, Qatar, April 19–20, 2004, 40.

89. ESCWA, "Globalization and Labour Markets," op cit., 53.

90. Farjani, op. cit., 53.

91. Ibid., 54.

92. ESCWA, "International Migration in the Arab World," op. cit., 54.

93. Ibid., 78.

94. Ibid., 114.

95. ESCWA, "Globalization and Labour Markets," op. cit., 60.

96. Ibid., 53.

97. Farjani, op cit., 65.

98. ESCWA, "International Migration in the Arab World," op. cit., 53.

99. ESCWA, "Globalization and Labour Markets," Ibid., 61.

100. Ibid., 61.

101. Al-Kawari, op cit., 47.

102. Ibid., 48.

103. Ibid., 68.

104. Maitha Al-Shamsi, "Population Policies and Demographic Transformation in the Arab World with Reference to the Arab Gulf Countries," Arab Population Forum, ESCWA, Beirut, 2004, 8.

105. Ahmad Abdul Nadhir, "Demographic Policies and their Relevance to Sustained Development," GCC Seminar on Demographic Policies, Qatar, April 19–20, 2004, 40.

106. Ibid., 31.

107. Al-Kawari, op cit, 62.

108. Ibid., 67.

109. The researcher is Abdullah Al-Madani, lecturer and expert on Asian affairs, quoted from Salman Al-Dosari, "Desired and Feared Labour Force," op. cit.

110. ESCWA, "International Migration in the Arab World," op. cit., 53.

111. Op. cit., 55.

112. Al-Kawari, op. cit., 76.

113. Op. cit., 34.

114. Maitha Al-Shamsi, "Substituting Nationals for Migrants in the GCC States" (in Arabic), op. cit., 34.

115. Wadie, op. cit., 44.

116. Maitha Al-Shamsi, "Substituting Nationals for Migrants in the GCC States," op. cit., 34.

BIBLIOGRAPHY

"A Secure Europe in a Better World." *EU Security Strategy*, Brussels, December 12, 2003 (http://www.consilium.europa.eu/uedocs/cmsUpload/78367.pdf).

Aaron, Sushil S. "Straddling Faultlines: India's Foreign Policy toward the Greater Middle East." *CSH Occasional Paper* no. 7 (New Delhi: Centre de Sciences Humaines, 2003).

Aarts, Paul and Gerd Nonneman (eds). *Saudi Arabia in the Balance: Political Economy, Society, Foreign Affairs* (London: Hurst & Co., 2005).

Adib-Moghaddam, Arshin. "Regional Security Complex Theory: A Critical Examination." *International Studies Journal*, vol. 3, no. 1 (Summer 2006).

Adib-Moghaddam, Arshin. *The International Politics of the Persian Gulf: A Cultural Genealogy* (London: Routledge, 2006).

Al 'Amoush, Ahmed Falah. "Asbab Intishar Zahirat al Irhab." Research study presented in *Terrorism and Globalization* (Riyadh: Naif University for Security Sciences, 1425 Hijri/2004).

Al Badaina, Ziyab. "al-Taqniya wa al Jariaim al Monzama." *Al Fikr al Shurti*, vol. 7, no. 4 (1999).

Al Dean, Ahmed Jalal Iz. *Al Irahab wa al Ounf al Siyasi* (Cairo: Dar al Huriya, 1986).

Al Dosari, Salman. "Desired and Feared Labour Force: Will 14 million migrant workers in the Gulf threaten the region and its demographic balance?" (in Arabic) *Asharq al-Awsat*, December 17, 2006.

Al-Faisal, Prince Turki. Speech delivered at the 12th ECSSR Annual Conference, March 7, 2007 (http://www.ecssr.ac.ae/CDA/en/ StaticContent/ShowStaticContentActivities/0,1626,40-00,00.html).

Al Hassan Nour, Othman. *The General Framework of Building a Population Strategy for the GCC* (in Arabic); (Riyadh: the Secretariat General of the GCC, 1416 Hijri).

Ali, Ali Abdel Gadir. "Building Human Capital for Economic Development in the Arab Countries." Paper presented at the conference on *Employment and Unemployment in Egypt*, held by the ECES in Cairo, January 13–14, 2002.

Aliboni, Roberto. "Europe's Role in the Gulf: A Transatlantic Perspective." *The International Spectator*, vol. 41, no. 2 (April–June 2006).

Al Kawari, Ali Khalifa. "Towards a better understanding of the population imbalance" (in Arabic). *Majalat Dirasat Al Khaleej wa al Jazeera al 'Arabiyya*, no. 10 (1983).

Al Mashhadani, Akram Abdul Razaq Jassem. "Criminal Statistics: The Use of Criminal Statistics in the Arab World" (in Arabic). Arab Institute for Training and Statistical Research (http://www.aitrs.org/ fasc/research.htm).

Al Nabi, Mahmoud Abdul. "Al Jamrima al Monazama 'Abr al Wataniya bain Jihoud Monazamat al Oumam al Motahida fi al Mokafahat wa Ta'theer al Motaghairat al Douwaliya." Research paper presented to the debate on *Security and Society* held at King Abdul Fahd Security College, Riyadh, 2001.

Al Najar, Baqir Salman. *The Dream of Migration for Wealth* (Beirut: Markaz Dirasast Al Wihda al Arabiya, 2001).

Al 'Omari, Ahmed bin Mohammed. *Jarimat ghasiyl al Amwal, Nazra li Jawanibiha al-Ijtima'iya w ail-Iqtasdiya* (al-Riyadh: Kitaab al-Riyadh, 2000).

[498]

Al Qaradawi, Yusuf. *Al Sahwas al Islamiyya bain al Jimoud wa al Tataruf* (Beirut: Muasasat Al Risala lil al Tiba'a was al Nashr was al Tawzi', 1419 Hihri/1998).

Al Shamrani, Mohammed. *Al Jarima al Monazama wa Siyasat al Mokafaha fir al Tashri' al Islami wa al Qanoun al Jina'iy*, MA thesis (Riyadh: Naif Arab University for Security Sciences, 2001).

Al Shamsi, Maitha. "Assessing Migration Policies in the GCC Countries: Future Lessons" (in Arabic). The Meeting of a Team of Experts on the challenges and Opportunities of International Migration in the Arab Countries, the Economic and Social Commission for Western Asia (ESCWA), Beirut, May 15–17, 2006.

Al Shamsi, Maitha. "Foreign Migration and Developing the Labour Force: A Study of the Service Sectors in the UAE Society" (in Arabic). (Dubai: Culture and Science Symposium, 1996.)

Al Shamsi, Maitha. "Labour Migration in the GCC States" (in Arabic). Study presented to the *Arab Conference on Implementing the Action Plan of the International Conference on Population and Development*, ESCWA, Beirut, September 22–25, 1998.

Al Shamsi, Maitha. "Substituting Nationals for Migrants in the GCC States" (in Arabic). *Fourth Forum of Human Resources*, the Chamber of Commerce and Industry, Riyadh, 2006.

Al Tamimi, Abdul Maalik Khalaf. "Foreign Settlement in the Arab World" (in Arabic). *'Alam al Ma'rifa* (Kuwait: the National Council for Culture, Arts and Letters, 1983).

Al Thaqafi, Mohammad. "The Role of Civil Organizations in Resisting Terror Crimes." Research study presented to the symposium *Security and Society*, King Fahd Security College, Riyadh.

Al Thaqafi, Sultan. "Obstacles to Tourist Security and Methods of Overcoming Them." Research study presented to the symposium entitled *Tourist Security*, Naif Arab University for Security Sciences, Riyadh, 1424 Hirji/2003.

Al Wadai', Saeed Misfir. "Al Amn al Fikri al Islami." *Majalat al Amn wa al Hayat* no. 187 (Naif Arab University for Security Sciences, 1418 Hijri/1997).

Anderson, Liam and Gareth Stansfield. *The Future of Iraq: Dictatorship, Democracy or Division?* (New York, NY: Palgrave Macmillan, 2005).

Arab League. *Arab Convention for the Suppression of Terrorism* (Council of Arab Ministers of Interior and Arab Ministers of Justice, 1998).

Arab League, Secretariat General. *The Regional Report on Arab Labour Migration*. Population Policies and Migration Department (Cairo: Secretariat General of the Arab League, 2006).

Arab League and the International Migration Organization. *The Regional Conference on Arab Migration in a Globalized World*, Cairo, September 2–4, 2003.

Arab News. February 3, 2002; July 10, 2002; September 26, 2002; October 28, 2002.

Asseburg, Muriel (ed.) *Regionale (Neu) Ordnung im Nahen und Mittleren Osten und die Rolle externer Akteure* (Berlin: Stiftung Wissenschaft und Politik, March 2007).

Aziz Mosa, Mustafa Abdul. "Migration and the Population Structure of the GCC Countries and the Repercussions of Globalization: a Futuristic Vision" (in Arabic). *Shioun Arabiya* (Arab Affairs), no. 116 (2003).

Bahgat, Gawdat. "Oil Security in the New Millennium: Geo-economy vs. Geo-strategy." *Strategic Review*, vol. 26 (Fall 1998).

Barnett, Thomas. *The Pentagon's New Map* (New York, NY: Putnam, 2004).

Berman, Ilan. "The Battleground: Central Asia and the Caucasus." *Washington Quarterly*, vol. 28, no. 1 (Winter 2004–2005).

Bhadrakumar, M.K. "China's Middle East Journey via Jerusalem." *Asia Times Online* January 13, 2007 (www.atimes.com/atimes/Middle_East/IA13Ak02.html).

Buzan, Barry and Ole Wæver. *Religions and Power: The Structure of International Security* (Cambridge: Cambridge University Press, 2003).

Campbell, Kurt M. and Celeste Johnson Ward. "New Battle Stations?" *Foreign Affairs* (September–October 2003).

Chubin, Shahram and Charles Tripp. *Iran and Iraq at War* (Boulder, CO: Westview Press, 1991).

Commins, David. *The Wahhabi Mission and Saudi Arabia* (London: I.B. Tauris, 2006).

Cooley, Alexander. "Base Politics." *Foreign Affairs*, vol. 84, no. 6 (November–December 2005).

De Boer, Kito and John M. Turner. "Beyond Oil: Reappraising the Gulf States." *The McKinsey Quarterly*, January 31, 2007.

Defense and Regional Security in the Arabian Peninsula and Gulf States, 1973–2004: An Annotated Bibliography (Dubai: Gulf Research Center, 2006).

Dirwish, Abdul Kareem. "al Jarima al Monazama 'Abr al Hidoud wa al Qarat." *al Aman wa al Qanoun*, third year, no. 2 (1995).

Dirwish, Abdula Kareem. "Tenth United Nations Congress on the Prevention of Crime and the Treatment of Offenders, Vienna, 10–17th April 2000." *Majalat a Amn al 'Aam*, no. 168, (January 2000).

Dito, Mohammed. "Managing Migrant Labour in the GCC States: Risk and Opportunities." *The Meeting of a Team of Experts on the challenges and Opportunities of International Migration in the Arab Countries.*

Economic and Social Commission for West Africa (ESCWA). *International Migration in the Arab World* (New York, NY: UN Publications, 1985).

Economic and Social Commission for West Africa (ESCWA). *The Demographic Window an Opportunity for Development in Arab Countries*, no. 2 (New York, NY: UN Publications, 2005).

Engelhardt, Tom. "Can You Say 'Permanent Bases'?" *The Nation*, March 27, 2006.

Espinosa, Ángeles. "Ahmadineyad visita Arabia Saudí, rival regional de Irán y aliado de Washington." *El País*, March 2, 2007.

EU Bilateral Trade and Trade with the Gulf Cooperation Council, Tradoc, September 15, 2006 (http://trade.ec.europa.eu/doclib/docs/2006/september/tradoc_113482.pdf).

European Commission. *EU Strategic Partnership with the Mediterranean and the Middle East*. Brussels, EUROMED Report no. 78, 2004 (http://ec.europa.eu/comm/external_relations/euromed/publication/2004/euromed_report_78_en.pdf).

Farjani, Nadir. "The Labour Markets in the GCC States: the Reality and the Future" (in Arabic). *Al Mustaqbal al Arabi*, no. 216 (1997).

Fair, Christine. "Indo–Iranian Ties: Thicker than Oil." *MERIA*, vol. 11, no.1 (March 2007).

Fawcett, Louise (ed.) *International Relations of the Middle East* (Oxford: Oxford University Press, 2005).

Freedman, Lawrence. "International Security: Changing Targets." *Foreign Policy* (Spring 1998).

Friedman, Milton. *Capitalism and Freedom* (Chicago, IL: University of Chicago Press, 1982).

Gadir, Ali Abdel. "Building Human Capital for Economic Development in the Arab Countries." Paper presented at the conference on *Employment and Unemployment in Egypt*, held by the ECES in Cairo on January 13–14, 2002.

Garner, Jonathan. *The Rise of the Chinese Consumer* (Princeton, NJ: John Wiley & Sons Ltd., 2006).

Girgis, Maurice. "Would Nationals and Asians Replace Arab Workers in the GCC?" Fourth Mediterranean Development Forum, Amman, Jordan, October 2002.

Graham-Brown, Sarah. *Sanctioning Saddam: The Politics of Intervention in Iraq* (London: I.B. Tauris, 1999).

Gulf Center for Strategic Studies. "Arab Labour Force and the Difficult Options" (in Arabic). *Kurasat istratigiyya khleejiya* (Gulf Strategic Notes) series (Cairo: 1997).

Gulf News. December 30, 2002.

Haass, Richard N. and Meghan L. O'Sullivan (eds). *Honey and Vinegar: Incentives, Sanctions, and Foreign Policy* (Washington, DC: Brookings Institution Press, 2000).

Harasymiw, Bohdan. "Putting Organized Crime in its Place ... within Political Science." *Canadian Political Science Association Annual Meetings,* 2003 (http://www.cpsa-acsp.ca/paper-2003/harasymiw.pdf).

Harkavy, Robert E. "Thinking About Basing." *Naval War College Review*, vol. 58, no. 3 (Summer 2005).

Harkavy, Robert E. *Bases Abroad: The Global Foreign Military Presence* (Oxford: Oxford University Press, 1989).

Hatata, Mohammed Niyazi. Mokafahat al Jarima wa Mo'amalat al Mujrimeen (Cairo: 1995).

Heller, Mark A. "The Iranian–Saudi Summit. A Microcosm of Middle Eastern Contradictions." *INSS–Insight*, 13 (March 18, 2007).

Hertog, Steffen. "Renewing an Old Geo-economic Axis." *Gulf Asia Research Bulletin*, 1 (January 2007).

Hiro, Dilip. *Neighbours, Not Friends: Iran and Iraq after the Gulf Wars* (London: Routledge, 2001).

International Bank for Reconstruction and Development. *Global Economic Prospects, 2005: Trade, Regionalism and Development* (New York, NY: World Bank Publications, November 2004).

International Labor Organization (ILO). *Decent Work in Asia: Reporting on Results 2001–2005* (Geneva: ILO, 2006).

International Labor Organization (ILO). "Realizing Decent Work in Asia." AsRM/XIV/D.7, conclusions of the ILO 14th Asian Regional Meeting, Busan, Republic of Korea, August 29–September 1, 2006.

International Monetary Fund (IMF). "Direction of Trade Statistics." IMF Yearbook, December 2006.

Jabar, Faleh A. *The Shi'ite Movement in Iraq* (London: Saqi Books, 2003).

Jain, Prakash C. "Indian Migration to Gulf Countries: Past and Present." *India Quarterly*, vol. 61, no. 2 (April–June 2005).

Jervis, Robert. *Perception and Misperception in International Politics* (Princeton, NJ: Princeton University Press, 1976).

Kantorova, Vladimira. "International Migration in the Arab Region." *Expert Meeting on International Migration and Development in the Arab World: Challenges and Opportunities*, Population Division, Department of Economic and Social Affairs, United Nations, Beirut, May 15–17, 2006.

Kapiszewski, Andrezej. "Arab Labour Migration to the GCC States." *The Regional conference on Arab Migration in a Globalized World*, the Arab League and the International Migration Organization, Cairo, September 2–4, 2003.

Karim, Abbas Abdal. "Internationalization of the Gulf Labour Markets: Changing Patterns and Contradictory Effects." *Gulf Economic Report 2004–2005* (Al Sharjah: Dar Al Khaleej lil Sahafa wa al Tiba'a wa al Nashr, 2005).

Kenney, Dennis and James Finckenauer. *Organized Crime in America (Criminal Justice)*; (New York, NY: Wadsworth Publishing, 1994).

Khalil, Sanaa. "Al Jarima al Monzama wa al 'Abr Wataniya- al Jihoud al Douwaliya wa Moshkilat al Molahaqa al Qaddiya." *Al Majala al Jinaiyya al Qawmiya* (July 1996).

Khan, Javed Ahmad. *India and West Asia – Emerging Markets in a Liberalisation Era* (New Delhi: Sage Publications, 1999).

Kissinger, Henry. *Does America Need a Foreign Policy?* (New York, NY: Simon & Shuster, 2001).

Klare, Michael T. "Imperial Reach: The Pentagon's New Basing Strategy." *The Nation*, April 25, 2005.

Koch, Christian and Felix Neugart (eds). *A Window of Opportunity: Europe, Gulf Security and the Aftermath of the Iraq War* (Dubai: Gulf Research Center, 2005).

Kolko, Gabriel. *The Age of War: The United States Confronts the World* (Boulder, CO: Lynne Rienner, 2006).

Kolodziej, Edward A. and Robert E. Harkavy (eds). *Security Policies of Developing Countries* (Lexington, MA: Lexington Books, 1982).

Kraig, Michael. "Gulf Security in a Globalizing World: Going Beyond US Hegemony." *Yale Global Online*, June 29, 2004.

[505]

Kraig, Michael Ryan. "Assessing Alternative Security Frameworks for the Persian Gulf." *Middle East Policy*, vol. 11, no. 3 (Fall 2004).

Kraig, Michael Ryan. "Forging a New Security Order for the Persian Gulf." *Middle East Policy*, vol. 13, no. 1 (Spring 2006).

Krause, Keith. "State-making and region-building: the interplay of domestic and regional security in the Middle East." *Journal of Strategic Studies*, vol. 26, no. 3, (September 2003).

Kurth, James. "Global Threat and American Strategies: From Communism in 1955 to Islamism in 2005." *Orbis*, vol. 49, issue 4 (Autumn 2005).

Le Billon, Philippe and Fouad El-Khatib. "From Free Oil to 'Freedom Oil': Terrorism, War and US Geopolitics in the Persian Gulf." *Geopolitics*, vol. 9, no. 1 (March 2004).

Levite, Ariel, Bruce W. Jentleson and Larry Berman (eds). *Foreign Military Intervention: The Dynamics of Protracted Conflict* (New York, NY: Columbia University Press, 1992).

Liddick, Donald R. "An Empirical, Theoretical, and Historical Overview of Organized Crime." *Criminology Studies* no.6 (Lewiston, NY: Edwin Mellen Press, 1999).

Luciani, Giacomo and Felix Neugart (eds). *The EU and the GCC – A New Partnership* (Munich: CAP, updated February 2005).

Marucelj, Irv. *Mature Peacekeeping Operations as Facilitators of Organized Crime* (Institute for Research on Public Policy, Working Paper Series no. 2005–1, 2005).

McMillan, Joseph, Richard Sokolsky and Andrew C. Winner. "Toward a New Regional Security Architecture." *Washington Quarterly*, vol. 26, no. 3 (Summer 2003).

Messick, Hank. *The Mobs and the Mafia: The Illustrated History of Organized Crime* (New York, NY: Ballantine Books, 1972).

Mikail, Barah. "Entre Mythes et Réalité: Considérations autour d'un 'Croissant Chiite'." *Maghreb–Machrek* no. 190 (2006–2007).

Mohamedou, M. *Iraq and the Second Gulf War: State Building and Regime Security* (Bethesda, MD: Autin & Winfield, 1997).

Monshipouri, M. "The Paradoxes of U.S. Policy in the Middle East." *Middle East Policy*, vol. 9, no. 3 (2002).

Mosa, Mustafa. "Al Inhiraf al Fikri wa al Irhab." Unpublished research paper presented at the coordination meeting of the Directors of Research, Criminal Justice and Combating Crime (Riyadh: Naif University for Security Sciences, 1425 Hijri/2004).

Müller, Friedemann. *Energie-Außenpolitik. Anforderungen veränderter Weltmarktkonstellationen an die internationale Politik* (Berlin: Stiftung Wissenschaft und Politik, November 2006 [S 33/06]).

Nakash, Yitzhak. *Reaching for Power: The Shi'a in the Modern Arab World* (Princeton, NJ: Princeton University Press, 2006).

Nasar, Hiba. "Demographic Transformation, Employment and Labour Migration in the *Mashriq* (Orient) Countries" (in Arabic). *The Meeting of a Team of Experts on the challenges and Opportunities of International Migration in the Arab Countries.*

Nasr, Vali. "Regional Implications of Shi'a Revival in Iraq." *The Washington Quarterly*, vol. 27, no. 3 (2004).

Nasr, Vali. *The Shia Revival: How Conflicts within Islam will Shape the Future* (New York & London: Norton, 2006).

National US–Arab Chamber of Commerce (ed.) *2007 Outlook: US Exports on Track to Reach $45 Billion: A Special Report from the National US–Arab Chamber of Commerce*, March 2007 (http://www.nusacc.org/tradeline/trdln0107e.pdf).

[507]

Niblock, Tim. *Pariah States and Sanctions in the Middle East: Iraq, Libya, Sudan* (London: Lynne Reinner, 2001).

Niblock, Tim. *Saudi Arabia: Power, Legitimacy and Survival* (London: Routledge, 2006).

Nolan, Janne E. (ed.) *Global Engagement: Cooperation and Security in the 21st Century* (Washington, DC: Brookings Institution Press, 1994).

Nonneman, Gerd. "EU–GCC Relations: Dynamics, Patterns and Perspectives." *The International Spectator*, 41 (July–September 2006).

Obeid, Ahmed bin Sulaiman bin. "Unemployment in Gulf Society and Potential Employment" (in Arabic). *The Population Policies of the GCC* symposium, Qatar, April 19–20, 2004.

O'Hanlon, Michael. "Can High Technology Bring US Troops Home?" *Foreign Policy* (Winter 1998–1999).

Paarlberg, Robert Lee. "Knowledge as Power: Science, Military Dominance and US Security." *International Security*, vol. 29, no. 1 (Summer 2004).

Pant, Girijesh. "Gulf NRIs: From Expatriates to Entrepreneurs." *World Focus*, vol. 22, no. 3, March 13 (2001).

Pape, Robert A. "Soft Balancing against the United States." *International Security*, vol. 30, no. 1 (Summer 2005).

Patankar, A.C. "Economic and Industrial Cooperation: Future Challenges." *GCC–India Research Bulletin*. Gulf Research Center, Issue 2 (June 2006).

Perthes, Volker (ed). *Germany and the Middle East* (Berlin: Heinrich-Böll-Stiftung/Stiftung Wissenschaft und Politik, 2002).

Perthes, Volker and Stefan Mair (eds). *European Foreign and Security Policy: Challenges and Opportunities for the German EU Presidency* (Berlin: Stiftung Wissenschaft und Politik, RP 10, October 2006).

Pollack, Ken. "Securing the Gulf." *Foreign Affairs* (July–August 2003).

Posch, Walter. "A CSCE-like process for the Gulf Region? – Neither Integration nor Isolation: Case-by-Case Cooperation." *Der Orient* 47 (2006).

Posen, Barry R. "Command of the Commons: The Military Foundation of US Hegemony." *International Security*, vol. 28, no. 1 (Summer 2003).

Potter, Lawrence G. and Gary G. Sick (eds). *Security in the Persian Gulf: Origins, Obstacles and the Search for Consensus* (New York, NY: Palgrave, 2001).

Prabhakar, Akhilesh Chandra. "India's Energy Security of supply and the Gulf." *India Quarterly*, vol. 60, no. 3 (July–September 2004).

Pradhan, Bansidhar. "Changing Dynamics of India's West Asia Policy." *International Studies*, vol. 41, no. 1 (2004).

Pradhan, Samir Ranjan. "India and GCC: Synergizing Interdependence in the Global Energy Regime." Unpublished Ph.D thesis.

Roy, Olivier. *Globalized Islam: The Search for a New Ummah* (New York, NY: Columbia University Press, 2004).

"Russia, Saudi Arabia energy partners, not rivals—Putin." *RIA–Novosti*, February 12, 2007 (http://en.rian.ru/russia/20070212/60580105.html).

Sandars, Christopher T. *America's Overseas Garrisons: The Leasehold Empire* (Oxford: Oxford University Press, 2000).

Sariolghalam, Mahmood. "Globalization and Iran's National Sovereignty: Challenges of Compatibility." *Discourse: An Iranian Quarterly*, vol. 5, no. 2 and 3 (Fall 2003 and Winter 2004).

Sariolghalam, Mahmood. "How Domestic Politics is linked to Iran's Foreign Policy." *La Vanguardia*, May 7, 2007.

Sariolghalam, Mahmood. Presentation at the *Council on Foreign Relations*, New York, April 5, 2006.

Sariolghalam, Mahmood. Review of *The Shia Revival* by Vali Nasr. *The Journal of International Affairs* University of Columbia, Spring 2007.

Sariolghalam, Mahmood. "The Foreign Policy of the Islamic Republic of Iran: Theoretical Renewal and a Search for Paradigm." *Discourse: An Iranian Quarterly*, vol 3, no. 3 and 4 (Winter 2000 and Spring 2002).

Shah, Nasrat. "Arab Migration Patterns in the Gulf." *The Regional Report on Arab Labor Migration in a Globalized World.*

Sharara, Yusuf. *Moshkilat al Qarn al Wahid wa al 'Ishrin wa al 'Aalaqat al Douwaliya* (Cario: al Hai'a al Misriya al 'Aama lil al Kitab, 1997).

Sheridan, James E. *China in Disintegration* (New York, NY: The Free Press, 1975).

Shtauber, Zvi and Yiftah S. Shapir (eds). *The Middle East Strategic Balance, 2004–2005* (Tel Aviv: Jaffee Center for Strategic Studies, 2006).

Singh, Jasjit. "Growing South Asian Interests in the Gulf Region: Problems and Opportunities." *Strategic Analyst*, vol. 23, no. 9 (December 1999).

Sirriyeh, Hussein. "Development of the Iraqi–Iranian Dispute, 1847–1975." *Journal of Contemporary History*, vol. 20, no. 3 (1985).

Sokar, Abdul Samad. "Mahiyat al Jarima al Dowalia." *majalat al Amn al 'Aam*, no. 159 (October 1997).

Standing, André. *Rival Views of Organized Crime*. ISS monographs, no. 77, 2003 (http://www.iss.co.za/Pubs/Monographs/No77/Content.html).

Stansfield, Gareth. *Iraq: People, History, Politics* (Cambridge: Polity Press, 2007).

Stolberg, Sheryl and John Holusha. "Bush: Iraq Victory Still Possible." *International Herald Tribune*, December 20, 2006.

Talbott, Strobe. *The Russia Hand* (New York, NY: Random House, 2002).

Terrill, W. Andrew. *Regional Fears of Western Primacy and the Future of US Middle East Eastern Basing Policy* (Carlisle, PA: US Army War College, Strategic Studies Institute, December 2006).

United Nations (UN) Department of Economic and Social Affairs. *World Migrant Stock: The 2005 Revision* (http://esa.un.org/migration/index.asp?panel=2).

United Nations (UN) Department of Economic and Social Affairs. *World Population Monitoring with Emphasis on Migration and Development* (New York, NY: UN Publications, 2006).

United Nations (UN). *World Population Prospects*: *The 2004 Revision* (New York, NY: UN, 2005).

US Department of Defense. *Quadrennial Defense Review Report* (February 2006).

Vaezi, Mahmoud. "tartibât-e amniyat-e khalij-e fars." *Rahbord*, 40 (16/05/1385).

Valbjørn, Morten and André Bank. "Signs of a New Arab Cold War: The 2006 Lebanon War and the Sunni–Shi`i Divide." *Middle East Report* 242 (Spring 2007).

Weisburd, A. Mark. *Use of Power: The Practice of States since World War II* (University Park, PA: Pennsylvania University Press, 1997).

Willoughby, John. "Ambivalent Anxieties of the South Asian–Gulf Arab Labor Exchange." Working Paper Series, March 2005 (http://www.american. edu/cas/econ/workingpaper/2005-02.pdf).

Yehiav, Ayellet. "The Anti-Iranian Front: Egypt, Saudi Arabia, and Jordan." *MERIA*, 11 (March 2007); (http://meria.idc.ac.il/journal/2007/issue1/jv11no1a2.html).

Yusuf, Abdulla. "Al Sahbab wa al Inhiraf." *Majalat al Fikr al Sharti*, vol. 13, no. 15 (Al Shariah: 2004).

Zachariah, K.C., E.T. Mathew and S. I. Rajan. "Migration in Kerala State, India: Dimensions, Determinants and Consequences." Working Paper I (Thiruvanthapuram, Kerala: Centre for Development Studies, 1999).

Zakaria, Fareed. *The Future of Freedom* (New York, NY: W.W. Norton & Company, 2003).